Advanced
grammar & vocabulary

Student's book

Mark Skipper

Express Publishing

Contents

Unit 1	Adjectives I (Behaviour and Traits)	4
Unit 2	Adjectives II	6
Unit 3	Adjectives III (Word formation)	8
Unit 4	... and ... Pair phrases	10
Unit 5	Anger and Annoyance - Animals	12
Unit 6	Arguing	14
Unit 7	Body	16
Unit 8	Body Idioms	18
Unit 9	Chance and Probability	20
Unit 10	Choosing and Decisions - Clothes (Adjectives)	22
Unit 11	Clothes II (Idioms) - Colours	24
Unit 12	Comparing	26
Unit 13	Cooking and Food	28
Unit 14	Crime I	30
Unit 15	Crime II (Vocabulary and Collocations)	32
Unit 16	Damage and Conditions	34
Unit 17	Determination - Likes-Dislikes	36
Unit 18	Driving	38
Unit 19	Eating and Drinking	40
Unit 20	Education	42
Unit 21	Emphasis (Extreme Adjectives - Very)	44
Unit 22	Entertainment	46
Unit 23	Face	48
Unit 24	Fire and Light	50
Unit 25	Food I	52
Unit 26	Food II	54
Unit 27	Hands – Holding, Pushing, Pulling, Taking	56
Unit 28	Health I	58
Unit 29	Health II	60
Unit 30	Im ... and En ...	62
Unit 31	Informal Language	64
Unit 32	-ing form vs to	66
Unit 33	Introductions	68
Unit 34	... it ...	70
Unit 35	Key Words I	72
Unit 36	Key Words II	74
Unit 37	Linking Words	76
Unit 38	Little Words - Modals	78
Unit 39	Looking / Seeing	80
Unit 40	Money I	82
Unit 41	Money II	84
Unit 42	Nature - Noise I	86
Unit 43	Noise II - Nouns I	88
Unit 44	Nouns II	90
Unit 45	Nouns III	92
Unit 46	Nouns IV	94
Unit 47	Numbers - Objects	96
Unit 48	... of ... I	98
Unit 49	... of ... II	100
Unit 50	People and Personality	102
Unit 51	Physical Description	104
Unit 52	Place (Adjectives)	106
Unit 53	Problems	108
Unit 54	Reactions - Short and Long	110
Unit 55	Sleep and Bed	112
Unit 56	Something, Anything, Nothing - Speaking and Communicating I	114
Unit 57	Speaking and Communicating II - Sport	116
Unit 58	Talking (Reporting verbs)	118
Unit 59	There is ... - Time I	120
Unit 60a	Time II	122

Unit	Title	Page
Unit 60b	Time III	124
Unit 61	Travel	126
Unit 62	Under, Over and Out	128
Unit 63	Unhappy and Happy	130
Unit 64	Verbs I	132
Unit 65	Verbs II	134
Unit 66	Verbs III	136
Unit 67	Walking and Running	138
Unit 68	Ways of ...	140
Unit 69	Weather I	142
Unit 70	Weather II	144
Unit 71	Wishing, Wanting, Requests, Permission and Preferences	146
Unit 72	Work and Earning a Living	148
Unit 73	Compound Adjectives - Adverb Combinations I	150
Unit 74	Adverb Combinations II	152
Unit 75	Noun Combinations I	154
Unit 76	Noun Combinations II	156
Unit 77	Noun Combinations III	158
Unit 78	Noun Combinations IV	160
Unit 79	Verb Combinations I	162
Unit 80	Verb Combinations II	164
Unit 81	Verb Combinations III	166
Unit 82	Verb Combinations IV	168
Unit 83	Verb Combinations V	170
Unit 84	A, B and C Prepositions	172
Unit 85	D to J Prepositions	174
Unit 86	K to P Prepositions	176
Unit 87	R and S Prepositions	178
Unit 88	T to W Prepositions - At ... Prepositional Phrases	180
Unit 89	In ... Prepositional Phrases	182
Unit 90	On ... Prepositional Phrases	184
Unit 91	Prepositional Phrases-Preposition ... Preposition I	186
Unit 92	Preposition ... Preposition II	188
Unit 93	A, B and C Phrasal Verbs	190
Unit 94	D, E and F Phrasal Verbs	192
Unit 95	G to M Phrasal Verbs	194
Unit 96	N, O and P Phrasal Verbs	196
Unit 97	R and S Phrasal Verbs	198
Unit 98	T and W Phrasal Verbs	200
Unit 99	Phrasal Verbs I	202
Unit 100	Phrasal Verbs II	204
Unit 101	Phrasal Nouns	206
Unit 102	Be (Phrases)	208
Unit 103	Break - Bring - Catch (Phrases)	210
Unit 104	Come (Expressions/Phrasal Verbs)	212
Unit 105	Do or Make	214
Unit 106	Fall (Expressions/Phrasal Verbs)	216
Unit 107	Get (Expressions I)	218
Unit 108	Get (Expressions II/Phrasal Verbs)	220
Unit 109	Give (Expressions/Phrasal Verbs)	222
Unit 110	Go (Expressions)	224
Unit 111	Go (Phrasal Verbs)/Have (Expressions)	226
Unit 112	Make (Combinations/Expressions I)	228
Unit 113	Make (Expressions II/Phrasal Verbs)	230
Unit 114	Put (Expressions/Phrasal Verbs)	232
Unit 115	Set (Combinations/Expressions/ Phrasal Verbs)	234
Unit 116	Take (Expressions/Phrasal Verbs)	236

2 Adjectives II

> Note: * = used before a noun, ** = used after a noun, generally with the verb to be, *** = can be used before or after a noun

Adjectives in collocations

avid: * very enthusiastic (for people)
an avid reader/football fan/stamp collector

blatant: * very obvious, done without shame or embarrassment (used to describe bad things)
a blatant lie/foul

breathtaking: *** very beautiful, surprising or impressive
breathtaking view/scenery
For a child of his age, his knowledge of the subject was breathtaking.

gripping: *** very exciting; for films and books
It was a gripping tale of murder and intrigue.

harrowing: *** shocking, making you feel very upset (not used to describe people)
a harrowing film/tale

lax: *** not strict or not careful enough (for safety measures, security, morals, discipline, laws, etc)

lenient: *** not strict; used to describe people in a position to punish (parents, teachers, etc)
The judge was lenient and let him off with a fine.

meteoric: *** very sudden and very quick (generally used with the noun *rise*)
He was unprepared for his meteoric rise to fame.

misleading: *** giving the wrong idea or impression
misleading information/ advertisements/comments, etc

piercing: * loud and high-pitched (for noises)
She let out a piercing scream of terror.

prolific: *** producing a large number of works (for artists, composers and writers)

sporadic: *** happening at irregular intervals
sporadic fighting/shots/violence/ outbreaks

staunch: * very loyal
staunch supporter/friend/ally/ Democrat, etc

sweeping: * (i) too general and therefore not valid (for statements and generalisations) (ii) large and affecting everyone (for changes and reforms)
'Women are bad drivers' is a sweeping generalisation that is all too common these days.
He proposed sweeping changes to the country's electoral system.

watertight: impossible to prove wrong or argue against
watertight arguments/court case/alibi

*

Adjectives with similar meanings

dreary: *** boring and depressing
a dreary day/life/town
Her apartment was dreary and depressing.

dull: *** boring, without life, excitement or colour
dull afternoon/people/colour/ weather

mundane: *** ordinary, boring, giving little satisfaction; often used to describe jobs
He had a mundane job in a local bank.

tedious: *** boring, and often frustrating
tedious journey/task/job

*

atrocious: *** extremely bad
atrocious film/mess/game, etc

dreadful: *** very bad
dreadful weather/mistakes/acting

lousy: *** (informal) very bad
lousy day/hotel/teacher/singer

*

flawless: *** perfect, with no faults
flawless complexion/performance

impeccable: *** perfect, faultless
impeccable appearance/reputation/ taste in clothes

unblemished: * sth that has not been spoilt or harmed
unblemished record/reputation/ character

*

arduous: *** tiring and involving a lot of effort

arduous journey/task

gruelling: *** tiring and lasting a long time
gruelling schedule/day/race

strenuous: * needing a lot of physical effort
strenuous activity/trip/effort/ objection

*

bedraggled: *** untidy, dirty and wet (for people)
The two bedraggled children trudged into the house.

dishevelled: *** untidy
dishevelled clothes/hair/ appearance/man

scruffy: *** untidy (for people/places) old and worn out (for clothes)
scruffy pair of jeans/flat/boy

*

astute: *** clever at understanding people and situations
astute politician/decision

crafty: *** clever and good at using deception to achieve success
crafty man/plan/look

shrewd: ** clever and showing good judgement of other people and situations
shrewd businessman/investment/ eyes

wily: * clever, experienced at deceiving people and not easily deceived (for people/behaviour)
wily businessman/manoeuvring

*

conventional: *** ordinary, normal
conventional people/opinions/ ideas

mainstream: *** ordinary, conventional, neither strange nor extreme
mainstream beliefs/ideas / organisations/politics

middle-of-the-road: *** ordinary, not extreme
middle of the road ideas/beliefs/ music, etc

run-of-the-mill: * ordinary, nothing special
run-of-the-mill computer/ supermarket

Practice

1. Match the nouns with the adjectives.

1	a breathtaking	a	view
2	a blatant	b	fighting
3	a prolific	c	documentaries on animal experiments
4	a gripping		
5	misleading	d	judge
6	a piercing	e	lie
7	sporadic	f	novelist
8	a sweeping	g	reader
9	a staunch	h	security
10	a watertight	i	Republican
11	harrowing	j	information
12	a lenient	k	generalisation
13	a meteoric	l	rise
14	an avid	m	alibi
15	lax	n	film
		o	scream

2. Group the adjectives in the box into categories by putting them next to the appropriate heading.

> flawless – arduous – dreadful – dreary – impeccable – dishevelled – middle-of-the-road – dull – tedious – strenuous – astute – mainstream – gruelling – mundane – shrewd – wily – run-of-the-mill – lousy – atrocious – unblemished – crafty – scruffy – bedraggled – conventional

Boring: ....

Difficult: ....

Untidy: ....

Bad: ....

Clever: ....

Ordinary: ....

Perfect: ....

3. Read the following review and replace the adjectives in bold with more sophisticated ones from exercise 2.

SPELLBINDING HARRY

For an entertaining evening, I highly recommend the film version of the first J.K. Rowling book, "Harry Potter and the Philosopher's Stone". It is the story of an otherwise **1) ordinary** boy who possesses magical powers. Orphaned as a baby when his parents were killed by an evil wizard, Harry is brought up by his **2) bad and unpleasant** relatives, the Dursleys. Everything changes, however, when an untidy stranger turns up on his doorstep. His name is Hagrid and he happens to be the keeper of keys at Hogwart's School for magicians. So begins Harry's education at the school and the **3) difficult** task of both learning magic and fighting evil. Under the tutelage of the kindly but **4) clever** Professor Dumbledore and with the help of his two faithful friends, Ron and Hermione, Harry achieves his goal. Daniel Radcliffe (as Harry) and his co-stars give **5) perfect** performances in this refreshing new film in which there's never a **6) boring** moment.

4. Decide whether the following adjective-noun combinations are possible or not. If you think that the combination is possible, tick the box that follows it. If not, correct it replacing the noun with an appropriate one. Then use the correct combinations in sentences.

1	a gruelling shirt	☐
2	a staunch enemy	☐
3	a flawless performance	☐
4	a scruffy pair of jeans	☐
5	a crafty plan	☐
6	a shrewd businessman	☐
7	strenuous exercise	☐
8	a tedious room	☐
9	an atrocious driver	☐
10	an astute look	☐
11	an arduous journey	☐
12	impeccable taste	☐
13	mainstream politics	☐
14	a mundane job	☐
15	a dreary journey	☐

3 Adjectives III (Word formation)

accessible: sth that can be easily reached/entered/obtained/used; accessibility (n) **Opp:** inaccessible, inaccessibility (n)

The northern part of the park is virtually inaccessible unless you have a four-wheel drive.

accurate: precise/correct; accuracy (n) **Opp:** inaccurate, inaccuracy (n)

It is not always easy to give accurate measurements for the strength of an earthquake.

apologetic: to say or show you are sorry for doing sth

Audrey was extremely apologetic for having kept us waiting so long.

arguable: debatable, may be questioned [Note: **it is arguable that**: it can be argued that]

Whether or not this is the way forward is arguable.

It is arguable that education leads to higher income.

argumentative: quarrelsome; always ready to disagree

I've never met anyone more argumentative than Jenny; she will tell you that black is white.

coherent: well-planned, clear and sensible; coherence (n) **Opp:** incoherent, incoherence (n)

This is a clear and coherent explanation of the workings of the internal combustion engine.

decisive: able to make quick decisions in a difficult situation; decisiveness (n) **Opp:** indecisive, indecision (n)

Winston Churchill's decisive policies rallied the country round him at a difficult and dangerous time.

discreet: careful in order to avoid embarrassing or offending sb; discretion (n) **Opp:** indiscreet, indiscretion (n)

Try to be as discreet as possible as he's very sensitive and easily upset.

excessive: more or higher than is necessary or reasonable

Don't you think that a 25% price increase is excessive, even allowing for inflation?

knowledgeable: well-informed

Malcolm is knowledgeable about computer hardware and will tell you everything you want to know.

legible: clear enough to read; legibility (n) **Opp:** illegible, illegibility [(n)-not common]

I can't possibly read this; her handwriting is illegible.

logical: reasonable/sensible; logic (n) **Opp:** illogical

There is no logical explanation for his behaviour.

loyal: faithful; loyalty (n) **Opp:** disloyal, disloyalty (n)

A loyal friend will stand by you through good and bad times.

normal: usual/ordinary; normality (n) **Opp:** abnormal, abnormality (n)

It's not abnormal for boys of his age to want to join the army.

obedient: sb who does what they are told to do; obedience (n) **Opp:** disobedient, disobedience (n)

Jo is a very disobedient child and refuses to do what she is told.

official: approved by sb in authority **Opp:** unofficial

This is the only official biography of the author currently on the market.

orthodox: accepted or used by most people; orthodoxy (n) **Opp:** unorthodox, unorthodoxy (n)

He always gets outstanding results, despite his unorthodox teaching methods.

plausible: likely to be true, valid; plausibility (n) **Opp:** implausible, implausibility (n)

The special effects in the film were excellent but I didn't think the plot was very plausible.

polite: with good manners, courteous; politeness (n) **Opp:** impolite, impoliteness (n)

Timothy was a polite young man with impeccable manners.

practical: down-to-earth (for people); effective/likely to be successful; practicality (n) **Opp:** impractical, impracticality (n)

(im)practical person/idea/plan

Banning all vehicles from the city centre is a lovely idea but I don't think it's practical at all.

precise: exact; precision (n) **Opp:** imprecision (n)

This machine has brought an unprecedented degree of precision to the business of dating trees.

preferential treatment: (to be) treated better than other people

Harry gets preferential treatment at work, with an office all to himself, just because he is the boss's nephew.

replaceable: disposable; **Opp:** irreplaceable

Many of the paintings lost in the fire were irreplaceable old masters.

responsible: behaving sensibly and properly; responsibility (n) **Opp:** irresponsible, irresponsibility (n)

Sharon is the perfect employee; hardworking and responsible.

ripe: fully grown, ready to eat (fruit, grain); ripeness (n), ripen (v) **Opp:** unripe, unripeness [(n)-not common]

I'm not buying these tomatoes; they're unripe.

scrupulous: sb who takes great care to do what is fair, honest or morally right; scruples (n) **Opp:** unscrupulous

Socrates was known for his scrupulous adherence to the truth and his refusal to compromise.

Practice

1. *Make the opposites of the adjectives below by adding one of the following prefixes: un-, dis-, ir-, il-, ab-, im-, in-*

1	plausible	→	...... plausible
2	polite	→	...... polite
3	scrupulous	→	...... scrupulous
4	ripe	→	...... ripe
5	decisive	→	...... decisive
6	accessible	→	...... accessible
7	normal	→	...... normal
8	orthodox	→	...... orthodox
9	logical	→	...... logical
10	replaceable	→	...... replaceable
11	practical	→	...... practical
12	accurate	→	...... accurate
13	discreet	→	...... discreet
14	obedient	→	...... obedient
15	loyal	→	...... loyal
16	precise	→	...... precise
17	coherent	→	...... coherent
18	legible	→	...... legible
19	responsible	→	...... responsible
20	official	→	...... official

2. *Complete the sentences by using the word that appears at the end of each line to form an appropriate adjective. Remember that you may have to add a prefix from exercise 1 or a suffix from the following:*
-ish, -ial, -ed, -able, -ive, -less, -ible, -ic

1. I may be related to the Managing Director, but believe me, I don't get .... treatment. **PREFER**
2. You are 25 years old and you are acting like a spoilt schoolboy. Stop being so .... **CHILD**
3. Ben hated it, but I thought it was a very interesting and .... programme. **INFORMATION**
4. This is the worst .... crisis that this country has had to face in over 100 years. **ECONOMY**
5. Why are you being so ....? You're disagreeing with everything I say. **ARGUE**
6. Appearances can be .... He might look aggressive but really he is as gentle as a lamb. **DECEIVE**
7. .... with the money he was receiving, Sid decided to leave the company. **SATISFY**
8. For some .... reason, she gave up her job, sold everything she owned and went to live on a desert island. **EXPLAIN**
9. All the judges gave her ten out of ten. She had given a .... performance. **FLAW**
10. He looked terrible. Too much work and too many .... nights. He had to get away. **SLEEP**
11. He can be very .... when he wants to. He can talk you into anything. **PERSUADE**
12. The best man was very embarrassed and very .... about forgetting the time that the wedding was to take place. **APOLOGISE**

3. *Read the text below. Use the word given in capitals at the end of some of the lines to form an adjective that fits the space in the same line.*

What kind of **0)** .... experience and background should we be giving our children? In a **1)** .... western economy, they need to be well-informed and **2)** .... In a complex ever-changing modern world, it is **3)** .... that the task of preparing the next generation cannot be carried out within the **4)** .... classroom framework, because acquiring a proper education in this way is simply **5)** .... This is where computer-aided learning steps in, providing children with the skills that they will need in tomorrow's world, in a one-to-one learner-centred environment. There are those who claim, however, that **6)** .... exposure to computers may prove to be harmful rather than **7)** .... to children and that it is more **8)** .... for education to take place in the classroom. They say that, although computers seem to hold a(n) **9)** .... appeal for some people, particularly young children, it is **10)** .... for children to have a person, rather than a machine, for a teacher.

EDUCATION
COMPETE
KNOW
ARGUE
TRADITION
POSSIBLE

EXCEED
BENEFIT
PRODUCE

RESIST
PREFER

4 ... and ... Pair Phrases

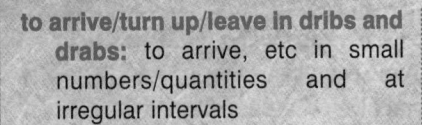

to arrive/turn up/leave in dribs and drabs: to arrive, etc in small numbers/quantities and at irregular intervals

We're receiving food, but it is only arriving in dribs and drabs.

bright and early: (to wake up/get up/leave) very early in the morning (has a positive connotation)

If we leave bright and early tomorrow morning, we should get there by midday.

by and large: generally

By and large, most people would prefer to have a badly paid job that they liked rather than a well paid job that they disliked.

to be few and far between: not to be very common/to be very difficult to find

Good jobs are few and far between in days of high unemployment.

to grin and bear it: to accept an unpleasant situation without complaining (probably because there is no choice)

A shorter lunch break is new company policy, so we'll just have to grin and bear it.

ins and outs: the details of a complicated situation/problem/system/proposal

We have yet to discuss all the ins and outs of his proposal.

to make a song and dance about: to complain too much about sth, in a way that seems unnecessary

I was only 10 minutes late. Why are you making such a song and dance about it?

odds and ends: small unimportant objects

Everything had been packed away in boxes except for a few odds and ends.

once and for all: definitely and finally so that you end all doubt and uncertainty

He set out to prove once and for all that Deakin's alibi was nothing but a tissue of lies.

one's own flesh and blood: a relative

We're talking about my family here, my own flesh and blood. Of course I trust them.

an out-and-out lie: a complete lie (used in reply to sb who has accused you of sth)

That is an out-and-out lie; you've made it all up!

to be part and parcel of: a basic and fundamental part of (life/a job/a problem)

Having your private life splashed across the front pages of newspapers and glossy magazines is part and parcel of being a celebrity.

peace and quiet: calm and tranquillity

We took a couple of days off and went to the country for a bit of peace and quiet.

pride and joy: sth/sb that a person is very proud of and which/who is very important to them

His car/daughter/garden is his pride and joy.

prim and proper: very conservative and easily offended (used to describe people)

She's far too prim and proper to have written anything as scandalous as that.

pushing and shoving: pushing (used with reference to crowded places)

After a lot of pushing and shoving, I finally made it to the counter where everything had been reduced by 50%.

safe and sound: safe and unharmed (used when sb has not been harmed despite being in a potentially dangerous situation)

The two children, who had been missing for three days, were found safe and sound hiding in an abandoned mine shaft.

spick and span: very clean

When I get back, I want this place looking spick and span.

touch and go: doubtful (used with reference to important or life-threatening situations)

It was touch and go whether they would allow us to leave the country.

up-and-coming: sb who shows a lot of promise and will probably be very successful in the future

up-and-coming artist/tennis player/pianist/writer

The government has introduced a scheme whereby up-and-coming young athletes will receive financial support.

to have ups and downs: to have good times and bad times

What family doesn't have its ups and downs?

wear and tear: damage caused to furniture/clothes/equipment, by daily use

Even allowing for wear and tear, these chair covers should last for at least fifteen years.

well and truly: completely (often used with *lost* and *beaten*)

After walking for three hours, we realised that we were well and truly lost.

As we had been well and truly beaten the Saturday before, the manager decided to make wholesale changes to the team.

to win fair and square: to win fairly (often used when you have been accused of cheating)

What do you mean I cheated? I won fair and square, and you know it.

Practice

1. a. Complete the sentences with an appropriate word from the box below.

> downs – early – quiet – sound – tear – outs – joy – blood – drabs – square – span – shoving

1. He won **fair and** ....
2. She got up **bright and** ....
3. We need some **peace and** ....
4. The guests arrived in **dribs and** ....
5. They got there **safe and** ....
6. There was a lot of **pushing and** ....
7. She's **their pride and** ....
8. That's **wear and** ....
9. Like any couple, they have **their ups and** ....
10. He's your own **flesh and** ....
11. We'll soon have this place looking **spick and** ....
12. I don't know the **ins and** ....

b. Make up appropriate responses to the following using pair phrases from exercise 1a, as in the example.

0. A: You cheated in the competition!
   B: *No, I won fair and square!*
1. A: Your garden looks wonderful!
   B: ....
2. A: So, how are things between you?
   B: ....
3. A: What was the rock concert like?
   B: ....
4. A: How about a weekend in the countryside?
   B: ....

2. In the sentences below, the bold parts of the pair phrases have been jumbled. Swap them around so as to form correct pair phrases.

1. I know it's not fair, but you'll just have to grin and **dance** it. ....
2. These carpets last for many years, even allowing for everyday wear and **bear**. ....
3. There was nothing in her bag but a few **outs** and ends. ....
4. As you can imagine, he's devastated. That Ferrari was his pride and **go**. ....
5. By and **once**, typed essays are much easier to read than hand-written ones. ....
6. She's far too prim and **parcel** to agree to anything as outrageous as that. ....
7. It's annoying, I know, but do you really have to make such a song and **far** about it? ....
8. Players of his calibre are few and **large** between, so keep him happy. ....
9. Making mistakes is part and **joy** of the learning process. ....
10. I don't know all the ins and **odds** of the situation, but the fact remains that the wrong diagnosis killed her. ....
11. Let's get this clear, **proper** and for all. I did not say that you hated Jane. ....
12. The doctors said it was touch and **tear** whether he would survive the operation. ....

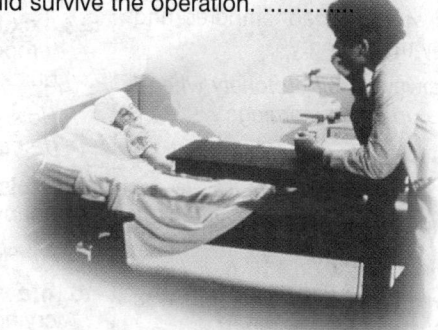

3. Rewrite the following sentences using a pair phrase from the two exercises above.

1. How could you have said such a thing to him? He is your brother.
   ....
2. You're just going to have to put up with it.
   ....
3. I want this room looking spotless when I get back.
   ....
4. He loves his tomato plants.
   ....
5. Cheap hotels are pretty hard to find in this neighbourhood.
   ....
6. She didn't cheat.
   ....
7. There is no need to make such a fuss about it.
   ....

5 Anger and Annoyance - Animals

Anger and Annoyance

a blazing row: an argument in which people are very angry and emotional
We had a blazing row.

to blow your top: to lose your temper and become very angry
When she told him, he blew his top and began shouting.

to be cross: to be a little angry (often used when speaking to children)
You'd better do what your teacher says, or she will get very cross.

to be crotchety: bad-tempered and easily made angry
I'm always a bit crotchety when I wake up in the mornings.

to drive sb up the wall: to annoy sb
That constant drilling noise outside my house is driving me up the wall.

furious: very angry
When they told him, he was furious and left the room.

galling: sth that is annoying, because it seems unfair or wrong
The most galling thing about his winning all that money is that he was already a millionaire!

to get on sb's nerves: to annoy sb
She gets on my nerves with her meaningless chatter.

a heated argument: a bad argument in which people are very angry
Raised voices told me that a heated argument was going on next door.

to hit the roof: to lose your temper and become very angry
He hit the roof when he saw my report card.

to be indignant: to be very angry because you think sth is wrong or unfair
She was indignant at the suggestion that she was lying.

infuriate: make angry
Rude people infuriate me.

irate: very angry
Within two minutes of coming off the air, we were inundated with phone calls from irate listeners.

to irritate: to annoy
His constant whistling irritates me.

to be livid: to be very angry (not used before a noun)
When she finds out that you told him, she'll be livid.

to be in no mood to: to be angry and not want to
I am in no mood to argue!

an outburst: a sudden explosion of anger
What was the reason for her sudden outburst?

a quick temper: if you have a quick temper, you lose your temper quickly and very easily
He's got a very quick temper, so be careful what you say to him.

to be sick and tired of sth/sb: to be annoyed and fed up with sth/sb
I'm sick and tired of your excuses!

to throw a tantrum: to start kicking, crying and shouting (generally used for children)
Whenever Tom didn't get his own way, he would throw a tantrum.

to be touchy: to be bad-tempered and easily made angry
I'm sorry I've been so touchy lately.

to be up in arms about sth: to be very angry and ready to protest (used to describe group reaction)
Local people are up in arms about the government's proposal to build a road through the village green.

Animals

the black sheep of the family: sb considered to be a failure/an embarrassment by relatives
I've always been the black sheep of the family. My father, mother and sister are all lawyers. Me? I'm a rock singer.

to be as blind as a bat: (informal) to have poor eyesight
She's as blind as a bat without her glasses.

you can... till the cows come home, but it won't: you can do sth for a very long time, but it won't change anything
You can ask till the cows come home, but I won't tell you.

a dark horse: sb who people know very little about
Sean is a dark horse, a bit of a mystery.

to be dogged by sth: sth bad keeps causing you trouble and it will not go away
I've been dogged by ill health ever since I left university.

for donkey's years: (informal) for a very long time
I've known Tom for donkey's years.

to duck: to avoid sth which is going to hit you by lowering your head
If he hadn't ducked, the ball would have hit him square in the face.

it is like water off a duck's back for sb: sth does not affect you because you are accustomed to it
His criticisms are like water off a duck's back.

fishy: suspicious
His proposal sounds a bit fishy, so I don't think we should trust him.

to hound sb: to persistently follow sb (used in connection with the press)
The paparazzi hounded her wherever she went.

the lion's share: the biggest part
Julie inherited the lion's share of Uncle Fester's fortune.

to rabbit on (about sth): to talk for a long time in a boring way
She rabbited on for ages.

ratty: bad-tempered/easily made angry
Sorry I was so ratty this morning. I didn't get much sleep last night.

to have a whale of a time: (informal) to really enjoy yourself
The kids had a whale of a time.

a wild goose chase: a search for sth that one is unlikely to find
Looking for him would be a wild goose chase.

to worm your way out of sth: to avoid doing sth you do not want to do
He wormed his way out of the work again!

Practice

1. Choose the correct item.

1. Angry? I was absolutely .... when our appointment was cancelled for the third time.
   A annoyed B irritated C livid D cross

2. The reason why he gets into trouble so often is that he has a .... temper.
   A fast B rapid C speedy D quick

3. What I find most .... about it is that he didn't even have the decency to say that he was sorry.
   A galling B furious C touchy D resentful

4. George wasn't in a particularly good mood, but then he is always a bit .... in the morning.
   A irate B crotchety C indignant D infuriated

5. Like many children of his age, he is prone to throwing a(n) ....
   A outburst B temper C mood D tantrum

6. Mum will hit the .... when she finds out that you've burnt a hole in her new sofa.
   A roof B wall C ceiling D top

7. How much longer do we have to wait? This is starting to get on my ....
   A mind B nerves C back D nose

8. "I'm .... to listen to your pathetic excuses," she said.
   A sick and tired
   B in no mood
   C having enough
   D sick to death

9. Stop that tapping, will you? I'm trying to concentrate and it is driving me up the ....
   A wall B roof C hill D house

10. The whole country is up in .... about the new tax the government has put on books.
    A rage B fists C anger D arms

11. It was so embarrassing. We were in the middle of a crowded restaurant when they suddenly had a .... row.
    A blazing B heated C stormy D smouldering

2. Complete the sentences with an appropriate word formed from the animals shown in the pictures below.

0. I've known them for **donkey's** years - since I was a child, in fact.

1. Throughout his playing career he was .... by injury.

2. He said we could double our money in two days? It sounds a bit .... to me.

3. At first, the criticism he got in the press used to affect him, but now it's like water off a .... back.

4. Of course she didn't see you. She's as blind as a ....

5. Did we enjoy the party? We most certainly did. We had a .... of a time.

6. You can sit there and argue till the .... come home, but I'm not changing my mind.

7. If I hadn't .... , the ball would have hit me square between the eyes.

8. Unlike the other players in the semi-finals, Popov is a bit of a dark ....

9. We're getting nowhere! This is a wild .... chase.

10. It's only fair. It was his idea, so he should get the .... share of the profits.

11. Ted has always been the black .... of the family. His parents are lawyers, his two brothers are doctors, while he dropped out of school at 15.

12. You're not going to .... your way out of doing the washing-up this time.

13. It was a nightmare. She .... on about her job for hours!

6 Arguing

according to sb/sth: this is what sb/sth (a report, the weather forecast, the rule book, a contract, etc) says
According to her mother, she is having second thoughts.

(by) far and away: used in superlative sentences for emphasis
By far and away the biggest flaw in his argument is... .

consequently: as a result of this
She is overworked and consequently suffering from stress.

for instance: for example
I can see a great many disadvantages to privatising hospitals. For instance, what happens to those people who cannot afford medical insurance?

given: when you consider/think about
Given her lack of experience, I think that she has done remarkably well.

granted/admittedly: used to accept that what the person one is arguing against says, is true; *granted* can be followed by *that* while *admittedly* cannot
Granted that by not joining the single currency we will preserve one facet of our national identity. But is it really worth it?
Admittedly, John is a brilliant athlete.

in accordance: conforming to
The estate will be divided among his heirs, in accordance with his will.

in addition to: and; followed by -ing form or noun
In addition to winning the Pulitzer Prize, she was also awarded the Nobel Prize for Literature.

in all: in total
There were about 5,000 people in all at the concert.

in case: because sb/sth might happen
Be quiet in case she hears us.

in comparison with: compared with
His hometown seemed dull in comparison with London.

in opposition: opposing, on the other side
There was a wave of protest in opposition to the new labour law.

in order to: so as to
He left the phone off the hook in order not to be disturbed.

in the event of: (formal) if sth occurs; for possible future happening
In the event of rain, the picnic will be postponed.

in (the) light of sth: taking sth into consideration; followed by a *noun* or *the fact that*
In (the) light of the new evidence, he will be tried for forgery as well.

key: (adj) the most important
the key point/argument/figure

Unemployment is likely to be a key issue in the debate tonight.

largely: mostly
The fact that he is in debt is largely his own fault, as he buys too much on credit.

much as: even though; typically used with **appreciate**, **sympathise** and verbs of **liking/disliking**
Much as I sympathise with your problems, I'm afraid that there is nothing I can do to help you.

nor: not... either (used to introduce another negative idea and is followed by inversion)
Finding somewhere to live is never easy in this part of Oxford. Nor is it particularly cheap.

notwithstanding: despite
Notwithstanding their different political views, they get on very well.

on top of: in addition to
The cat dug up the bulbs I had planted and then, on top of that, left muddy footprints all over the floor.

particularly: especially
I am particularly fond of this restaurant and dine here often.

while: (i) whereas, (ii) although
While Harry liked the idea, Jerry didn't think it would work.
While the government acknowledges the existence of the problem, it is unwilling to do anything about it.

Practice

1. a. Match the statements with their responses.

   1. **Given** the increasing depletion of the earth's resources,
   2. **According** to the experts,
   3. **In addition to** recycling paper, glass and aluminium,
   4. **Much as** some local authorities encourage recycling,

   a there are many other ways we can help the environment in the home.
   b others do little to address the problem.
   c the earth's resources are finite.
   d it is vital to recycle on a wider scale than we do at present.

   b. Discuss the following debate issue with a partner, using words/phrases from this unit and the prompts below, as well as your own ideas. Use exercise 1a as a model to construct your arguments.

   SHOULD VOTING IN ELECTIONS BE COMPULSORY?

   Yes
   - people/not vote/otherwise;
   - civic obligation;
   - no vote/no change

   No
   - freedom/choice;
   - if/not like/alternatives;
   - few votes/change nothing

14

2. Read the text and decide which answer (A, B, C or D) best fits each gap.

Arguing vs Quarrelling

Oscar Wilde once remarked that he disliked arguments as they were always vulgar and often convincing. What, 0) *then*, is the difference between an argument and a quarrel? Look the word "quarrel" up in a dictionary and you will find it defined 1) .... an "angry argument". It seems that "angry" is the 2) .... word here. Both quarrelling and arguing involve disagreements 3) .... it is only during the former that we become angry or upset. We may raise our voices or even display aggressive behaviour when quarrelling, 4) .... in an argument, we maintain a 5) .... tone of voice and refrain from physically threatening our opponent. 6) ...., should we forget the differences in content. An argument is a discussion or debate in which two or more people put forward different or opposing views. They may not be personally concerned in the issues under discussion. 7) ...., the process is an objective, intellectual one. Evidence and logic may be used 8) .... to support the speaker's point of view and possibly to convince the other(s). A quarrel, 9) ...., is personal, bound up with the ego and the participants' sense of self. 10) ...., things that the opponent may have said or done in the past are often dragged up at random as and when they occur to the speaker, in 11) .... the logical marshalling of ideas which arguing involves. A quarrel may result from a clash of personalities, may hurt the participants and may be sincerely regretted afterwards. 12) .... that there are hot-tempered people around, they may get carried away in an argument 13) .... it degenerates into a quarrel, but it should, 14) .... speaking, be a dispassionate exchange of views 15) .... a shouting match.

0	A particularly	B then	C although	D say
1	A as	B like	C by	D such
2	A key	B basic	C code	D main
3	A notwithstanding	B while	C consequently	D but
4	A nevertheless	B when	C whereas	D however
5	A steady	B level	C plain	D monotonous
6	A In addition	B Also	C Nor	D In all
7	A Largely	B Admittedly	C Particularly	D Consequently
8	A in order	B in case	C in the event	D in effect
9	A notwithstanding	B despite	C however	D no matter
10	A For that	B For instance	C In fact	D That is
11	A comparison with	B tandem with	C opposition to	D contradiction
12	A Allowing	B Granted	C Given	D Knowing
13	A so there	B so much	C so as	D so that
14	A generally	B usually	C normally	D habitually
15	A better than	B rather than	C more than	D other than

3. The linkers (1-7) used in the text are jumbled. Read the text and swap them around so that they function properly.

The Silent Killer

A 27-year-old British hospital doctor collapses and dies. **1) In addition to** the coroner's report, he died of natural causes. However, **2) while** the fact that the young medic had just completed an 86-hour working week, could it not be that he died as a result of stress and overwork? We ignore stress at our peril, and **3) far and away** we acknowledge its existence, we choose to pay very little attention to the effects it has on our health. Stress, **4) in light of** resulting from overwork, an unhealthy liestyle or a combination of the two, is a potent and unforgiving killer. Something must be done because things can only get worse. Modern life favours and nurtures stress. **5) According to** living in work-orientated cultures in which overwork is the norm, we seem to be incapable of leading stable and balanced personal lives. Stress upon stress. So what are we to do? The first step for most of us is to face up to the truth: stress causes heart problems, cancer and depression and, as a result, in today's world it is **6) if** the biggest threat to our well-being. At least **7) whether** the young doctor had died in a Japanese hospital his death certificate would have read 'karoshi' - death by overwork.

1 .... 2 .... 3 ....
4 .... 5 .... 6 ....
7 ....

7 Body

Posture and Movement

to crouch: to sit with legs bent under you so that you are close to the ground and leaning forward slightly
Soldiers in camouflage crouched silently in the bushes.

to curl up: to move into a position where your body makes a rounded shape
The cat was curled up on the sofa, nose to tail, fast asleep.

to duck: to quickly lower your head in order to avoid being hit by sth, or so as not to be seen
If he hadn't ducked, the ball would have hit him square in the face.

to fidget: to be constantly moving your hands or your feet
Children often fidget and fuss around restlessly when they are bored.

to flinch: to make a sudden small movement because sth has hurt you or has made you jump
I'm going to put a little drop of this in your eye so try not to flinch.

to frown: to lower your eyebrows because you are angry or you do not understand
He frowned in frustration as he tried to add the sums one more time.

to kneel: to bend your legs so that your knees are touching the ground
He knelt before the Queen to be knighted.

to nod: to move your head up and down (in most countries, you nod when you say yes)
"Are you all happy with today's programme?" she asked. Everyone nodded in agreement.

to nudge: to gently push sb with your elbow to attract their attention
She nudged him. "Look," she said. "I think that's Elton John over there."

to shiver: if you are shivering, your body is shaking because you are cold
He had forgotten to take his coat and was shivering.

to shudder: if you shudder, your whole body shakes for a short time because you have seen, heard or tasted sth unpleasant
The surgeon then proceeded to describe the operation in graphic detail. Mr Forth shuddered.

to tremble: if you are trembling, your body or part of your body is shaking because you are frightened or very nervous
I was so scared that I couldn't stop trembling.

Compound Body Adjectives

bloodcurdling (scream): very frightening
We heard a bloodcurdling scream and then we saw the vampire.

eye-catching: so attractive or unusual that you can't help noticing it
A good advertising poster must be simple but eye-catching.

first-hand: if you have first-hand experience of sth, you have experienced it personally
Now, Gary, you have first-hand experience of teaching in Paraguay.

hair-raising: very frightening; used to describe experiences and journeys
How we didn't crash I do not know. It was one of the most hair-raising bus rides I've ever been on.

head-on: used to describe a collision between two moving vehicles where the front part of one vehicle hits the front part of another vehicle
The car he was driving was involved in a head-on collision with a lorry.

light-hearted: funny and not very serious
light-hearted films/ television programmes/books
It's a comedy, but I wouldn't describe it as being a light-hearted film.

mouth-watering: food that looks and/or smells very good
... a shop full of mouth-watering cakes.

nail-biting: very exciting and dramatic, because you do not know what is going to happen
The final would be decided on penalty kicks. It was going to be a nail-biting five minutes.

narrow-minded: not accepting and positively disliking anything new, different or radical **Opp:** broad-minded
My parents are very broad-minded and accept new ideas easily.

well-thumbed: a book or magazine that has been read so much that the edges and corners of the pages are dirty and in poor condition
Some of the second-hand books were well-thumbed.

Verb-Noun Combinations

not to bat an eyelid: not to show any visible signs of surprise
When I told him that his bill came to £25,000, he didn't bat an eyelid. His face remained expressionless.

to clear your throat: to cough in order to speak more clearly
He stood up, cleared his throat and started to speak.

to clench your fist: to curl your fingers up very tightly, usually because you are very angry (also: **to clench your teeth**)
He clenched his fists and went to punch me.

to cross your legs: while sitting, to put one leg on top of the other
I had hardly enough room in my airline seat to cross my legs, let alone stretch them.

to flex your muscles: to strike a pose and show your muscles
The strong man at the fairground was proudly flexing his muscles.

to fold your arms: to bring your arms together and link them
She folded her arms over her chest and glared at him defiantly.

to grit your teeth: to press your teeth tightly together, often because you are angry or distressed (also: **to clench your teeth**)

Joe gritted his teeth as the bullet was extracted from his arm.

to pluck your eyebrows: to pull out some of the hairs of your eyebrows, using tweezers

For this season's look, pluck your eyebrows and pencil them into a half-moon shape.

sb's heart is pounding: sb's heart is beating very hard

As he took the envelope containing his results, his hands were shaking and his heart was pounding.

to rumble (of stomach): to make a noise because it is empty and you are hungry

I hadn't had breakfast and in the middle of the interview my stomach started rumbling.

to shake your head: to move your head from side to side; in most countries, you shake your head when you say no

He shook his head as a sign of refusal.

to shrug your shoulders: to move your shoulders up and down

The boy shrugged his shoulders and said: "Who cares?"

to sprain (your ankle/wrist): to twist and hurt (your ankle/wrist)

She fell down the stairs and sprained her ankle.

to stub your toe: to hit your toe against sth

She stubbed her toe against the leg of the chair.

Practice

1. Match the verbs in the box with their definitions (sentences 1 to 12).

> nudge – duck – kneel – crouch – tremble – fidget – curl up – shudder – frown – nod – shiver – flinch

1 You do it when you make a small sudden movement because something has hurt you (an injection, for example) or something has made you jump. ....
2 Some people do it when they pray. ....
3 You do it to avoid something that has been thrown at your head. ....
4 You do it with your elbow to get someone's attention. ....
5 You do it on the floor or on a big sofa, often whilst reading a book or watching television. ....
6 You do it when you lower your body to the ground by bending your knees. When a football team is having its photograph taken, the players in the front row do it. ....
7 When you shake because you are cold, you do it. ....
8 When you shake momentarily because you have seen, heard or eaten something unpleasant, you do it. ....
9 When you shake because you are frightened, you do it. ....
10 You do it with your eyebrows when you are angry or you don't understand. ....
11 You do it with your head when you are agreeing with someone or when you are saying yes. ....
12 Kids do it when they can't keep still. ....

2. Each of the compound body adjectives below is followed by two nouns. Only one of the nouns goes with the adjective. Circle the correct one. Then use the correct combinations in sentences.

1	a well-thumbed	**book / road**
2	a nail-biting	**finish / animal**
3	a mouth-watering	**nap / dessert**
4	an eye-catching	**disease / dress**
5	a light-hearted	**comedy / fruit**
6	narrow-minded	**streets / parents**
7	a blood-curdling	**recipe / scream**
8	a hair-raising	**shampoo / bus journey**
9	a head-on	**collision / decision**
10	first-hand	**cars / knowledge**

3. a. Complete the collocations with an appropriate part of the body from the box below.

> shoulders – heart – teeth – fist – eyebrows – legs – muscles – eyelid – toe – throat – head – stomach – ankle – arms

1 He cleared his ....
2 He didn't bat an ....
3 He shrugged his ....
4 He crossed his ....
5 She folded her ....
6 He stubbed his ....
7 He flexed his ....
8 He clenched his ....
9 His .... was pounding.
10 He shook his ....
11 She sprained her ....
12 She plucked her ....
13 My .... was rumbling.
14 She gritted her ....

b. Describe the pictures using appropriate collocations from exercise 3a.

8 Body Idioms

a pain in the neck: a very annoying person, thing or task

All he does is complain all the time. He is a real pain in the neck.

at the foot of: at the bottom of (a hill, mountain, the stairs, a tree, your bed, etc)

He fell asleep at the foot of a tree.

to cost an arm and a leg: to be very expensive

Getting this roof fixed will cost us an arm and a leg.

to cry your eyes out: to cry a lot

It was a very sad film. I cried my eyes out all the way through it.

to face a team: to play against another team

If they win this match, they will have to face Lazio in the next round.

to fall head over heels in love (with sb): to fall madly and completely in love (with sb)

He spotted her across a crowded room and fell head over heels in love with her.

to foot the bill: to pay the bill at a restaurant or hotel (used to emphasise that you thought sb else was going to pay)

Not only did I sit there waiting for him for over an hour but he left me to foot the bill!

to get cold feet: to suddenly feel that you are not brave enough to do sth important

He got cold feet at the last minute and withdrew from the competition.

to get sth off your chest: to tell sb sth that has been worrying you

He told them the secret to get it off his chest.

to get up sb's nose: to annoy sb

My neighbours deliberately play their radio at maximum volume to get up my nose.

to give sb a hand (with sth): to help sb do sth

I'm sure Tim will give you a hand to move the fridge.

to be glad to see the back of sb/sth: to be happy when sb leaves or when sth is finished

She's so irritating! I'd be glad to see the back of her.

to have sth on the brain: to be obsessed by sth and think about it all the time

He's got motorbikes on the brain. It's all he ever thinks about.

to have your eye on sth: to have seen sth (in a shop, for example) that you want to buy/have

I've had my eye on a ring from Munn's Stores for ages.

to have/give sb a head start: to have/give sb an advantage over a competitor (in business)/other people (in life)

We sent him to a private school to give him a head start in life.

to head home: to leave somewhere in order to go home

I think we'd better head home. It's getting late.

I can't put my finger on: to know that sth is wrong or different, but be unable to say exactly what it is

I couldn't put my finger on what it was, but there was something different about her appearance.

I couldn't keep a straight face: I couldn't stop laughing

He couldn't keep a straight face during the interview.

I don't know off-hand: (informal) I can't tell/answer until I have checked first

"What time do we land?" "I don't know off-hand. I'll have to check the tickets."

I'd give my right arm to: I would really like to

I'd give my right arm to have a fantastic job like his.

in the eyes of the law: legally, according to the laws of the land

You knowingly drove through a red light and in the eyes of the law that is a criminal offence.

to keep an eye on sth/sb: to look after sth/sb

Could you keep an eye on my plants while we are away?

to know somewhere like the back of your hand: to know a particular place very well (not used for people)

I know Venice like the back of my hand.

to learn to stand on one's own two feet: to learn not to depend on others (e.g. one's parents)

He's 36, so it's time he learned to stand on his own two feet.

to make/lose money hand over fist: to rapidly make or lose large sums of money

We had to close the business because we were losing money hand over fist.

off the top of one's head: information given immediately without full knowledge of the facts

Off the top off my head, I would say that it will cost about £2,000.

sth is on its last legs: sth (a car, a television, etc) is in very bad condition and will very soon stop working

This car is on its last legs. It's time we bought a new one.

to pull sb's leg: to play a joke on sb and make them believe sth that is not true

He wasn't being serious. He was pulling your leg.

to put your foot down: to become strict and tell sb (generally a child) that they must/can't do sth

Well, you'll have to put your foot down and tell him he can't do whatever he likes.

to set eyes on sb: to see sb, often for the first time

The minute he set eyes on her, he knew she was the one.

to set your heart on sth: to really want sth

I'd set my heart on that house and I was devastated when it was sold.

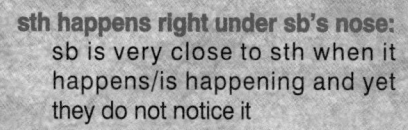

sth happens right under sb's nose: sb is very close to sth when it happens/is happening and yet they do not notice it

The children were copying from each other during the test, right under the teacher's nose.

to stick your nose into other people's business/affairs: to interfere in a situation which does not concern you, with the result that you cause other people problems

Now she hates you. That's what you get for sticking your nose into her affairs.

to think on your feet: to be able to give good answers to unexpected questions

The ability to think on your feet is essential if you want to be a politician.

with an eye to: in order to (+ noun or -ing form)

He married her with an eye to getting his hands on her money.

(it's) written all over your face: to show by the expression on your face how you really feel

She said she wasn't angry, but clearly she was. It was written all over her face.

you have to hand it to sb: you have to admire and respect sb (for sth they have done)

You may not like the way Charles runs his business, but you have to hand it to him, he gets results.

Practice

1. Complete the sentences using an appropriate body word.

1 I was born and bred in London so I know the city like the back of my ....
2 He's got football on the .... It's all he ever talks about.
3 It was a joke! I was just pulling your ....
4 They're so lucky! I'd give my right .... for a house like theirs.
5 He fell .... over .... in love the minute she walked into the room.
6 Business has been awful. We've been losing money .... over ....
7 Do you see how much better you feel now that you have got it off your .... ?
8 "There's no way we can afford it," she said. "It'll cost an .... and a ...."
9 She had set her .... on studying at Oxford but they turned her down.
10 Something was different about the place, but I just couldn't put my .... on what it was.
11 She stayed with us for six weeks and she was a real pain in the .... All she did was criticise me and complain about everything. When she left, I was glad to see the .... of her.
12 I think it's time we got a new television. This one is on its last ....

2. Circle the correct item.

1 It's impossible to anticipate all the questions that you are going to be asked. You're going to have to think on your **head / feet**.
2 It's a terrible car and what really gets up my **teeth / nose** is that I paid a fortune for it.
3 Everything you need for your climb can be found in the village situated at the **head / foot** of the mountain.
4 I don't know off- **heart / hand**. I'll have to look it up in the encyclopaedia.
5 You have to **back / hand** it to Joe – his company is a roaring success.
6 The lecturer had such a ridiculous voice that neither of us could keep a straight **eye / face**.
7 Mum had her **heart / eye** on the painting for months, so we bought it for her on her birthday.
8 We were the first company to set up business in China, so we have a **neck / head** start over our competitors.
9 Now it looks like I'm going to have to **hand / foot** the bill for the repairs.
10 He bought the cottage with a(n) **eye / heart** to doing it up and selling it at a later date.
11 He had always said yes. But this time he was going to put his **hand / foot** down.
12 It was happening right under my **eye / nose**, and I didn't realise it. I feel so stupid.
13 The little girl was obviously very upset as she was sitting on the step crying her **eyes / chest** out.
14 We ought to **hand / head** home. It's late and I'm working early tomorrow.
15 Why do you always have to stick your **hand / nose** into other people's affairs?
16 I don't think he's really determined. In the end, he'll get cold **feet / heart** and cancel the whole thing.

9 Chance and Probability

to be bound to happen: to be certain to happen (because it always happens)

There's bound to be heavy traffic at this time of day.

to be certain to happen: sth will very probably happen

They are certain to find out.

to be in with a chance of + ing form: there is a good possibility that

Only six people have applied for the scholarship, so Joanna is in with a good chance of winning it.

to be unlikely to/it is unlikely that: one/sth probably won't

They are unlikely to accept, but we can still try.

It is unlikely that they will let us in without tickets.

to blow your chances: to ruin your chances (of getting/achieving sth)

He blew his chances of a promotion when his boss overheard him criticising the firm's methods.

to grab an opportunity/chance (with both hands): to quickly accept a good opportunity, especially because you think you will not get that opportunity again

When the opportunity to work abroad presented itself, he grabbed it with both hands.

(sth will), in all probability, (happen): sth will very probably happen

He will, in all probability, deny having had anything to do with it and put the blame on us.

it is doubtful whether/that sth will happen: sth probably won't happen

Given his injury, his doctors say that it is doubtful whether he will ever play again.

it was purely by chance that ...: it was complete chance that sth happened

It was purely by chance that I found out about the job.

to jump at the chance/opportunity: to quickly accept a good opportunity

She was offered a free holiday in the Caribbean and, of course, she jumped at the chance.

(to do sth) on the off-chance: do sth hoping it will succeed although you think it is unlikely

We knew they would be fully booked, but we still went there on the off-chance that somebody might have cancelled at the last minute.

to pass up a chance/opportunity: to say no to a good opportunity (a good job offer, etc)

She'd be a fool to pass up a chance like that/pass a chance like that up.

(not) to stand a chance: to have no possibility (of achieving/getting sth) [Note: **to stand no/little/a (very) good chance of + ing form**]

Win the lottery? You don't stand a chance.

With Senator Fox withdrawing from the race, she stands a good chance of winning the election.

the chances are that sth will happen: sth will probably happen

Man will definitely walk on Mars and the chances are that this will happen in the next thirty years.

the chances of sth happening are very remote: there is very little possibility that sth will happen

The chances of his winning the next election are very remote.

the odds are against sth happening: sth probably won't happen

The odds are against her passing the exam, as so few people get through first time.

there's a slim/remote/little chance that sth will/could happen: there is not much possibility of sth happening

Opp: there's every chance that sth will happen

There is, I suppose, a slim chance that you'll get your money back, but I wouldn't bank on it.

There's every chance that she'll win the race.

there's every indication (to suggest) that sth will happen: all the signs show that sth will very probably happen

There's every indication to suggest that by the end of the year the economy will be on its feet again.

there's every likelihood of sth happening/that sth will happen: sth will very probably happen; **Opp:** there's little/no likelihood of sth happening/that sth will happen

There's every likelihood of his being re-elected in next month's general election.

There's little likelihood that they will agree to such a deal, as they stand to gain so little from it.

Practice

1. Work with a partner. Make predictions about the environment and the future of our planet using expressions from this unit and the prompts below, as well as your own ideas.

- hole in ozone layer/grow bigger/incidence/skin cancer
- rainforests/be/completely destroyed/build cities
- be/ban/use of CFCs
- recycling/be/enforce/by law
- supplies/fossil fuels - coal, gas, oil/run out

2. Choose the correct item.

1 Harry was offered a scholarship to study in Spain and he .... the opportunity with both hands.
   A grasped   B grabbed   C held   D passed

2 No way will you beat him. You don't .... a chance. He's a hundred times better than you are.
   A hold   B run   C possess   D stand

3 It was .... by chance that we managed to find her.
   A sheerly   B purely   C plainly   D highly

4 Both the favourite and then the second favourite pulled out. Naturally, we thought we were .... a chance.
   A in with   B up for   C in for   D up with

5 A full scholarship to Harvard and you're worried about leaving your job? Get real! You'd be a fool to .... up a chance like that.
   A turn   B brush   C pass   D cast

6 We knew the concert was sold out, but we still went to the stadium .... the off-chance that someone might want to sell us their tickets.
   A with   B by   C on   D in

7 He admitted taking a bribe and he doesn't think he's .... his chances of getting re-elected?
   A pulled   B wiped   C thrown   D blown

8 Given the appalling weather conditions on top of the mountain, I'd say the chances of their finding any survivors are very .... indeed.
   A narrow   B lean   C remote   D shallow

9 I suppose that there is a .... chance that he could win, but I can't see it happening, myself.
   A thin   B slim   C meagre   D short

10 If someone offered me a posting in South Africa, I'd .... at the chance.
   A bound   B jump   C grab   D seize

3.
For questions 1 to 10 below, complete the second sentence so that it has a similar meaning to the first sentence, using 3 to 8 words. You must include the word given in bold, which cannot be changed in any way.

1 Tom's coach said that he didn't think he would be fit enough to compete.
   doubtful   Tom's coach said .... enough to compete.

2 I'm sure they will complain about the delay.
   certain   They .... about the delay.

3 It's very unlikely that he will continue racing once this season has finished.
   probability   He will, ... once this season has finished.

4 All the signs point to a steady economic recovery over the next two years.
   indication   There's .... economic recovery over the next two years.

5 He stands little chance of winning.
   odds   The .... winning.

6 "He will probably fail in the attempt," she said.
   unlikely   She said that he was ....

7 It's more than likely that he will call an election in the next two months.
   likelihood   There's .... in the next two months.

8 Meteorologists say that we will probably have a hard winter this year.
   chances   According to meteorologists, ... a hard winter this year.

9 I'm sure he knows by now.
   bound   He's .... out by now.

10 He never planned to become an actor. It just happened.
   purely   It was .... an actor.

21

10 Choosing and Decisions - Clothes I (Adjectives)

Choosing and Decisions

to be in a quandary: not to be able to decide what to do because you find yourself in a difficult situation

He was in a quandary as to whether to accept the new job, even though it was better-paid, as it would involve moving to a new area.

to be in two minds about sth/ whether to do sth: can't decide whether or not to do sth

I'm in two minds about going to Jennifer's party, as I have to get up very early for work tomorrow.

to be shortlisted: to be chosen from a large number of applicants for a job to join a much smaller group, all of whom will be interviewed and one of whom will be given the job

Three hundred people applied for the job, but only six were shortlisted for interview.

to be spoilt for choice: to have a lot of (similar) things to choose from

As for somewhere to stay, you will be spoilt for choice. This stretch of the Black Sea boasts over fifty top-class hotels.

to be torn between sth and sth else: to find two things attractive and as a result not to be able to decide between them

I'm torn between a degree course in pure maths and one in computer engineering.

hand-picked: especially chosen to do a particular job

Most of the people on the advisory body had been hand-picked by the Chancellor himself.

to have a change of heart: to change the way you feel about sth/sb

I wasn't going to take the children to the theatre but I had a change of heart and took them after all.

to have no alternative but to...: the only choice sb has is to; often used in formal threats

If you do not pay this bill within 14 days, we will have no alternative but to take legal action against you.

to opt for/to do sth: (formal) to choose (to do) sth

My choice was between a company car or a 5% increase in my salary. After much deliberation, I opted for the car.

to reach/come to/arrive at a decision: to decide after careful consideration (generally used for juries, committees, boards of directors, governments, etc)

The jury were unable to reach a decision.

to single (sth/sb) out: to choose and pay special attention to sth/sb from a group of similar things/people, usually in order to praise or criticise them

He said that all the paintings were excellent, but he singled mine out for special praise.

to sit on the fence: not to commit oneself in an argument; to neither agree nor disagree

Gary refuses to become involved in other people's arguments. He just sits on the fence.

Clothes I (Adjectives)

baggy: very loose

a baggy jumper/pair of jeans

creased/crumpled: unironed, full of lines and wrinkles

a creased/crumpled jacket/shirt

faded: having lost its original colour or brightness

a faded pair of jeans/sweatshirt

fancy: special and unusual, with a lot of decoration

The pretty lace blouse had a fancy embroidered trimming.

fetching: attractive; can be used to describe a person (generally a woman) or an article of clothing

She was wearing a particularly fetching dress.

flared: wide at the bottom

flared trousers/jeans

flat: with very low or no heels

I'd wear flat shoes for your walking holiday if I were you.

garish: very colourful, in a way that is not in good taste

He was a paragon of bad taste in his checked trousers and garish pink shirt.

grubby: dirty

grubby coat/face

loud: very colourful, in a way that some might find unpleasant

That tie is far too loud, especially with that brightly coloured shirt.

moth-eaten: full of holes

Does he have to dress so scruffily? Look at that moth-eaten jumper he is wearing.

patched: with pieces of material sewn on to cover holes

The tramp looked a sad sight in his ragged jacket and patched trousers.

platform: platform shoes have thick high heels and an elevated sole

Flared trousers, wide lapels and platform shoes – de rigueur for the fashion-conscious in the 1970's.

shabby: looking old and in bad condition

This costume is so shabby that I'll have to throw it out.

sturdy: strong

Cordelia was wearing sturdy riding gear.

synthetic: made from artificial substances/material

Clothes that are part natural fabric and part synthetic are easy to wash and care for.

tailored: designed to fit close to the body

A tailored suit is the best thing to wear for formal occasions.

worn-out: old and ready to be thrown away

Those worn-out gardening trousers are only fit to be torn up and used as dusters.

10

Practice

1. Choose the correct item.

1. Chris was .... between buying a new house and going on a round-the-world cruise.
   A pulled B torn C moving D leaning

2. It was a difficult decision, but in the end we .... for a state rather than a private pension scheme.
   A chose B preferred C opted D selected

3. Of all the entries received, his was .... out for special praise.
   A isolated B brought C opted D singled

4. If you need a decent suit, go to Munns Stores. You'll be .... for choice.
   A overcome B ruined C spoilt D overwhelmed

5. I have to admit I'm in two .... about whether to tell her or not.
   A minds B choices C camps D options

6. Royson had deliberately disobeyed her orders. She had no alternative .... punish him.
   A but to B to C apart from D than

7. They were the best economic analysts in the United States – a team hand-.................. by the President himself.
   A selected B picked C named D settled

8. I was in a .... as to what to do. If I told the truth, he would get into trouble, but if I said nothing I would be in more trouble.
   A doubt B quandary C hitch D complexity

9. It took the selection panel only twenty minutes to .... to a decision.
   A reach B arrive C come D clinch

10. I wish you would stop sitting on the .... and decide whose side you're on.
    A fence B crossroads C wall D middle

11. At first, her father was against her studying abroad, but later on he had a change of .... and let her go to Paris.
    A thought B feeling C mind D heart

12. Two hundred and fifty people applied for the job. Of these, only twenty applicants were .... for interview.
    A shortcut
    B short-staffed
    C short-changed
    D shortlisted

2. Fill in the gaps with an appropriate adjective from the box below. Each gap is followed by a definition of the adjective you need. You may have to use some of the adjectives twice and there are some extra adjectives which you do not need to use.

> tailored – worn-out – flared – baggy – garish – loud – shabby – fetching – flat – fancy – grubby – crumpled – creased – synthetic – patched – moth-eaten – sturdy – platform – faded

A When on safari, it is important not to wear 1) .... (very colourful) or 2) .... (very colourful) clothes, as bright colours will only scare animals away. Stick to muted colours. If going on a walking safari, remember to pack a pair of 3) .... (strong), 4) .... (without heels) shoes – hiking boots are best.

B You wouldn't think that man over there is Doctor Fredricks, would you? Look at him, standing there in those 1) .... (dirty) jeans and that 2) .... (full of holes) cardigan.

C She breezed into the room wearing 1) .... (unironed), 2) .... (having lost its original colour or brightness), 3) .... (very loose) trousers and black 4) .... (old and ready to be thrown away) shoes. Looking up, her father almost choked on his tea. "I'm off to school," she said.

D Neither of us looked particularly 1) .... (attractive) on the day we first met. I'd crawled out of bed and thrown on the first things that came to hand: a 2) .... (old) pair of jeans, a 3) .... (unironed) shirt and a pair of tennis shoes. She had walked in dressed in a hideous pair of 4) .... (wide at the bottom) corduroy trousers and a huge 5) .... (very loose) jumper. Sartorially, we were made for each other.

23

11 Clothes II (Idioms) - Colours

Clothes II (Idioms)

and, to cap it all: and finally; used to introduce the last and often worst thing in a list

It rained all the time, the hotel was horrible, and, to cap it all, we lost our passports.

at the drop of a hat: immediately and without thinking

If he proposed to her, she would definitely marry him at the drop of a hat.

to be out of pocket: to have less money than you should have [Note: **I don't want you to be out of pocket:** an expression used to check if sb will have enough money themselves if they lend you money]

My expenses cost me more than they paid me, so I worked and ended up out of pocket.

below the belt: unfair and cruel; for a criticism/remark/comment

You should apologise to Jo. What you said to her last night was really below the belt.

to fit like a glove: to fit perfectly; used for clothes

I was sure this coat was going to be too big for me, but it fits like a glove.

to get the boot: (informal) be dismissed from your job [Note: **to give/be given the boot**]

Jim got the boot last week for persistently being late.

to get hot under the collar about sth: to get angry about sth; generally used to describe sb else - not yourself

What are you getting so hot under the collar about?

to get/have sth under your belt: to have already achieved or done sth

Once they had got their first championship under their belts, there was no stopping them.

to have sth up your sleeve: to have a secret plan or idea

It seemed to be a hopeless case but his lawyer had something up his sleeve.

if I were in your/his/etc shoes: if I were you/him/etc

If I were in their shoes, I would seriously think about taking him to court.

to pull your socks up: to work harder and start trying to improve your work/behaviour/performance

If you don't pull your socks up, you are going to fail these exams.

sb wears the trousers (in that house): (informal) to be the dominant partner of the two people involved; generally used about women

Jenny wears the trousers in that house. Nathan won't breathe unless she gives him permission!

Colours

to be black and blue all over: to be bruised everywhere

I didn't break any bones, but I was black and blue all over after falling down the stairs.

to give sb a black look: to look angrily at sb

Everyone gave me black looks when I said I was bored.

in black and white: written or printed [Note: **to have sth down in black and white:** to have written proof of sth]

There it was, in black and white; he had passed!

the black market: the illegal buying and selling of goods or the illegal changing of money

He bought the tickets on the black market.

once in a blue moon: not very often

He still writes, but only once in a blue moon.

out of the blue: suddenly and unexpectedly

I hadn't heard from him for ten years, then, out of the blue, I got a fax from him.

you can ... until you are blue in the face, but ...: you can (scream/argue) as much as you like but (I won't change my mind/ we won't let you ...)

You can scream and shout until you're blue in the face, but you're not borrowing the car.

the green belt: an area of countryside that surrounds a city and in which the construction of houses is strictly controlled

Living in the green belt is both peaceful and convenient.

to give sb the green light (to do sth): to give sb (especially a business) permission to do sth

All we need is the council to give us the green light, and we can go ahead with the project.

to have green fingers: to be very good at growing and looking after plants

Cedric's garden is lovely, but then, he does have green fingers.

red tape: complicated official rules and regulations/ bureaucracy

We decided against setting up an office there because of the red tape that would be involved.

to be in the red: to have spent more money than is in your account – so that you owe the bank money

We can't still be in the red. I put £3,000 into our account last week.

to catch sb red-handed: to catch or discover sb while they are in the middle of doing sth wrong

Of course I'm going to plead guilty. What else can I do? I was caught red-handed.

a white-collar job: an office job [Note: **blue-collar work:** manual labour]

White collar jobs may be routine but they are less tiring than factory work.

to go as white as a sheet: to lose all the colour in your face because you are very shocked or sick

When I told her the news, she went as white as a sheet.

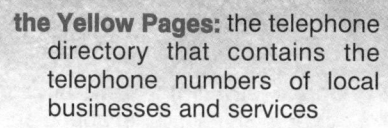

the Yellow Pages: the telephone directory that contains the telephone numbers of local businesses and services
Why don't you look up their number in the Yellow Pages?

a double yellow line: two yellow lines along the side of a road which mean no parking
If you park on a double yellow line, you will be fined.

to be yellow: to be a coward
It is better to face a bully rather than be yellow and run away.

Practice

1. *Complete the idioms in the following sentences with an article of clothing from the box below.*

> socks – belt – trousers – hat – boot – cap – shoes – pocket – sleeve – belt – glove – collar

1 Your coach is right. What you need is two or three years' playing experience under your ....
2 We were delayed taking off, the cabin crew were rude, and, to .... it all, when we arrived in Prague, we were told that our luggage had been lost.
3 It's not difficult to see who wears the .... in that house. Look at the way she orders him around.
4 These trousers fit me like a ....
5 If you can't afford to lend me the money, tell me. I don't want you to be out of ....
6 My opponent had a look of quiet confidence on his face. What did he have up his ....?
7 It's time you pulled your .... up and got down to some serious work. Your exam's next week.
8 I don't know what I'd do if I were in her .... I guess I'd take the promotion.
9 He bought luxury cars, jewels and he'd throw large, extravagant parties at the drop of a ....
10 Why are you getting so hot under the ....? I only said I'd think about their suggestion.
11 Granted he's not our most talented player, but calling him the worst football player on the planet was a bit below the ....
12 No, he didn't resign. He got the ....

2. 🎧 *You will hear someone talking about an incident at customs. Listen to the recording and decide whether the sentences below are true or false.*

1 The customs official looked angrily at Martin. ......
2 Martin had bought the camera at a retail outlet. ......
3 Martin was fed up with bureaucracy. ......
4 The person behind Martin was hot. ......
5 The camera would still be cheap, even with a fine. ......
6 Martin decided that arguing would be a waste of time. ......

3. *Circle the correct item.*

1 I didn't believe I'd won the prize until I saw it in black and **red / white**.
2 She went as **white / blue** as a sheet when I mentioned his name. I had touched a raw and painful nerve.
3 You wouldn't believe how much **red / green** tape is involved in getting a work permit here.
4 I wish I had **yellow / green** fingers like you. I only have to look at a plant and it dies.
5 I parked and quickly ran into the bank. I didn't realise I'd left my car on a double **yellow / white** line.
6 You should have seen the **black / blue** look she gave him when he criticised her work.
7 You can't deny that you did it. You were caught **red / black** - handed.
8 Now that the chairman has given us the **red / green** light, we can go ahead and buy Proudfoot's company.
9 We live in the **green / black** belt just outside London. It's ideal as we live in the country but the city is right on the doorstep.
10 If you don't know the company's number, look it up in the **Blue / Yellow** Pages.
11 I didn't realise hockey was such a violent game. I'm **mauve / black** and blue all over.
12 You're a coward. You're **yellow / green**. You were afraid to do it.
13 You can shout and argue until you're **red / blue** in the face, but I'm not going to change my mind.
14 The bank refused to lend me any more money as my account was in the **black / red**.
15 We hadn't seen her in years and then the other day she came to visit us out of the **red / blue**.
16 We only see each other once in a **blue / white** moon, which is a shame really.
17 He doesn't want a **blue / white** -collar job. He'd rather work outside than be stuck in an office all day.

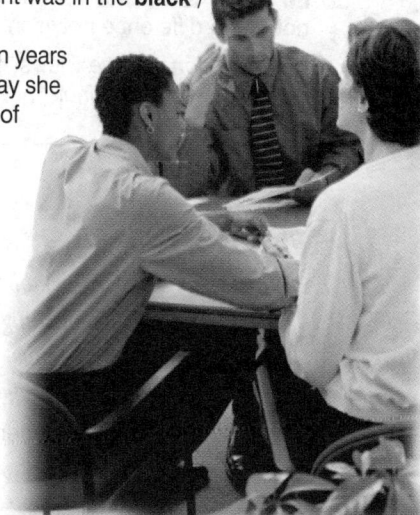

12 Comparing

not to be a patch on: to be much inferior to

I like Krispy burgers, but they are not a patch on Krusty burgers.

to be at odds with: (i) (of two things e.g. results, alibis, etc which should be the same) to be different (ii) (of two people) not to agree with one another about sth or not to share the same opinions or outlook on life

Richards was at odds with his colleagues over the decision.

to be by far (and away) + superlative: by far (and away) is used to emphasise superlatives

Of the two players, Franks is by far and away the most experienced.

It is by far and away the prettiest island along the coast.

to be every bit/just as + adjective + as: to be equally + adjective (used when sb has made a comparison you don't agree with)

My job is every bit as demanding as your job.

to be identical to: to be exactly the same as

Your answers to the maths problems are identical to mine.

to be in a league of one's own: to be much better than the other people who share the same activity

When it comes to modern dance music, The Chemicals are in a league of their own.

to be much the same as: there is not much difference between

Her reaction to the news was much the same as mine.

sb/sth was more of a + noun than a + noun/was not so much a + noun as a + noun: the structures are used (i) when you contradict sb because you think they are exaggerating (ii) to highlight the fact that sth was/is not what you expect(ed) it to be or what it should be

It wasn't so much a river as a stream.

She was more of a mother to me than a sister.

not to be nearly as + adjective + as: to be much inferior to

He is not nearly as talented as she is.

to be nothing like as + adjective + as: to be much inferior to

The reds are nothing like as good as the blues.

to be nowhere near as + adjective + as: to be much inferior to

His second book is nowhere near as good as his first book.

to be on a different wavelength: to have very different ideas and attitudes

My parents and I are on a different wavelength when it comes to taste in music.

to be streets ahead of/to be head and shoulders above: to be much better than

He is streets ahead of the other players in the competition.

Sweden are head and shoulders above the other teams in the tournament.

to be (totally, quite) unlike: to be different from

The new Vectron V is unlike any other computer on the market.

to bear a (striking) resemblance to: to be (very) similar in appearance or character **Opp**: to bear little/no resemblance to

He bears a striking resemblance to his grandfather.

to have nothing in common (with sb): not to share the same ideas, background, qualities, etc

He was very nice, but I won't be seeing him again. We had nothing in common with each other.

to pale in comparison (to sth): to seem small or unimportant when compared to sth else (used for problems)

Our problems pale in comparison to theirs.

to tell apart: to recognise differences between

Only their own mother can tell Simon and Mike apart.

there is a world of difference between: there is a very big difference between

There is a world of difference between butter and margarine.

to think/say/do otherwise: to say/think/do sth different from what has already been mentioned; always comes in the second half of a sentence

It was clearly a penalty, but the referee thought otherwise.

to vary (in): to be different from each other

Cats may vary in size, shape, colour and character, but they make wonderful pets.

Practice

1. For questions 1 to 23, complete the second sentence so that it has a similar meaning to the first sentence, using 3 to 8 words. You must include the word given in bold, which cannot be changed in any way.

1 Buenos Aires is much hotter than London.
   nowhere   London .... Buenos Aires.

2 It's much easier than everyone makes out.
   nothing   It is .... as everyone makes out.

3 Her dress is just as nice as mine.
   bit   Her dress is .... mine.

4 "When you lose someone you love everything else seems pointless," he said.
   pales   "When you lose someone you love ...." he said.

5 Fred is the scruffiest person in the class.
   scruffy   Nobody ....
   .... Fred.

6 His latest film is not nearly as good as his earlier ones.
   patch   His latest film ....
   .... ones.

7 He is a much better swimmer than the others.
   streets   As a swimmer, ...
   .... others.

8 It wasn't so much an order as a request.
   more   It was ....
   .... an order.

9 Of all the teams competing in this year's World Cup, England is in a league of its own.
   far   England is ....
   .... the competition.

10 Simon had never seen anything like it.
   unlike   It was ....
   .... before.

11 We are very different indeed.
   common   We have ....
   .... another.

12 The final version of the report was very different from the initial draft.
   resemblance The final version of the report ....
   .... initial draft.

13 Jack and I obviously think very differently from one another.
   wavelength Jack and I are ....
   ...., as you can see.

14 Jerry thought it was an excellent idea. Unfortunately, his wife found it terrible.
   otherwise Jerry thought it was an excellent idea but ....I'm afraid.

15 Why are my findings different from yours?
   odds   Why are my findings ....
   .... yours?

16 They come in different shapes and sizes.
   vary   They .... size.

17 I can't tell the difference between them; they're identical.
   apart   I ....
   .... the same.

18 With constant practice, you'll be a much better pianist than the others.
   shoulders If you practice constantly, ...
   .... other pianists.

19 Saying something is not the same as doing it.
   world   There ....
   .... and doing it.

20 There is little, if any, difference between brown eggs and white ones.
   much   Brown eggs are ....
   .... white ones.

21 You'll find it difficult to tell them apart.
   identical They .... other.

22 His house is half as big as mine.
   twice   My house .... his.

23 As it gets hotter, I drink more water.
   the   The ....
   .... drink.

2. *Work with a partner. Compare and contrast the two holiday destinations, using expressions from this unit and adjectives from the boxes below each set of pictures, as well as your own ideas.*

A

varied – lively – bustling – exciting – noisy – interesting – historical – boring – polluted – entertaining

B

exhilarating – picturesque – breathtaking – isolated – monotonous – relaxing – exotic – idyllic – secluded

27

13 Cooking and Food

Verbs – Nouns

to bake: to cook e.g. cakes and bread in the oven

to baste: to pour oil or liquid fat over meat while it is cooking

to beat eggs: to mix the white and the yolk together in a bowl with a fork

to bring sth to the boil: to boil sth

to carve: to cut a piece of meat, usually into slices

to chop: to cut sth (usually vegetables) into small pieces

cuisine: a particular style of cooking

Italian cuisine is my favourite.

to defrost: to allow or cause sth to become unfrozen

a dish: (i) a shallow container with a wide uncovered top, used to eat/serve/cook food (ii) a particular kind of food prepared in a particular way

My favourite Chinese dish is sweet and sour chicken.

to dress: to put a mixture of oil, vinegar, salt, etc (salad dressing) on a salad

foil: metal paper used in cooking

to grate: to rub sth (especially cheese and carrots) into small, long, thin pieces, using a grater

a grater: a kitchen tool which has a rough surface (used for cutting food into very small pieces)

to grind: to crush pepper corns or coffee beans into powder or very small pieces

freshly ground coffee

to ice: to put icing (a coating of soft sugar) on the outside of a cake

kettle: a covered container used for boiling water

to knead: to press and stretch dough (the mixture of flour, water, etc used to make bread)

to marinade: to leave food (before it is cooked) in a specially prepared liquid (often a mixture of oil and spices) so as to make it more tender or to give it a special taste

pan: a round, metal container used for cooking things in

to peel: to remove the skin from fruit or vegetables

plate: a round flat dish used for holding food

to pluck: to pull out the feathers from a chicken, turkey, etc so as to prepare it for cooking

to poach: to cook eggs (without their shells) in a special pan in which the eggs are cooked above boiling water

pot: deep round container used for cooking soups, stews, etc

a recipe: cooking instructions

to rinse: to quickly wash sth, generally using running water

to roast: to cook meat or vegetables in the oven

roast potatoes; roast lamb

to rustle up: to quickly cook sth (often when you were not expecting to cook)

to scrub: to wash sth vigorously, sometimes by using a special brush

to season: to add salt, pepper or spices to food, especially when it is being cooked

to shell: to remove the hard outside covering of nuts, some seeds and some sea creatures (crabs, prawns, etc)

sieve: a tool used for separating solids from liquids

to sizzle: describes the noise sth makes when it is being fried

to soak: to leave food (especially beans) in water so that it becomes soft or so that it absorbs the water

to sprinkle: to drop small pieces of salt, cheese, sugar, etc on sth, using a spoon or your fingers

to stuff: to fill the inside of sth (often a chicken or turkey) with a bread or rice mixture, etc

to thicken: to make a sauce thicker

to toss a salad: to mix a salad

to whip: to stir cream very quickly so that it becomes stiff

Idioms, verbs, expressions

to go bananas: to become very angry or very excited

She'll go bananas when she finds out that you have lost her watch.

a breadwinner: a person who supports a family with the money she or he earns

After my father died, I became the family's only breadwinner.

to butter sb up: to be very pleasant to sb (and often pay them compliments) because you want sth from them

Don't try to butter me up! I won't let you have my car.

as different as chalk and cheese: very different from each other

Although they're twins, they're as different as chalk and cheese.

sth is not my cup of tea: (informal) I don't particularly like sth

Opera isn't really my cup of tea.

to grill sb: to ask sb a lot of questions (often in an aggressive way) to make them confess to sth

The police grilled him for 4 hours but he told them nothing.

it's like an oven in here: this room is very hot

How can you study in this room? It's like an oven in here!

peanuts: (said of a sum of money) very small

I like my job but it pays peanuts!

a piece of cake: very easy to do

Don't worry about the exam. It'll be a piece of cake.

to simmer down (of feelings): to calm down, having been very angry

I'd wait for him to simmer down before talking to him.

to take sth with a pinch of salt: not to believe that sth is completely accurate or true

He may say he's a top golfer, but you have to take everything he says with a pinch of salt.

Practice

1. Fill in the gaps that follow the verbs with food items from the box below.

> a turkey – eggs – sugar – a frozen chicken – dough – cream – a sauce –
> a cake – cheese – coffee beans – prawns – meat

1 You grate ....
2 You baste ....
3 You stuff ....
4 You grind ....
5 You beat ....
6 You knead ....
7 You pluck ....
8 You whip ....
9 You sprinkle .... on sth
10 You thicken ....
11 You shell ....
12 You defrost ....
13 You roast ....
14 You ice ....

2. a. Choose the option (A, B, C or D) which best fits each gap in the recipe below.

0) *Soak* two cups of haricot beans for six to eight hours. Drain, add fresh water, garlic and seasoning. **1)** .... to the boil and then **2)** .... gently until the beans are tender. Drain again. Finely **3)** .... some onions, add some peeled tomatoes and cook the onions and tomatoes to a puree. When the puree is ready, add the beans. Meanwhile, **4)** .... a joint of beef and cover it with butter in **5)** .... **6)** .... the beef in a preheated oven at gas mark 5 or 190°C. **7)** .... the beef every ten minutes for an hour, discarding the wrapping for the last ten minutes to **8)** .... the joint. Warm the beans and puree in a **9)** .... Do not **10)** .... , as the beans will break. **11)** .... the beef into slices and then serve on top of the beans. Traditionally, this **12)** .... is **13)** .... with potatoes and leeks.

0	A Rinse	B Scrub	C Soak	D Pluck
1	A Take	B Induce	C Bring	D Render
2	A simmer	B sizzle	C bubble	D stand
3	A shred	B carve	C chop	D peel
4	A season	B toss	C dress	D peel
5	A paper	B foil	C covering	D bag
6	A Bake	B Poach	C Marinade	D Roast
7	A Bake	B Grate	C Grind	D Baste
8	A breathe	B crackle	C evaporate	D brown
9	A grater	B pot	C sieve	D kettle
10	A revolve	B beat	C knead	D stir
11	A Sever	B Carve	C Chop	D Dismantle
12	A plate	B cuisine	C dish	D recipe
13	A served	B tasted	C sprinkled	D rustled up

b. Which of the following would you use in making the dish?

3. Complete the sentences with an appropriate word related to cooking and food.

1 It is difficult to make ends meet when you are the sole ....:............ for a large family.
2 They said I was the best boss they had ever had, but I think they were just trying to .... me up.
3 The police .... the suspects for over six hours.
4 My exam was a piece of .... It couldn't have been easier.
5 Malcolm's still angry about being passed over for promotion but he should soon .... down.
6 You pay her £25 a week! That's .... for a woman of her experience.
7 "Turn on the air conditioning," she said. "It's like a(n) .... in here."
8 I'm afraid an adventure holiday is not really my cup of .... I'd rather laze by the pool at a luxury hotel.
9 The boss went .... when I told him that Jamieson plc. had pulled out of the merger deal.
10 My sister and I may look alike, but in character we're as different as chalk and ....
11 She exaggerates everything, so take anything she says with a pinch of ....

29

14 Crime I

to act on a tip-off: if the police act on a tip-off, they use information they have been given to try to prevent a crime or seize a criminal/illegal goods

Acting on a tip-off, the police raided a house in central London and seized £30,000 worth of stolen goods.

to break out of prison/jail: to escape from prison

Only one prisoner has ever broken out of this jail.

to be convicted of a crime: to be found guilty in a court of law of a crime you have been accused of committing

He was convicted of a crime which he hadn't committed.

to cordon (an area/building) off: to place a barrier around an area or building so as to prevent people leaving or entering

The area around the bank was cordoned off while bomb disposal experts tried to defuse the bomb.

to be fined for (committing) a crime: to have to pay a certain amount of money as punishment for committing a crime

I was fined £300 for driving without a seatbelt on.

to be found (not) guilty of: to be in a court of law where a judge or jury decide that sb committed/did not commit the crime they have been accused of

He was found guilty of arson.

to get away with sth: to do sth wrong or illegal and not be punished for it

If you think you can get away with blackmailing the president, then you've got another think coming.

to hold (sb/sth) up: to rob a person or a place, using a weapon [Note: a **hold-up**: a robbery]

The bandits held up the stage coach at gunpoint.

an inquiry into (+ noun): an official investigation

An inquiry into alleged government involvement in the scandal will be held next week.

to let sb off (with a fine/caution, etc): to be given a lighter punishment (a fine/a caution) than you deserve

You should count yourself lucky he let you off with a fine. You could have gone to jail.

to make off with sth: to steal and escape with sth

A group of armed men held up a restaurant in the northern suburbs of Quito and made off with £2,000 from the till.

to be on the loose: to have escaped from prison and not been captured by the authorities

Of the four inmates that broke out of Maidstone prison last week, only one is still on the loose.

to be on the run: to be trying to escape or hide from the police

He decided to give himself up to the police after being on the run for two years.

to be on trial for (committing) a crime: to be in a court of law, where a judge and/or jury are deciding whether you are guilty of a crime

He's on trial for forgery.

to plead (not) guilty (to the charges): to say in a court of law that you are (not) guilty of the crime you have been accused of committing

He pleaded guilty to all the charges that had been brought against him.

to be released from prison: to be set free from prison

Having served twelve years of his sentence, he was released from prison in 1995.

to rule out (the possibility of) sth: to say that sth is not possible

We can't rule out the possibility that this was a politically motivated crime.

to be sentenced to (a number of years in prison): if a judge sentences sb, he or she states in court what their punishment is going to be

He was convicted of theft and sentenced to two years in prison.

to stand up (in court): to be accepted as true or satisfactory when it is carefully examined in court

It's a forced confession. They won't use it because they know it won't stand up in court.

to testify against sb: to provide the court with information that shows that sb is guilty of the crime that they have been accused of committing

If you want to see him sent to prison, you will have to testify against him in court.

to tip (sb) off: to tell the police where and when a crime will be committed or where a criminal or illegal, stolen goods can be found [Note: **a tip-off**: a piece of information given to the police, usually in secret]

How did the police know? Did someone tip them off?

to track (sb/sth) down: to look for and find

They tried to flee the country, but the police tracked them down.

14

Practice

1. Read the news excerpt below and decide if each preposition in bold is correct. If yes, put a tick. If not, write the correct one next to the line in which it appears.

... had no alternative but to plead guilty **over** the ....
charges. The Minister was cautioned and fined
£1,000 **for** disturbing the peace. ....
And finally, the police, acting **on** a tip-off, arrested ....
Ben Nutt and Tito Anderson yesterday in a
downtown Miami hotel. The two men had been **at** ....
the run for three weeks following Nutt's dramatic
escape from Miami State Penitentiary. Anderson,
in trial for the bank robbery at the time Nutt broke ....
out **of** prison, allegedly masterminded his cousin's ....
escape. Nutt was convicted **with** fraud six months ....
ago and was sentenced **with** ten years in prison. ....
He caused a sensation at his trial when, having
been found guilty **of** the charges brought against ....
him, he vowed that when he was released **of** prison ....
he would personally 'deal with' those people who
had testified **against** him. Fortunately, none of the ....
witnesses who appeared **in** court during Nutt's trial ....
was harmed while the two men were **at** the loose. ....
An inquiry **about** Nutt's escape is to be held on ... .

2. For questions 1 to 10 below, complete the second sentence so that it has a similar meaning to the first sentence, using 3 to 8 words. You must include the word given in bold, which cannot be changed in any way.

1 The thief robbed him at gunpoint outside his very own home.
   held   He ....
               .... outside his very own home.
2 Ten inmates escaped from Wandsworth Prison last night.
   out   Ten inmates ....
               .... Wandsworth Prison last night.
3 The judge was lenient, fining him instead of sending him to prison.
   let   The judge ....
               .... a fine.
4 He thought he would be able to steal the money and not be caught and punished for it.
   get   He thought he could ....
               .... the money.
5 The thieves took everything in her safe.
   made   The thieves ....
               .... the contents of her safe.
6 Someone undoubtedly told the police that he was going to rob the bank.
   tipped   The police must ....
               .... about the robbery.
7 The court will dismiss this evidence as being unsatisfactory and unacceptable.
   stand   This evidence .... in court.
8 The police stand little chance of finding the missing jewels.
   track   It is doubtful ....
               .... the missing jewels.
9 The police surrounded the entire area and prevented people from entering it while they dusted for fingerprints.
   cordoned The area ....
               .... dust for fingerprints.
10 "It would be foolish not to consider the possibility of foul play," said the policeman.
   rule   The policeman refused ....
               .... of foul play.

3. What do you think has happened/is happening in each photograph? Talk about them, using the prompts, as well as your own ideas.

barrister / question / witness / court / testify / against / defendant / be / trial / serious / crime / if / be / found / guilty / be convicted

he / sentence / years / prison / theft / police / tip off / track / down

31

15 Crime II (Vocabulary and Collocations)

an alibi: a person or story which proves that sb was not in a place when a crime was committed [Note: **watertight alibi:** alibi that is impossible to disprove]

We checked out his alibi and it is watertight. He was at a party when the robbery took place.

an appeal: a request to a court asking for a previous decision to be changed

The defendant's appeal was rejected.

blackmail: threatening to reveal a secret about sb unless they do sth the other person wants

The two men are thought to be behind the recent spate of blackmailing of local restaurant owners.

a brush with the law: dealings with the police for a very minor crime

Most people have had at least one brush with the law in their lives.

a cache of: a hidden number of, used for explosives, weapons, etc

The police uncovered a cache of protection money during the raid.

a criminal record: a list of crimes which sb has been found guilty of, which is kept by the police

The jury should bear in mind that my client has no criminal record.

to drop the charges against sb: (police) to decide that sb did not commit the crime that they are charged with

All the charges brought against Genski were dropped when it was revealed that ...

to fit a description: to look exactly like sb (a criminal) that has been described

If you see a man who fits this description, please contact your local police station immediately.

to be found (not) guilty of: a judge decides that sb did (not) commit the crime that they have been charged with

He was found guilty of shoplifting and fined £500.

to hand down a sentence: (a judge) to announce in a court of law what sentence a criminal will receive

It was one of the longest prison sentences ever handed down in an American court of law.

to handle sb's defence: (a lawyer) to defend sb in a court of law

Who is handling his defence?

a hardened criminal: an experienced criminal who is unlikely to ever abide by the law

He was a hardened criminal.

a law-abiding citizen: a person who does not break the law

This new law is an insult to all law-abiding citizens.

not a shred of evidence: not a single piece of evidence

There may not be a shred of evidence to connect him with the crime, but he's still the main suspect.

to pass sentence: (a judge) to tell a court what punishment a convicted person will receive

Passing sentence, Judge Rand described Smith as a menace to society.

to place sb under arrest: (formal, police language) to arrest sb

He was placed under arrest last Monday.

a plain-clothes policeman: a policeman who does not wear a uniform

How was I to know that he was a plain-clothes policeman?

to plead guilty: to say (in a court of law) that you are guilty of a crime that you have been charged with

He pleaded guilty to the crime and was sentenced to six months in prison.

to be in/taken into police custody: arrested and kept in prison while waiting to go to court

He was taken into police custody pending trial.

to press charges against sb: to make an official accusation against sb, which has to be decided in a court of law

Will the police be pressing charges, after all?

a previous conviction for ...: to have previously been found guilty of a crime in a court of law

He asked for previous convictions to be taken into account.

protection money: money paid to sb who threatens to hurt or blackmail the other person

The nightclub owner refused to pay protection money to Mr Big.

to be quashed: to be rejected; for an appeal/a decision

Lord Chief Justice Bates quashed the lower court's decision and Jenkins walked free.

to raid: if the police raid a place, they arrive without warning and search it because they believe that a criminal or sth illegal is hidden there [Note: a raid (n)]

The police raided the house and arrested two people.

to reach a verdict: to decide in a court of law whether sb is guilty or not guilty of a crime

It took the jury five days to reach a verdict.

to be released on bail: sb who is waiting to go on trial does not have to wait in prison because a large sum of money has been paid as a guarantee that they will not run away

He should never have been released on bail. It was obvious that he would flee the country.

a spate of...: a spate of robberies/break-ins/attacks/etc is a series of these things that follow each other, often in the same area, over a short period of time

A spate of muggings has the police and the public worried.

to stand trial: to go to a court of law and be judged

Jennifer Mills will stand trial for embezzlement.

to trace the whereabouts of sb: (police language)/(formal) to look for sb

The police are trying to trace the whereabouts of the driver.

Practice

1. Complete the text with words from the box below.

> shred – custody – trace – brushes – fit – abiding – whereabouts – cache – plain – record – watertight – raid – hardened – spate – previous

The Metropolitan police are trying to 1) .... the 2) .... of a Mr Nobby Redston, following a 3) .... on his East London flat yesterday afternoon. The police are reported to have uncovered £10,000 worth of stolen goods and a 4) .... of weapons. Mr Redston is believed to be behind the recent 5) .... of robberies that have terrorised Londoners over the last six months. The police were alerted to the possibility of Redston being The Man in the Mask when he was photographed by a 6) ....-clothes policeman outside a bank in the Isle of Dogs. The policeman who photographed Mr Redston said, "We received a call saying that there was a suspicious character hanging around outside one of the city's largest banks. Rather than jump straight in, I took a photo of him. I matched the picture with a man called Redston. Redston has a long criminal 7) ...., being a 8) .... criminal with 9) .... convictions for armed robbery, extortion and the illegal use of arms." Redston's flatmate, who is now in police 10) ...., said that the police were looking for the wrong man and claimed that there was not a 11) .... of evidence to connect Redston to the robberies. Redston's lawyer issued the following statement an hour ago: "My client has a 12) .... alibi and does not 13) .... the description of the man the police had previously been looking for. Whilst Mr Redston has admittedly had one or two 14) .... with the law in the past, he is basically an upstanding and law- 15) .... citizen who abhors violence of any kind. He is appalled by these allegations. Unfortunately, my client is currently unavailable for questioning as this afternoon he went on a business trip to Austria, but he wishes to make it known that when he returns he will be in immediate contact with the police."

2. Passage B is a summary of passage A. Using passage A as a guideline, complete passage B with words from the box below.

> reach – quashed – stand – passed – handed – pressed – released – placed – found – drop – taken – plead – handling

A It was my neck or his. I was arrested in connection with one of the robberies and after spending the night in a police cell, I cut a deal. I had to go to Austria, wear a microphone and get Redston to talk. The police said they'd let me go, you see. I had my reservations but the police reckoned once he was on trial he'd have to admit that he'd done it, and that even if he didn't, what with my testimony and old man, Hobday, being his lawyer, he didn't stand a chance. I'd be safe, they said. So I went along with it. I got the police what they wanted and I even got him to come back home. I was there when the police arrested him, and I was there when the judge gave him ten years. It had only taken the jury one hour to decide that he was guilty. I wasn't that worried when Hobday announced there would be an appeal. Even the police said the courts would reject it. They didn't. He was allowed to go free before a retrial. That's why I'm not helping the police any more.

B On the day he was 1) .... into custody on charges of theft, Mr Russell Franks agreed to help the Metropolitan Police Force capture his one-time associate, Mr Norbert Redston. He did this on the understanding that in exchange the police would 2) .... all outstanding charges against him and that he would not 3) .... trial. The police assured Mr Franks that Mr Redston was certain to 4) .... guilty at his trial and that even if he didn't, the fact that Mr Redston had Anthony Hobday 5) .... his defence would almost certainly guarantee a favourable outcome. Mr Franks wore a microphone and recorded Mr Redston admitting his involvement in six robberies. Mr Franks was present when the police 6) .... Mr Redston under arrest and testified against Mr Redston during the subsequent trial. Thanks to Mr Franks' testimony, Mr Redston was 7) .... guilty of all the charges 8) .... against him. Mr Franks was in court when the Lord Chief Justice Ross 9) .... sentence. Given the length of the sentence 10) .... down and the fact that it took the jury only one hour to 11) .... a verdict, Mr Franks was not concerned when Mr Hobday lodged an appeal. He had also been assured that Mr Redston's appeal would be 12) .... It was not, and Mr Redston was 13) .... on bail pending a retrial. As a result of this, Mr Franks no longer wishes to co-operate with the police.

16 Damage and Conditions

blocked: (for sinks or toilets) sth is stopping the water from leaving it
The kitchen sink is blocked.

blunt: not sharp
blunt pencils, scissors/knives
You should sharpen these knives. They're all blunt.

to break/cut in half: to break/cut sth into two pieces
He broke the bar of chocolate in half and gave Jo one piece.

bruised: (for a piece of fruit) with brown marks on it (under which the flesh of the fruit is soft and tastes unpleasant)
There were only two bruised pears in the cupboard.

to burst: to explode, letting water or air escape
I stepped on the balloon and it burst with a loud noise.

chipped: with a small piece broken off
I chipped a tooth while biting into an apple.

to come off: to fall from/become separated from
The top came off in my hand.

cracked: slightly damaged, with lines appearing on the surface
She dropped the mirror and it cracked.

to be crumbling off: (for plaster) small pieces of plaster are falling off because it is very old and very dry
Lumps of plaster were crumbling off the wall.

to crush: to press or squeeze sth hard so as to change its shape or completely destroy it
Be careful with these ornaments when you pack them. I don't want you to crush them.

dented: with a hollow in the surface caused by hitting or pressing (for metals)
The car was badly dented in the accident.

(sth is) falling to pieces: sth is very old and in very bad condition
We've got to get rid of this car. It's falling to pieces.

filthy: very dirty
filthy clothes/car/room/hands, etc

flat: (i) (of a fizzy drink) having lost its bubbles and tasting unpleasant (ii) (of a tyre) without enough air
That flat tyre needs to be seen to.

frayed/fraying: with loose threads at the edges
fraying jeans/rugs/a frayed carpet

grimy: very dirty
Cities were grimy, squalid places to live in during the Industrial Revolution.

grubby: dirty
His hands were grubby from working in the garden.

sth has seen better days: sth (a television, a car, etc) is now old and not in very good condition
The TV doesn't work and the fridge is on its last legs. Even the beds have seen better days.

moth-eaten: old, in poor condition and with holes (for material)
a moth-eaten tablecloth

mouldy: with mould on it (i.e. a soft growth which looks like green/blue fur and grows on old food)
The bread was mouldy.

sth is on its last legs: sth is in very bad condition and very soon it will stop working
This television is on its last legs. It's time we got rid of it and bought a new one.

to be peeling off: (for wallpaper/paint) to be falling off a surface
Strips of yellowing wallpaper were peeling off the walls.

rickety: (for furniture) old, weak and unstable
He entered a dark, gloomy room, full of rickety furniture.

to rip: to tear sth badly/to get badly torn
She caught her skirt in the car door, and it ripped.

to rip sth to shreds: to tear paper or material into little pieces
The dog ripped the paper to shreds.

rusty: with rust on it (i.e. a red-brown substance that covers some metals when they get wet)
The problem with this particular make of car is that it goes rusty very quickly.

to scrape: to scratch
Dad won't be amused when he finds out that you have scraped his car.

to shatter (into a thousand/million pieces): to break into many tiny pieces (generally used for things made of glass or china)
A rock hit the windscreen of the car causing it to shatter into a million pieces.

to smash to smithereens/into tiny pieces: to break into very small pieces
The vase fell to the floor and smashed to smithereens.

to snap sth in two: to break sth (made of a hard material) in two pieces
He took the little boy's ruler and snapped it in two.

to split: to separate (not necessarily completely) into two pieces, often along a straight line
Seeing a large tear in my sleeve, I realised that the seam had split.

sth is still in one piece: if you drop sth (a cup, glass, etc) and it is still in one piece, it has not broken
Amazingly, the bowl I dropped was still in one piece.

stained: with a mark that is difficult to remove
You can't wear that shirt to work. Look at it! It's stained!

stale: not fresh
stale bread/cake/biscuits

threadbare: the material sth is made of has become very old, weak and thin
threadbare carpet/sofa/chair

16

Practice

1. *Each adjective is followed by two nouns. Cross out the noun which does not go with it. Then use the correct combinations to complete the sentences below.*

a a rickety **fork**/chair
b a chipped cup/**tyre**
c fraying curtains/**bread**
d a blocked sink/**carpet**
e a rusty **banana**/fork
f flat **cola**/scissors
g a flat tyre/**sink**
h mouldy cheese/**pens**
i a dented peach/bumper
j a bruised **ceiling**/peach
k a cracked ceiling/**cheese**
l a blunt **mirror**/knife
m moth-eaten clothing/**bread**
n a threadbare carpet/**knife**
o stale bread/**curtains**

1 He gave us a piece of .... and a glass of ....
2 On the way home the car stopped. He had a ....
3 I nearly slipped on the ....
4 Don't sit on that ....
5 Well, if you keep putting tea bags down it, no wonder you've got a ....
6 He lay on the bed and looked up at the ....
7 They were drinking tea out of ....
8 The only fruit in the house was a single ....
9 I tore what was in the wardrobe up for dusters, as it was only a bundle of ....
10 That he wasn't very good at driving could be seen from his ....
11 You'll never be able to cut anything with that ....
12 She went to the window and drew the ....
13 Even a mouse wouldn't eat that ....
14 Haven't you got any better cutlery than this? There's only a ....

2. *Choose the correct item.*

1 The vase slipped from his hands and, on hitting the floor, it .... into a thousand pieces.
   A split   B crumbled   C cracked   D shattered

2 The kitchen is flooded. One of the water pipes must have ....
   A ripped   B burst   C torn   D parted

3 The doors were hanging off their hinges and the paint was .... off the walls.
   A splitting   B scraping   C peeling   D snapping

4 She's even broken the door! Look, the handle has .... off.
   A come   B parted   C gone   D split

5 Pulling the contract out of the envelope, she ripped it to ....
   A smithereens   C tiny pieces
   B shreds   D half

6 It's time we bought some new furniture. Look at these chairs. They're .... to pieces.
   A battered   B crumbling   C falling   D going

7 You dropped it down the stairs? You're lucky it is still in one .... !
   A piece   B whole   C entirety   D unit

8 Grabbing the twig, he .... it in two.
   A crumbled   B crushed   C snapped   D tore

3. *Read the following passage and decide if the words in bold have been used correctly. If not, replace each word with (a) more appropriate one(s). All the words in bold and the possible replacements can be found in this unit.*

Unshaven and smelling of cat food, he stood in the doorway and beckoned me straight into the living room. "This is the living room," he said. I had never seen anything like it. The wallpaper was **1) scraping** off the walls and the **2) stained** and **3) bruised** carpet was littered with old newspapers and ageing sandwiches. A single **4) crumbling**, **5) moth-eaten** curtain hung like a dirty handkerchief at the **6) grimy** window. "This is my chair," he said. "Take a seat, and I'll make you a coffee." I sat down. The chair was unusually uncomfortable. On the table next to me there was an overflowing ashtray and a **7) stale** piece of cheese. I wanted to leave. He came back and handed me a cup. The cup was not only **8) filthy** but it was also **9) shattered**. I said "thank you." "Oh," he said. "Here's your spoon." He pulled a **10) rusty** spoon out of his trouser pocket and handed it to me. "Of course, there are one or two problems with the flat. The pipes **11) burst** in the kitchen last winter, so it's a bit smelly in there and I'm afraid in the bathroom the sink and the toilet are both **12) blunt**, so you can't really use them." I smiled. He smiled back. "Oh, and the cooker is on its last **13) feet**, the central heating doesn't work and there is a hole in the roof... The rent's cheap, though." I put my cup down. "Well," I said, "I think..." He interrupted. "Just one other thing," he said. I looked at him. "Yes?" I replied. He pointed at his chair. "You're sitting on my sandwiches."

35

17 Determination – Likes - Dislikes

Determination

but rest assured: but do not worry

We are sorry that your luggage has been mislaid by the airline but, rest assured, we will find it.

to go to any lengths to do sth: to do anything to get or achieve sth

Some people will go to any lengths to get on television.

to have (absolutely) no intention (whatsoever) of doing sth: will definitely not do sth/act in a certain way

I have absolutely no intention whatsoever of handing in my resignation.

to be hell-bent on doing sth: to be absolutely determined to do sth (often sth dangerous or potentially harmful)

He simply won't do as he is told. He seems hell-bent on completely destroying his career.

if sb thinks he/she is going to/can ..., then they have got another think coming: (spoken phrase) if sb thinks they can do sth bad and that nothing will happen, then they are wrong

If he thinks he can get away with writing such things in the press, then he's got another think coming. I'm going to take him to court.

I'm not prepared to: I refuse to ...

I'm not prepared to put up with this any longer. I'm going to complain to the manager.

one way or another I'm going to...: It doesn't matter how I do it or how it happens; the important thing is I'll do it/it will happen

One way or another, he'll make sure he gets that leading role.

there's no way: I absolutely refuse to (used to show that you will not change your mind) [Note: when **No way** ... begins a sentence it is followed by an inversion]

There's no way I am going to apologise.

No way am I going to tell you.

sb will stop at nothing to ...: sb will do anything – no matter how illegal or cruel it is – to get sth

She'll stop at nothing to get that promotion and she'll crush anyone who gets in her way.

Likes – Dislikes

to appeal: if sth appeals to sb, they find it attractive and interesting

The idea of living abroad has always appealed to me.

to be besotted/madly in love with sb: to be absolutely in love with sb

He's besotted with her, head over heels in love.

to detest sth: really hate

I detest doing the washing-up, although I don't mind cooking.

to be devoted to sb: to love sb a lot and be very loyal towards them; often used for husband – wife or parent – child relationships; also used as an adjective before a noun

He is devoted to his wife.

She has always been a devoted mother.

to go off sth/sb: to stop liking sth/sb that you used to like in the past

I used to love steak but I've gone off it.

I went off him when he said those horrible things about his brother.

to hate the sight of: to really hate

They look so happy together when you see them on television, but apparently they hate the sight of each other.

to have a soft spot for sb: (informal) to have a special liking for sb

I like all my classes, but I've got a soft spot for my proficiency group.

to have no time for sb: to dislike and have no respect for sb because of their attitude or the way they behave

I've got no time for Jim. He's so arrogant.

not to be overly keen on sth: to dislike, but not intensely

I'm not overly keen on horror movies, to tell you the truth. Let's go and see a comedy instead.

to loathe: to really hate sb/sth

He loathes driving to work.

to object to sth: to dislike sth and feel angry about it because you think it is wrong or unfair

I object to having to pay so much money for an ink cartridge.

I object to the way she orders me about. (or: I object to her ordering me about).

to be partial to sth: to like; especially used for food and drink

I like anything that's sweet, but I'm particularly partial to chocolate.

to take an instant dislike to sb: to dislike sb the moment you meet them

Ray and Ted took an instant dislike to one another and avoid each other as much as they can.

to take a shine to sb: (informal) to begin to like sb, having only known them for a short time

Mrs Harris has taken a real shine to him, hasn't she?

to take to sb/sth: to like sb/sth

I really got on with Jill, but I didn't take to her husband at all.

The children took to the new school immediately, and made lots of new friends there.

not to think much of sth/sb: not to think sth/sb is very good

She didn't think much of his attempts at oil painting, but said nothing for fear of hurting his feelings.

to think the world of sb: to like, respect and admire sb

His children think the world of him.

Practice

1. *Complete each sentence opening (1 to 9) with an appropriate ending (a-i).*

1	If he thinks he is going to get away with this, then he's got	a	any lengths to get what he wants.
2	I have no intention whatsoever	b	nothing to get what he wants.
3	He'll stop at	c	I'm going to give in to their demands.
4	She seems to be hell-bent	d	another think coming.
5	Don't worry. One way or	e	of giving in to their demands.
6	I'm not prepared	f	on destroying her career.
7	He'll go to	g	assured, we'll get him next time.
8	There's no way	h	another, he'll pay for what he's done.
9	He might have got away this time, but rest	i	to put up with such behaviour any longer.

2. *For questions 1 to 8 below, complete the second sentence so that it has a similar meaning to the first sentence, using 3 to 8 words. You must include the word given in bold, which cannot be changed in any way.*

1 I don't like it when people I don't respect tell me what to do.
 object I .... do by people I don't respect.
2 She detests him.
 sight She .... of him.
3 Fred disliked Viviana the minute he set eyes on her.
 instant Fred .... the minute he set eyes on her.
4 She had a low opinion of his poetry.
 much She .... his poetry.
5 I'm sure young children will love this new film.
 appeal I'm sure this .... young children.
6 David is very loving and loyal towards his family.
 devoted David .... his family.
7 Sue is crazy about Alan.
 madly Sue .... Alan.
8 The students disliked their new teacher.
 take The students .... new teacher.

3. *Complete the following sentences with an appropriate word taken from the box below.*

> besotted – overly – spot – world – time – partial – gone – taken – detested – loathes

1 George has .... off heavy metal music. He used to like it, but not any more.
2 Susan .... him. She hated everything about him.
3 I'm not .... keen on those kinds of films. They're all the same, as far as I'm concerned.
4 I've got no .... for people like Ian. He does nothing but complain and whinge all the time.
5 It's true that she really .... him but I find it very difficult to believe that she'd say such a thing.
6 He's only known Becky for a week, but I think he's .... quite a shine to her.
7 Anna's .... with him. It's as if she's been hit by a ten-ton truck!
8 She was devastated when she found out that he was a liar. She had thought the .... of him.
9 He loves cheese. He's particularly .... to Stilton.
10 He had always had a soft .... for Carla. His favourite niece, he called her.

4. *Work with a partner. Take it in turns to ask each other questions about your own likes and dislikes and answer them using expressions from this unit, as in the example.*

A: Have you ever gone off something?
B: Yes, I used to like hip hop music some years ago but now I've gone off it.

18 Driving

a blind corner: a corner around which you cannot see
Never overtake on a blind corner.

a collision: a crash in which two moving vehicles hit each other
He was injured when the car he was in was involved in a collision.

the crash barrier: strong low fence built along the side of a road or between two halves of a motorway to prevent accidents
He swerved to avoid the dog and smashed into the crash barrier.

to dent a car: to damage the metal (the door, the bumper, the bonnet, etc) of a car
I dropped a can of paint on the car roof and dented it.

to do ... kph: to drive at ... kph
He was caught doing 60 kph in a 40 kph speed zone.

to draw up: to stop in a vehicle
I drew up at the traffic lights.
A taxi drew up outside my house.

(to be on) full beam: if your lights are on full beam, they are raised so that you can see more
Dip your lights. They're on full beam and you are blinding the poor man in front of you.

to get out (of a car): to leave a car, taxi, van, lorry [Note: for all other forms of transport (plane, train, bike, etc) you use **to get off**]
Opp: to get in/into a car [Note: for all other forms of transport you use **to get on**]
Help grandma get out of the car while I unlock the front door.
You get off the bus at the next bus stop.
We got on the train, the whistle blew and we pulled out of the station.

a hairpin bend: sharp bend in road, where road turns back in opposite direction
Hairpin bends are always signposted.

heavy traffic: lots of traffic
The traffic was heavy that night.

to hit/slam on the brakes: to brake quickly and suddenly
Seeing the boy, he hit the brakes and the car screeched to a halt.

to jump a red light: to pass through a traffic light that is red
I was fined £40 for jumping a red light.

a lane: large, wide roads are divided into lanes (most motorways have 3 or more lanes)
The dual carriageway was divided into two lanes in each direction.

the lights changed: the traffic lights turned red or green
It took ages for the lights to change.

to mount the pavement: to go up on the pavement while driving
I mounted the pavement and crashed into a tree!

to overtake: to pass a car which is in front of you
Never overtake on a hill.

to pull away: to start driving, having previously stopped (e.g. at traffic lights) or having previously been parked
She checked her rear view mirror and pulled away.

to pull into somewhere: to leave the road in order to stop somewhere [Note: **to pull in:** to move to the side of the road in order to let another vehicle pass]
Pull into the next petrol station and I'll ask where the bank is.
We pulled in so that the ambulance could pass.

to pull out: to join the traffic, having previously stopped
Never pull out into heavy traffic without due care and attention.

to pull (sb) over: to stop at the side of the road
The car was making a funny noise so I pulled over, parked and looked under the bonnet.

to pull up: to stop in a vehicle
I pulled up at the traffic lights.

to put a car into reverse: to change into reverse gear so that you can move backwards
He put the car into reverse and backed into the drive.

to skid: to slide on the road
He started skidding towards an oncoming lorry!

to speed: to go faster than the speed limit
He was fined for speeding, as he was doing twice the speed limit.

to stall: if sb/a car stalls, the engine of the car stops suddenly
She tried to pull away, but she stalled.

to swerve to avoid sth: to suddenly move one's car sideways so as to avoid sth in the road
In swerving to avoid the fox, he crashed into a telephone box.

to tow: if one vehicle tows another, it pulls that vehicle behind it, often by means of a rope or a chain
The car in front of us was towing a caravan.

to tow (sth) away: to remove a vehicle that has been illegally parked or that has been involved in an accident by towing it
I'd parked on a double yellow line and my car had been towed away by the police.

a windscreen: the front window of a car
The windscreen was so dirty that we could hardly see through it.

to write (a car) off: to damage a car so badly that repairing it would cost more than buying a new one [Note: **a write-off:** sth that has been written off]
He was fine, thank goodness, but the car was a write-off.

38

18

Practice

1. Read the two texts below and decide which answer (A, B, C or D) best fits each gap.

She had 1) .... Her foot must have slipped. Either way, the five seconds it took her to restart the car had seemed an eternity. The drivers behind her had impatiently sounded their horns and she had been flustered. How it happened she didn't know, but she had put the car into reverse and driven into the car behind her. Nothing had happened to the car behind, but she had 2) .... the back of her own. Her husband would be livid. Five minutes later, she was still thinking about her husband. Perhaps that was why she was not paying attention. Perhaps that's why she didn't see the boy kick his football into the road. Perhaps that's why when she saw the ball she couldn't rationalise that it was only a ball. She 3) .... to avoid it and then 4) .... the brakes as she realised she was heading for a ditch. Smash. It happened in slow motion. She watched the windscreen shatter, she heard the metal crumple. But she was okay.
She had 5) .... off her husband's car. Destroyed it. She watched the recovery van 6) .... away the wreckage of what was once her husband's pride and joy. The van, with the car rolling unsteadily behind it, disappeared. She watched it go, turned, picked up the football and started walking home.

1	**A** arrested	**B** halted	**C** stalled	**D** jolted
2	**A** bruised	**B** dented	**C** creased	**D** snapped
3	**A** swerved	**B** swung	**C** twisted	**D** spun
4	**A** hit	**B** slapped	**C** struck	**D** hammered
5	**A** dashed	**B** written	**C** cast	**D** signed
6	**A** tow	**B** draw	**C** tug	**D** drive

He pulled 1) .... at the traffic lights and a horde of children crowded round his car trying to scrub off yesterday's dirt from his windscreen. He shooed them away. His mind was running at a hundred miles an hour. What was he going to say?
The minute the policeman had pulled him 2) .... he knew he was in trouble. The policeman had been sitting at the side of the road and he hadn't seen him. The policeman had walked over to his car and as he wound down his window the night air had hit him. It felt like a slap. "You do realise you were 3) ....?" he said. "I clocked you doing 75". He found it difficult to talk. Before he knew it he had been arrested and his parents had been notified. He spent the night at the police station and was now on his way home. He 4) .... up outside his home. What were they going to say? He turned off the engine, got 5) .... the car and slowly walked towards the door.

1	**A** up	**B** out	**C** into	**D** away
2	**A** over	**B** in	**C** along	**D** away
3	**A** exceeding	**B** crawling	**C** dashing	**D** speeding
4	**A** parked	**B** stopped	**C** crawled	**D** drew
5	**A** down	**B** off	**C** out of	**D** away

2. 🎧 You will hear a conversation between a driving instructor and a learner driver. Listen to the recording and answer the questions below.

1. How fast was Mr Barnes driving when he was on the highway?
....
2. Why was the lorry driving towards Mr Barnes?
....
....
3. Why could Mr Barnes see the lorry driver's face?
....
....
4. What happened when Mr Barnes hit the brakes?
....
....
5. What were the three incidents that occured before Mr Barnes got on the highway?
....
....
6. What did Mr Barnes try to do in order to impress Mr Huggins?
....
....
7. Why couldn't Mr Barnes see if there was any traffic coming when he tried to pull out?
....
....
8. How did Mr Huggins knock himself out?
....
....

3. What do you think has happened/is happening in the photograph? Talk about it, using the prompts.

Pete and Jack/drive along/country lane/come across/flock of sheep/road/ not able/swerve/avoid/animals/so/hit brakes/not able/put car/reverse/sheep in front and behind/Pete/get out/car/ Jack/look/map/see/where/be/realise/ get/lost

39

19 Eating and Drinking

Eating and Food

appetite: desire to eat
I was hungry before I watched that documentary on plastic surgery. Now I have lost my appetite.

a big eater: a person who eats a lot and has big meals
We are all big eaters in my family, so none of us is thin.

to bolt (sth) down: to eat very quickly, generally because you are in a hurry
He ran into the kitchen, bolted down his breakfast and ran out of the door.

canned/tinned goods: food put into a metal container and sealed to remain fresh
If you're taking canned food with you on your camping trip, don't forget to pack a tin opener.

I could eat a horse: I'm very hungry; often preceded by *I'm starving*
"I'm starving," he said. "I could eat a horse."

crockery: the collective noun for plates, cups, mugs, bowls, dishes, etc
I'll wash the crockery later.

cutlery: the collective noun for knives, forks and spoons
Could you put the cutlery on the table?

dig in!: (informal) start eating
"Dig in," he said, as he got up to answer the door.

to eat sb out of house and home: if sb visits or stays with sb and eats them out of house and home, they eat all the food in the house
My nephews came to stay with me for a week and they ate me out of house and home.

to be famished/starving/ravenous: to be very hungry
When is dinner? I'm famished.

a gadget: a small, useful and clever machine or tool
She had one gadget I had never seen before - it was called an automatic butter softener.

to grab a bite to eat: to quickly have sth to eat; generally in a fast food restaurant
"I'm going to grab a bite to eat. Do you want to come?" he asked.

the larder: the cupboard in the kitchen where food is kept
You'll find all our tinned food in the larder.

to be/feel peckish: to be a little hungry
I felt a bit peckish, so I popped out to the supermarket and bought myself a cake.

to pick at your food: to eat your food very slowly and without enthusiasm (generally when you are unhappy/unwell/do not like the food)
Henrietta picked listlessly at her food and then pushed her plate aside.

to spoil your appetite: to eat sth before a meal, so that you are no longer hungry when it is mealtime
No, you can't have another slice of toast. I don't want you to spoil your appetite.

to wolf sth down: to eat sth very quickly, often because you are very hungry or in a hurry
"Well, you wolfed that down quickly enough, didn't you? Do you want some more?" she asked.

to work up an appetite: to do sth (generally some kind of physical exercise) which makes you hungry
Playing a sport is a good way of working up an appetite.

Drinking

fizzy drinks: carbonated soft drinks
Opp: still
Will you have a fizzy orangeade or a still orange drink?

to be gasping for a drink: to be extremely thirsty
It was hot and we had walked for miles. Both of us were gasping for a drink of water.

mineral water: bottled water, generally taken from spas and considered to be healthier that tap water
Some claim that drinking mineral water improves your health.

on the house: if you go to a café or a restaurant and you are given sth (a drink, a dessert, etc) on the house, you do not have to pay for it
Our children's meals contain a special offer this week: as much ice cream as they can eat - on the house!

to be parched: to be very thirsty
I'm parched. Let's get something to drink.

to quench your thirst: to satisfy your thirst so that you are no longer thirsty
This glass of lemonade will quench your thirst.

soft drinks: cold (often fizzy) drinks that do not contain alcohol
We only sell soft drinks like lemonade and coca cola.

Practice

1. Choose the correct item.

1 I'm absolutely .... ! I could eat a horse.
  A parched **B** peckish **C** hungry **D** famished

2 Sid has always been a .... eater.
  A heavy **B** strong **C** grand **D** big

3 We were starving but mum wouldn't let us eat before dinner as it would .... our appetites.
  A damage **B** spoil **C** dent **D** prejudice

4 He must have been hungry. Did you see the way he
   .... his dinner down?
   A wolfed   C demolished
   B swallowed   D polished

5 That's the last time they're coming to stay for the weekend. They ate us out of house and ....!
   A kitchen   B garden   C home   D larder

6 "There's no need to stand on ceremony. .... in," said a disembodied voice from the kitchen.
   A Plough   B Burrow   C Fork   D Dig

7 I'm just going to .... a bite to eat and then we can meet. Is that all right?
   A grasp   B clutch   C clasp   D grab

8 Feeling off-colour, she .... at her food.
   A bolted   C worked
   B picked   D grabbed

9 We couldn't find a single knife, fork or spoon anywhere. Apparently, for them, fully equipped meant everything except ....
   A crockery   B cutlery   C utensils   D gadgets

10 There's nothing like a good cup of tea to .... your thirst.
   A draw   B quench   C safe   D work up

11 After three hours of walking in the hot summer sun, we were .... for a drink.
   A gasping   B gulping   C panting   D sighing

12 He prefers .... water to tap water.
   A canned   B well   C mineral   D fresh

13 Fresh fruit juice is better for you than .... drinks.
   A fuzzy   B fizzy   C saccharine   D bubbly

14 They don't sell tea or coffee. They only sell .... drinks.
   A mild   B sweet   C plain   D soft

15 We had to pay for our food but not for the drinks - they were on the ....
   A house   C compliment
   B café   D consumption

16 There's plenty of .... food in the larder.
   A spoiled   C frozen
   B raw   D canned

2. *Read the restaurant review below. Using the highlighted word that appears at the end of some of the lines, form a word that fits the space in the same line. An example has been done for you.*

We found out about our next restaurant when an **0)** *invitation* from one of its owners found its way on to my desk. Situated in a **1)** .... overflowing with themed Irish and American eateries, the Wedge stands out not only for the **2)** .... of its décor (bare brick walls, polished floorboards and white linen tablecloths) but also because of its uniquely British menu. **3)** .... to say, we were intrigued and we chose to dine out at the Wedge last Monday. We were welcomed by a team of excellent and switched-on staff who, **4)** .... our meal, were attentive and **5)** .... without being overbearing. The menu was extensive, interesting and **6)** .... for all budgets. The emphasis, as you might expect, was on traditional British fare - roast meats, pies, baked puddings - though a number of more **7)** .... dishes were thrown in for those with an adventurous palate. We were spoilt for **8)** .... and in the end, I plumped for crab soup as a starter and roast beef and Yorkshire pudding for my main course. The **9)** .... we were served were generous, our food arrived promptly, and nice intervals of time were left between courses. Superior service, a relaxing ambience, an imaginative menu and **10)** .... prices – it would seem that the Wedge has hit on a winning formula. It is a shame, therefore, that our food tasted like industrial strength soap.

INVITE

NEIGHBOUR

SIMPLE

NEED

THROUGH
COURTESY

SUIT

INNOVATION

CHOOSE

HELP

AFFORD

3. *Describe your favourite restaurant, using words and expressions from this unit.*

20 Education

a borderline candidate: a person who has equal chances of passing or failing an exam

Our policy is not to allow borderline candidates to take the Higher exams.

a certificate: official document sb receives on completing course of study or training

Her Beginner's Swimming Certificate is framed on the wall.

to cheat in an exam: to use dishonest methods (e.g. copying from the student next to you) in order to pass an exam

He cheated in every exam he sat for, being too lazy to study.

to come top of your class: to be the best in your class

I came top of my class in history.

a course: a series of lessons in a particular subject (you can do a course at a training institute, at a language institute, etc)

I'm doing a course in radio journalism at the local technical college.

a degree: the qualification you receive when you have finished studying a course at university; [Note: **to do a degree**: to study for a degree]

I've got a degree in biochemistry.

I'm doing a degree in zoology.

diploma: qualification awarded to student by college, or by high school in USA

The two-year course leads to the City & Guilds Diploma in Printing.

to drop out of university: to leave university before finishing your degree

She dropped out of Oxford, having spent less than two terms there.

edutainment: sth designed to be both educational and entertaining

Some people would say that computer games are edutainment.

to excel at: to be very good at

He excelled at maths and physics, later winning the Nobel prize.

to be expelled from school: to be dismissed from school permanently because you have done sth very bad

She was expelled from school for insolence to her teacher.

a gifted student: a student with natural ability to do sth well

The headmaster was dismayed that such a gifted and hardworking student should choose to leave school at the age of sixteen.

a grade: mark received by students in examination or for written work, usually in form of a letter

I got a grade B in my composition.

a graduate: a person who has received a degree from a university

Mike is a graduate of Kent University.

to graduate from university: to leave university, having finished your degree course and having got your qualifications

Rebecca graduated from York in 1995.

to learn sth by heart: to learn sth so well that you do not need to read it

Margaret had learned the poem by heart so that she could recite it in class.

to lecture in: to teach a particular subject at university

Steven lectures in Roman Law at Exeter University.

a lenient teacher: a teacher who is not strict and does not punish students who deserve to be punished

If you are too lenient with your students, you can be sure that they will take advantage of you.

a mark: point given for correct answer or for doing well in examination

Percy got top marks in his maths test.

a mock exam: a practice exam usually taken a short time before a real and important exam

I passed my mock proficiency exam, so I'm confident that I will do well in the real thing.

to pass an exam with flying colours: to do very well in an exam and get very good marks

Laura is a very bright student and I'm sure she will pass all her exams with flying colours.

to play truant: to miss school without permission

He was playing truant again and this time he had been caught.

to be popular: if you are popular, everybody likes you

He was a popular teacher and his students really enjoyed his lessons.

a post-graduate: sb who is studying for an advanced degree (a master's degree or a doctorate) at university

Postgraduates must apply for research funding before the end of the academic year.

to research/to do research into: to do advanced studies in a particular subject (often done by people who have a university doctorate) [research is an uncountable noun]

Having gained a PhD in nuclear physics, he went on to do research into atomic particles.

to revise: to study for an exam [Note: revision (n)]

Paul is revising for his geography test.

to sail through an exam: to pass an exam very easily and with a good mark

I sailed through my end of year exams.

to sit (for) an exam: to take an exam

I am going to sit for my proficiency exam next week.

an undergraduate: sb who is studying for their first degree at university

Penny loved every moment of being a university undergraduate.

to win a scholarship: to be given money to help pay for the education you receive (you often win a scholarship by doing well in an entrance exam)

He won a scholarship to Cambridge.

Practice

1. Match the words in column A with the correct definition in column B. Then complete the sentences below with words from column A.

Column A

1. grade
2. to learn sth by heart
3. diploma
4. edutainment
5. mark
6. certificate
7. undergraduate
8. to revise

Column B

a. sth officially received on completion of training
b. educational and entertaining
c. mark of A, B, C, etc
d. grade out of 10 or 20, etc
e. to learn sth for a test or exam
f. sb studying for first university degree
g. paper awarded by college or by U.S. high school
h. to know sth very well

1 .... 3 .... 5 .... 7 ....
2 .... 4 .... 6 .... 8 ....

1. On graduation day, all the high school graduates received their ....
2. I can't come out tonight as I'm .... for tomorrow's test.
3. Ten out of ten is the best .... anyone can get.
4. He didn't need notes as he had learned the speech ....
5. We will need to see photocopies of your G.C.S.E ....
6. Is this video series really ...., or is it just a gimmick?
7. Although Eric got a D .... in the exam, it was a narrow fail.
8. In the USA, first-year .... are called freshmen.

2. Read the text below and fill each blank with one suitable word.

Lionel Mendax: Curriculum

I was a child prodigy, and went to the most expensive and most academically demanding schools in the country. I was a model student and was popular both 1) .... my teachers and my classmates. I was elected class president for six years 2) .... I passed every exam I 3) .... for with flying 4) .... and came 5) .... of my class in every subject I took. I also excelled 6) .... sports. In my final year at school, I 7) .... a scholarship to Cambridge University. Cambridge was child's play and I sailed 8) .... every exam I took, finally getting a first class honours degree 9) .... natural sciences. On graduating 10) .... Cambridge, I went on to Oxford to 11) .... research 12) .... atomic particles. 13) .... completed my research, I took 14) .... a teaching post at Harvard, where I lectured 15) .... astrophysics. I am presently teaching post– 16) .... students everything they do not know about nuclear physics at the Sorbonne University in Paris. Oh well, it keeps me occupied, and it's a job.

3. Read the text below and decide which option (A, B, C or D) best fits each gap.

Lionel Mendax: The Truth

It was my misfortune to be Lionel Mendax's form master in his last year at school. Lionel was a **0)** *compulsive* liar and an inveterate cheat who, when not **1)** .... truant, plagued the hell out of both myself and my teaching colleagues. Contrary to his own inflated opinion of his intellectual abilities, Lionel was not a **2)** .... student. Far from it. He was at best a **3)** .... candidate for his GCSE exams and as such it was perhaps a blessing that he was **4)** .... from the school before he took them. It is only fair, however, that I should give Lionel credit where credit is due. No one had ever been **5)** .... out of Greyfriars School before. Notwithstanding that, even our ridiculously **6)** .... and excessively liberal headmaster could not ignore the fact that Lionel had been caught cheating **7)** .... every single one of his **8)** .... GCSE Exams. After his **9)** ...., he **10)** .... a course in printing and design at the local technical college, but soon **11)** .... out.

0	A hardened	B heavy	**C compulsive**	D addictive
1	A running	B playing	C making	D doing
2	A gifted	B upstanding	C skilled	D strict
3	A grey	B borderline	C futile	D debatable
4	A evacuated	B expelled	C evicted	D expired
5	A thrown	B pitched	C discarded	D hurled
6	A harsh	B light	C stringent	D lenient
7	A on	B at	C in	D by
8	A false	B pretend	C mock	D fake
9	A eviction	B extraction	C expulsion	D evacuation
10	A made	B did	C assisted	D sat
11	A fell	B went	C let	D dropped

21 Emphasis (Extreme Adjectives - Very)

> **Note 1:** * = used before a noun, ** = used after a noun, generally with the verb *to be*, *** = can be used before or after a noun. **Note 2:** To strengthen extreme adjectives you must use the word **absolutely**; you cannot use the word **very**. *It was absolutely hilarious.* ✓ *It was very hilarious.* ✗

Emphasis I - Extreme Adjectives

delicious: *** very tasty indeed
  delicious cake
  The pudding was delicious.

dreadful: *** very bad indeed
  I made a dreadful mistake when I told him the truth.

drenched/soaked: *** very wet
  After walking in the rain for twenty minutes we were drenched.
  We got soaked. That's how I caught that cold.

distraught: *** very upset indeed, probably because sth very bad has happened
  She had been missing for a week. Her parents were distraught.

famished: ** very hungry indeed
  We were famished.

filthy: *** very dirty indeed
  My hands were filthy after I'd been gardening all day.

flabbergasted: ** very surprised indeed
  I was flabbergasted by the news.

hilarious: *** very funny indeed
  I've never laughed so much in my life. It was hilarious.

livid: ** very angry indeed
  She'll be livid when she finds out that you smashed her favourite vase.

packed: *** (i) very crowded indeed (ii) full of
  a packed cinema
  The train was packed.
  This book is packed with useful information.

parched: *** extremely thirsty
  Why don't we get a drink? I'm parched.

priceless: *** extremely valuable
  a priceless painting/Ming vase
  Of the many works of art lost in the fire, six or seven were thought to have been priceless.

riveting: *** very interesting
  a riveting documentary/speech
  Everybody found her speech riveting.

superb: *** very good indeed
  a superb performance/restaurant
  The food was superb. The singer was superb. In short, we loved it.

Emphasis II - Very

brand-new: *** completely new
  a brand-new bike
  The gleaming car parked outside his house was brand-new.

to sit/stand bolt upright: to sit/stand with a very straight back
  Suddenly he sat bolt upright, shouted, "the bell!" and then slumped back down on the bed.

bone idle: (informal) very lazy
  Your problem is that you are bone idle and do nothing all day.

crystal clear: (i) *** (for water) very transparent and clean (ii) ** (for an explanation) very clear and easy to understand
  We swam in the crystal-clear waters of the Caribbean.
  He made his position on the subject crystal clear.

dirt cheap: ** (informal) very cheap [Note: it can also follow the verbs **buy** and **sell**]
  Of course we bought them. They were dirt cheap.
  We bought it dirt cheap at the local market.

freezing (cold): *** very cold (used to describe the weather or how you feel)
  freezing cold weather
  I was wet and it was freezing cold.
  I'm freezing! Could you shut the door?

paper thin: *** very thin (used to describe walls, particularly inside houses and hotels)
  The bed was hard, the floorboards creaked and the walls were paper thin.

pitch-black/dark: *** completely dark
  It was a pitch-black starless night.

razor-sharp: *** very sharp
  razor-sharp teeth
  The needles on the cactus were razor-sharp.

red-hot: *** very hot (used to describe metals, plates, etc that have become very hot)
  a red-hot knife
  Be careful with these plates. They are red-hot.

sound/fast asleep: ** completely asleep
  He put his head round the door; the boy was sound asleep.

stone cold: ** completely cold (used to describe food or drink that should be hot)
  By the time he got off the phone, his dinner was stone cold.

stone deaf: ** totally deaf
  He is stone deaf.

stuck fast: ** stuck very firmly and unable to move
  The plaster was stuck fast to my finger and I couldn't get it off.

wide awake: ** completely awake
  Although I hadn't slept for two days, I felt wide awake.

wide open: ** completely open [Note: if a **competition/election** is *wide open*, there are lots of teams/candidates that may possibly win it]
  You left the door wide open!
  With no favourites left in the competition, the tournament is wide open.

21

Practice

1. *Match the adjectives in column A with their definitions in column B. Then use the adjectives to complete the sentences below.*

	A			B
1	livid	....	a	very thirsty
2	packed	....	b	very dirty
3	flabbergasted	....	c	very angry
4	famished	....	d	very tasty
5	parched	....	e	very wet
6	filthy	....	f	very crowded
7	distraught	....	g	very upset
8	hilarious	....	h	very surprised
9	superb	....	i	very interesting
10	drenched	....	j	very hungry
11	dreadful	....	k	very bad
12	priceless	....	l	very funny
13	riveting	....	m	very valuable
14	delicious	....	n	very good

1 The novel was so .... that he couldn't put it down.
2 The film was .... and we laughed all the way through.
3 He went out without an umbrella in the storm and got ....
4 Your hands are ...., so wash them before you come and have your dinner.
5 Sam was beside himself, really ...., when he found out that he hadn't got the promotion.
6 Will you make a cup of tea? I'm ....
7 They couldn't get a table in the restaurant, as it was absolutely ....
8 Did you hear the news about that .... train crash this morning?
9 What's for dinner? I'm ....
10 She was .... when she saw the sum on the cheque and could hardly believe her eyes.

2. *Complete the sentences using the words from the box below.*

> cheap – sharp – fast – hot – clear – idle – black – deaf – thin

1 The glue was stuck ....
2 They were dirt ....
3 It was pitch- ....
4 He is bone ....
5 She is stone ....
6 The walls were paper ....
7 Don't touch it. It's red- ....
8 Be careful. That knife is razor- ....
9 His explanation was crystal ....

3. *Read the texts below and replace the words/phrases in bold with an appropriate adjective or phrase from this unit.*

A What did he expect? He had left his front door **1) completely open**. It was an open invitation to every thief in the city. While he was upstairs, **2) completely asleep**, there were hordes of thieves downstairs, stealing everything he owned. He lost his television, a **3) completely new** DVD player, his CDs, his hi fi... the list was endless. Maria, his wife, was **4) very angry**. She couldn't understand how he could have been so stupid. And you know what he does for a living, don't you? He's a security guard. He looks after all those **5) very valuable** paintings in the museum.

B What was the restaurant like? Terrible. The food was **1) very bad** and the service was worse. I waited an hour for my soup, which –when it arrived– was **2) horribly cold**. I complained, of course.

C It was **1) very cold** inside the room. The window had a gaping hole in it. She couldn't sleep. The walls that divided the rooms were **2) very thin** and she could hear the man in the next room snoring. In truth, she didn't want to sleep. She didn't want to get into the bed. It was damp and the sheets were **3) very dirty**. So there she was, **4) completely awake**, sitting **5) up straight** in a rocking chair, staring into the night and waiting for the morning. It was going to be a long holiday.

45

22 Entertainment

Films and Plays

an act: plays are normally divided into acts
The play is a comedy in three acts.

backstage: behind the stage in a theatre where the dressing room, toilets, etc are
After the performance, we went backstage to meet the cast.

a blockbuster: a very successful film which makes a lot of money
"Ben Hur" is one of the biggest blockbusters of all time.

the box office: the place in a theatre or cinema where you buy tickets [Note: **a box-office success**: a film or play which makes a lot of money because many people go to see it]
There was a long queue at the box office.

the cast: the actors and actresses who perfom in a film or play [Note: **a star-studded cast**: a cast in which many of the actors and actresses are famous]
"Cleopatra" boasted a cast of thousands.

the credits: the credits appear in written form at the very end or the very beginning of a film and tell you who was in the film and who was involved in making it
Come on, we haven't missed any of the film except the credits.

to be dubbed (into a language): to have the original language of a film replaced by another language
I hate films that have been dubbed.

a flop: a film or play that is not successful
Although the film cost a lot to make, it was a box-office flop.

the plot: the story in a play or film [Note: **a weak plot**: a plot that is not very good or believable]
The plot was weak and the characters were unconvincing.

a (rave) review: a (very good) written or spoken opinion of a film or play by a critic

[Note: if a play, book or film gets/is given/receives **mixed reviews**, some critics liked it while others did not]
The film has been given rave reviews.

a remake: a new version of an older film
It is a remake of Hitchcock's classic, 'Rear Window'.

a scene: in a play, an act is divided into scenes
Scene two is set in a forest.

the script: the written form of a film or play
Having read the script, the actress accepted the part.

the soundtrack: the music in a film
You can buy the soundtrack to the film on CD.

a stunt: dangerous and spectacular actions in a film [Note: **a stuntman**: sb who performs stunts]
Rocky Hardman, the actor, performs all his own stunts.

subtitles: written translations for a foreign film which appear at the bottom of the screen
Was it dubbed or did it have subtitles?

a trailer: an advertisement often shown before you watch a film in the cinema showing extracts from a forthcoming film
Have you seen the trailer for 'Lethal Hammer 8'?

a twist: a surprise in the plot of a film or play
Far from being predictable, the film has a surprising twist at the end.

Reviews

appalling: very bad
appalling film/director/acting

contemptible: without anything to recommend it so that you have absolutely no respect for it
contemptible behaviour/performance

deep: serious, full of meaning
It was hardly what you would call a deep, thought-provoking film.

dreary: boring, without life
It was a dreary film about contemporary life in Europe.

electrifying: very exciting
an electrifying performance/opening sequence

first-rate: excellent [Note: **third-rate**: very poor quality or standard]
first-rate film/cast

flawless: perfect, without mistakes or imperfections
Jade Swinger gave a flawless performance.

gratuitous: unnecessary; most commonly used in the combination: **gratuitous violence**
It was a good film spoilt by too much gratuitous violence.

gripping: exciting
a gripping finale/car chase

incoherent: impossible to understand
incoherent plot

lacklustre: without life or energy
a lacklustre performance

lousy: (informal) bad
lousy script/special effects

mediocre: no more than average in quality
mediocre performance

mindless: stupid; senseless
mindless film/violence

outstanding: very good
an outstanding playwright

praiseworthy: deserving to be admired and respected because it is very good
praiseworthy effort

predictable: when what is going to happen is obvious
predictable ending

shallow: superficial, not deep
The play comes across as shallow and pretentious.

22

slick: attractive, cleverly made and well produced (but probably not very deep)
  a slick Hollywood production
sparkling: full of life and energy
  sparkling dialogue/performance
tedious: boring, and rather frustrating
  a tedious art film
wooden: without life, energy or passion
  wooden characters
unconvincing acting: acting you do not believe in – you see an actor as opposed to the character portrayed
  He gave an unconvincing performance as Hamlet.

Practice

1. Are the words/phrases below connected with films, plays, or both films and plays?

> a rave review – the plot – a twist – a trailer – the credits – subtitles – an act – a scene – a remake – a stunt – the box office – a blockbuster – backstage – the soundtrack – a flop – a star-studded cast – dubbed into English – the script

2. Decide whether the adjectives in bold in the film review below have been used appropriately or not. Replace each inappropriate adjective with a more suitable one from this unit.

Despite its star-studded cast and the many millions of dollars that went into its making, *Half Way to Heaven* has to be one of the most **1) outstanding** films ever to come out of a Hollywood studio. **2) Mindless**, and about as compelling as making a dental appointment, it is a classic case of formula film-making at its worst. Like its many predecessors, not only are the main characters **3) wooden**, **4) deep** and crudely drawn but it also relies on almighty explosions and a surfeit of **5) gratuitous** violence for its impact. Unlike its predecessors, it is neither **6) slick** nor particularly **7) riveting**, lurching as it does from one cliché to another until it stumbles to its thoroughly **8) surprising** and thoroughly disappointing climax. What, I ask, were actors of the calibre of Jordi Hutton, Lori Poynton and Sean Vetch doing in this film? Not acting, that's for sure. Vetch gives a **9) flawless** and utterly **10) unconvincing** performance as the wayward cop, Buck Jansen, whilst the normally **11) electrifying** Poynton's portrayal of Laura Beck is **12) lacklustre** at best. It is greatly to their credit that, **13) lousy** as the film is, their acting is worse. Tack on to this a **14) first-rate** supporting cast, an overabundance of **15) gripping** car chases, massive inconsistencies in the plot and hours of **16) sparkling** (and at times totally **17) incoherent**) dialogue and what you have got is a monument to all that is **18) intelligent** and **19) praiseworthy** in contemporary American film-making.

3. Read the text below. Use the word given in capitals at the end of some of the lines to form a word that fits the space in the same line. An example has been done for you.

Septon's Secret is a rich and startling collection of twelve short stories from the **0)** *actress* Shelly Rodger, best known for her **ACT**
1) .... of Melon in Tim Deal's **PORTRAY**
Oscar-winning film, *Nowhere*. With a deftness of touch reminiscent of John Kennedy Toole, the twelve stories draw the reader into the numerous worlds enveloping Septon, the book's **2)** .... **CENTRE**
character. Septon is surrounded by a cast of eccentric and generally unpleasant miscreants, including his **3)** .... **NEUROSIS**
and possessive wife, his ambitious friends and his malicious and thoroughly **4)** .... business partner. With each **SCRUPLE**
successive story, more is revealed about Septon, and with each **5)** .... we **REVEAL**
get closer to the secret referred to in the book's title. Plot lines and the principal characters are brought crashing together in the appropriately titled *Shock*, the book's **6)** .... and final story. All is **TWELVE**
revealed in a cleverly worked climax that is as disturbing as it is unexpected.
Shelly Rodger is a master of her craft. Her characters are vividly drawn and wholly convincing, her writing is **7)** .... **EVOKE**
without being pretentious or overbearing and her plotting is assured and compelling. On its **8)** .... in the United States **PUBLISH**
two months ago, *Septon's Secret* met with great **9)** .... acclaim. Within a **CRITICISE**
month it had shot to the top of US bestseller lists. A work of **10)** .... power by **ORDINARY**
an exceptionally gifted writer, *Septon's Secret* comes out in the UK next week.

47

23 Face

Verbs

to blink: to quickly open and close your eyes

They blinked as they came out into the daylight again.

to blush: to go red when you are embarrassed

Sarah blushes when people pay her compliments.

to frown: to draw one's eyebrows together because one is either annoyed or concentrating

She looked at the piece of paper and frowned. "I don't understand what it means," she said.

to grin: smile broadly because you are very pleased – though a grin can also be sinister

He grinned at me, then laughed out loud.

to grit your teeth: to put your teeth tightly together, especially because sth is hurting you

I gritted my teeth as the plaster was pulled off my arm.

to lick: move your tongue across the surface of sth

The children were walking along licking lollipops.

to scowl: to have an angry or hostile expression when you disapprove of sth

She scowled at me. "That's disgusting," she said.

to sneer: you sneer to show your contempt/lack of respect

She's a snob and sneers at people who have less money than her.

to wince: to grimace when sth is hurting you or when you are remembering sth embarrassing

He winced as the needle went in.

to wink: to look towards sb and close one eye briefly, usually as a signal that sth is a joke or a secret

It wasn't until he winked at me that I realised he was pulling my leg.

to yawn: you yawn when you are tired or bored

He yawned. "I'm going to bed," he said.

Idioms and Expressions

to keep/have an/your ear to the ground: to be attentive of what is happening or is about to happen

Jack keeps his ear to the ground and can usually let us know what the boss's mood is like.

to lie through your teeth: to tell an outright lie

He's lying through his teeth. What a ridiculous excuse!

to lose face: to lose the respect of other people

If he admitted to making such a terrible mistake, he'd lose face.

to play it by ear: to decide what to do according to how a situation develops

We won't organise the holiday. We'll just play it by ear.

to do sth by the skin of your teeth: to only just manage to do sth

He passed the exam by the skin of his teeth.

to see eye to eye on sth: to agree about sth

We will never see eye to eye on this. Let's just agree to differ.

to turn a blind eye to sth: to deliberately ignore sth

It is illegal to sing in the street, but at Christmas the police tend to turn a blind eye to it.

to turn your nose up at sth: to think sth is not good enough for you

He got her a ring and all she could do was turn her nose up at it.

not to be able to get one's tongue round: (for a word or phrase) to find a word or phrase very difficult to pronounce

I can't get my tongue round even the simplest word in Spanish.

sth catches your eye: you notice sth because it is particularly attractive, unusual or interesting

I was reading the local paper when this ad caught my eye.

I'm all ears: I can't wait to hear

"Come on, tell me. I'm all ears."

my lips are sealed: (informal) I will not tell anyone what you have just told me

I promise I won't tell him. My lips are sealed.

I'll never be able to show my face in there/here again: I feel too embarrassed to go to a particular place because I have previously done sth embarrassing there

He'll never be able to show his face in that restaurant again after the fuss he made last time.

it's on the tip of my tongue: I know it but (annoyingly) I just can't recall it

What was the name of the hotel we stayed at? Oh, it's on the tip of my tongue!

Practice

1. a. Use the verbs below to answer questions 1 to 11.

> yawn – wince – wink – sneer – blush – lick – frown – grin – grit – blink – scowl

1 What do you do when you are tired or bored?
You ....

2 What do you do when you are embarrassed?
You ....

3 What do you do when you are angry?
You ....

4 What do you do when you are happy?
You ....

5 What do you do when something hurts you?
You ....

48

6   What do you do to a stamp before you put it on a letter?
    You .... it.
7   What might do you do in anticipation of pain?
    You might .... your teeth.
8   How do some people show that they have no respect for what someone has said or done?
    They .... at the other person.
9   What would you do if someone shone a light into your eyes?
    You would ....
10 What might you do when you disapprove of something or when you don't understand something?
    You might ....
11 What might somebody do when they say something to someone but don't mean it seriously?
    They might .... at them.

   b. *Can you match the pictures to any of the verbs in 1a?*

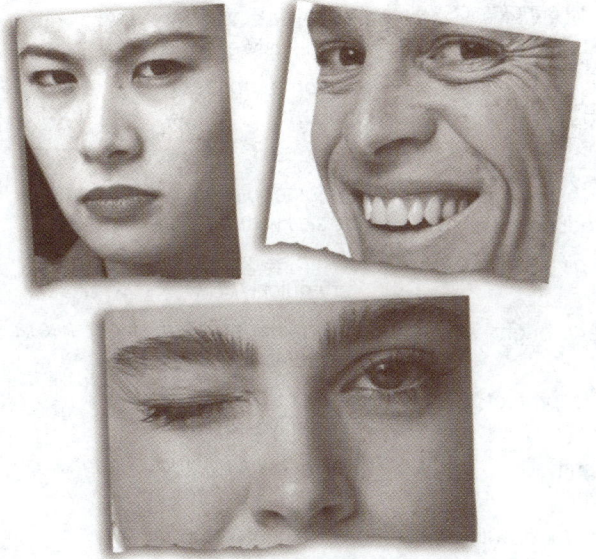

6   We're always arguing. We never see .... to .... on anything.
7   I passed, but only by the skin of my .... The pass mark was 55 and I got 56.
8   A: "You'll never guess what happened to Julie last night."
    B: "Tell me. I'm all ...."
9   I made an utter fool of myself. I'll never be able to show my .... in there again.
10 We don't know what they'll say, so we can't plan our next move. We'll have to play it by ....
11 Oh, what's his name? It's ... it's ... oh... it's on the tip of my ....
12 I know it's only a small part but you shouldn't turn your .... up at it. It's a major film and if they like your acting it may lead to bigger things.
13 The police in this country tend to turn a blind .... to minor traffic offences.
14 I was looking through the Sunday supplement and this article on Vietnam caught my .... I thought you might be interested in it.

2. Complete the idioms in the sentences with words from the box below.

    ear(s) – tongue – face – nose – mouth – teeth – eye(s) – lips

1   A: Just promise not to tell anyone about this.
    B: Of course. My .... are sealed.
2   I've given up studying German. I can't get my .... round all those long words.
3   It was a dilemma indeed – how to admit that he had done something that was incredibly stupid and yet not lose .... ?
4   Of course it's not the truth. He's lying through his ....
5   A good businessman always keeps his .... to the ground and rarely takes pot luck.

3. You will hear an account of an incident that took place in a French restaurant. Listen to the recording, decide whether the sentences below are true (T) or false (F) and tick the correct box.

		T	F
1	Matthew was fluent in French.		
2	Norma was sleepy.		
3	Norma liked most dishes.		
4	Matthew was afraid of making a fool of himself.		
5	Matthew had everything planned.		
6	Matthew was unable to pronounce some French words.		
7	Matthew was deeply embarrassed by his mistake.		

24 Fire and Light

Fire

to billow: (for smoke or clouds) to move slowly upwards or across the sky

Smoke was billowing out of the top-storey windows.

a blaze: a large and dangerous fire [Note: **to tackle a blaze**: to try to put a blaze out]

Two firemen were injured as fire crews from around the city were called in to tackle the blaze.

to catch fire: to start to burn

Don't put those candles near the window or the curtains may catch fire.

to be engulfed in flames: if sth (a car, a building, etc) is engulfed in flames, every part of it is on fire

Soon the whole house was engulfed in flames.

to gut: if a fire guts a building, it completely destroys everything inside the building, leaving only the outside standing

The west wing of the castle was completely gutted by fire.

to light a fire: to start a small fire (to cook on it or to provide heat for a room)

The scouts lit a camp fire to cook their supper on.

to rage: to burn intensely and be out of control

The forest fires have been raging for over a week now.

to scorch: if sb scorches sth, or if sth is scorched, its surface burns – without catching fire – so that a black mark is left behind

I scorched my favourite shirt while I was ironing it.

to set fire to sth: to deliberately start a fire in order to damage or destroy sth

The protestors set fire to every shop along the High Street.

to smoulder: to be burning but with no flames

The burnt-out shell of what had once been the museum was still smouldering.

Light

to be ablaze with light: if sth is ablaze with light, a lot of light is coming from it

A cruise ship, ablaze with light, lit up the night sky as it made its way past the island.

in broad daylight: in the middle of the day; used for things (especially crimes) that you would expect to happen at night

Sometimes crimes are committed in broad daylight.

to be dazzled: to be unable to see because a bright light is shining into your eyes

The bright sunshine dazzled him and he reached for his sunglasses.

to dim: to make a light less bright/to become less bright

The lights began to dim; the film was about to start.

Shall I dim the lights?

to give off light: to produce light

This lamp doesn't give off much light, does it?

the glare of: the very bright and unpleasant light of

You'll need a hat to protect you from the glare of the sun.

to gleam: to shine brightly, especially in the sun

His brand-new car stood outside the garage, gleaming in the sun.

to glimmer: to produce a weak, unsteady light

We could see the city lights glimmering in the distance.

to glisten: if sth glistens, it shines, usually because it is wet

It had been raining. The road glistened in the moonlight.

the gloom: the darkness

In the gloom, we could just make out the street sign.

to glow: to shine with a very soft, warm red light, often used for sth that is burning (without flames) in the dark

The charcoal on the barbecue still glowed in the dark.

to be plunged into darkness: (for a place) to suddenly become very dark

A power cut plunged the city into darkness.

Fire and Light Idioms, Expressions and Verbs

to burn yourself out: to work so hard over a period of time that you become too ill or too tired to work any more

They work 15 hours a day, 6 days a week. They'll burn themselves out by the time they are 30.

to come to light: to become known

If the truth ever comes to light, it will bring down the government.

that's daylight robbery: that's ridiculously expensive

£5 for a coffee! That's daylight robbery!

to be dazzled: to be very impressed

The other players were dazzled by his skill with the ball.

to have a fiery temper: to get angry very quickly

That famous opera singer has a fiery temper.

to flare up: (for violence) to suddenly start

Violence has flared up again on the streets of Paris.

flashy: expensive and showy

After he became a millionaire, he drove around in a flashy car.

to get on like a house on fire: if two people get on like a house on fire, they really like each other

I thought they would hate each other, but when they met, they got on like a house on fire.

a glowing report: a report that is full of praise

The government inspectors gave the school a glowing report.

a glimmer of hope: a little bit of hope

There was still a faint glimmer of hope that an agreement would be reached.

24

sb's face lights up: sb's face suddenly shows that they are very happy or excited
When they saw the Christmas tree, their little faces lit up.

a shot in the dark: a complete guess based on absolutely no information at all
It's a shot in the dark, but it might work.

to spark off: to cause sth to happen
Their decision not to prosecute the minister sparked off widespread rioting throughout the country.

Practice

1. Choose the correct item.

1 The lights slowly ...., the curtain went up, and the audience went wild.
   A dulled   B darkened   C diminished   D dimmed

2 That wasn't an accident. It was arson. Someone intentionally .... fire to that building.
   A put   B lit   C caught   D set

3 Such was its intensity that it took forty firemen to tackle the ....
   A flame   B sparks   C blaze   D rage

4 Within minutes the building was .... in flames.
   A engulfed   B engrossed   C engaged   D entangled

5 We were alerted to the fire when we saw thick, heavy smoke .... out of the window.
   A clouding   B billowing   C choking   D pushing

6 The fire .... for days until the monsoon rains put it out.
   A ignited   B scorched   C flashed   D raged

7 The city below her was .... with neon lights.
   A afresh   B alight   C ablaze   D acute

8 I could see the lantern .... in the dark.
   A gleaming   B glowing   C glistening   D glimmering

9 It's only a small lamp, so it doesn't .... off much light.
   A cast   B spend   C shed   D give

10 The fire hardly touched the exterior of the building. The inside, however, was completely ....
   A swept   B gutted   C smouldered   D blazed

11 It's freezing in here. Why don't we .... a fire?
   A catch   B light   C set   D start

12 The lights went out and the room was .... into total darkness.
   A covered   B plunged   C taken   D put

13 Sunglasses protect you from the .... of the sun.
   A ray   B gloom   C glare   D blaze

14 It was a daring robbery, which took place in .... daylight.
   A broad   B total   C wide   D absolute

15 I was .... by his headlights.
   A dazzled   B flared   C inflamed   D ablaze

2. Complete the sentences with an appropriate word from the box below.

> dazzled – glimmer – flashy – dark – lit – fire – glowing – sparked – fiery – flared – daylight – light – burnt

1 You know Steve! He's got a .... temper and likes to get his own way.

2 Suddenly, violence .... up among the striking miners.

3 Apparently, they got on like a house on ....

4 Straight A's! That's another .... report to take home to his parents.

5 I accused him of embezzlement. It was a shot in the ...., as I didn't know anything for sure.

6 It's not over yet. There's still a .... of hope.

7 Widespread rioting, ... off by Abele's arrest, has paralysed the country.

8 He was completely .... by her beauty.

9 Her face .... up. "We're going to the Caribbean? Are you serious?"

10 The first thing he did after winning the lottery was to buy himself a .... car.

11 £10 for a toothbrush?! That's .... robbery!

12 Unfortunately, the athlete .... himself out before reaching his peak.

13 The truth about the scandal only came to .... years later.

51

25 Food I

a bunch of grapes: a group of grapes growing on the same stem

a clove of garlic: a single segment of garlic

core: the central part of certain fruit (apples, pears)

He ate the apple, leaving only the core.

a dash of milk: a drop of milk

Just a dash of milk in my coffee, please!

diced carrots: carrots that have been cut into small cubes [Note: **grated carrot:** carrots that have been shredded into small pieces using a grater]

a dollop of jam: a large spoonful of jam

a drumstick: a cooked leg of chicken

fresh milk: today's milk [Note: **skimmed milk:** milk with a low fat content; **powdered milk:** milk in powdered form]

grated cheese: cheese that has been rubbed over a grater [Note: **melted cheese:** cheese that has been heated until it is very soft]

gristle: hard and chewy bits of tissue in meat which are difficult and unpleasant to eat

My steak was full of gristle. I couldn't eat it.

kipper: a herring (a kind of fish) that is smoked (preserved by being hung up in smoke)

lean: lean meat has very little fat on it **Opp.:** fatty

a loaf of bread: bread which has been shaped and baked in one large piece

a lump of sugar: a small cube of sugar

mature: if cheese is mature, it has a strong flavour **Opp.:** mild

This is a mature cheese with a strong but pleasant flavour.

minced beef: beef that has been cut into small pieces in a mincer. [Note: **roast beef:** beef cooked in the oven]

a pat of butter: a small lump of butter

peel: the skin of certain fruit (orange, apple, lemon, etc) and of potatoes

pickled onions: small onions which have been left in vinegar for a long time

a pinch of salt: a little bit of salt

pips: small seeds inside certain fruit (apples, oranges, tomatoes, grapes, lemons, etc)

plain chocolate: chocolate that is very dark because it does not contain much milk

plain yoghurt: yoghurt without any flavouring (strawberry, vanilla, etc)

rancid butter: butter that is not fresh and that tastes and smells very unpleasant

The smell of rancid butter wafted out of the fridge.

rind: the skin that covers some cheeses or the peel of an orange or a lemon

roast potatoes: potatoes cooked in an oven. [Note: **baked potato:** potato cooked in its skin, either in an oven or in a fire]

a round of sandwiches: a number of sandwiches

seedless grapes: grapes that do not have pips

scrambled eggs: eggs cooked in a pan with milk [Note: **poached eggs:** eggs (without their shells) cooked in or over boiling water]

smoked salmon: cold salmon (prepared by leaving it in smoke to give it a smoky taste) which is an orange/pink colour

sour: milk that has gone off and is no longer fresh

Throw that milk out. It's sour.

sparkling water: water with gas, carbonated water [Note: **mineral water:** very pure bottled water from a spa]

a stick of celery: an individual piece of celery

still: when a drink is still, it is not fizzy (carbonated)

stone: large hard seed in the middle of fruit such as peaches, plums or cherries

tender: meat or other food which is soft and easy to cut

The steak was tender and juicy.

tough: meat or other food which is hard and difficult to cut

unripe: fruit that is not ready to eat

veal: the meat from a calf

I'll have the veal cutlets, please.

a wedge of cheese: a thick piece of cheese in a triangular shape

a white coffee: a cup of coffee with milk [Note: **a black coffee:** a cup of coffee without milk]

whipped cream: cream that has been stirred very quickly so that it has become stiff [Note: **sour cream:** cream with lemon juice added to give it a sour taste]

Practice

1. *The food items below are preceded by three adjectives. Cross out any adjectives that do not go with the food item. An example has been done for you.*

0 ground / a white / ~~grated~~ **coffee**
1 sparkling / mineral / gas **water**
2 scrambled / skimmed / poached **eggs**
3 roast / baked / mashed **potato**
4 grated / melted / ground **cheese**
5 smoked / whipped / crushed **salmon**
6 pickled / minced / roast **beef**
7 beaten / whipped / sour **cream**
8 pickled / whipped / smoked **onions**
9 fresh / skimmed / powdered **milk**
10 smoked / chilled / baked **herring**
11 diced / melted / grated **carrots**

2. a. *Match an '..of.. phrase' from Column A with an appropriate food item from Column B.*

	A		B
1	a bunch of	a	salt
2	a dash of	b	garlic
3	a wedge of	c	cheese
4	a stick of	d	sandwiches
5	a clove of	e	lamb
6	a lump of	f	butter
7	a pinch of	g	sugar
8	a leg of	h	grapes
9	a loaf of	i	celery
10	a pat of	j	milk
11	a round of	k	jam
12	a dollop of	l	bread

b. *Now match the pictures to the food items.*

c. *Complete the sentences with correct combinations from exercise 2a.*

1 There was a crusty bread roll and a .... on the plate.

2 There's a .... on the saucer if you like your tea sweet.
3 Audrey took the .... and cut some slices to make sandwiches.
4 A .... was roasting in the oven.
5 She added a .... to the soup just before serving it.
6 If you want some fruit, there's a .... on the kitchen table.
7 I've packed a .... for you to eat at lunchtime.

3. a. *Are the following words connected with MEAT, FRUIT and VEGETABLES, DAIRY PRODUCTS or DRINK? (Some words are connected with more than one category). Write M for meat, FV for fruit and vegetables, DP for dairy products and D for drinks in the spaces that follow each word. An example has been done for you.*

mature ....
sour .... core .... a drumstick ....
pips .... lean .... peel ....
tender .... seedless ....
unripe .... rind .... sparkling ....
tough .... rancid .... soft ....
plain .... gristle .... still .... stone ....

b. *Which of the above words do you associate with the following?*

1 butter   ....
2 chicken   ....
3 apples   ....
4 strong cheese   ....
5 meat that is easy to cut   ....
6 grapes   ....
7 oranges   ....
8 lemonade   ....
9 chocolate or yoghurt   ....
10 meat that is difficult to cut   ....
11 meat that is not fatty   ....
12 fruit that is not ready to eat   ....

c. *Find the odd one out, then briefly explain why it doesn't fit its group.*

1	gristle	rancid	sour	rind
2	lean	mature	plain	veal
3	sparkling	still	scrambled	soft
4	stick	bunch	clove	core
5	roast	smoked	baked	grated

26 Food II

a bed of: a layer of sth (rice, lettuce, etc) that other things are put on top of

The main course is a lightly grilled steak served on a bed of fluffy long-grain rice.

chewy: sth you have to chew a lot in order to eat (some things should be chewy e.g. toffee - while others should not e.g. meat)

The meat was tough and chewy and full of fat.

to chop: to cut sth (generally vegetables) into small pieces

Chop the mushrooms and stir-fry for five minutes.

a course: a stage of a meal [Note: **three-course dinner:** dinner that has three stages – the **starter** or **first course**, the **main course** and finally the **pudding** or **dessert**]

What are you going to have for your main course? I fancy fish.

crusty: bread or rolls that are crusty have a hard, crisp crust [Note: **soft rolls:** rolls that have a soft crust]

I'm going to have soup and a crusty roll.

French fries/chips: fried potatoes

Fish and chips are traditionally eaten out of newspaper.

to be garnished with: to be decorated with

She prepared rump steak garnished with a few leaves of basil.

to grind: to crush pepper corns or coffee beans into powder or very small pieces [Note: **ground** (adj)]

I love waking up to the smell of freshly ground coffee.

lashings of: lots of a particular kind of food (esp. cream and sauces)

... served with lashings of whipped cream.

a mixed salad: a salad containing two or three salad vegetables (lettuce, tomato and one other - cucumber, onion, carrot, etc)

I'll have steak and chips and my wife will have fish with a mixed salad.

mouth-watering: (food) that looks and/or smells very good

They found a shop full of mouth-watering cakes.

parsley sauce: sauce made with a plant called parsley

Garnish with lemon and serve with parsley sauce.

piping hot: very hot; used to describe food

This soup is best served piping hot.

plaice: kind of fish

Plaice is my favourite fish.

seasoned with: with salt and/or pepper and/or spices added to improve the taste

Season the sauce with salt and pepper, then sprinkle with herbs.

in season: if vegetables or fruit are in season it is the time of the year when they are ready to eat and as a result are available in large quantities

The dish of the day is Chicken Kiev accompanied by vegetables in season.

smothered in/with: to be covered thickly in

He ate a sticky chocolate cake, smothered in/with cream.

stodgy: solid, heavy and difficult to digest

That spaghetti we had was so stodgy!

stringy: if meat is stringy, it has an unpleasant texture because it is full of long thin pieces (that are like string) and it is therefore difficult and unpleasant to eat

It was a pie full of stringy, fatty meat.

succulent: juicy and tasty (for meat and vegetables)

The Chinese dish consisted of succulent stir-fried vegetables.

The steak was tender and succulent; absolutely delicious!

topped with: if sth is topped with sth else then the latter is put on top of it (generally used for desserts)

I ordered a slice of apple tart topped with a generous helping of ice cream.

Practice

1. Ten words in the menu are either incorrect or inappropriate. Underline them and replace them with a word that is more appropriate.

SET MENU

First Plate
Traditional French onion soup, served with a chewy roll and rancid butter
– . –
Main Course
Either: Steak à la Jansen
Stringy pieces of steak served on a cushion of spinach and accompanied by vegetables in station
– . –
or: Fish and Chips
Fillets of plaice and French fries with flushings of red-hot parsley sauce
– . –
Desert
Choose from a selection of our eye-watering pies and puddings

2. Read the menu below and decide which option (A, B, C or D) best fits each gap.

Hors d' oeuvres and Salad

Iced Melon

1) .... salad with vinaigrette dressing
2) .... rolls and butter

Main 3) .... of Your Choice

Chicken Ugarteche

4) .... pieces of chicken in a creamy sauce served on a
5) .... of basmati rice and 6) .... with mangetout and baby sweetcorn

or

Steak Sennett

tender strips of sirloin steak in a rich mustard sauce 7) ....
by fresh vegetables in 8) ....

Dessert of Your Choice

Strawberry Surrender

a mouth-9) .... mousse 10) .... in cream and served with 11) .... of 12) .... hot strawberry sauce

or

American Pie

Home-made apple pie, served hot and 13) .... with vanilla ice cream

Freshly 14) .... coffee from the highlands of Colombia

1	A Combined	B Mixed	C Blended	D Mingled
2	A Crackly	B Crusty	C Chewy	D Brittle
3	A Food	B Plate	C Course	D Menu
4	A succulent	B stringy	C suppurating	D stodgy
5	A mattress	B base	C bed	D foundation
6	A joined	B added	C elaborated	D garnished
7	A decorated	B accompanied	C adorned	D combined
8	A station	B harvest	C season	D stock
9	A watering	B licking	C tempting	D provoking
10	A teeming	B loaded	C smothered	D swarming
11	A floods	B lashings	C rivers	D flowings
12	A piping	B baking	C boiling	D red
13	A mounted	B seasoned	C topped	D capped
14	A crushed	B ground	C grated	D pulverised

3. Make your own menu using the vocabulary presented in the unit.

27 Hands – Holding, Pushing, Pulling, Taking

Hands

to fiddle with sth: to play with sth small (a pencil, a box of matches, etc) in your fingers, especially when you are bored or nervous

Will you please stop fiddling with the catch on that bag. You'll break it.

to fumble: to hold sth or try to reach for sth with your hands or fingers, but in an awkward and clumsy way

He fumbled with his lighter and dropped it on the floor.

to pat: to repeatedly touch sb lightly with the hand held flat

"Well done," he said, patting him on the back.

to rub: to move your hand or fingers over sth, applying pressure

"That hurts," he said, rubbing his arm where he had banged it.

to slap sb: to hit sb (generally on the face) with an open hand, often because sb has said or done sth to offend or hurt you

"How dare you say that to me!" she screamed and she slapped him across the face.

to smack sb: to hit a child with an open hand in order to punish him or her

You should never punish children by smacking them.

to stroke: to gently move an open hand back and forth over sth (generally for animals)

He might look like the gentlest dog on the planet, but he'll bite you if you try to stroke him.

to tamper with sb: to touch or move sth without permission and in doing so change it or damage it

That was no accident. Somebody had tampered with his brakes.

to tickle sb: to make sb laugh by touching them with your fingers

She tickled the baby's feet.

to toy with sth: to play with sth in your hands or fingers, often while you are deep in thought

She toyed with her hair as she read her book.

to twiddle sth: to turn sth (a dial, a knob, etc), especially when you are trying to make sth work

He could see a small knob. He twiddled it but nothing happened.

Holding, Pushing, Pulling, Taking

to cling: to hold on to sth very tightly because you are frightened that you will fall or you will lose it

She clung to her suitcase, frightened of losing it if she relaxed her grip.

clingy: i) (for clothes) very tight and showing the shape of your body ii) (for people) too attached and dependent on others

She was wearing a very clingy and not particularly flattering dress.

The little boy is too clingy and won't leave his mother's side.

to clutch: to hold sth tightly because you are in pain

He fell to the ground, clutching his leg and crying.

to drag: to pull sth that is heavy

It took three of us to drag the grand piano outside.

to embrace: to put your arms around sb

We embraced and said goodbye.

to grab: (i) to quickly take sth (ii) to manage to get some food/drink/sleep

He grabbed his coat and ran out of the room.

I'm going to the canteen to grab something to eat.

to grasp: to take sth and hold it very tightly

She swam to the rope and grasped it with both hands.

to have an excellent grasp of: to have an excellent understanding of

We need someone with an excellent grasp of computers.

to grip: to hold sth very tightly

He gripped the edge of his seat as she overtook the car in front.

to be in the grip of: to be experiencing sth that cannot be controlled (an economic crisis, a famine, bad weather, etc); generally for (a region or the people of) a country

Switzerland is in the grip of its worst winter on record.

to let go of sth: to stop holding sth so that it is no longer in your hand

She let go of the bird and it flew away.

to manhandle: to push sb roughly

The police manhandled him into a van.

to pull your weight: to do your fair share of the work

If you don't start pulling your weight in this office, you will be asked to resign.

to seize: to take sth illegal (stolen goods, etc) away from sb

The police seized a cache of counterfeit money during a raid on a house in north-east London.

to shove: to push sb roughly

Two men shoved rudely past me.

to snatch: to quickly take sth (especially sth that does not belong to you) from sb

The naughty girl snatched her friend's sweets.

to tow: to pull a vehicle, often by means of a rope or a chain

Our car broke down so it had to be towed to the garage.

to tug: to pull sth with short but forceful pulls

The little boy tugged at his mother's skirt to get her attention.

to wrench: to pull sth forcefully and quickly, in order to open it/remove it from where it is

The door was stuck. He wrenched it open and continued running.

to yank: to pull sth with one quick, forcefull pull

He yanked the sheets off the bed.

56

Practice

1. Complete each sentence in Section A by adding an appropriate ending from Section B.

A 1 She obviously took exception to something he said because she suddenly
2 In England it is quite common for parents to
3 Anna couldn't stop laughing because her sister was
4 Still under influence of the anaesthetic, he staggered to the door. He
5 His car wouldn't start. He looked under the bonnet. Some wires had been cut. Someone had
6 The little girl sat
7 Interviews, how he hated them! He sat outside the room, nervously
8 "Well done," he said,
9 "That didn't hurt," he said. But I knew differently because he kept
10 I had no idea what wavelength Radio Codfish was on, so I suggested he kept
11 "Ahh, it's so cute," she said, bending down and

B
| a | **fumbled** with his keys, swayed and unceremoniously fell to the ground.
| b | **patting** his son on the back.
| c | **stroking** the little kitten that was curled up on the sofa.
| d | **slapped** him across the face.
| e | **fiddling** with his pen. He was next.
| f | **twiddling** the dial until he found it.
| g | **tickling** her.
| h | **toying** with her hair.
| i | **smack** their children when they have been naughty.
| j | **tampered** with the engine, someone who didn't want him to get to court.
| k | **rubbing** his leg and wincing.

2. Choose the correct item.

1 At that point the hero is .... into a car, which then speeds away.
   A seized   B manhandled
   C snatched   D grabbed

2 He .... of the vase and it dropped to the floor, shattering into a thousand tiny pieces.
   A left hold   B released   C loosened   D let go

3 The man let out a scream, ... his stomach and staggered towards the window. It was a very realistic scene.
   A gripped   B embraced   C clutched   D snatched

4 She reached the lifeboat. She was exhausted and she .... to its side, waiting for someone to pull her in.
   A gripped   B grasped   C clutched   D clung

5 Tim looked up and .... at his mother's dress. "Can I have an ice cream?" he asked.
   A let go   B tugged   C gripped   D heaved

6 As the train pulled in, she .... him into its path. At that point the novel ends.
   A shoved   B yanked   C wrenched   D snatched

7 There she was, walking out of customs, ... a huge suitcase behind her.
   A towing   B manhandling   C pushing   D dragging

8 I'm packed and everything's ready. I'm going to .... a couple of hours sleep before we leave.
   A seize   B embrace   C grab   D grasp

9 My ideal partner would have to be someone who wasn't too dependent on me, someone who wasn't too ....
   A graspy   B grippy   C huggy   D clingy

10 At the time, Mexico was in the .... of its worst economic recession on record.
   A grip   B tug   C hug   D grab

11 Of course you'll pass. You write well and you have an excellent .... of the subject.
   A grip   B seizure   C embrace   D grasp

12 Everybody was busy with the spring cleaning, except Stanley, who always refused to pull his ....
   A socks   B weight   C finger   D share

13 I really don't want to get involved in your problems. Why are you .... me into it?
   A pulling   B dragging   C wrenching   D towing

14 "How silly of me to have tried to move the sofa all by myself," he said, ... his back.
   A tugging   B stroking   C rubbing   D patting

15 I picked up the letter. She darted forward and .... it. "That's mine!" she said.
   A gripped   B grabbed   C yanked   D wrenched

28 Health I

Collocations

to alleviate (the) pain/symptoms: to reduce the amount/effect of pain/symptoms. [Note: alleviate is also used with **boredom, a problem, anxiety, poverty**]

Take two of these. They'll alleviate the pain.

to contract a disease/illness: to catch/fall ill with a disease/illness: not used with minor illnesses in spoken English

It was during his trip down the Amazon that he contracted malaria.

to give blood: to voluntarily have blood taken from you so that it can be stored and used for sb else at a later date

Hospitals are appealing to donors to come forward and give blood.

to make a recovery: to recover, to get better [Note: **to make a full recovery**: to recover completely]

It was a simple operation and the doctors expected him to make a full recovery.

to nurse sb back to health: to help sb get better

After the operation, his sister nursed him back to health.

to perform an operation: (formal) to operate on sb

The man performing your operation is the best heart surgeon in the country.

to reduce the swelling: do sth (put ice on the swelling) or take some medicine which will return the swollen part of your body back to its normal size

We can't put it in plaster yet. We have to reduce the swelling first.

to regain consciousness: to 'wake up' having previously fainted/been unconscious; to come round/to

He regained consciousness in the hospital ward.

to respond to treatment: to get better as a result of taking a particular medicine, etc

For some reason, he is not responding to treatment.

to take effect: to start to work (for a medicine, a painkiller, an anaesthetic)

You'll feel much better when the painkillers take effect.

to treat an illness: to try and cure an illness

It's one of those illnesses that you just can't treat with conventional medicine.

to undergo surgery: (formal) to have a surgeon operate on you

The Vice President underwent surgery late last night and his condition is said to be stable.

Prepositions

to be admitted to hospital: to be taken into hospital

He was admitted to hospital after complaining of pains in his chest.

to be allergic to sth: if you are allergic to sth (cats, dust, nuts, etc), your body reacts to it in a negative way – perhaps you start sneezing, or perhaps you get a rash

I'm allergic to pollen.

to be on antibiotics: to be taking antibiotic medicine

I'm on antibiotics and they make me feel a bit sleepy.

a cure for a disease: a medicine or medical treatment that will get rid of an illness or a disease

Scientists have recently discovered a cure for Redstein's disease.

to die of sth: if sb dies of a particular disease/illness, it kills them

He died of pneumonia.

to be discharged from hospital: to be allowed to leave hospital

The President was discharged from hospital last night.

to be in intensive care: to be in a hospital ward where people who are very ill are treated and looked after

It was very serious. He was in intensive care for two weeks.

to be on the mend: to be getting better

Although not yet fully recovered, he is on the mend.

to operate on sb: to treat sb by cutting open part of their body and removing or repairing sth

He's being operated on tomorrow.

to get medicine on prescription: you must have a prescription to obtain it [Note: buy medicine **over the counter**: you do not need a prescription to buy it]

Here you cannot buy tranquillisers over the counter; you can only get them on prescription.

to be rushed to/into hospital: to be taken to hospital very quickly

He collapsed at work and was rushed to the city hospital.

to be in good shape: to be fit and healthy

It's an extremely difficult climb, but we're in very good shape.

to be under a lot of stress: to be unable to relax because you are worrying a lot

I know he's been bad-tempered recently, but he's under a lot of stress at the office at the moment.

to suffer from sth: to have a particular illness or disease

Kelly suffers from migraine.

to be susceptible to sth: to be the kind of person who easily catches a disease or illness

The vaccination is being given to those groups in society who are particularly susceptible to flu.

to hang by a thread: if one's life is hanging by a thread they are very ill and likely to die

The doctors later told her how her life had hung by a thread during the operation.

to take its toll/a heavy toll on: to have a bad effect on

Working down the mines for so many years had taken its toll on his health.

Practice

1. The following exercise has been done by a fellow student. Are his/her answers correct? Put a tick (✓) if the answer is correct or, if not, supply the correct answer.

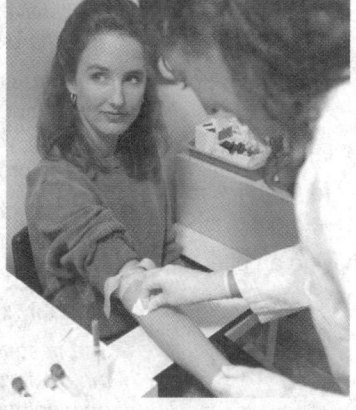

1 So you have to **give** blood. It won't hurt. ....
2 These pills will help to **alleviate** the pain. ....
3 He has to **undergo** surgery on his left knee and will therefore not play in Milan. ....
4 Bathing your ankle in cold water should **contract** the swelling. ....
5 These pain killers will **make** effect almost immediately. ....
6 I **took** the disease in Africa last summer. ....
7 It was his wife who **regained** him back to health, tending to his every need. ....
8 She was out cold. It was seven hours before she **reduced** consciousness. ....
9 If it doesn't **respond** to this treatment, we'll have to operate. ....
10 The hospital's senior eye specialist was going to **nurse** the operation, so she was in good hands. ....
11 Most common infections can be **treated** with antibiotics. ....
12 Thankfully, he **performed** a complete recovery. ....

2. Complete the sentences below with an appropriate preposition.

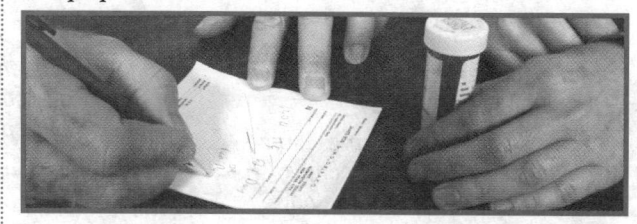

1 "You can't buy these tablets .... the counter. You have to get them .... prescription."
2 There is no known cure .... Sterrits disease.
3 He was rushed .... hospital with suspected appendicitis.
4 He couldn't eat what she had prepared for him because he was allergic .... cheese.
5 He had been .... a lot of stress, and it was beginning to take its toll .... his health.
6 You are supposed to finish the course if you are .... antibiotics.
7 Her grandfather died .... cancer.
8 Both of her sons suffer .... hayfever.
9 He was .... pretty good shape for a man of his age.
10 They operated .... him on Monday and he was discharged .... hospital on Tuesday!
11 He was .... intensive care, his life hanging .... a thread.
12 She takes vitamin supplements in winter because she is susceptible .... colds and flu.
13 She was admitted .... hospital with third-degree burns.
14 There's a long way to go before my leg is totally better but at least it is .... the mend.

3. What do you think is happening/has happened in the pictures? Use the prompts, as well as your own ideas, to talk about them.

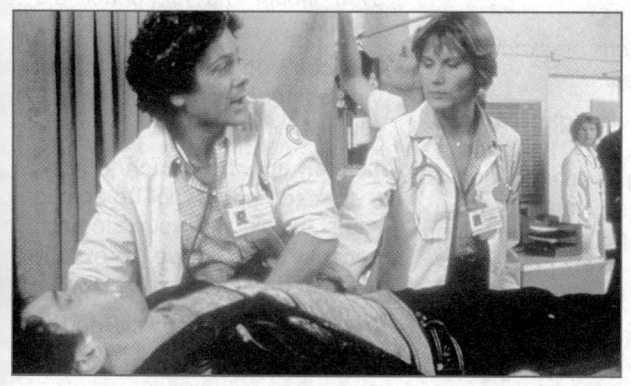

A rush to hospital/suffer from heart attack/undergo surgery/life/hang by a thread/intensive care/respond to treatment/on the mend

B suffer from migraine and back pain/stress/take medicine on prescription/no effect/take up yoga and relaxation techniques/alleviate pain/in good shape now

29 Health II

Phrasal Verbs

to clear up: if a rash or a cold clears up, it goes away

The doctor gave me some ointment and told me that the rash should clear up within five days.

to come out in a rash/spots: if you come out in a rash/spots, a rash or spots start covering part or all of your body

I'm allergic to feathers. I only have to look at a bird and I come out in a rash.

to come out of a coma: to wake up from a coma

It was two months before he came out of his coma.

to come round/come to: to regain consciousness after you have fainted

When I came round/to, I was in an ambulance.

to go down with sth: to become ill with sth

Tommy's gone down with measles.

to pass out: to faint, to lose consciousness

My finger bled so badly that I very nearly passed out.

to pull through: to survive and recover from a serious illness

He's in critical condition but the doctors have assured us that he will pull through.

to put sb on sth: if a doctor puts you on a particular course of medicine, he prescribes that medicine for you to take [Note: a doctor can also **put you on a diet**]

The doctor has put me on a course of antibiotics.

to put your back out: to hurt your back, often because you have tried to lift sth very heavy

John won't be playing for us today. He's put his back out.

to shake (sth) off: to get rid of sth

Angela has been on antibiotics for a week but she can't seem to shake off her cold.

to take a tooth out: to remove a tooth

The last time I went to the dentist, he took four of my teeth out.

to wear off: to stop having an effect

When the anaesthetic wears off, you will be in some pain.

Illness, Aches, and Pains

a blinding/splitting/thumping headache: a very bad headache

Give me some aspirin; I've got that thumping headache again.

a bug: an illness which is easily caught but which is not serious and probably lasts for two or three days [Note: **a stomach/tummy bug**: a bug which affects the stomach]

I hope I don't pick up that bug which is going round the school at the moment.

to feel as right as rain: to feel 100% well, after having previously felt ill

Helen went to bed with a blinding headache but in the morning she felt as right as rain.

a highly infectious disease: a disease that is very easily passed from one person to another

Bushell's disease is highly infectious. You only need someone to sneeze near you and you will get it.

to have/suffer a nervous breakdown: to become extremely depressed and unable to cope

He's had two nervous breakdowns in the last three years.

to have (got) poor eyesight: not to be able to see very well and probably needing to wear glasses or contact lenses [Note: **to be hard of hearing**: not to be able to hear very well and probably needing to use a hearing aid]

We all wear glasses in my family. We've all got very poor eyesight. You'll have to speak up a bit; he's quite hard of hearing.

a runny nose: if you have (got) a runny nose or if your **nose is running**, you have a cold and your nose is producing a lot of liquid

I've just got a bit of runny nose and a bit of a sore throat, that's all.

to be seriously-ill: to be very ill and probably in hospital as a result

She is seriously ill in hospital and the doctors say that it is touch and go whether she will pull through.

shooting pains: sudden, sharp pains which do not last for a long time but which do repeat themselves

I keep getting shooting pains like needles in my back.

a sore throat: if you have (got) a sore throat, your throat hurts so that you find it difficult to swallow and sometimes even to speak

These lozenges are very good for a sore throat.

a stinking cold: a very bad cold

I'm not going into work today. I've got a stinking cold.

to have a touch of flu: to have some of the symptoms of flu (a runny nose, a headache, etc) but not be so ill that you need to go to bed

I've just got a touch of flu. It's nothing a few paracetamol won't fix.

to feel (a bit) under the weather/off-colour: to feel slightly ill

Geoff went to work yesterday, even though he felt under the weather.

You don't normally need to visit the doctor or take any medicine if you just feel off-colour.

to have an upset stomach/to have a stomach upset: not be able to keep anything in your stomach because you have probably eaten or drunk sth bad

The last time I ate that, I got an upset stomach.

Practice

1. Complete the sentences with an appropriate phrasal verb from the box below. You may have to change the tense or form of the verbs.

> go down with – take out – come out of – pass out –
> come out in – put on – pull through – shake off –
> come round/to – put out – wear off – clear up

1. Ted .... his back .... trying to lift a very heavy box of books.
2. Chris is allergic to cheese, and if she has even a slice of it she .... a rash all over her body.
3. I can't seem to .... this cold. I've tried everything, but it just won't go away.
4. He .... One minute he was standing, chatting to Mark, and the next he was on the floor.
5. I didn't feel anything because I was anaesthetised, but when the anaesthetic .... I was in agony.
6. Naturally, we're all incredibly relieved, as at one point it was touch and go whether he would ....
7. Her tooth was so decayed she had to have it ....
8. When he .... his coma, the first words he said were "Where am I?"
9. We're so short-staffed because half our teachers have .... food poisoning.
10. As Emi's throat infection hadn't ...., the doctor decided to .... her .... a stronger course of antibiotics.
11. I don't know how long I had been unconscious, but when I ...., I found myself neatly tucked up in a hospital bed.
12. The doctor .... Anna .... a special diet for diabetics.

2. Make up questions for the following answers.

1. A: ....
   B: I'm sure he'll pull through.
2. A: ....
   B: Yes. I can't seem to shake it off.
3. A: ....
   B: It'll clear up within a couple of days.
4. A: ....
   B: She just passed out!

3. *a.* Complete the sentences in Section A with an appropriate noun from Section B.

A

1. I've got a stinking ....
2. She's got a runny ....
3. He's got a sore ....
4. I shouldn't have eaten that curry. It's given me an upset ....
5. I think I've got a touch of ....
6. I've got a blinding ....
7. Before he collapsed, he complained of a shooting .... in his chest.
8. He's not coming into work today. He says he feels a bit off–.................. .
9. It's a highly infectious ....
10. I've got a stomach ....
11. She is seriously ....
12. He had a nervous ....
13. I'm feeling a bit under the ....
14. She's got very poor ....
15. Take two of these and you'll feel as right as .... in the morning.

B

flu
cold
colour
throat
weather
nose
headache
eyesight
ill
breakdown
rain
pain
bug
disease
stomach

b. Can you match the pictures to any of the sentences in 3a?

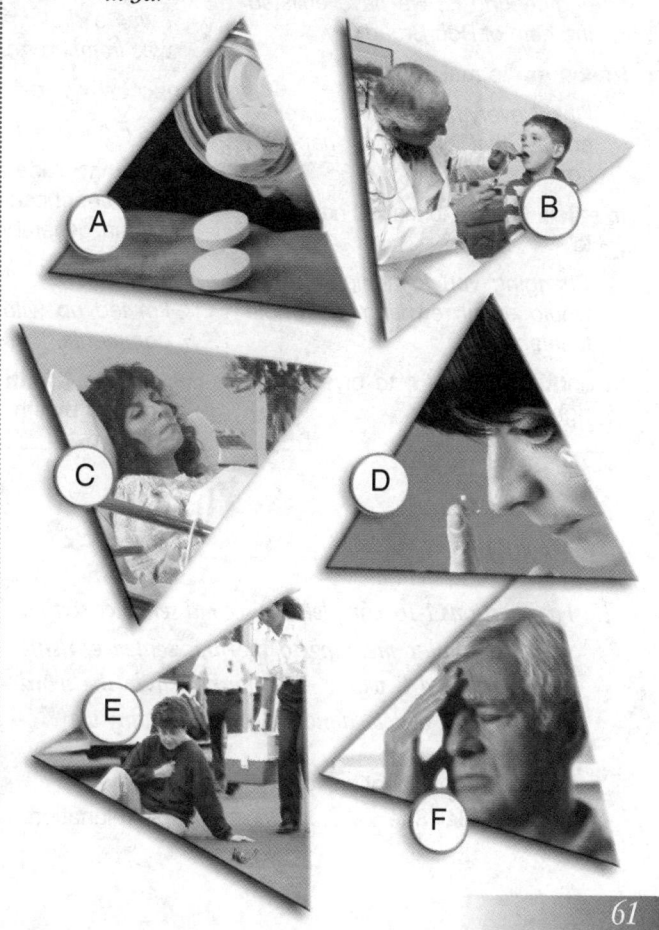

30 Im ... and En ...

to enable sb do sth: to make it possible for sb to do sth

Using e-mail has enabled us to reduce our costs by 45%.

to encourage sb (to do sth/in sth): to say or do things that give sb the courage or confidence to do sth

My parents encouraged me to apply to Oxford.

She encouraged me in my decision to give up work and set up my own business.

engrossed in sth: paying all your attention to sth (a book, a film, your work, your own thoughts, etc)

So engrossed was she in her thoughts that she forgot to get off the train.

to enlist (in the army/navy/airforce): to join (the army/navy/airforce) voluntarily [Note: **to enlist the help of sb**: to get sb to help]

On leaving school, he enlisted in the navy.

To explain to you what genetic engineering is, we have enlisted the help of Bob Broadway.

to ensure: to make sure

I'll do everything in my power to ensure that this never happens again.

to entail: (formal) to make it necessary to

Changing you to senior classes would entail rewriting the whole timetable.

to entitle sb to sth: to give sb the right to have sth

Being with the firm for twenty years does not entitle you to boss everybody else around.

to envisage: to expect

We do not envisage having any problems.

It is envisaged that by the year 2010 nearly 80% of the population will own a computer.

immaterial: not important or relevant; *immaterial* comes after a noun and generally follows the verb *to be*

What we think is immaterial. It is what the jury thinks that counts.

immune to sth: if you are immune to a particular illness or disease, you cannot catch it (because you have a natural resistance to it, or because you have been vaccinated against it) [Note: **immune from prosecution**: cannot be arrested or charged with a crime]

As nobody is immune to this disease, we strongly recommend that you be vaccinated against it.

I was a diplomat and, as such, I was immune from prosecution.

impeccable: perfect and without faults

His French is impeccable.

impertinent: rude and disrespectful; *impertinent* can go before or after a noun, generally with the verb *to be*

impertinent child/remark/question

I'm fed up with your impertinent comments.

impervious to sth: not bothered or affected by sth

Donald is totally impervious to criticism and doesn't care what people say about him.

implausible: not very convincing and probably not true

Jamie was the master of implausible excuses.

impressive: great in size or degree or done with great skill (only used for **positive** things)

an impressive speech / performance, etc

We knew he was good but we didn't expect his results to be as impressive as they were.

imposing: big and impressive [Note: **imposing person**: important, with a strong character] *imposing* can go before a noun or after a noun, generally with the verb *to be*

It's a big city, full of wide open spaces and imposing buildings.

He was a very imposing man and everyone in the office was in awe of him.

impromptu: without advanced preparation or practice; generally used before a noun

The Beatles gave an impromptu performance on the rooftop of the Apple building in central London.

impulsive: doing things suddenly without thinking about them carefully first

It was impulsive and perhaps rather foolish of Jonathan to give up a good job to become an actor.

Practice

1. For questions 1-16, complete the second sentence so that it has a similar meaning to the first sentence, using between 3 and 8 words. You must include the word given in bold, which cannot be changed in any way.

1 I found her explanation very difficult to believe.
   implausible She .... explanation.

2 Analysts believe that interest rates will remain the same for the next six months.
   envisage Analysts do not .... in interest rates for the next six months.

3 She was wrong to have said such a rude and disrespectful thing.
   impertinent She shouldn't ....
   .... remark.

4 She found her book so interesting that she didn't even hear me.
   engrossed   She .... that she didn't even hear me.

5 They told him that, as long as he co-operated, he would not be brought to trial.
   immune   He was .... prosecution if he co-operated.

6 No other building in the city has such a big and impressive entrance as The Park Towers.
   imposing   The Park Towers has .... any building in the city.

7 He acts without considering the possible risks involved, which is why he didn't get promoted.
   impulsive   Were .... promoted.

8 Helen speaks excellent Spanish.
   impressive   Helen has .... of Spanish.

9 If they built a by-pass, they would have to spend a lot of money.
   entail   Building a bypass .... of money.

10 It was by using a four-wheel drive that they reached the more inaccessible regions of the park.
    enabled   Using a four-wheel drive jeep .... to the more inaccessible regions of the park.

11 With this voucher you can get a free drink with every doughnut you buy.
    entitles   This voucher .... when you purchase a doughnut.

12 I left school and then joined the army.
    enlisted   On .... the army.

13 I don't care if he meant it or not. The fact is, he said it.
    immaterial   Whether .... The fact is, he said it.

14 His mother said it would be a good idea for him to start playing tennis.
    encouraged   He .... up tennis.

15 We will endeavour to make sure that this never happens again.
    ensure   We will do our very .... that this never happens again.

16 Quite without preparation, the minister spoke about the effects the new law would have.
    impromptu   The minister .... about the effects the new law would have.

2. Complete the sentences using the vocabulary presented in this unit.

1 Sylvie gave an .... rendering of the sonata, with no faults at all.
2 Hector is totally .... to criticism and doesn't let anything people say affect him.
3 A massive vaccination programme made people .... to the disease.
4 Geoff suddenly realised that accepting the promotion would .... moving to head office.
5 They .... the help of local volunteers in setting up a shelter for homeless people.
6 Although he had prepared nothing in advance, Brendan made a marvellous .... speech.
7 That the dog ate your homework seems a rather .... excuse to me.
8 As she was so talented, her parents .... her to go on the stage.
9 Please .... that all lights are switched off when you leave the building.
10 My grandfather was an .... individual, with a larger than life personality.

31 Informal Language

Verbs

to beat it: to go away
Beat it before I lose my temper.

to bug: to annoy
If it bugs you so much, why don't you do something about it?

to bung: throw/give/put
Can you bung me the newspaper?
They are easy to prepare. You just bung them in the microwave.
Don't leave it on the floor. Bung it in the bin.

to chuck: to throw or give [Note: you can substitute **chuck** for **throw** in most **throw** phrasal verbs]
Can you chuck me the lighter?
It's no good. Chuck it away.

to flog: to sell
I flogged it to my next door neighbour.

to hammer sb: to beat sb/another team very easily and very convincingly
We hammered them 6 – 0 last season!

to knock: criticise
I'm not knocking your car. All I'm saying is that it's a little bit noisy.

to nip to: to go somewhere for a short time
I'm just nipping to the shops. Do you want anything?
I'm going to nip out for an hour or two and get some fresh air.

to pop: to quickly put
Pop the kettle on, will you?

to scoff: to eat quickly and greedily
Fred scoffed all the pancakes and then got indigestion.

to scrounge: to borrow, especially money [Note: **can I scrounge?**: will you give me ...?]
I'll see if I can scrounge some money from my mum.
Can I scrounge a lift with you?

to stink: to have a bad smell
The kitchen stinks of burnt meat.

Adjectives

airy-fairy: not practical or realistic
They want to charge a fee of £6 for every car that enters the city? Who comes up with these airy-fairy ideas?

chock-a-block: very crowded with people or cars (not used before a noun)
The main road was chock-a-block with traffic.

clapped-out: old and in bad condition (for cars and machines)
He's got lots of money, yet he insists on driving around in that horrible clapped-out Austin.

daft: silly, not sensible
Don't be daft! Of course he still loves you.

dodgy: (i) risky and dangerous (ii) dishonest and untrustworthy (for people) (iii) weak (for parts of the body)
Lying to the police is a bit dodgy, isn't it?
He's a dodgy character. I don't trust him.
I can't help you lift that. I've got a dodgy back.

gross: disgusting to look at, taste or think about
Why do some people behave in such a gross way?

hush-hush: secret
I don't know what he does. It's obviously very hush-hush.

lousy: bad
a lousy film/hotel/actor
The weather was lousy all week.

mucky: dirty
mucky hands/pair of jeans
My car is a bit mucky inside.

nippy: cold (used for weather)
Take a coat with you if you are going out. It's quite nippy outside.

posh: expensive and upper class
posh hotel/restaurant/dress/car/accent/people

tacky: poor quality, cheap and showing a lack of good taste
tacky furniture/jewellery/shoes/ornaments

tatty: old and in bad condition
a tatty shirt/pair of jeans/suitcase/carpet/book

weird: strange
a weird noise/film/man/sense of humour

Phrasal Verbs

to chicken out: not to do sth because you are afraid
He says he's going to tell them tonight, but I bet he chickens out.

to chuck (sth) out: to get rid of sth
If the TV doesn't work any more, we should chuck it out.

to conk out: to break down (for machines and cars)
My car conked out last night so it's at the garage.

to cough up: to pay sb money (often used as a request)
You lost the bet, so come on, cough up.

to hit it off: if two people hit it off, they really like one another (generally used when two people meet for the first time and mainly with the pronouns 'we' and 'they')
We hit it off immediately and have been friends ever since.

to rip sb off: to cheat sb out of money
When I looked at my change, I realised that the shopkeeper had ripped me off.

to set sb back: to cost
How much did that set you back?

to slag sb off: to criticise sb
It is unkind to slag people off behind their backs.

to wind (sb) up: to tease sb in order to annoy or provoke them
You only say those ridiculous things to wind me up.

31

Practice

1. *The verbs in bold in the sentences below are informal verbs. What does each verb mean?*

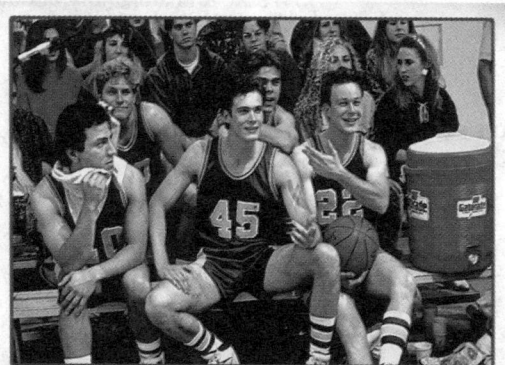

1. I don't understand why everyone **knocks** our team. After all, we are at the top of the league. ....
2. Karen? She'll be back in a couple of minutes. She's just **nipped** to the shops. ....
3. You **scoffed** all the cakes, you greedy thing! ....
4. I haven't got it anymore. I **flogged** it to the guy down the road. He gave me £40 for it. ....
5. **Pop** the kettle on, will you? I'm dying for a cup of tea. ....
6. A: I'm not buying this. It **stinks**. ....
   B: It's supposed to. It's blue cheese.
7. Dad, I don't suppose I could **scrounge** a couple of pounds off you, could I? I'll pay you back tomorrow. ....
8. It really **bugs** me when he complains about how poor he is. I know for a fact that he earns a small fortune. ....
9. These TV dinners are so simple that you take them out of the freezer, **bung** them in the oven and they're ready in 5 minutes. ....
10. There's no milk because it went off and I had to **chuck** it away. ....
11. All I did was ask him what the time was and he told me to **beat it**. ....
12. Manchester United **hammered** A. C. Milan 8 – 0 last night in the semi–final of the European Cup. ....

2. *The sentences below contain an informal adjective in bold. Replace the informal adjective with an appropriate neutral synonym or phrase. An example has been done for you.*

0. It's a bit **nippy** in here. Could you close the window?   *cold*
1. The hotel was awful, the food was horrible and the weather was **lousy**. We'd have been better off staying at home.   ....
2. Did we enjoy the horror film? No, it was so **gross** that we left before it finished.   ....
3. I've had enough of your **airy-fairy** ideas. What we need are sensible, no-nonsense solutions.   ....
4. The city centre was **chock-a-block with** people shopping in the sales.   ....
5. You can't wear that **tatty** old jacket to the interview. It'll create a bad impression.   ....
6. Look at you, you **mucky** boy! You've got chocolate everywhere!   ....
7. Pink fur and plastic! She's says it is fashionable. I think it's downright **tacky**.   ....
8. It's a bit **dodgy**, don't you think? I mean, if they find out, you'll almost certainly get the sack.   ....
9. His job is so **hush-hush** that he can't even tell me what he does – and I'm his wife.   ....
10. He was a very **weird** person. He didn't have any furniture in his living room except for a huge rock in the middle of the room.   ....
11. Well, it was a **daft** question, wasn't it? Of course winning all that money will change his life!   ....
12. I don't see any point in getting rid of it. Granted it's a bit **clapped-out**, but we only need it to get us round town.   ....
13. I'd much rather stay in a little bed and breakfast than one of those **posh** five-star hotels.   ....

3. 🎧 *You will hear 9 short extracts. In each extract you will hear an informal phrasal verb. Based on what you hear, explain what each phrasal verb means.*

1. to rip someone off: ....
2. to cough up: ....
3. to set someone back: ....
4. to chicken out: ....
5. to conk out: ....
6. to chuck something/someone out: ....
7. to hit it off: ....
8. to wind someone up: ....
9. to slag someone off: ....

65

32 -ing form vs to

Words and phrases followed by ...ing

to have sb doing sth: to make sb do sth (through persuasion, by giving them orders, etc) that they probably do not want to do

Be careful or Frank will have you doing his work as well as your own.

to be pointless: to have no sense or purpose

It's pointless having meetings because nothing ever gets decided.

to resent sth happening/sb doing sth: to feel angry and bitter about sth, probably because you think it is unfair or wrong

He resented taking orders from a man half his age.

to be (well) worth doing: it would be a good idea to do

'The Test' is an excellent novel. It's well worth reading.

you would be better off doing sth: used to introduce advice

You really ought to move out. You'd be much better off living on your own.

Words and phrases followed by to

to be the first/second/last person to: sb is the first/second/last person that

In fact, I was the last person to go.

You are not the first person to have been bitten by that dog.

can't be bothered to do sth: don't feel like making the effort to do sth [Note: when **can't be bothered** is used about sb else, the speaker is being critical, implying that sb is lazy]

I can't be bothered to cook tonight. Let's go to a restaurant.

He obviously can't be bothered to write to us.

sth/sb is bound to...: sth/sb is certain to happen/do sth because it has happened/they have done it before

He's bound to be late. He never arrives on time.

to be certain to: to be sure sth will happen or sb will do sth

They are certain to refuse.

to fail to/neglect to do sth: not to do what you should have done

He failed to hand in his homework on time.

to know better than to do sth: to be old or experienced enough to know sth is the wrong thing to do

He should have known better than to try and do something so risky.

not to know how best to do sth: not to know the best way to do sth

I don't know how best to tell him the truth.

to manage to do sth: to succeed in doing sth difficult

The window was stuck, but after a lot of pushing and pulling I managed to open it.

to wish to do sth: (formal) would like to do sth

If you wish to contact us, you can do so via our website.

Words and phrases followed by to + ...ing

to come close to doing sth: to almost do sth

She came close to winning the election.

to be committed to sth: to believe strongly in sth, to want it to happen and succeed and to be prepared to work very hard in order to make it happen

This government is committed to tackling unemployment.

not to feel up to doing sth: not to feel well enough to do sth

I don't feel up to going to the gym.

to object to doing sth/sb doing sth: to dislike and feel angry about sth because you think it is wrong or unfair

I object to her ordering me about.

to resort to doing sth: to do sth you disapprove of because you feel that it is the only way you can succeed or deal with a problem

Much as he disliked the idea, he had to resort to borrowing the money from his parents.

Words and phrases followed by both to and ...ing

to dread: (i) **to dread + to** appears in the phrase **I dread to think** and generally followed by **what** (ii) **to dread +ing:** to dislike and be frightened of sth you have to do

I dread to think what she will say when she finds out the truth.

to go on: (i) **to go on + to:** to proceed, after doing sth else (ii) **to go on +ing:** to continue

Having won the silver medal in the 200m, he then went on to win the gold in the 100m.

He went on speaking, even though nobody was listening.

to mean: (i) **to mean + to:** to intend (ii) **to mean +ing:** to involve, entail

Harvey didn't mean to criticise; he merely wanted to tell the truth.

Catching the six o'clock ferry will mean getting up at five.

to regret: (i) **to regret + to:** to be sorry to (used with the verbs say, tell, inform, announce) (ii) **to regret +ing:** to be sorry about sth that has/hasn't happened

We regret to inform you that your application has been unsuccessful.

I regret passing up that marvellous opportunity.

Practice

1. Categorise the following words/phrases according to whether they are followed by -ing form, to (inf), to +ing or both -ing and to. Then use them in sentences. The first one has been done for you.

0	mean	both -ing and to
1	manage	....
2	I was the last person	....
3	come close	....
4	can't be bothered	....
5	neglect	....
6	It's pointless	....
7	is certain	....
8	should've known better than	....
9	go on	....
10	feel up	....
11	regret	....
12	dread	....
13	how best	....
14	resent	....
15	want	....
16	is bound	....
17	wish	....
18	object	....
19	resort	....
20	committed	....
21	well worth	....
22	be better off	....
23	he'll have you	....

0 *Taking this job means moving to Canada, so I'm not too sure. I'm sorry, I didn't mean to be rude.*

2. For questions 1 to 13, complete the second sentence so that it has a similar meaning to the first sentence, using 3 to 8 words. You must include the word given in bold, which cannot be changed in any way.

1 He was the runner-up in three men's singles finals at Wimbledon.
   close   He .... the men's singles title at Wimbledon on three separate occasions.

2 I wish I hadn't lied to him.
   regret   I .... truth.

3 She won the National Championship two months after she had won the Regional Championship.
   went   Two months after she had won .... the National Championship.

4 We will have to lay off 25 of our employees if we want to reduce our costs.
   mean   Reducing our costs .... 25 of our employees redundant.

5 Everyone knew before me.
   person   I was .... told.

6 I'm sure he will be found guilty.
   certain   He .... guilty.

7 I'm almost certain she won't still be at home.
   bound   She .... by now.

8 He didn't take kindly to his boss telling him that his work was not up to standard.
   resented   He .... that his work was not up to standard.

9 She didn't tell the Inland Revenue that she had a second job.
   neglected   She .... had two jobs.

10 I think you should go by bus. A taxi will cost you an arm and a leg.
   off   You'd .... by bus.

11 I don't feel like doing the washing-up now.
   bothered   I .... the dishes now.

12 You have been friends with Brian long enough to know that lending him your car was stupid.
   better   You .... Brian your car.

13 It was a serious operation and it took John two months before he felt well enough to go out.
   up   John didn't .... out for two months after his operation.

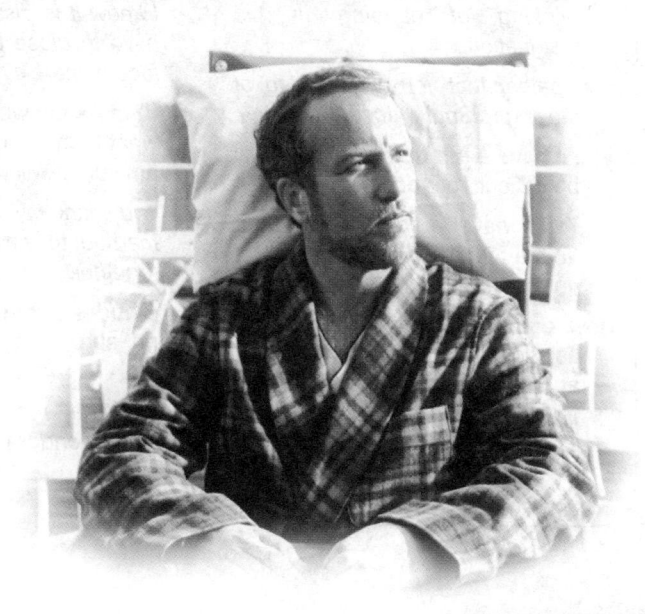

33 Introductions

as far as I know, ...: I don't know for sure, but I think ...

As far as I know, they are still living in Japan.

but all the same ...: but nevertheless, but despite this...

I'm sure they are correct but all the same I'd better have a look at them.

but I'll say this for ...: but you can't criticise sb/ sth for... (used to balance criticisms that you have made or that another person has just made about sb or sth)

That was the gloomiest restaurant I have ever been to, but I will say this for it, it was remarkably cheap.

but rest assured ...: but I promise you

We are not sure where the meteor is going to hit, but rest assured that, as soon as we know, you'll know.

by the sound of it, ...: based on what sb has told me/what I have read/heard ...

I haven't seen Andy for ages, but by the sound of it, he is doing really well.

from what I can gather/I gather that ...: based on the information I have, I think I am right when I say ...

From what I can gather, he's thinking of handing in his resignation.

I gather that you are thinking of moving to South Africa.

you'll have a job doing sth ...: it will be difficult for you to do sth

You'll have a job finding their house. It's in the middle of nowhere.

how come ...: an informal way of asking *why*; followed by clause and not used with an auxiliary

How come you got a bonus and I didn't?

I don't know about you, but I ...: used when you are telling sb what you would like to do (often used as an indirect way of inviting sb to join you)

I don't know about you, but I wouldn't mind something to eat.

I know for a fact that ...: I know for sure that ...

I overheard her talking to Jenny so I know for a fact that she's got the job.

it's all very well ...: it's okay for you but not for me because my circumstances are different (used to criticise or reject sb/sth)

It's all very well for you to go to bed at 3 a.m. You don't have to go to work in the morning.

I was led to believe that ...: sb told me that sth was true/possible

We were led to believe that our hotel was a short distance from the beach, which was far from true.

I wish to goodness ...: (followed by pronoun + would) I really wish; used when you want sb to do or stop doing sth or when you are complaining about sth annoying that sb habitually does

I wish to goodness you'd hurry up!

let's face it, ...: we must accept that

I know it is disappointing that we have to close the shop, but let's face it, there's nothing we can do.

(you) mark my words, ...: remember what I am about to say because I am sure it will happen

You mark my words, if they get married, they will be very unhappy together.

no wonder .../small wonder ...: it's not surprising

The last time you ate was yesterday morning?! No wonder/ small wonder you're hungry!

to be perfectly honest ...: to be completely truthful

To be perfectly honest, I didn't understand a word of what he said.

sb struck me as ...: it seemed to me that sb was (often used to give your first impressions of sb) [Note: **what struck me most ...:** the thing I particularly noticed]

He struck me as an honest and trustworthy person.

What strikes me most about this picture is the way the man in the foreground is looking at the camera.

surely you are not (doing sth) ...: I think that sth would be a mistake [Note: **surely:** I believe that]

Surely you are not going to take them up on their offer.

Surely that is illegal?

whatever possessed you to ...?: why did you ...? (used instead of *why* in order to show great surprise)

Whatever possessed you to suddenly give up your job like that?

where/what/who/etc on earth ...?: *on earth* is used after question words to emphasise surprise or anger in a question

Where on earth has he gone off to now?

What on earth is he complaining about?

Who on earth does she think she is, putting on airs and graces like that?

with all due respect, ...: (formal) polite way to introduce criticism, contradiction, etc

But sir, with all due respect, you can't do that. It's only going to cause more problems.

33

Practice

1. Match the sentence openings (1 - 21) from Section A with an appropriate ending (a-u) from Section B.

A

0	I wish to	0
1	I know we can't afford it, but all the	....
2	I know you don't like Anne, but I'll say this	....
3	From what I can	....
4	You want to move again ?! You'll have a	....
5	Surely you're	....
6	To be perfectly	....
7	No	....
8	He struck me	....
9	By the sound	....
10	How	....
11	He's lying. I know for a	....
12	I don't know about you,	....
13	It's all very	....
14	He may think it's a great idea, but mark my	....
15	They may have got away this time, but rest	....
16	Whatever	....
17	Where on	....
18	With all due	....
19	As far	....
20	I was led	....
21	Let's	....

B

0 **goodness** you would consult me before you make decisions that concern both of us.
a **honest**, I really don't care what you think.
b **fact** that he didn't come home on Friday night.
c **job** persuading your wife to leave this area. I know for a fact that she loves it here.
d **respect**, sir, I don't think a decision like that can be taken without consulting a lawyer.
e **face it**, neither of us has ever been any good at hiding our feelings.
f **come** you weren't at work today?
g **possessed** her to do such a thing?
h **not thinking** of telling her? That would be a terrible idea.
i **as** being a very honest and very generous man.
j **same**, I can't help feeling that we'd be missing out on a wonderful opportunity.
k **for her**, she's always been there for me when I've needed a shoulder to cry on.
l **earth** did I put my keys?
m **as I know**, he is still working for that company.
n **wonder** she dislikes him. I can't believe he said those things.
o **gather**, they're doing very well over there.
p **well** for Simon to say that we should take a pay cut – he doesn't have a family to feed.
q **assured**, we will be doing everything in our power to bring these people to justice.
r **of it**, they're having the time of their lives.
s **but** I could do with a cup of tea.
t **to believe** that the price of the holiday was all-inclusive.
u **words**, this will end in tears!

2. Act out short dialogues using the introductions from Exercise 1, as in the example.

A: *I wish to goodness you would consult me before you make decisions that concern both of us.*
B: *I'm really sorry. Honestly, I didn't think you'd mind and it seemed like a perfect opportunity.*

3. Complete the sentences using appropriate introductions from this unit.

1 She .... as the kind of person that would fit in perfectly at our company.
2 Julie left without saying goodbye to him? .... he's upset!
3 ...., there's no point trying any more. It's a hopeless case.
4 ...., I have no idea.
5 ...., we've got the deal!
6 .... getting there on time. Traffic is really bad in the centre.

69

34 ..it..

... and to cap it all: used to introduce the last and worst thing in a list of bad things

I left my keys at home, I missed the bus and to cap it all it started raining.

to get it over (and done) with: to do sth unpleasant so that you no longer have to think or worry about it

Why don't you tell him now and get it over and done with?

I can't bear/hate/love, etc it when: used to emphasise how you feel about sth

I hate it when she shouts at him like that.

I can't bear it when the neighbours play loud music.

I love it when I have a Sunday to myself with nothing to do.

I'll see to it: I will make sure that sth happens/is done

I will see to it personally that the tickets are sent to you this morning.

I/we would appreciate it if you could: (formal) please could you ...

We would appreciate it if you could return the form to us within the next five days.

I'd appreciate it if you didn't tell anyone about this.

I would prefer it if you + past tense: a polite way of saying please do sth/please don't do sth

I'd prefer it if you left the door open.

legend has it that: there is a legend that says ... [Note: **rumour has it that:** there are rumours that say]

Legend has it that if you pull the sword from the stone, you will become king of England.

Rumour has it that his wife wrote all of his novels.

to put it bluntly: used to introduce sth which is very direct and which might offend or surprise

Well, to put it bluntly, I think that what you did was inexcusable.

to put your foot in it: accidentally do or say sth that embarrasses or upsets sb

I really put my foot in it when I told her we had all been invited to the party. She was the only one who hadn't.

to take it for granted that: to believe or assume that sth is a fact without thinking about it

He took it for granted that we all understood French, and he started reading us a poem by Rimbaud.

to take it in turns to do sth/to take turns doing sth: if two people take it in turns to do sth/take turns doing sth, one of them does it first, then the other and so on

It was a long journey, so we took it in turns to drive/took turns driving.

sth take(s) it out of you: sth makes you very tired

Teaching adolescents can certainly take it out of you.

Practice

1. *All the sentences below contain mistakes. Find the mistakes and correct them.*

1 We took it in turns steering the boat. ....
2 I'd prefer it if you don't sit there. ....
3 It's not going to be easy, so let's get over it and done with. ....
4 I really put my foot in it to tell him that Shirley had told me about it. ....
5 I would appreciate if you don't tell him who gave you this information. ....
6 Bringing up two small children certainly takes you out of it. ....
7 I took for granted she would say yes ....
8 Rumour is giving it that they are thinking of closing down the factory. ....
9 I'll see it that the letters get posted. ....
10 To put bluntly, it seems Petra isn't capable of handling the job. ....

2. *For questions 1 to 12, complete the second sentence so that it has a similar meaning to the first sentence, using 3 to 8 words. You must include the word given in bold, which cannot be changed in any way, and the word 'it'.*

1 I said that our company would do the job without checking with my partner as I was sure that she would say yes.
granted I .... that my partner would say yes to our company doing the job.

2 Please don't tell anyone what I said.
appreciate I .... tell anyone what I said.

3 I'd rather you didn't talk in the reference library.
  prefer I ....
  .... in the reference library.

4 If we hadn't borrowed that money from your father, we would have gone bankrupt.
  lending Had ....
  that money, we would have gone bankrupt.

5 Looking after two young children is certainly exhausting.
  takes Looking after two young children ....
  .... you.

6 I'll be honest and frank. I think his new book is really overrated.
  bluntly Well, to ....
  .... is really overrated.

7 We have to tell Reilly that he has been made redundant, so let's do it now.
  over We have to tell Reilly that he has been made redundant, so let's ....
  .... immediately.

8 I hate people saying things like that.
  stand I ....
  .... like that.

9 I feed the baby on Monday night and Jo feeds him on Tuesday, then it is my turn on Wednesday and so on.
  turns Jo and I .... to feed the baby.

10 There is an old story that says that Elizabeth I slept in this castle.
  has Legend ....
  .... Elizabeth I slept in this castle.

11 I'll make sure that you are not disturbed.
  see I'll .... that you're not disturbed.

12 It was so embarrassing. How was I to know that he had said he wouldn't accept the promotion?
  foot I really .... when I told his wife that he was going to accept the promotion.

3. *Make up appropriate questions for the following answers, using expressions from this unit.*

1 A: ....?
  B: No, I took it for granted that he would.
2 A: ....?
  B: Yes, I really put my foot in it!
3 A: ....?
  B: No, let's get it over with.
4 A: ....?
  B: Well, it really takes it out of you.
5 A: ....?
  B: No, we take turns.
6 A: ....?
  B: And, to cap it all, we didn't get in!
7 A: ....?
  B: Yes, to put it bluntly.
8 A: ....?
  B: Actually, I'd prefer it if you didn't.
9 A: ....?
  B: Well, rumour has it they will.
10 A: ....?
  B: No, I love it.

4. 🎧 *You will hear five short extracts (1-5). In each extract a man is talking. Match the extracts as you hear them with the statements, listed A-H. Write the correct letter in the appropriate extract box.*

A He offended someone.
B He shared something with someone.
C He thinks something has happened, but he doesn't know for sure.
D He will make sure that something happens.
E He made a terrible mistake.
F He assumed that something would happen.
G He has to do something unpleasant.
H He knew for sure that something would happen.

Extract 1 ☐
Extract 2 ☐
Extract 3 ☐
Extract 4 ☐
Extract 5 ☐

35 Key Words I

all told: in total and including everyone or everything; used for time, money and when you are counting

There were six of us, as well as three guides, so all told there were nine of us.

I imagine it is going to take you three hours all told.

to be all for sth/to be all in favour of sth: to totally agree with/support (normally used in spoken English)

I don't know what you think but I'm all for private education.

(when) all of a sudden: (when) suddenly

We were talking about the weather when all of a sudden she burst out crying.

to count yourself lucky: to consider yourself lucky (used to say that, even though sth bad has happened to sb, it could have been a lot worse)

You should count yourself lucky your house is not damaged. Some people have had to be evacuated from their homes.

sth doesn't count: sth is not valid

He's put the ball in the back of the net! No, no, it doesn't count. He was offside.

to count for: to be regarded as important or valuable [generally used in the expression: (**sb's experience**, **record**, etc) **must/will count for sth**]

Surely the fact that I've never been in trouble before must count for something.

at the end of the day: (informal, spoken) the most important thing is/what you must remember is

You may disagree with him, but at the end of the day, he is your boss and as such you have to respect his decisions.

let's call it a day: let's stop working (generally used after you have done a lot of work)

We've been painting for seven hours now. Let's call it a day, shall we?

to have a field day: to have the opportunity to criticise and write a lot about sb (generally used about the press)

When the press finds out that the Minister of Transport has been arrested for speeding, they will have a field day.

to be due back: to be expected to return

He's due back from work in half an hour.

in due course: at some time in the future, when the time is right

Our roads are far too congested and we will be addressing this problem in due course.

it's just as well: it is a good thing (or a lucky thing) that

It's just as well I didn't make a meat pie. I've just found out that Polly is a vegetarian.

only just: (i) very nearly did not happen (ii) only recently (used with the present perfect tense)

I only just got there in time.

I've only just got up.

to be just about to do sth: will do sth in the next few seconds or minutes; [Note: **sb was just about to do sth:** it was sb's intention to do sth in the next few seconds or minutes, but they didn't]

The film is just about to start.

I was just about to phone you.

to put you in mind of sth: to remind you of sth

That puts me in mind of the time we had to take Chris to hospital.

sth crosses your mind: to have a particular thought

It never crossed my mind that he might be lying to me.

no one in their right mind would: only a crazy person would...

No one in their right mind would invest in that company.

first thing: before you do anything else

I've got a meeting first thing on Friday.

to have a real thing about: to have an obsession about

George has got a real thing about people touching his books.

He's got a thing about cleanliness. (= he dislikes dirt)

to make a big thing out of sth: (informal) to exaggerate the importance of sth

Calm down. Why are you making such a big thing out of it?

to treat an illness: to try and cure an illness

It's one of those illnesses that you just can't treat with conventional medicine.

to treat sb like dirt: to treat sb very badly

He treats her like dirt. I don't know why she puts up with it.

to treat sb to sth: to buy or pay for sth special for sb because you know that they will really enjoy it

To say thank you for all her support, I decided to treat her to a weekend in New York.

way too ...: way can be used to emphasise too.

It's way too far to walk.

I'm way too tired to go out tonight.

to go out of your way to do sth: to make a special effort to do sth for sb, even if it is inconvenient for you

They went out of their way to make me feel at home.

the wrong way round: opposite to how it should be

No wonder the audience were laughing; he was holding the cue card the wrong way round.

35

not to breathe a word about sth to sb: not to reveal a secret

It's a secret, so don't breathe a word about it to anyone.

word soon got round: everyone soon found out that ...

Word soon got round that her novel had been accepted by a major publisher.

to want a word with sb: to want to speak to sb in private

I want a word with you about that broken window, young man.

Practice

1. Complete the sentences below using one of the words in the box. You may have to change the form of the word you choose.

> just – treat – mind – all – count – day – word – way – thing – due

1 I can't afford a trip to India. It's .... too expensive.
2 Seeing that documentary on Cambridge put me in .... of my university days.
3 Stop complaining, will you? You should .... yourself lucky that the judge let you off with a fine.
4 It's .... as well we didn't go out in the boat this afternoon. We'd have got soaked.
5 Mr Jones wants to see me first .... on Monday morning.
6 I was .... about to leave when the telephone rang.
7 Actually, I think you've got it the wrong .... round. Louise is studying archaeology and Laura's doing philosophy.
8 Well, at the end of the .... what matters is if they won or not.
9 Flights, tickets, car hire and a night in a hotel. .... told, the trip should cost £300.
10 It never crossed her .... that a prestigious firm like Mijinns would try to sell her a fake.
11 It is a very dangerous illness and if it is not .... quickly it can lead to blindness.
12 He passed, but only .... .The pass mark was 50 and he got 52.
13 All I said to her was hello. I don't know why you are making such a big .... out of it.
14 Surely the fact that I passed my mid-term exam must .... for something.
15 It was Rosie's birthday, so I .... her to a day's shopping in London and then tea at the Ritz.
16 It's blowing a howling gale. No one in their right .... would go sailing in this weather.
17 We were in this restaurant, talking about the wedding when .... of a sudden she fainted.
18 We've been working for nine hours solid. I'm tired. Let's call it a .... , shall we?
19 Mr. Jenkins wants a .... with you in his office.
20 .... soon got round that the factory was closing down.
21 I wonder where they are. They were .... back over an hour ago!

2. Circle the correct item.

1 Is it any wonder he hates you? You took him completely for granted and **counted / treated** him like dirt.
2 He's a government minister. If the press find out he was involved, they'll have a **field / word** day.
3 The boss has got a **real / mind** thing about punctuality. He's actually sacked people for being ten minutes late.
4 George and Milly were wonderful to me. They went out of their **day / way** to make me feel at home.
5 Don't breathe a **thing / word** of this to anyone, but I think they are going to give Thompson the sack.
6 Well, those first games don't **mind / count**. My hand control wasn't working properly.
7 I'm **way / all** for people enjoying themselves, but not when it involves being cruel to others.
8 I thought Pedro was **due / way** back from school two hours ago.
9 Obviously, Mr Philips was wrong and we'll deal with that in **real / due** course, but first I want to know how this all started.

36 Key Words II

to board: to live and sleep at a school during term time; used for students (but not teachers) [Note: **a boarding school:** a school where students live and sleep during term time]

What I hated most about school was the fact that I had to board.

a board meeting: a meeting of the directors of a company
[Note: **a board of directors:** all the directors of a company]

I've got a board meeting this afternoon, so I may be late.

to go by the board: to be abandoned because it is no longer practicable

My plan to buy a bookshop went by the board when the bank refused to lend me any money.

to be hard to come by: to be difficult to get or find

Nowadays, these books are very hard to come by.

to feel hard done by: to feel that you have been unfairly treated

Of course we feel hard done by. Everyone had the day off except us.

(to come) hard on the heels of sth: to happen soon after sth happens

This latest tragedy comes hard on the heels of the Diddington train crash.

in a matter of seconds: very quickly

I know you hate injections, but I promise it will be over in a matter of seconds.

(it) is no easy matter (to do sth): it is difficult to do sth

Running a business is no easy matter.

there's sth the matter with: there is sth wrong with

There is something the matter with our computer.

to come to one's notice: (formal) to find out about sth

It has come to our notice that you have not paid your council tax for the past six months.

to hand in your notice: to resign from your job

He handed in his notice because he had found a better job.

at such short notice: with little advance warning so that you are probably unprepared for it

'The meeting has been moved to tomorrow afternoon', he said and apologised for telling us at such short notice.

to be plain sailing: to be easy and uncomplicated to do

Once we had secured financial backing, setting up the business was plain sailing.

to make it plain that: to make it very obvious/clear that

She made it plain that he would be expelled if he did not behave himself.

plain English: English that is clear and easy to understand

I like this particular manual because it is written in plain English.

it's got to the point where: it has reached a stage where

It's got to the point where we can't afford to keep two cars anymore.

to be on the point of doing sth: to be going to do sth in the next few minutes/hours

We were on the point of signing the contract when he said that the deal was off.

what's the point of doing sth: used when you think that sth is not worth doing

What's the point of doing that? You know it won't work.

right away: immediately

I could tell right away that something was wrong.

it is only right that: it is only fair and correct/understandable that

It is only right that you should feel upset. They have treated you terribly.

it serves sb right: sb deserves the bad thing that has happened to them

Nobody is speaking to him? It serves him right for lying.

to follow suit: to do the same or to act in the same way

Once one of the High Street banks lowers its interest rates, you can be sure all the others will follow suit.

suit yourself (used in orders): do sth just because you are determined to, even though I find it wrong.

Suit yourself, but don't blame me if you catch pneumonia.

to suit sb down to the ground: to be perfect for sb

The ZXY model would suit you down to the ground. It's small, economical and comfortable.

a tip: a place that is very untidy and messy

This room is a tip. Tidy it up now!

to leave a tip: to leave money for a waiter in a restaurant after you have paid the bill

Shall we leave a tip?

to tip sb to do/be sth: to predict that sb will do or be sth (usually in passive voice)

He is widely tipped to be Fergal's successor at Manchester United.

stiff competition: difficult/severe competition

You'll face stiff competition in the semi-finals.

to be scared stiff: to be very scared

He was scared stiff when he saw the tiger.

to have (got) a stiff neck: when the muscles in your neck hurt when you try to move

I've got a stiff neck from sitting in a draught.

don't get me wrong: don't misunderstand me

Don't get me wrong; I wasn't criticising you.

to get on the wrong side of sb: to annoy sb so that they dislike you

If he likes you, you are fine and you'll enjoy working here, but if you get on the wrong side of him, he'll make your life a misery.

Practice

1. Circle the correct item.

1 This place is a **board / tip**. You'd better tidy it up before your landlady comes back.
2 Violent crime has increased so dramatically in this neighbourhood that it has got to the **tip / point** where we are all afraid to go out at night.
3 Whenever I sleep on planes, I wake up with a **stiff / hard** neck.
4 What with his comments and the off-hand way he treated us, he had made it **plain / wrong** that we were not welcome in his house, so we left.
5 He cheated but they caught him and he was punished. It serves him **hard / right**.
6 If you really feel like that about your job, you should hand in your **notice / suit**.
7 Once they had deactivated the alarm, it was **right / plain** sailing. They got into the office, took the plans and were out and away in under ten minutes.
8 Whatever you do, don't get on the **wrong / plain** side of Mr Evans.
9 I'm afraid the Managing Director is not available at the moment. He's in a **notice / board** meeting.
10 **Hard / Stiff** on the heels of last week's scandal comes news of yet another embarrassment for the government, as the Minister for Public Works was accused of nepotism yesterday.
11 He is very stubborn. Persuading him to change his mind will be no easy **matter / point**.
12 We're boycotting their products and we're hoping that other companies in the area will follow **right / suit**.
13 Now that we've qualified, we'll be up against **wrong / stiff** competition in every match we play.

2. Complete the sentences, using the words in the box below in the appropriate form.

> tip – suit – plain – point – matter – right –
> board – notice – wrong – hard – stiff

1 You did most of the work, so it is only .... that you should get most of the money.
2 What's the .... of our each buying her a small present? Why don't we all chip in and buy her a big present?
3 The government were on the .... of declaring a state of emergency.
4 Look at this contract. What with all this legal jargon, I can't understand a word of it. Why can't they write these things in .... English?
5 Using fax and e-mail, it is possible to get information through in a .... of seconds.
6 Most political commentators .... Pickering as the most likely candidate to take over from Mr Ryan.
7 Don't get me .... I think your book is very well-written. It's just that I'm not into detective fiction.
8 It has come to our .... that you have not paid last month's Council Tax.
9 The students at this school .... during the week but go home to their parents at the weekend.
10 There's something the .... with my car. I can't get it to start.
11 He said it is very rare. Apparently, Roman coins in this condition are pretty .... to come by.
12 I'm sorry to ask you this at such short .... , but could you stand in for George at tomorrow's presentation?
13 It says that service is included, but even so, I think we should leave a ....
14 My idea soon went by the .... when I discovered how much money I would need to invest.
15 She didn't have to speak. I could tell .... away that something was wrong.
16 Okay, ... yourself. I'm not going to argue with you.
17 Of course I feel .... done by. I was the only person in the office who didn't receive a bonus.
18 I found a job for Tim which will .... him down to the ground. A video reviewer. It's ideal for him.
19 Frightened? I was scared .... !

75

37 Linking Words

Cause and Result

to attribute sth to: to say that sth was caused by

Most historians attribute his downfall to his involvement in the Redgate scandal.

to be/come as a consequence of: to happen because of

Acid rain is a consequence of the burning of fossil fuels.

sth can be put down to: sth happens because of

The doctors put his ill health down to the fact that he was working too much.

The doctor said that his ill health could be put down to the fact that he was working too much.

due to/owing to + noun/- ing form: because of the fact that

The match had to be called off due to adverse weather conditions.

We had to call the match off owing to the fact that the pitch was waterlogged.

sth led to + noun/- ing form: sth happened because of sth else

Her refusal to give a blood sample after the match led to her disqualification.

to be responsible for + noun/-ing from: to be the reason for sth happening

Though he denied everything, he was clearly responsible for the fire.

to result in + noun/-ing form: to cause to happen

The scandal resulted in his resignation/resigning.

to stem from: to happen because of; often used for problems, unrest, discontent, trouble, etc

Most of their economic problems stem from the fact that their government is so incompetent.

to trigger off: to cause sth to happen

The government's decision to tax savings triggered off widespread rioting thoughout the country.

Concession

* The following words and phrases are concession linkers: **adjective + though/as, all the same, although, and yet, but, despite, even so, even though, for all, however, in spite of, might ... but, much as, nevertheless, nonetheless, though**

* Concession linking words and phrases join a fact and a surprise that is related to that fact

*Although they don't earn very much, (**fact**) they still go to the Caribbean every year. (**surprise**)*

* Some concession linking words and phrases introduce the fact, others introduce the surprise

Introducing the fact

adjective + though/as + subject + verb: (formal) this structure starts a sentence

Crazy though it sounds, I think he actually enjoys being hounded by the press.

although/even though + clause: the second part of the sentence often includes the word **still**

Although/even though he tried hard, he still didn't succeed.

despite/in spite of: (i) **(my/his/her/our, etc + ing form** (ii) **+ noun**; [Note: sometimes **despite/in spite of** is followed by **this**, referring to the previous sentence] (iii) **+ the fact that + clause**

Despite/In spite of his having a lot of experience, they decided not to offer him the post.

Despite/In spite of gaining straight A's in all his exams, he was unable to get a place at university.

Despite the terrible weather, we decided to go ahead with the match.

He was well-qualified and highly experienced. Despite this, he found it difficult to get a job.

We have decided to continue showing the programme, despite the fact that we have received a great many complaints about it.

for all + (my/his/her etc) + noun: generally starts a sentence

For all the mayhem and misery that war causes, there are many people who believe it is necessary.

might ... but ...: **might** appears in the fact part of the concession sentence, whilst **but** introduces the surprise; for past tense sentences you must use **might + have + past participle;** this structure is particularly common in spoken English

He might be 93, but he still jogs around the park every day.

She might have been well-prepared, but she still didn't pass the exam.

much as + clause: although; generally starts a sentence [Note: is only used with certain verbs: **admire, appreciate, respect, sympathise, would like**, and verbs of **liking (detest, love**, etc)]

Much as I sympathise with your problems, I'm afraid that there is nothing I can do to help you.

Much as I like his music, I would never go to one of his concerts.

though + clause: **though** can also be used at the end of the surprise part of a concession sentence (this usage is common in spoken English)

Though she was the best candidate, she didn't get the job.

She was the best candidate. She didn't get the job, though.

Introducing the surprise

The most common way of introducing the surprise part of a concession sentence is with the word **but**. Sometimes other words are added to it: **but ... still, but all the same, but even so, nevertheless, but nonetheless**

She knew the truth, but (nonetheless) she didn't say anything.

37

Practice

1. Read the following extract and, based on what you have read, complete the sentences that appear below it.

The directors lost everything because they were incompetent. They had made a number of unwise investments and were losing a lot of money. Blaming the company's problems on a recession, the directors made twenty factory workers redundant. The redundancies so angered the workforce that their leader, Marvin Tressle, called everyone out on strike. The directors responded quickly and sacked Tressle. The workers, incensed by Tressle's dismissal, rioted and in the general confusion the factory caught fire and was burnt down. Uninsured, the directors had no alternative but to file for bankruptcy.

1 All the directors' problems **stem** ....
2 The company was doing badly **owing** ....
3 The directors **attributed** the company's economic problems ....
4 The redundancies **were a consequence** ....
5 The redundancies **led** ....
6 Marvin Tressle's decision to strike **resulted** ....
7 Tressle's dismissal **triggered** ....
8 The general confusion **was** ....
9 The directors couldn't claim for fire damage **due to the** ....
10 The fact that the directors lost everything **can be put down** ....

2. Listen to the text and, based on what you hear, complete the notes in the table below.

1	Neville's parents were	BUT	they were ....
2	Neville was weak and	BUT	Neville never refused ....
3	Neville was an extremely .... young man	BUT	he still managed to ....
4	Neville's poetry was	BUT	but it sold ....
5	Neville was rich and	BUT	he was not a ....man.
6	Neville was afraid of	BUT	he managed to ....
7	Rami Rama was	BUT	Neville learnt ....
8	Neville was .... and well-known	BUT	he was still ....
9	In the supermarket, Neville was in	BUT	Belinda still ....
10	Neville knew very little about	BUT	Belinda still offered him ....

3. Write a new sentence for each of the sentences in the table above. Sentence 1 below corresponds to sentence 1 in the table, sentence 2 corresponds to sentence 2 in the table, etc. Each new sentence must include the word(s) given.

1 and yet ....
2 Even though ....
3 Adjective+ though ....
4 but even so ....
5 For all ....
6 Despite + noun ....
7 Despite the fact that ....
8 However ....
9 might ....
10 Despite + ing ....

77

38 Little Words – Modals

Little Words

as long as: if (and only if) (followed by the present tense)
I'll lend you the money as long as you promise to pay me back.

both ... and: used to connect two qualities/facts (not used in negative sentences)
Both Otto and Elizabeth are lawyers.

to be bound to: to be certain to
She's so talented that she's bound to get that film part.

but for: if it had not been for
But for our goalkeeper, we would have lost the match.

sb could hardly: sb found it difficult to ...
He was so tired that he could hardly keep his eyes open.

to do nothing but: the only thing sb does is ... (followed by bare infinitive)
I don't know why he came on holiday. He did nothing but complain the whole time.

hardly/scarcely any: very few or very little (cannot follow a negative form of a verb or be followed by 'no' words **nobody**, **none**, etc.
There were hardly any complaints.

I've yet to: I haven't ... yet
I've heard Ana's side of the story. I've yet to hear what Pablo has to say about it.

in case: because it might; followed by a present tense when referring to the future or a past tense when referring to the past
Take a sandwich with you in case you get hungry.

lest: (formal, literary) in order to make sure that sth will not happen (followed by subject + (should) bare infinitive) [Note: **lest** often follows **afraid**, **scared**, **frightened**, **anxious**, etc, in which case it means because of the possibility that]
They tied him up lest he escape.
She was frightened lest he find out her terrible secret.

neither ... nor: used to connect two similar negative qualities/states/actions etc
Neither John nor Mary went to the party.

no matter: it does not matter; (followed by most question words **what**, **where**, **how much**, etc but not **why**)
No matter where you go in the world, you will always find someone who speaks English.

otherwise: because if not (often follows an **imperative** or **had better**)
Do as he says, otherwise he'll get angry.
You'd better do as he says, otherwise he'll get angry.

whatsoever: absolutely (used to emphasise the words **no** and **none**; **no** + noun + **whatsoever** and **none** + **whatsover**)
"You must have had some money." "No. We had none whatsoever."

not least because: especially because
We did not go for a number of reasons, not least because it was so expensive.

Modal Verbs – Expressions

sb could/might have done sth: a spoken construction used to say that you are annoyed with sb for not doing sth
You might/could have given me a ring. I was worried sick!

sth/sb couldn't have been + comparative: couldn't have been before a comparative, e.g. **easier/hotter** etc, is used to emphasise how easy/hot etc sth was
We had a wonderful time. The weather couldn't have been better.

I might have guessed/known that: I am not surprised sb was involved in doing sth bad because it would be typical of them
I might have known Sam was involved. It's just the kind of stupid thing he'd do.

sb may/might well: it is possible that sb will, it was possible that sb would
You could try phoning him, but he may well have left by now.

sb might as well: it would be advisable in the circumstances
The show will have started now, so we might as well go home.

might/may ... but ...: although
They might argue all the time, but they love each other dearly.
She might have been well-qualified, but she still didn't get the promotion.

sb should have known better than to ...: sb is old/intelligent enough to know that the kind of things they did were foolish
He should have known better than to make such a comment.

I should imagine/think that: should is often used with **think** or **imagine** to make opinions less direct
I should imagine that the play will have started by now.

try as I might: however hard I tried
Try as I might, I couldn't open the door.

78

38

Practice

1. *For questions 1 to 12, complete the second sentence so that it has a similar meaning to the first sentence, using 3 to 8 words. You must include the word given in bold, which cannot be changed in any way.*

1 Try as we might, we could not get the car to start.
   matter   No .... tried, we could not get the car to start.
2 I'm sure Milan will beat Lazio. They always do.
   bound   Lazio .... Milan.
3 All he did for the whole journey was complain.
   nothing   He .... for the whole journey.
4 "Take an umbrella with you because I think it might rain," she said.
   case   "You'd better take an umbrella with you ....," she said.
5 We are running short of coffee, so we'd better buy some more.
   hardly   We ...., so we'd better buy some more.
6 The main reason we decided not to go was that it was too hot there at that time of year.
   least   We decided not to go for a variety of reasons, ... it was the hottest season.
7 Both John and Jane disliked the film.
   thought   Neither .... of the film.
8 You can borrow my bicycle only if you promise to look after it.
   long   I'll .... you promise to look after it.
9 She covered her face because she didn't want him to see her cry.
   lest   She covered her face .... cry.
10 If the fire services hadn't responded so rapidly, our house would have burned to the ground.
   rapid   But .... of the fire services, our house would have burned to the ground.
11 There is absolutely no way I am going to resign.
   whatsoever   I have .... in my resignation.
12 Nobody I know likes her.
   yet   I've .... likes her.

2. *Complete the sentences with an appropriate modal verb.*

1 It .... look harmless, but it is in fact one of the most dangerous reptiles known to man.
2 So it was Tommy who let off the fire extinguisher. I .... have known he'd be involved.
3 When she finds out that he has spent all their savings, I .... imagine that she is going to be very angry indeed.
4 He lost his licence and it serves him right. He .... have known better than to speed in the city centre.
5 You .... have told me you were going to be late. I've been waiting for hours.
6 The exam was a piece of cake. It .... have been easier.
7 No one has put their name down for the seminar and it is only two days away. We .... as well call it off.
8 Take your raincoat with you. It .... well rain later this afternoon.
9 Try as I ...., I couldn't get the car to start.
10 You .... open the windows if you find it warm in here.

3. *Fill in the gaps in the text with an appropriate word or phrase from the box below. There are three extra items that do not fit.*

> in case – neither – might – should – may – could hardly – but for – otherwise – bound – as long as – both

There I stood, clutching my speech, waiting to go on stage. I was so nervous that I 1) .... breathe and 2) .... the fact that my boss, Mr. Crofts, was in the audience and had personally asked me to speak, I would have run away there and then. "Don't worry, Harry. 3) .... you include a few jokes, you'll be fine," said Nora, patting me on the back. "Come on, smile 4) .... they will think you don't want to be up there talking to them." I didn't want to be up there talking to them. I smiled weakly to appease her. "They're a great audience," said George. 5) .... George and Nora had given their speeches and were waiting behind the curtain trying to give me moral support. And they were good speeches too, which didn't help. Besides, they 6) .... have been a great audience, but I was most certainly not a great speaker. "Something is 7) .... to go wrong," I said. "Don't be silly," said George, "you've got nothing to worry about. And if Mr Crofts likes it, you 8) .... well get a promotion." Oh great I thought. There was no pressure, then. I took a deep breath, looked at my notes and walked through the curtain...

79

39 Looking/Seeing

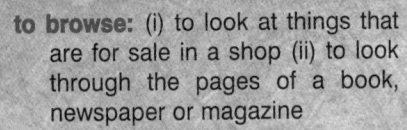

to browse: (i) to look at things that are for sale in a shop (ii) to look through the pages of a book, newspaper or magazine

"Can I help?"
"No thanks. I'm just browsing."

I was browsing through 'The Times' when I saw an article about tropical fish.

to cast an eye over sth: to have a quick look at sth (a report, a composition, calculations, etc) in order to check it for any obvious mistakes

Can you please cast an eye over my essay and see if it makes sense before I hand it in?

to catch a (fleeting) glimpse of: to get a quick look at sth/sb when moving

We caught a glimpse of the President as he sped past in his limousine.

to be colour blind: to be unable to tell the difference between certain colours

They say that if you're colour blind, you cannot tell the difference between green and red.

to gape: to stare at sb/sth; often with your mouth open

Her parents gaped at her in astonishment. They had no idea about the surprise party.

to gaze: to look for a long time without really seeing what you are looking at (when, for example, you are bored, in love, thinking about sth, very attracted to sth)

As I gazed out of the window, I thought about Mary and what she had told me just before I left.

to give sb a black look: to quickly look at sb angrily, often in response to sth that person has said or done

You should have seen the black look she gave me. How was I to know it was a secret?

to glance: to take a quick look at sth often by moving your eyes but not moving your head

He glanced at his watch. It was late and they were still only halfway through the meeting.

to glare: to stare at sb angrily

The two motorists sat in their cars glaring at each other.

look me (straight) in the eye and tell me ...: an expression which is used when you confront sb and want them to tell you the truth

Look me straight in the eye and tell me that you had nothing to do with it.

to look daggers at sb: to look at sb angrily and in a threatening way, because that person has done or said sth really annoying

Sally looked daggers at me. She was livid.

to look over a property: to look at a house or flat, to see if you are interested in buying it

Having looked over the house, we decided that it wasn't what we were looking for.

to make (sth) out to see sth/sb, but often with difficulty

Up ahead in the distance we could just make out the silhouette of a motel.

to peek: to take a quick look at sth you are not supposed to see

He had promised not to look. But, as soon as she was out of the room, he peeked under the bed.

to peer: to look with difficulty because one cannot see properly (because it is dark/foggy/you have poor eyesight)

He peered at his watch.

to peruse: to read (formal)

She perused the contract before signing it.

to pore over: to read very carefully and for a long time, probably because you are very interested in what you are reading or you have to study it

He was in his office poring over the document.

to set eyes on sb: to see sb (often prefaced by **the minute**)

The minute we set eyes on it, we knew that we'd found our dream house.

to squint at sb/sth: to look at sb/sth with eyes partly closed

She squinted at him in the bright sunlight.

to stare: to look at sth/sb fixedly or for a long time

Why are you staring at me?

to view: to walk around and look at a house or paintings in art exhibition

A number of people have viewed the house, but nobody seems interested in buying it.

to witness: to see sth bad (a crime, an accident, etc) or sth important (the fall of the Berlin wall, sb win an Olympic medal, etc) happen

We witnessed the historic signing of the peace treaty between our two countries.

Practice

1. Complete the sentences with an appropriate word from the box below. There are two extra words, which you do not need to use.

> withering – deficient – daggers – in – out – over – set
> squinting – blind – straight – cast – witnessed – fleeting

1 We caught a .... glimpse of him as he sped past in his limousine.
2 The minute I .... eyes on him, I fell head over heels in love.
3 My wife looked .... at me. I had obviously put my foot in it.
4 Look me .... in the eye and tell me that you're not lying.

5 Could you .... an eye over these figures and check that I haven't made a mistake?
6 He just stood there, gaping .... astonishment.
7 Always look .... a property before you buy it. Estate agents have a habit of being economical with the truth.
8 It could be red, but then again it could be green. How should I know? I'm colour ....
9 Peering through the window, he could just make .... two figures standing at the counter.
10 One person .... the robbery, but understandably – given the alleged culprit – she is reluctant to testify.
11 'I'll just go and get my sunglasses,' she said, ... in the brilliant sunshine.

2. *The sentences below each contain a **looking** verb in bold. Read each sentence and decide whether the statements that follow are true or false. An example has been done for you.*

0 "You go on," she said. "I'd like to **browse** for a while."
  a They are in a shop. *T*
  b She wants desperately to buy something. *F*
  c She is in a hurry. *F*
1 "Don't just stand there **gaping**! Say something!" she said to him.
  a He is very surprised. .....
  b His mouth is probably open. .....
  c He is staring at her. .....
2 He **glared** at her.
  a He was angry. .....
  b He looked fixedly at her. .....
  c He was in love with her. .....
3 They **gazed** into each other's eyes.
  a They are in love. .....
  b They are carefully examining each other's face. .....
  c They couldn't see properly. .....
4 He **caught a glimpse** of her as she left the theatre.
  a He looked at her for a long time. .....
  b He was moving or she was moving when he saw her. .....
  c He was surprised to see her. .....

5 She **glanced** at her watch.
  a She looked at her watch for a long time. .....
  b She moved her head in order to look at her watch. .....
  c She had a quick look at her watch. .....
6 She **peered** at her watch.
  a She could be somewhere dark. .....
  b She might have poor eyesight. .....
  c She looked at her watch for only a second. .....
7 "You **peeked**," she said.
  a He took a quick look. .....
  b He wasn't supposed to look. .....
  c He saw something bad. .....
8 She **gave him a black look**.
  a She is in a situation where she can't speak. .....
  b She is happy. .....
  c He has probably said or done something which she disapproves of. .....
9 The woman told her small son that it was rude to **stare at** people.
  a She is annoyed with her son. .....
  b He is looking at her. .....
  c He is looking at someone else. .....
10 We'll **view** it tomorrow.
  a They are going to look at a holiday brochure. .....
  b They are going to look at a house. .....
  c They will make some kind of decision based on what they have seen. .....
11 He was **poring** over a book in the reference library.
  a He looked quickly at the book. .....
  b He wasn't interested in the book. .....
  c He was interested in the book. .....
12 She **perused** the content of the letter.
  a She had a quick look at the letter. .....
  b She read the letter. .....
  c She looked at the letter without actually seeing it. .....

3. *Can you match the pictures to any of the verbs presented in this unit?*

40 Money I

abject poverty: terrible poverty
Half the people in this country are living in abject poverty.

to be/fall behind with sth: not to do/produce/pay sth in time
Mark's fallen behind with most of his payments.

capital: the amount of money you need to start a business
I wanted to set up a business, but because I didn't have any capital, I had to shelve the idea.

close on: nearly; can be used with the verbs **cost**, **charge**, **buy**, **spend**, **sell**, **invest**, etc
We bought it for close on £25,000.

counterfeit money: false money, copied to look like real money
Be careful when shopping or you'll get back to your hotel with a wad of counterfeit money.

economic: related to a country's economy
economic situation/crisis/growth

economical: cheap to use (used particularly for cars)
My car is very economical to use.

(the) economy: a country's financial framework – its money, what it produces, its trade, etc [Note: as an adjective for food and drink, **economy** means cheap]
This country's economy is healthier than it has ever been.
I usually buy economy tea bags.

to eke out a living: to earn just enough money to survive
He ekes out a living selling doughnuts in Victoria Station.

exclusive: so expensive that very few people can afford to go to/use/buy
She lives in an exclusive, upmarket part of town.

extravagant: spending more money than you can afford
No wonder she's in debt. She leads a very extravagant lifestyle.

finance: (i) funds/capital (n) (ii) to provide funds/capital (v)
The bank may give you the finance to start up your own business.

He took out a loan to finance the purchase of a car.

fiscal: related to government or public money, especially taxes
The government will probably tighten fiscal policy.

to be heavily in debt: to owe sb/an institution a lot of money
We are heavily in debt to the bank.

an invoice: a bill sent to you by a company or organisation to tell you how much you owe for a service or for sth that you have bought
Please find enclosed our official invoice.

to live from hand to mouth: to barely manage financially
Many people are so poor that they live from hand to mouth.

to live in the lap of luxury: to have lots of money and lead a very comfortable life
Who wouldn't want to spend their life living in the lap of luxury?

to make ends meet: to manage financially
On a salary like his, it's not suprising that he finds it hard to make ends meet.

an outstanding debt: a debt that you have not paid
You must pay these outstanding debts immediately.

to be overdrawn: to be in debt to the bank because you have spent more money than you have in your account
Mary is £100 overdrawn at the bank.

to pay off/clear your debts: to pay the money you owe
We'll buy a new car once we have paid off all our debts.

(to earn) a pittance: (to earn) a very low salary;
I earn a pittance and can hardly manage to survive.

prosperous: rich, wealthy
He came from a prosperous family of landowners.

return on an investment: the profit one makes on an investment
If you buy antiques, you can get a good return on your investment.

to be rolling in it: (informal) to be very rich (only used after a noun)
Of course they can afford it! They're rolling in it!" he exclaimed.

royalties: the money a writer/musician receives annually from the sales of their book(s)/music
He lives on the money he gets from the royalties on his books.

to scrimp and save: to save as much money as you can, even though you earn very little
He bought this house after years of scrimping and saving.

a (large/small/considerable) sum of money: an amount of money
It cost me only a small sum of money but I like it.

to tighten one's belt: (informal) to try to spend less than usual
"We'll manage. We are just going to have to tighten our belts," she said.

to be tight-fisted: to be mean, to dislike spending money
Like his father, he was very tight-fisted, a real miser.

to have sth tucked away: to store sth valuable, e.g. money
She's got her bank book tucked away in her drawer.

the turnover: the amount of money earned by a business during a particular period of time
ABM has an annual turnover of 2 million.

well-to-do: (informal) rich and often belonging to a high social class
His parents are quite well-to-do.

well-heeled: (informal) rich
well-heeled businessman

a windfall: a large amount of money you receive unexpectedly (e.g. an inheritance or a win on the lottery)
An aunt left us £300,000 in her will. Thanks to this windfall, we bought the house.

40

Practice

1. *For each of the texts below decide which answer (A, B, C or D) best fits each gap.*

Life is a circle. Beginning to end, end to beginning. Take Bob. This is Bob five years ago, alone in a shabby flat, no car, no television, **1)** .... in debt. Bob is a mess, barely keeping his head above water. He **2)** .... out a living selling burgers and he is paid a **3)** .... He is **4)** .... at the bank and horribly **5)** .... with his rent. His life is a succession of unpaid bills, **6)** .... debts and angry exchanges with his bank manager. Bob needs a plan.

So he asks his parents for money. It's not a bad plan as plans go. His parents aren't short of a bob or two. They could help him to **7)** .... his debts and get back on his feet again. *"Money doesn't grow on trees, Bob. We can't afford* **8)** .... *you that kind of money."* His mother. The woman who spends money like there is no tomorrow. *"Tighten your* **9)** ....*, son. We haven't got that kind of money."* His father. The man who spent close **10)** .... £3,000 on a set of plastic chairs for the garden, who's got thousands tucked **11)** .... in a Swiss bank. Rejected, dejected, Bob returns to his miserable flat and the ever-shifting mountain of brown envelopes that are stacked high on his doormat. Despair gathers him in and whispers in his ear - he is doomed to a life of **12)** .... poverty.

1	A strongly	B heavily	C flatly	D wholly
2	A works	B ekes	C digs	D ploughs
3	A pittance	B misery	C snip	D steal
4	A overtaken	B overrated	C overdrawn	D overcast
5	A back	B liable	C behind	D detained
6	A outstanding	B outdated	C underpaid	D underhand
7	A pay for	B pay off	C pay up	D pay through
8	A giving	B to give	C given	D to have given
9	A pocket	B fist	C shirt	D belt
10	A by	B at	C on	D about
11	A off	B in	C around	D away
12	A object	B reject	C abject	D subject

And then something happens, something magical. The circle never stands still. Where do you go from rock bottom? From overtime at a burger bar, **13)** .... meals, empty pockets and overdrafts, from a life of **14)** .... and saving to pay a £20 gas bill? There's only one direction. Perhaps that's why, out of nowhere, a large **15)** .... of money comes crashing into Bob's life. Money, irresistible money - and Bob's got it, bundles of it. Where does it come from? It wasn't a(n) **16)** .... on the lottery, nor an inheritance from a long-lost aunt. Neither was it a **17)** .... on an inspired investment, nor a change of heart from his tight- **18)** .... parents. No, the money that comes crashing into Bob's life does so literally. A suitcase falls through the rotting ceiling of his living room. It is full of money. Bursting at the seams. His mother was right - money doesn't grow on trees. It comes in suitcases that fall through the ceiling!

From rags to riches. Living in the **19)** .... of luxury, his life becomes a sudden giddy whirl of **20)** .... restaurants, penthouses and upmarket stores. This is the new Bob with his flashy cars and new-found circle of **21)** .... friends. Well-off, well - **22)** .... Bob is **23)** .... in it ... and he is riding for a fall. Never forget the circle. A simple knock on the door and Bob's life comes crashing down about his ears. It's the police. It's about a suitcase stuffed with **24)** .... money!

13	A economic	B economy	C economical	D fiscal
14	A scraping	B scratching	C scrimping	D scrapping
15	A fortune	B deal	C figure	D sum
16	A capital	B windfall	C invoice	D turnover
17	A sum	B stake	C royalty	D return
18	A fisted	B handed	C minded	D hearted
19	A state	B height	C crest	D lap
20	A exclusive	B elusive	C evocative	D effusive
21	A well-appointed	B well-kept	C earned	D well-to-do
22	A heeled	B tailored	C cut	D shod
23	A rolling	B swimming	C bathing	D tumbling
24	A duplicate	B imitation	C false	D counterfeit

83

41 Money II

to appreciate in value: (used for things) the value of sth will increase with the passing of time (often used for investments) **Opp: to depreciate in value**

He buys modern paintings, hoping they will appreciate in value.

Unlike other cars, a Rolls Royce will never depreciate in value.

to borrow: to get money from sb or from a bank, which must be paid back at a later date [Note: **to borrow heavily**: to borrow a lot of money]

I borrowed £50 from him last week.

to be on a (strict/tight) budget: to have decided that you cannot spend more than a certain (normally small) amount of money over a particular period of time

During our trip round India we were on a budget of £25 a day.

to charge sb an amount of money for sth: to ask for/take money for sth that you are selling

I had bought so much in his shop that they didn't charge me for one of the magazines.

to cost a (small) fortune/a bomb/the earth: to cost a lot of money

Look at the car he has got. It must have cost him a fortune.

I'd love to go to the Caribbean, but a holiday in Barbados would cost a bomb.

to go halves on sth: to share the cost of sth

Let's go halves on this bill.

(in) instalments: (in) small monthly payments

I'm buying a TV in twelve monthly instalments.

in a sale: on special offer

If you buy electrical goods in a sale, you can normally save a lot of money.

in the region/neighbourhood of: approximately

If it's about five years old, it will cost you in the neighbourhood/region of £40,000.

to knock an amount of money off (the price of) sth: to reduce the price of sth

It was damaged, so he knocked £20 off the price.

to lend: to give sb money for a period of time, after which they have to pay it back

The bank refused to lend him any more money.

to make the cheque payable to: to put sb's name on the cheque so that they receive the money

Shall I make the cheque payable to you?

to make out a cheque: to write sb's name on the cheque (i.e. they will receive the money)

Who do I make this out to?

to be on a salary of: to earn

I don't know how he can afford it. He's on a salary of only £400 a month!

on the market: available to buy/on sale

This model has only been on the market for two weeks.

to pay by cheque: to use a cheque in order to pay [Note: **to pay by credit card/to pay cash**]

Can I pay by cheque or do you only accept cash?

to put down a deposit on sth: to pay part of the price of a product in order to reserve it

Would it be okay if I put down a deposit of £30 on it now and you put it aside for me?

a reduction in: a decrease in; a reduction in the **number/cost amount/price of sth** [Note: **a steady/gradual reduction**: a slow but continual reduction]

There's been a significant reduction in the price of petrol.

a dramatic/marked reduction: a big reduction

The sales period was extended because of a dramatic/marked reduction in consumer spending.

to retail at/for: to be on sale in a shop for (advertising language)

We are offering this unique exercise bike, normally retailing at £350, for only £230.

to run up a bill: to owe money, acquire debts (either by buying a lot of things or borrowing money)

It is easy to run up a high bill when you have a credit card.

to sell sth at a profit: to sell sth at a higher price than you bought it

I can't buy it at that price because I wouldn't be able to sell it at a profit.

to be strapped for cash/hard up/short of money: to have very little money

I'd love to go, but I'm a bit strapped for cash at the moment.

I'd lend you the money, but I'm a bit hard up myself at the moment.

He's always short of money.

a tax on sth: money you have to pay to the government for provision of public services.

I wouldn't be surprised if the government put a tax on the air we breathe!

to be up to one's ears in debt: to owe a lot of money

If I weren't up to my ears in debt, I'd buy a new car.

(to be) valued at: to be said to be worth

The painting, valued at £3 million, was stolen last night.

Practice

1. Complete the sentences by putting a preposition into each gap.

1 Can I pay .... cheque?
2 Who do I make this cheque payable ....?
3 You can pay .... instalments .... only 1% interest.
4 This watch normally retails .... £600, but I got it for only £250.
5 I was travelling for six months and was .... a strict budget of £20 a day.
6 I put .... a deposit .... a new car.
7 Her house has been valued .... £600,000.
8 Property in this area is bound to appreciate .... value.
9 He knocked £10 .... the price, so instead of £50 it cost me £40.
10 I'm a bit strapped .... cash at the moment, so I'm afraid I won't be able to join you on the trip.
11 With all the bills I've had to pay this month, I'm a bit hard .... at the moment.
12 The Finex PC150 is the cheapest computer .... the market.
13 I can't afford to do anything. I'm .... to my ears .... debt.
14 The government intends to introduce a new tax .... books.
15 We knew that at a later date we would be able to sell the cottage .... a profit.
16 If you're so short .... money, how come you can afford to eat out every night?
17 A house like that would cost you .... the neighbourhood .... £250,000.
18 Who would you like me to make the cheque ....?

2. For questions 1 to 11, complete the second sentence so that it has a similar meaning to the first sentence, using 3 to 8 words. You must include the word given in bold, which cannot be changed in any way.

1 We will have to pay a lot of money to repair this.
   fortune   It will .... this repaired.
2 She suggested sharing the cost of the meal.
   halves   She suggested that .... the bill.
3 She put her house up for sale over a year ago and she is still waiting for someone to buy it.
   market   Her house .... over a year.
4 The only calls we've made have been local ones, so our bill can't possibly come to this much.
   run   We can't .... when we've only made local calls.
5 A car like that will cost you approximately £50,000.
   region   A car like that .... £50,000.
6 Without a loan from the bank, we would have gone bankrupt.
   borrowed   Had ...., we would have gone bankrupt.
7 This outfit was on special offer in the High St.
   sale   I bought this outfit .... in the High St.
8 I spent a small fortune on this.
   charged   I .... this.
9 There is nothing to suggest that house prices will come down.
   sign   There's no .... house prices.
10 He is very well-paid. His annual income is £68,000.
   salary   He is very well-paid; he's .... £68,000 p.a.
11 Always check the rate of interest when you ask a finance house for a loan.
   lend   Always check the rate of interest .... you money.

3. Use the prompts to act out dialogues.

1 A: pay/cash/credit card/madam?
   B: cheque/if all right
   A: certainly madam/cheque payable/ Wright Bros Ltd

2 A: like/buy/new video recorder/but/bit/strapped/cash/moment
   B: why not buy/instalments?
   A: good idea!/not as if/up/ears/debt/just a bit/ hard

3 A: Victorian ring/value/ region/£3,000
   B: antique jewellery always/appreciate/cost
   A: yes, it/be good investment/and you/sell/it/profit

42 Nature - Noise I

Nature

to beat about the bush: avoid or delay talking about sth embarrassing or unpleasant

Come on, stop beating about the bush and tell me what you think. If you hated it, say so.

to have a field day: to have the opportunity to criticise and write a lot about sb (generally used about the press)

When the press find out he has been lying, they will have a field day.

grass roots: ordinary people (used in connection with politics, most commonly in the phrases: (i) **grass roots support**: the support of ordinary people who are members of a political party (ii) **at grass roots level**: among/with ordinary people who belong to a political party)

None of the senior party members liked him, but at grass roots level he was very popular.

to be on the rocks: (used for marriages or relationships) to be close to failing [Note: a **rocky marriage/relationship**]

It's hardly surprising they broke up; their relationship had been on the rocks for years.

the root cause: the main reason for

The root cause of his discontent is his being passed over for promotion.

to put sb/sth in the shade: to be so good that it makes sb/sth else look unimportant/ordinary/uninteresting

They have got a brilliant team. It puts all the other teams in the division completely in the shade.

to stem from: be caused by

Most of their economic problems stem from government corruption.

to be stone deaf: to be completely deaf

She wouldn't have heard anything. She's stone deaf.

(not) to have enough money to tide you over: (not) to have enough money to survive (pay your bills, buy food, etc) until a particular time in the future

Could you lend me £30 to tide me over until Monday?

to be barking up the wrong tree: to be wrongly accusing sb of sth

You are barking up the wrong tree if you think that I did it.

an argument doesn't hold water: an argument is illogical

Your argument doesn't hold water and I'll explain why.

a wave of: a sudden increase in a particular emotion / behaviour affecting a large number of people

News that the volcano was about to erupt sent a wave of panic throughout the city.

to weed (sb) out: to get rid of unwanted people from a group or organisation

On taking over the company, we weeded out those employees who were not pulling their weight.

not to be out of the woods yet: not to be out of danger or trouble yet

We're not out of the woods yet. We're still heavily in debt to the bank.

Noise I

🎧 **Note:** You will hear the noises for each verb on the tape. As you listen, read the notes below.

to backfire: to make a sudden loud noise (like a bang; made by an old car whose engine is not working properly)

He turned the key. The car rocked into life, backfiring twice and then spluttering off down the road.

to bleep: to make a short, high-pitched, electronic sound (made by alarm clocks, computers, etc) [Note: **a bleeper**: a small device which bleeps, used to tell you that sb wants to speak to you or needs you]

My alarm clock was bleeping. It was time to get up.

to clatter: describes the noise made when sth metal (like a tray) hits the ground

The tray clattered to the ground.

to creak: describes the noise made by a door opening or by floorboards when you walk on them
[Note: **creaky** (adj)]

The old door creaked as we pushed it open.

to hiss: to make a sound like a long 's'

The air hissed out of the tyre.

to howl: to make a long, loud cry (a wolf/dog/a strong wind/sb in pain or laughing howls)

At night we could hear the wolves howling outside our cabin.

The wind was howling.

She howled with laughter.

It's blowing a howling gale outside.

to patter: describes the sound of quick light steps (a baby walking on a wooden floor) or taps (rain against a window)

The rain was gently pattering against the window pane.

to rustle: describes the soft, dry sound made by leaves when they move in the wind

The leaves were rustling in the breeze.

to screech: describes the high-pitched noise made by a car when it brakes suddenly

The taxi screeched to a halt.

to shriek: describes a high-pitched scream or shout

A mouse ran from under the table. Lisa shrieked.

The audience shrieked with laughter.

to sizzle: describes the noise made by food products being fried in oil

We could hear eggs sizzling in a pan.

to thud: describes sound of a heavy object hitting the floor

He fainted, hitting the floor with a thud.

to tick: describes the regular series of short sounds made by a clock as it works

The loud ticking of the old clock kept me awake all night.

Practice

1. Complete the sentences, using an appropriate word from the box below.

> stone – field – bush – shade – water – woods – weed – rocks – tree – tide – grass – stem – root – wave

1. I have to say that our new ZX200 model puts the ZX100 in the ....
2. When the press found out that she had lied about her qualifications, they had a .... day.
3. Business has picked up. Having said that, we are still heavily in debt, so we're not out of the .... yet.
4. He was popular at the .... roots level of the party, but his cabinet colleagues couldn't stand him.
5. If you think he stole the money, then you are barking up the wrong ....
6. I'm afraid your argument doesn't hold .... You say mobile phones can cause brain tumours and yet scientists have found no evidence of this.
7. Rumours that there was going to be a petrol shortage sent a .... of panic throughout the country.
8. I just need to borrow enough money to .... me over until Friday.
9. Most people would agree that the .... cause of vandalism is boredom.
10. Their separation didn't come as much of a surprise as their marriage had been on the .... for quite some time.
11. The country's economic problems .... from the government's inadequate financial planning.
12. I won't beat about the ...., I'll come straight to the point – there have been complaints about the way you have been treating your staff.
13. The selection process begins with an aptitude test. This helps us to .... out those applicants who are clearly unsuited to a career in the diplomatic service.
14. She can't hear us. She's .... deaf.

2. Three options appear next to each of the following *noise* verbs. Circle those options (one or more) which make the noise described by the verb.

1. **rustle**
   A leaves on a tree moving in the breeze
   B an angry dog
   C a waterfall

2. **clatter**
   A a metal tray hitting the ground
   B an alarm clock
   C someone walking through fresh snow

3. **sizzle**
   A someone moving in a leather armchair
   B a boiling kettle
   C chicken frying in a pan

4. **tick**
   A a computer starting up
   B your heart
   C a clock or watch

5. **backfire**
   A a rocket being launched
   B a typewriter
   C an old car

6. **shriek**
   A a frightened woman on seeing a rat
   B a telephone
   C distant traffic

7. **howl**
   A a wolf
   B a child throwing a tantrum
   C a gale-force wind

8. **thud**
   A a stone dropped into a river
   B a door closing
   C a heavy object hitting the ground

9. **screech**
   A a car when it suddenly brakes
   B a horse
   C a vehicle horn

10. **patter**
    A rain hitting a window
    B a train
    C the distant sound of people talking

11. **creak**
    A someone climbing an old staircase
    B an old door as it closes
    C a mouse

12. **bleep**
    A water flowing through a pipe
    B an alarm clock
    C a small bell

13. **hiss**
    A a snake
    B an audience applauding a play
    C a punctured tyre

43 Noise II - Nouns I

Noise II (Mouth Verbs)

to chatter: (i) to keep talking quickly (ii) (for teeth) to knock together

I was so cold that my teeth were chattering.

to chew: break food in your mouth before you swallow it

It was such a tough steak that I found it difficult to chew.

to gargle: you gargle in order to freshen your breath or to soothe a sore throat

He advised me to gargle with salt water three times a day for my sore throat.

to gasp: to inhale quickly [Note: **I'm gasping (for a drink)**: I really want a drink]

He came up to the surface of the water, gasping for air.

Have you got any lemonade? I'm gasping.

to groan: to make a long, low sound because you're in pain or unhappy

"Do I have to go?" she groaned.

Every time we tried to move the patient he groaned.

to gulp sth down: to eat or drink sth very quickly

He ran into the kitchen, gulped down some cereal and ran out.

to hum: to sing a tune with your lips closed

She sat on the bus, humming a tune, oblivious to everything.

to lick sth: to move your tongue across the surface of sth

lick stamps/an ice cream

At six o' clock my dog would jump onto my bed and lick my face.

to moan: to make a low sound of pain or unhappiness [Note: **to moan about sth**: (informal) to complain about sth]

The wounded man moaned as we lifted him up.

All you do is moan about your job. Why don't you just quit?

to mumble: not to speak clearly

He mumbled sth about being uncomfortable.

to puff: to breathe loudly and quickly after a lot of physical effort [Note: **to be puffed out**: to be physically tired]

After the seventh flight of stairs, I was beginning to puff.

I'd run two kilometres and I was puffed out.

to sigh: to let out a deep breath expressing happiness, pleasure, disappointment, tiredness

She looked at his photograph and sighed. She was in love.

to sip: to take a quick, short drink of something [Note: **a sip**: a small amount of drink]

Can I have a sip of that?

to snore: to make a loud noise when you breathe while asleep

David's snoring kept me awake.

to yawn: you yawn when you are tired or bored

I was so tired that I couldn't stop yawning.

Nouns I (Houses)

attic: a room or space under the roof of a house

banister: a rail supported by posts and fixed along the side of a staircase

beam: a long thick bar of wood, metal or concrete used to support the roof of a building

cot: a bed for a baby with bars or panels so that the baby cannot fall out

double-glazing: two layers of glass fitted to windows to reduce heat loss or noise

drainpipe: a pipe attached to the side of a building through which rainwater falls from the roof into a drain

drive: a wide piece of hard ground or private road that leads from the road to a house

duvet: a large cover filled with feathers used instead of a sheet or blankets

fence: a barrier which separates two pieces of land (esp. gardens) or which surrounds one piece of land

floorboards: long pieces of wood that a wooden floor is made up of

gate: a kind of door at the entrance to a garden

gutter/guttering: a plastic or metal channel fixed to the lower edge of the roof which rain water drains into

hedge: a row of bushes along the edge of a garden, field or path

landing: the floor at the top of a flight of stairs

larder: a cupboard in the kitchen where people keep their food

lawn: an area of grass, tended and kept short

ledge: a narrow shelf along the top or bottom edge of a window or on a cliff face

mattress: a large, flat layer of padding put on a bed to sleep on

mantelpiece: a wood or stone shelf which is the top part of a border round a fireplace

radiator: a hollow metal device connected to a central heating system, used to heat a room

rug: a small carpet; mat

settee: a couch, sofa

sill: a shelf along the bottom edge of a window

shed: a small building in the garden used for storing things such as garden tools

shutters: wooden or metal covers fitted on the outside of a window

socket: (i) a device on a piece of electrical equipment into which you can put a bulb or plug (ii) a device or point in a wall where you can connect electrical equipment to the power supply

tile: a flat, generally square piece of baked clay used for covering roofs, floors and kitchen or bathroom walls

wardrobe: a tall cupboard or cabinet in which you can hang your clothes

43

Practice

1. a. Match the verbs in the box below with their corresponding definitions.

> snore – chew – gulp down – groan – sip – sigh – puff – mumble – yawn – gasp – hum – gargle – chatter – lick – moan

1. You do it with salt water when you have got a sore throat. ....
2. You do it when you are asleep. ....
3. You do it when you are tired or bored. ....
4. You do it when you are drinking something very hot. ....
5. Your teeth do it when you are cold. ....
6. You do it to your food before you swallow. ....
7. You do it to a stamp or an ice cream. ....
8. You do it when you swallow something very quickly. ....
9. You do it when you've just been told a particularly bad joke. ....
10. People who don't speak clearly do it. ....
11. You do it when you are surprised or you desperately need air. ....
12. You do it when you sing the tune but not the words of a song. ....
13. You do it when you are disappointed, in love or incredibly happy. ....
14. People in pain do it. ....
15. You do it after walking up sixteen flights of stairs. ....

b. Use the verbs in the box to describe the pictures. What do you think is happening/has happened to each person?

2. a. Would you find the following things inside or outside a house? (some items are for both)

> drive – banister – gutter/guttering – duvet – cot – tile – floorboards – radiator – sill – larder – ledge – mantelpiece – shutters – beam – rug – attic – drainpipe – fence – double-glazing – mattress – socket – wardrobe – shed – landing – settee – gate – hedge – lawn

b. Which of the above

1. would you associate with windows?
2. would you associate with gardens?
3. would you keep your clothes in?
4. would have bedrooms leading off it?
5. keeps you warm?
6. would you walk on?
7. would you sit on?
8. would you associate with electricity?
9. are a kind of cupboard?
10. might you find above a fireplace?
11. would lead to your garage?
12. collects rain water from the roof?
13. would you associate with the stairs?
14. would a baby sleep in?
15. would you find on a ceiling?
16. would you keep tools and gardening equipment in?
17. would you find on the roof, or in a kitchen or bathroom?
18. is a room in the roof of a house?
19. would you find in a bedroom?
20. would you find in a living room?

3. 🎧 You will hear someone describing a house. Listen and decide whether the sentences below are true or false.

1. There was a neat hedge in front of 205 Grecian Street. .....
2. The attic had a broken window. .....
3. The roof tiles were made into a mosaic. .....
4. The garden gate opened noiselessly. .....
5. The lawn was strewn with rubbish. .....
6. The garden shed was obviously new. .....
7. Several window shutters had fallen off. .....
8. There were a number of photos on top of the fireplace. .....
9. There was an unpleasant smell in the writer's room. .....
10. The bed in the writer's room was probably comfortable. .....
11. There was a heating charge, even though the radiator didn't work. .....
12. Our overall impression of 205 Grecian Street is not favourable. .....

89

44 Nouns II

Deception

forgery: a copy of a letter/picture/official document made in order to trick people into believing it is real

The painting is a clever forgery.

hoax: a lie that is told to make people believe that sth bad is happening (e.g. a fire) or will happen

We evacuated the building because we had been told a fire had broken out - as it turned out, it was all a hoax.

a smokescreen: sth said or done to hide the true nature of sb's activities

His embassy post is nothing but a smokescreen to cover up his real activities.

Edges

brim: the wide part that sticks out at the bottom of a hat [Note: **full to the brim:** filled right up to the top]

She was wearing a hat with a broad brim.

crust: the hard outer part of a loaf/slice of bread

We had to cut the crust off every slice of bread.

rim: the outside edge of a circular object

the rim of a glass/round mirror/ rims of spectacles

Fighting

brawl: a fight between two groups of people, generally in a public place or between players during a sports event

The match was spoiled by a last minute brawl which involved all players and both managers.

clash: a short fight between two armies/two politically opposed groups/the police and protestors

A number of people were injured in clashes between the police and anti-government protestors.

scuffle: a short fight which is not very violent and generally involving only pushing and shouting

It was more of a scuffle than a brawl.

skirmish: a short fight between two small groups of soldiers

It wasn't a battle, just a skirmish in which nobody was hurt.

Films or TV Programmes

clip: a short piece of action taken from a film and shown separately (e.g. in a programme reviewing new films)

In tonight's show we will be showing two clips from Redston's latest film.

series: a number of TV programmes shown over a period of weeks containing the same characters [Note: **episode/instalment**: one programme in a series]

Did you see last night's episode/instalment of "Friends"?

trailer: an advertisement for a forthcoming film, shown in the cinema/on TV

We had to sit through 15 minutes of trailers before the film came on.

Future

a weather/economic/sales forecast: a prediction of what the weather/economy/sales will be like [Note: **to forecast:** to predict the weather/sales, etc]

According to the weather forecast, it will rain tomorrow.

premonition: a strange feeling that sth (unpleasant) will happen

I've had a premonition that there will be a huge train crash next week.

prognosis: what a doctor thinks will happen to sb who is ill

"What's your prognosis, doctor?" "He'll live, but I don't think he will walk again."

prophecy: a statement of what sb with religious or mystical powers believes will happen in the future

He claims that all of Nostradamus' prophecies have come true.

Mistakes

blunder: a stupid mistake

The government made a huge blunder when it passed that law.

misprint: a word that is wrongly spelled in a book or newspaper

Some of the misprints in this newspaper are hilarious.

oversight: a mistake made by not noticing sth/forgetting to do sth

Due to an administrative oversight, 25% of people in this area have not been sent their telephone bills.

Parts of Books

appendix: a part at the end of a non-fiction book giving additional information

For more information on Barthes, see appendix II.

foreword: a preface normally written by a friend of the author

The foreword to Isherwood's novel was written by W H Auden.

index: an alphabetical list at the back of a non-fiction book containing names, subjects, etc and the page numbers where you can find them

Look it up in the index.

preface: an introduction to a book

The preface to the novel was written by E M Forster.

Smell

aroma: a pleasant smell given off by e.g. coffee or food

I just love the aroma of freshly brewed coffee.

reek: a very strong, unpleasant smell [Note: **to reek** (v)]

The reek of spicy food stung his nose.

He reeked of garlic.

scent: pleasant smell

The scent of roses filled the air.

stench: a strong, unpleasant smell

The stench of cleaning fluid was unbearable.

Parts

the blade: the part of a knife/axe/saw which is used for cutting

claws: thin, hard, curved nails of a bird or animal

the cockpit: the part of a plane where the pilot sits

a cuff: the part at the end of a sleeve or the leg of a pair of trousers

the eye: (of a needle) a small hole at one end

a hand: (of a clock) thick piece of metal or plastic that indicates what time it is

lapels: two top parts at the front of a jacket/coat which are folded back on each side and join on to the collar

the nib: a pointed piece of metal at the end of a pen, which controls the flow of ink

rungs: wooden or metal bars that form the steps of a ladder

the spine: (i) row of bones down your back (ii) the narrow, stiff part of a book to which pages and cover are attached

spokes: bars of a wheel which connect the outer ring to the centre

the stem: the thin upright part of a plant on which the flowers and leaves grow

a string: thin piece of wire or nylon stretched across a musical instrument that makes sounds when the instrument is played

the wick: a piece of string in a candle which burns when it is lit

the trigger: a small lever of a gun which you pull to fire it

the yolk: the yellow part of an egg Opp: white

Practice

1. a. Group the words in the box by putting them next to the appropriate category.

misprint – brim – instalment – prognosis – forecast – aroma – clip – smokescreen – skirmish – reek – oversight – index – rim – scuffle – clash – hoax – crust – premonition – stench – blunder – prophecy – trailer – forgery – brawl – preface – episode – appendix – scent – foreword – series

Edges: ....
Deception: ....
Mistakes: ....
Fighting: ....
Smell: ....
Future: ....
Parts of books: ....
Films or TV programmes: ....

b. Are the nouns in bold used correctly? If not, explain why they are wrong and replace each one with a more appropriate noun from exercise 1a.

1 Why don't you look up the date in the **foreword** at the end of the book?
2 Stop being superstitious. There's no such thing as a **forecast**.
3 There were a few **scuffles** as people jostled each other in the sales.
4 The kitchen was filled with a lovely **reek** of freshly baked bread.
5 As soon as she looked at his passport, she realised that it was a **forgery**.
6 It's my grandmother's favourite **trailer**; she never misses an episode.
7 Read the advertisement again. Are you sure it's not a **misprint**?
8 We needn't have worried in the end; it was all a **hoax**.

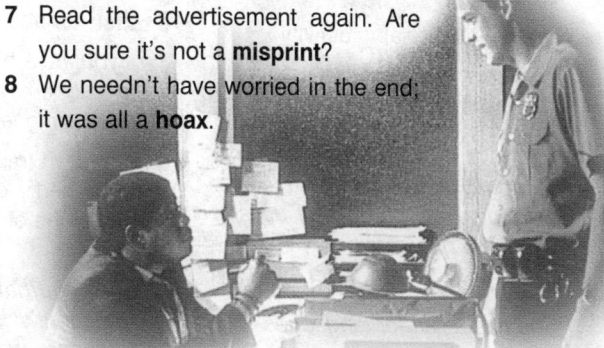

2. Match the "part(s)" in Column A with what they are a part of in Column B. Then, use the combinations in sentences.

	A			B
1	a hand	....	a	a ladder
2	the nib	....	b	a needle
3	the stem	....	c	a guitar
4	the trigger	....	d	a knife
5	the yolk	....	e	a gun
6	the spine	....	f	a pen
7	the eye	....	g	a candle
8	a string	....	h	a cat's or dog's paw
9	a lapel	....	i	an egg
10	rungs	....	j	a bicycle wheel
11	the wick	....	k	a book
12	spokes	....	l	a plane
13	the blade	....	m	a jacket
14	a claw	....	n	a flower
15	the cockpit	....	o	a clock
16	a cuff	....	p	a sleeve

45 Nouns III

the aftermath of: the period of time following a war, tragedy or natural disaster (e.g. earthquake, volcanic eruption)

In the aftermath of catastrophes like this, it is not unusual for governments to appeal for aid from the international community.

a brainwave: a sudden, clever idea

I've just had a brainwave. Why don't we ...

a catch: a hidden trick

So, if I fill in this form, I get a free holiday in Scotland. What's the catch?

clout: influence and power

The president of the republic is a figurehead only and carries no clout.

a craze: a fashionable activity

The latest craze to hit the streets of New York is motor skateboarding.

a fiasco: a complete disaster

The party was a complete fiasco. Only nine people turned up and we had a power cut.

a flair: a natural ability to do sth well

She has a flair for languages.

gibberish: words that do not make sense

The old man opposite was looking at me and talking absolute gibberish.

a hitch: a problem that causes a small delay (often used in the phrase: **to go off without a hitch**: to happen successfully, without any problems)

[Note: a **technical hitch**: a technical problem, generally affecting a television programme]

Everything went off without a hitch and the conference was a great success.

We are experiencing one or two technical hitches, but rest assured that we are doing everything in our power to sort them out.

a hunch: an idea based on a strong intuitive feeling, and not on evidence

"How did you know we would find her there?" "I didn't. It was just a hunch."

might: power/strength

He pushed the door open with all his might.

a must: an absolute necessity

If you are a beginner and you want to truly enjoy your skiing holiday, then skiing lessons are a must.

a scoop: an important piece of news published in one newspaper before any of the other newspapers know about it

The journalist overheard the President's wife saying that her husband was going to resign. What a scoop it was going to be!

scruples: moral principles; [Note: **unscrupulous:** without scruples]

This is an administration that had no scruples about raising taxation to its highest level ever.

The unscrupulous salesman swindled the elderly couple out of their life savings.

a slur: an unfair accusation or criticism which hurts sb's reputation

Every week they printed something about him. It was just one slur on his character after another.

a snag: a small problem (often used ironically when the problem is big)

I'd love to go to the Caribbean with you next week. There's just one snag - I have to work next week.

squalor: dirt and untidiness [Note: **squalid** (adj)]

He lived in squalor. (= his room/house was very dirty and untidy)

He lived in a squalid room in an equally squalid block of flats.

a stalemate: (i) a situation where no further progress can be made (ii) (in chess) a position in which neither player can make a move allowed by the rules so the game ends with neither player winning

The management weren't prepared to make any concessions, so negotiations reached a stalemate.

The chess game between the two Grandmasters ended in stalemate.

standpoint: point of view

From the government's standpoint, the results of these local elections are very encouraging indeed.

Practice

1. Circle the correct item.

1 Unable to bear the **squalor / slur** on his reputation, the minister took the newspaper to court.
2 The offer seems too good to be true, so there must be a **catch / hitch**.
3 Some trade unions are very powerful and carry a lot of **clout / might**.
4 If you look at it from his **stalemate / standpoint**, you'll see that he is right.
5 An interior decorator needs to have a **flair / craze** for combining colours and textures.
6 Although he is a successful businessman, Mr Harding is a person with strong **scoop / scruples**.
7 A good sunblock is a **must / might** for anyone who wants to go sunbathing.
8 I can't explain why I thought we would find it there; it was just a **brainwave / hunch**.

2. *Replace the words/phrases in bold in the sentences with a noun from the box below.*

> scruples – might – a stalemate – a fiasco – craze – squalor – a brainwave – snag – hitch – a flair – gibberish – standpoint – a scoop – clout – a must – slur on – a hunch – aftermath of – a catch

1 Read the small print. There is bound to be **a hidden trick**.
2 A: What makes you think that Sandonato had a hand in this?
   B: It's a **strong intuitive feeling**, that's all.
3 The meeting was **a complete disaster**. Half the delegates didn't turn up and those that did started fighting during the afternoon session.
4 "I'd be only too glad to lend you the money you need," he said. "There's just one **problem**, though. I'm completely broke at the moment."
5 She has **an instinctive and natural talent** for business.
6 What **an important piece of news published in one newspaper before any of the other newspaper knows anything about it**!
7 He's the consummate businessman. He is driven, ambitious and he has no **moral principles** whatsoever.
8 "Read this," he said, handing me a scrappy piece of paper. "It's **absolute nonsense**. He must have been mad when he wrote it!"
9 Rollerblading is the latest **fashionable activity** to hit the streets of London.
10 For students taking the optional translation paper in December's exam, Professor Forth's two-week intensive course on literary language is **an absolute necessity**.
11 The talks between the management and the unions ended in **a situation where no further progress could be made**, as neither side was willing to make concessions.
12 The introduction of identity cards made perfect sense to the government, but from the **point of view** of the ordinary man on the street it was yet another infringement of civil liberties.
13 Due to a technical **problem**, we will not be broadcasting tonight's European Cup match between Monaco and Parma.
14 He said hello, took Mr Firtelli's hand and squeezed it with all his **strength**.
15 Yet another article about her, yet another **unfair criticism of** her character.
16 What does it say about the president's **influence and power** in international affairs when both countries have summarily rejected his advice?
17 We were broke. We needed £100,000 and we had no idea how to get it. Then Laura had **a sudden, clever idea** ...
18 He opened the door to his apartment. She had never seen such **dirt and untidiness**.
19 In the **period of time following** the Second World War, many families decided to leave Europe in search of a better and happier life in the New World.

3. *Make up appropriate questions for the following answers/responses.*

1 A: .... ?
   B: OK. What's the catch?
2 A: .... ?
   B: It was a fiasco!
3 A: .... ?
   B: Well, I think you need to have a flair for it.
4 A: .... ?
   B: Yes, it's the latest craze.
5 A: .... ?
   B: It's just a hunch.
6 A: .... ?
   B: Yes, they're a must.

46 Nouns IV

Making nouns from adjectives

accurate: accuracy (n); Opp: inaccurate (adj); inaccuracy (n)

anxious: anxiety (n)

brave: bravery (n)

boring: boredom (n)

discreet: discretion (n); Opp: indiscreet (adj); indiscretion (n)

flattered: flattery (n); to flatter (v) [Note: **to flatter**: to praise – generally in order to get sth]

grateful: gratitude (n); Opp: ungrateful (adj); ingratitude (n)

mediocre: mediocrity (n) [Note: **mediocre**: not very good]

a mediocre film/performance/team/actor, etc

mischievous: mischief (n) [Note: **mischievous**: naughty]

nostalgic: nostalgia (n); [Note: **nostalgia**: a feeling of sadness mixed with pleasure when you think about happy times in your past]

poor: poverty (n)

Half the world's population live in abject poverty.

popular: popularity (n); Opp: unpopular (adj); unpopularity (n)

precise: precision (n); Opp: imprecise (adj); imprecision (n)

prestigious: prestige (n) [Note: **prestigious**: important and well-respected]

a prestigious company/job/award

proud: pride (n)

satisfied: satisfaction (n); Opp: dissatisfied/unsatisfied (adj); dissatisfaction (n)

sincere: sincerity (n); Opp: insincere (adj); insincerity (n)

stupid: stupidity (n)

vain: vanity (n)

versatile: versatility (n) [Note: **versatile**: good at different things]

Making Nouns from Verbs

to analyse: analysis (n); analyst (n)

a political analyst

to approve: approval (n); disapprove (v); disapproval (n)

to belong: belongings (n) [Note: **belongings**: the things that you carry with you (luggage, coat, handbag, etc)]

Marie collected her belongings and left.

to break: breakage (n) [Note: **breakage**: sth (a cup, a plate, a vase, etc) you break in a shop or restaurant]

All breakages must be paid for.

to collide: collision (n)

The getaway car was involved in a collision with an articulated lorry.

to compete: competition (n); competitor (n)

to complain: complaint (n)

We've received thousands of complaints about last night's programme.

to criticise: criticism (n) [Note: **a critic**: sb who criticises or who writes reviews (of films, books, etc)]

to deepen: depth (n)

We've been trying to calculate the depth of the lake.

to deter: deterrent (n) [Note: **deterrent**: sth that stops you doing sth bad or illegal]

It is hoped that the possibility of going to prison will act as a deterrent to people who repeatedly break the speed limit when driving.

to destroy: destruction (n) destructive (adj)

to emphasise: emphasis (n); emphatic (adj)

More emphasis has been put on reading skills.

to evade: evasion (n) [Note: **evade**: deliberately avoid sth you are supposed to do; **tax evasion**: the crime of not paying your taxes]

to fail: failure (n)

Their failure to qualify for the next round of the tournament was wholly unexpected.

to grow: growth (n)

The government's new tax concessions are designed to stimulate economic growth.

to portray: portrayal (n)

He is best remembered for his portrayal of Mr Blue in Tarantino's 'Reservoir Dogs'.

to pursue: pursuit (n) [Note: **pursue**: carry out/follow]

We are in pursuit of a green car travelling at 165 kph down the wrong side of the motorway.

to recollect: recollection (n) [Note: **recollect**: to remember]

I know her face, but I don't recollect her name.

I have no recollection of saying those things.

to receive: receipt (n) [Note: **receipt**: piece of paper that is proof of purchase]

to refuse: refusal (n) [Note: **refusal**: non-acceptance to do or take sth]

to resign: resignation (n)

to reveal: revelation (n) [Note: **revelation**: a surprising fact which was secret but is suddenly made known]

to solve: solution (n)

It was Baljinder who came up with a solution to our problem.

to withdraw: withdrawal (n)

I'd like to make a withdrawal of £60 from my bank account.

Practice

1. Give the nouns for the following adjectives. An example has been done for you.

0	vain	→	vanity
1	popular	→	....
2	satisfied	→	....
3	mediocre	→	....
4	grateful	→	....
5	precise	→	....
6	sincere	→	....
7	accurate	→	....
8	prestigious	→	....
9	mischievous	→	....
10	poor	→	....
11	brave	→	....
12	discreet	→	....
13	versatile	→	....
14	anxious	→	....
15	stupid	→	....
16	boring	→	....
17	nostalgic	→	....
18	proud	→	....
19	flattered	→	....

2. Use the word given in capitals at the end of some of the lines to form a word that fits the space in the same line.

1 England are bound to win, especially after Germany's unexpected .... from the tournament. **WITHDRAW**

2 At this company we do not tolerate .... **FAIL**

3 We have decided to give you the executive suite on the top floor. We hope it meets with your .... **APPROVE**

4 I'm going to write a letter of .... **COMPLAIN**

5 I'm afraid we can't give you your money back if you haven't got a .... **RECEIVE**

6 On all our courses, we place a great deal of .... on communicative skills. **EMPHASISE**

7 In big bold letters the sign read: All .... must be paid for. **BREAK**

8 She says she has no .... of the accident. **RECOLLECT**

9 The new law is believed to act as a .... to potential criminals. **DETER**

10 He was injured in a head-on .... with a lorry. **COLLIDE**

11 Her .... to carry out her superior's orders resulted in her being court-martialled. **REFUSE**

12 The press were very .... of the way the police handled the matter. **CRITICISE**

13 The hurricane ripped though the outskirts of the city, leaving behind it a trail of .... **DESTROY**

14 There were 600 .... in the race. **COMPETE**

15 He won an Oscar for his .... of Martin Luther King in Spike Dee's film, *Power*. **PORTRAY**

16 I was out of my .... They started talking about philosophy and I didn't understand a thing. **DEEP**

17 If we don't find a .... to this problem in the next few days, we're going to lose the contract. **SOLVE**

18 We were all very surprised when she handed in her .... **RESIGN**

19 He was forced to stand down following a number of .... about his private life in the press. **REVEAL**

20 If you are found guilty of tax .... in this country, you can be sent to prison. **EVADE**

21 When you leave the aircraft, please make sure that you have all your .... with you. **BELONG**

22 The thieves ran out of the bank with two policemen running behind them in hot .... **PURSUE**

23 Political .... believe that we will have an election in May. **ANALYSE**

24 The .... in interest in Latin American music is due, in part, to the success of films such as *Salsa*. **GROW**

47 Numbers – Objects

Numbers

to see double: to see two, when there is only one of sth

I'll have to consult an optician. I'm seeing double.

sth has increased fourfold: sth has increased four times; particularly used with verbs related to statistics (increase, rise, fall decrease, etc) [Note: **threefold:** three times, **eightfold:** eight times, etc]

The number of people with access to the internet has increased tenfold over the past eight months.

never in a million years: emphasises that sth will/would definitely not happen (+ inversion)

Never in a million years will he agree to something like that.

to be second to none: to be, at the very least, as good as the very best

Their in-flight entertainment is second to none.

to be back to square one: to return to the very beginning of a plan/project/attempt because no progress has been made

When planning permission for the new sports complex was refused, they were back to square one.

to have second thoughts: to change your mind [Note: **to be having second thoughts:** to be having doubts about a decision]

Are you sure you won't have second thoughts about emigrating?

to flee somewhere in their thousands: to escape from a place in great numbers

Fearing for their lives, people fled the country in their thousands.

to stand on your own two feet: to stop depending on others because you are old enough to do things for yourself

Frank is an adult now, capable of standing on his own two feet.

Everyday Objects, Implements and Tools – Idioms and Expressions

to axe: i) to make sb redundant from their job ii) to get rid of a plan, system or service

PCL Ltd have announced that 200 jobs are to be axed next year.

The government have decided to axe the controversial voting tax.

to have an axe to grind: to have private reason for doing sth/being involved in/being unhappy about sth

No, there's no problem; I have no axe to grind with you.

sth rings a bell: sth sounds familiar

Smee? That name rings a bell.

to be in the same boat: to have the same problems

Times are hard, but we're all in the same boat.

in my book ...: in my opinion

He took it without permission. In my book, that is unacceptable.

if sb plays their cards right: if sb is clever and uses the right tactics

I'm sure that, if you play your cards right, they will appoint you as the President's successor.

to chair a meeting: to be in charge of a meeting

They have asked me to chair the meeting.

on your doorstep: very near where you live or where you are staying

I have all the shops and services I need right on my doorstep.

frame of mind: how you feel, the mood you are in

It might not bother him but it all depends on his frame of mind at the time.

to hammer out an agreement: to reach an agreement after long and difficult negotiations

It took three long days for the management and the unions to hammer out a mutually acceptable agreement.

to hinge on: to depend on

In the end, his future hinged on a decision that was to be made by the Florida Supreme Court.

to iron out problems: to solve and get rid of small problems

His job is to help people who have just set up a business to iron out any problems they might have.

sth is a different kettle of fish: sth is very different from the thing that has previously been mentioned

Teaching adults is relatively easy. Teaching kids, on the other hand, is a different kettle of fish.

to have hit the nail on the head: to have just said sth that is exactly right

You've hit the nail on the head. What they need is publicity.

(it was so quiet) you could hear a pin drop: it was very quiet (informal)

Nothing lived in this desert. It was so quiet you could hear a pin drop.

to have (got) a lot on your plate: to have a lot of problems to worry about /be very busy

I've a lot on my plate at the moment, what with reorganising the department and everything.

to pull strings: to use influence/ connections

We had to pull strings to push the business deal through quickly.

it's like talking to a brick wall: to talk to sb without getting any response

I'd like to be able to discuss my problem with the boss but it would be like talking to a brick wall.

47

Practice

1. a. Complete the sentence beginnings in A with an appropriate ending from B.

A

1 Resign? **Never in a** .....
2 First she says she's sure about it, now she says she's having **second** .....
3 That didn't work, so we are **back to square** .....
4 As a holiday destination, it is **second to** .....
5 The value of this property has **increased** .....
6 34 and still living with his parents? It's about time he learned how to **stand on his own** .....
7 After hitting my head, I was feeling dizzy and **seeing** .....
8 People fled the city **in their** .....

B

a fourfold.
b double.
c million years!
d thousands.
e thoughts.
f one.
g two feet.
h none.

b. Now, use the phrases in bold in sentences.

2. Complete the sentences with an appropriate word formed from the objects shown in the pictures below.

1 I think you have hit the .... on the head. The sales have started early to boost consumer spending.
2 This paperwork needs sorting out but I'm just not in the .... of mind to do it.
3 As the President of the company was ill, Mrs Allen, was asked to .... the meeting.
4 Amateur football is one thing, but playing professionally is a different .... of fish.
5 He pushed right in front of us in the queue. In my .... , that's sheer bad manners.
6 Neither side was prepared to make concessions, so it took them six days to .... out a mutually acceptable agreement.
7 If you play your .... right, you can get that promotion, you know.
8 She has a lot on her .... just now, what with those three projects to finish.
9 If you have an .... to grind, I suggest that you take it up with the management.

3. The words in bold have been jumbled. Swap them around so as to make correct collocations.

1 It won't be long before our website is ready. We've just got to **axe** out one or two problems with the graphics.
2 I don't know why I bother saying anything to you. It's like talking to a brick **boat**.
3 The government were forced to **iron** student grants and replace them with a student loan system.
4 The success of the peace plan **strings** on their willingness to disarm.
5 It was so quiet in the library that you could hear a **wall** drop.
6 Gabi's father knows the head of the Immigration Department, so he pulled a few **hinges** for me.
7 The name certainly rings a **pin**.
8 We rented a villa by the sea and the beach was (literally!) on our **bell**.
9 Please stop complaining. I know there's a power cut but we're all in the same **doorstep**, you know.

97

48 ... of ... I

- **an article of clothing:** one piece of clothing

    An accessory may be as important as other articles of clothing in achieving a total look.

- **a blade of grass:** a single leaf of grass

    She tickled him with a blade of grass.

- **a board of directors:** the group of people in charge of a company/business

    I know someone on the board of directors who could help you.

- **a bunch of keys:** a number of keys together

    An enormous bunch of keys hung from his belt.

- **a coat of paint:** a single layer of paint

    All it needs is a coat of paint and it will look as good as new.

- **the dead of night:** the middle of the night

    He walked around in the dead of night, enjoying the silence.

- **a fit of jealousy:** an attack of jealousy

    Don't pay too much attention to his younger sister or he'll probably have a fit of jealousy.

- **a flash of brilliance:** a sudden burst of excellence

    Apart from one or two flashes of brilliance from Owen, England put on a rather poor performance.

- **a flight of stairs:** a set of stairs

    He was out of breath after climbing ten flights of stairs.

- **a grain of sand:** a single piece of sand

    This tiny insect, no bigger than a grain of sand, is responsible for the destruction of the country's potato crop.

- **a leg of a journey:** one part of a journey

    The first leg of the journey, Rio to Buenos Aires, was overland.

- **a load of rubbish:** (informal) no good/stupid

    I saw that film everyone's been raving on about but I thought it was a load of rubbish.

- **a means/mode of transport:** one particular kind of transport (car, train, bus, horse, etc)

    The most popular means of transport in this area is the camel.

- **a pack of lies:** if sth such as a story, an excuse, etc is a pack of lies, it is completely untrue

    Everything she told me was a pack of lies.

- **a pane of glass:** a flat, single piece of glass used in a window or door

    The bedroom window was made up of three large panes of glass.

- **a piece of advice:** one bit of advice (advice: uncountable noun)

    When he left, he gave me two very valuable pieces of advice.

- **a piece of furniture:** one bit of furniture (a chair, a table, a chest of drawers, etc) (furniture: uncountable noun)

    They had one piece of furniture in the room – an incredibly small chair.

- **a plank of wood:** a long, thin piece of wood

    "The bridge is over there," he said, pointing to a flimsy plank of wood that traversed the ravine.

- **a spate of robberies/price increases, etc:** a series of robberies/price increases, etc

    The recent spate of price increases has fuelled inflation.

- **a speck of dust:** a single piece of dust

    Even a tiny speck of dust on a camera lens can affect the quality of the pictures you take.

- **a spell of good/bad/sunny, etc weather:** a period of weather

    Last week's spell of unusually warm weather has had disastrous consequences for ski resorts.

- **stacks of time:** (informal) lots of time

    The film doesn't start for another two hours. We've got stacks of time.

- **a storm of protest:** a very angry and critical reaction from a large number of people

    The Minister's decision to reintroduce the tax provoked a storm of protest in Parliament.

- **a stretch of (the) motorway:** a section of the motorway

    There are always hold-ups on the stretch of motorway between Maidstone and Rochester.

- **a stroke of luck:** an unexpected piece of good fortune

    What a stroke of luck that you're here today! You're just the person I wanted to see.

- **a wealth of information:** a lot of information [Note: **a wealth of experience/knowledge**: a lot of experience/knowledge]

    This book contains a wealth of information on the country's schools and universities.

48

Practice

1. Complete the *of* combinations by providing the missing word in column B. The first letter of the missing word is given and the spaces that follow indicate the number of missing letters. The **Association Word** box will provide clues to help you get the missing column B word. Meanings for the words in column A are given in the **Meaning column**. Then use the correct combinations in sentences.

	A	B	Meaning of Column A	Association Words for B
0	a blade of	G R A S S	a single leaf of	green, field
1	a pane of	G _ _ _ _	a big, flat piece of	window
2	an article of	C _ _ _ _ _ _ _	one item of	trousers, shirt
3	a means of	T _ _ _ _ _ _ _ _	one kind of	bus, train
4	a piece of	A _ _ _ _ _	one/some	problem, help
5	a stroke of	L _ _ _	a piece of	fortune, fingers crossed
6	a grain of	S _ _ _	a single particle of	beach
7	a piece of	F _ _ _ _ _ _ _	one item of	chair, table
8	a fit of	J _ _ _ _ _ _ _	an attack of	suspicion, betrayal
9	a flash of	B _ _ _ _ _ _ _ _ _	a sudden burst of	genius, light
10	a plank of	W _ _ _	a long, thin piece of	trees
11	a speck of	D _ _ _	a tiny piece of	powder, unclean, old
12	a spell of	BAD W _ _ _ _ _ _	a period of	forecast
13	a spate of	R _ _ _ _ _ _ _ _	a series of	crime, thief
14	a pack of	L _ _ _	a lot of	dishonesty
15	a wealth of	I _ _ _ _ _ _ _ _ _	a lot of	facts, details
16	a flight of	S _ _ _ _ _	a set of	house, steps
17	a storm of	P _ _ _ _ _ _	a lot of	unfair, demonstration
18	the dead of	N _ _ _ _	in the middle of	late, black
19	a coat of	P _ _ _ _	a single layer of	Picasso, brush
20	a leg of a	J _ _ _ _ _ _	one part of a	travel, trip
21	a stretch of	M _ _ _ _ _ _ _ _	a section of	road, fast, lanes
22	a bunch of	K _ _ _	a group of (together)	lock, door, open
23	a board of	D _ _ _ _ _ _ _ _	a group of	company, bosses
24	stacks of	T _ _ _	a lot of	minutes, seconds
25	a load of	R _ _ _ _ _ _	a lot of	dustbin, nonsense

2. Can you match the pictures to any of the items above?

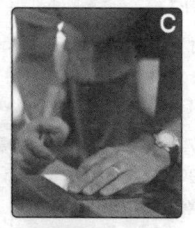

3. Complete the responses to the questions/statements, using phrases from this unit.

0 Don't you think the hallway is looking rather shabby?
Yes, it could do with a coat of paint.

1 I've got to do some research on this term paper about trends in modern architecture.
You'll find ....
....

2 The crime rate is rising alarmingly, isn't it?
Yes, there has been ....

3 Come on, get a move on, or we'll be late for the meeting.
No, we won't. We've still ....

4 The government has just put purchase tax up.
I know. There has been a ....

5 Why are you so out of breath?
I've just climbed ....

99

49 ... of ... II

not to take a blind bit of notice: to completely ignore

I told you not to interfere but you didn't take a blind bit of notice of what I said and went ahead anyway.

a breach of contract: an action which breaks agreements you have made in a contract

If you teach any of the school's students privately, you will be in breach of contract.

a clean bill of health: a formal statement that you are 100% fit and healthy

Having recovered from his injury, the sprinter was given a clean bill of health by his doctor.

the crack of dawn: very early in the morning, at sunrise

Catching the six o'clock ferry will mean getting up at the crack of dawn.

the cradle of sth: the place where sth (e.g. civilisation, democracy, etc) started

Greece is the cradle of Western civilisation.

a figment of sb's imagination: sth that you think is real but which in fact is not

What he thought he saw was a figment of his imagination. He's been watching too much TV.

(to point) the finger of suspicion: to suspect sb of sth

Since the door was not forced, the finger of suspicion points at the cleaning lady.

to dissolve into a flood of tears: to suddenly start crying a lot

On hearing the news, she dissolved into a flood of tears.

a glimmer of hope: a little bit of hope/a faint hope

There was still a faint glimmer of hope that some kind of agreement would be reached before the call came for an all-out strike.

the heat of the moment: if you do sth in the heat of the moment, you do it without thinking (because you are very angry or very excited)

She only said those hurtful things in the heat of the moment.

to live in the lap of luxury: to have lots of money, lots of possessions and lead a very comfortable life

Many people say that their dream is to win the pools and live in the lap of luxury.

a means of identification: sth that shows your name and address (an identity document, a passport, a driving licence, etc)

The only means of identification I carry with me is my driving licence.

a miscarriage of justice: a situation where the law (through decisions made in a court) treats a person unfairly

That our legal system permits such an obvious miscarriage of justice is a cause for grave concern.

the nick of time: if sth happens in the nick of time, it happens just in time to prevent sth bad from happening

The firemen arrived in the nick of time to save our house from being burned to the ground.

a ring of truth: if you think a story/excuse/alibi has a ring of truth about it, you think that it could possibly be true

Normally, when he was late, he gave a pathetic excuse, but not this time; what he said had a ring of truth about it.

not a shadow of (a) doubt: no doubt at all that sth is true

There is not a shadow of doubt in my mind that Healey committed this crime.

not a shred of truth in sth: sth completely untrue [Note: **not a shred of evidence:** no evidence at all]

Mr Trematis claims that there is not a shred of truth in the allegations that have been made against him.

There is not a shred of evidence to suggest that my client is guilty.

a smattering of sth: a very small amount of sth, especially used for knowledge of foreign languages

I speak Spanish, Italian and a smattering of Polish.

sb's standard of living: the level of comfort and wealth a person has

I moved to Australia because I knew I would enjoy a higher standard of living than I did in England.

a touch of sth: (i) a little of sth (ii) a hint of sth

As a student, he did a touch of creative writing but soon gave up and turned to accountancy.

She congratulated him, of course, but her words conveyed a touch of bitterness.

a trail of destruction: if sth (such as a storm, hurricane, tornado, etc) leaves behind it a trail of destruction, it passes through a large area of land and destroys everything as it passes

The tornado hit the south of Miami early on Monday morning and left behind it a trail of destruction.

Practice

1. Complete the *of* combinations in Section A with an appropriate word/phrase from the box below. Completing the situations in Section B with the correct word(s) in bold from Section A will help.

> touch – finger – nick – ring – clean bill – standard – figment – shred – smattering – flood – lap – trail – breach – blind bit – means – crack – cradle – beat – miscarriage – glimmer – shadow

Section A

the .... of **suspicion**
the .... of **luxury**
the .... of **time**
the .... of **the moment**
the .... of **dawn**
a .... or .... of **truth**
a .... of **Dutch**
a .... of **destruction**
a .... of **identification**
a .... of **tears**
a .... of **justice**
not a .... of **doubt**
a .... of **hope**
a .... of **notice**
one's .... of **living**
a .... of **contract**
a .... of **health**
a .... of **one's imagination**
a .... of **arthritis**
the .... of **human evolution**

Section B

1 The ambulance arrived in **the nick of** .... Ten minutes later and he probably would have died.
2 To her surprise, the doctor gave Sue **a clean bill of** .... He even suggested she was a hypochondriac and that her shooting pains, dizzy spells and raging fevers were nothing but **a figment of her** ....
3 He tells her he no longer loves her. She is devastated and she dissolves into a **flood of** ....
4 The fact that Rita passed gave me **a glimmer of** .... If Rita can pass, anyone can!
5 I regret saying those things to him. I was angry and they were said in **the heat of the** ....
6 You don't want much, do you? All you want is to win the lottery so that you can give up working and **live in the lap of** .... for the rest of your life!
7 He doesn't have a national identity document. His only **means of** .... is his passport.
8 How will you survive in Amsterdam? You only speak **a smattering of** ....
9 They are positive that she's guilty. There's not **a shadow of** .... in their mind.
10 Was she lying? We had to admit that her story had **a ring of** .... about it. Maybe we are gullible, who knows?
11 He's only got himself to blame. I warned him that if the police stopped him for speeding he'd be in trouble but he didn't take **a blind bit of** ....
12 Simon works downtown and lives in the suburbs. He has to get up at the **crack of** .... to get to work on time!
13 The red-faced man in front of him was pointing at his signature, shouting that he was going to sue him for **breach of** ....
14 **A miscarriage of** ....? You bet it was! She went to prison for a crime she didn't commit.
15 The forest fire raged on for days, leaving a **trail of** .... in its wake.
16 Human life first appeared in Africa, which is the **cradle of** ....
17 I get these twinges every now and again; it's just a **touch of** ....
18 From the beginning of the story, the .... **of suspicion** was pointed at the butler.
19 He's got lots of money and he can afford to do whatever he wants. His **standard of** .... couldn't be better.

50 People and Personality

Note: Adjectives with a negative connotation are followed by (-), those with a positive connotation are followed by (+), and those that are either negative or positive are followed by (-/+).

Nouns

an all-rounder: sb who is good at everything

Rupert is an all-rounder, good at academic subjects and at sports.

a bystander: sb standing near sth (generally an accident or a crime) when it happens

A number of bystanders witnessed the accident.

a daredevil: sb who gets a thrill out of taking unnecessary risks

Going bungee jumping again? You daredevil, you!

a gatecrasher: sb who goes to a party that he/she has not been invited to

Who are those people? They must be gatecrashers.

a has-been: sb who is no longer famous or important

In his time he had been a big star but now he was a has-been.

a minor: sb who is under the age of full legal responsibility (usually 18 or 21 years of age)

Being a minor, she was not entitled to vote.

a name-dropper: sb who likes mentioning the names of famous people they know (or pretend they know) to impress other people

Gary thinks he impresses people, but he's just a name-dropper.

an opportunist: sb who takes advantage of any situation, in any way, to get on

Being an ambitious opportunist, he will do anything to get on the board of directors.

a smart alec: sb who always knows the right answer/says clever things to such an extent that other people find it annoying

All right, smart alec, you tell us the answer.

a snob: a middle or upper class person who thinks they are better than people from a lower class

You don't like him because he has got a working class accent?! You're such a snob.

a spoilsport: sb who ruins the fun and enjoyment of others

"The party must finish at midnight." "Oh come on, Dad! Don't be such a spoilsport."

a squatter: sb who lives in an empty building without permission and without paying rent

The house can only have been empty for a week before squatters moved in.

a tomboy: a young girl who enjoys doing the same things and playing the same games as boys

She was a bit of a tomboy when she was a kid.

a troublemaker: sb who causes trouble

Simon is a troublemaker who loves to start arguments.

a wimp: a weak and pathetic person

If you don't stand up for yourself, they'll think you're a wimp.

a yuppy: a young professional person who earns a lot of money

The area has been smartened up by the arrival of yuppy residents.

Adjectives

blunt: sb who says exactly what he/she thinks even if it offends or upsets people (+/-) [Note: **bluntness** (n)]

conceited: far too proud of one's abilities, achievements (-) [Note: **conceit** (n)]

crafty: good at getting what one wants by means of clever planning or deceiving other people (+/-) [Note: **craftiness** (n)]

easy-going: sb who is not easily annoyed, worried or upset (+)

gullible: sb who will believe anything you tell them (-) [Note: **gullibility** (n)]

highly-strung: sb who is very nervous, and easily gets upset or angry (-)

impulsive: sb who has a tendency to do things suddenly and without thinking about them carefully (+/-) [Note: **impulsiveness** (n)]

modest: sb who does not like talking about their abilities/achievements (+) [Note: **modesty** (n)]

outgoing: sb who likes to meet and talk to new people (+)

petty: sb who gives far too much importance to insignificant things and is often unnecessarily mean and unkind (-) [Note: **pettiness** (n)]

reserved: sb who does not show their feelings or share their opinions with others (+/-)

ruthless: cruel, showing no mercy to others when trying to achieve his/her objectives (-) [Note: **ruthlessness** (n)]

sensible: sb who has common sense (+) [Note: **sense** (n)]

sensitive: sb who is easily offended or hurt by things other people say about them (+/-) [Note: **Opp:** insensitive (adj) **sensitivity** (n)]

spiteful: deliberately cruel (-) [Note: **spite** (n)]

stubborn: sb who is determined not to change their mind even when they know they are wrong (-) [Note: **stubbornness** (n)]

sympathetic: sb who will try to understand sb else's problems and give them help (+) [Note: **sympathy** (n)]

tactful: careful not to offend or upset sb else (+) [Note: **Opp:** tactless; **tact** (n)]

vain: having extreme pride in one's own beauty, intelligence, etc (-) [Note: **vanity** (n)]

vindictive: sb who never forgets that they have been harmed in some way and is only satisfied when they have taken revenge on the person who harmed them [Note: **vindictiveness** (n)]

Practice

1. Give the word that each of the sentences below defines.

0 He/She gets a thrill out of taking unnecessary risks. *daredevil*
1 He/She is a weak and pathetic person. ....
2 She/He ruins other people's fun. ....
3 He/She is a young professional who earns and spends a lot of money. ....
4 She/He is present when something bad (a crime, an accident) happens. ....
5 He/She likes talking about all the famous people he/she knows or has met. ....
6 She/He is still legally a child. ....
7 He/She takes advantage of any situation in order to gain advancement in any way he/she can. ....
8 He/She wants nothing to do with people who belong to a lower social class. ....
9 She is a young girl who likes playing the same games as boys. ....
10 He/She deliberately causes trouble. ....
11 He/She always has something clever to say. ....
12 She/He was once important or popular. ....
13 She/He goes to parties that she/he has not been invited to. ....
14 She/He is good at everything (e.g. academic subjects and sports, etc) ....
15 He/She has made his/her home in an empty building, without the owner's permission. ....

2. a. A friend fills in the following questionnaire. Based on his/her answers, describe him/her, using the adjectives that appear below.

> blunt – outgoing – vain – petty – modest – gullible – ruthless – highly-strung –tactful – impulsive – sensible – sensitive – reserved – sympathetic – crafty – conceited – easy-going – vindictive – spiteful – stubborn

0 A sensitive friend has written a book. You don't think it is very good. He wants your opinion of it. Would you
   Ⓐ say that it's rubbish?
   B say that the book shows great promise but could do with some changes here and there?

1 You are at a party. Do you
   A sit in a corner, and hope that nobody talks to you?
   Ⓑ talk to friends and strangers alike?
2 You've just won a scholarship to Oxford. Do you
   Ⓐ make a point of telling the whole world that it is hardly surprising as you are a brilliant scholar?
   B smile in an embarrassed sort of way and say that you were lucky?
3 You've just had your hair cut. A friend says he doesn't like it and that it makes you look older. Would you
   A burst into tears?
   Ⓑ rush to a mirror and examine yourself for two hours?
   C ignore it but spread nasty gossip about your friend?
4 A friend, not known for his reliability, says that a friend of a friend owns a farm in Australia and might give you some work. Do you
   A go to Australia?
   Ⓑ say no?
5 You have had an argument with a friend. The next day, you see each other and your friend has an incredibly large and obvious red spot on the end of his/her nose. Would you
   A point at it and laugh uncontrollably because you know your friend is very sensitive about this kind of thing?
   Ⓑ say that it is nothing to worry about as the spot will soon go away?
6 You are the boss of a company and one of your employees is 40 minutes late for work. He has never been late before. Would you
   A fire him?
   Ⓑ make sure that he is not paid for those forty minutes?
7 You are in a supermarket and have been in a queue, waiting to pay, for thirty minutes. When you reach the cash desk, the woman at the till says the cash desk is closed and that you have to join another queue. Do you
   Ⓐ lose control and start shouting?
   B smile and go to the other queue?
   C refuse to move, even after the manager has offered you free shopping at the supermarket for the rest of the week?
8 A friend of yours tells you that she is an alien. Would you
   A believe her and ask her what her planet is like?
   Ⓑ decide that she must be completely insane but realise that now is the time to ask her for a large loan?

b. Now match the adjectives in the box with the question options. You must use all the adjectives in the box. An example has been done for you.

0 A *blunt*   B *tactful*

51 Physical Description

Note: All the words that appear below are adjectives

Hair

glossy: shiny and in good condition [Note: **a glossy magazine** a well-produced magazine printed on shiny paper, with lots of colourful pictures]
The dog had bright eyes and a thick, glossy coat.

greasy: dirty and oily
Greasy hair has to be washed frequently.

lacklustre: lacking life and without shine [Note: **a lacklustre performance:** a poor quality and unenthusiastic performance]
'Bio Shampoo' - the perfect remedy for lacklustre hair!

lank: thin, straight and unattractive
His long lank hair needed cutting.

permed: that has been made curly by means of a chemical treatment
It is not recommended that this product be used on permed hair.

tangled: very untidy and, because it has not been combed, full of knots
He looked a mess, unshaven, scruffy, his hair a tangled mess.

unkempt: very untidy, hasn't been combed and probably needs to be cut
He smiled, running an unwashed hand through his unkempt hair.

Fat

chubby: fat but in a pleasant, healthy way (often used for children; used to describe a whole body or parts of the body)
chubby fingers/cheeks
He was a chubby little baby.

flabby: having loose fat where there should be muscle (used to describe a whole body or parts of the body)
flabby arms/legs
I'm getting old and flabby and could do with some exercise.

plump: pleasantly fat (often used instead of the word fat, because it is not as strong and potentially offensive a word; used to describe a whole body)
She was a plump, elderly woman with rosy cheeks and a welcoming smile.

tubby: short and a little fat (often with a large stomach) (used to describe a whole body)
a tubby man in a pin-stripe suit

Thin/Weak

bony: very thin, so that all you can see is flesh-covered bone (used to describe parts of the body)
long bony fingers, bony ankles

frail: thin and very weak (used to describe a whole body and often used to describe old people)
For Serpil, life is hard. Frail and alone, she has been forced to give up her job because of ill health.

lanky: unattractively tall and thin (used to describe a whole body and often used in the phrase **tall and lanky**)
I was a tall and lanky adolescent.

puny: weak, thin and without muscles (used to describe a whole body or parts of the body)
puny arms/shoulders
Don't tell me you are frightened of that puny little guy who works in the fish and chip shop.

scrawny: unattractively thin and weak-looking, used to describe a whole body or parts of the body
a scrawny neck/scrawny arms
"You used to be such a scrawny, awkward child," he said. "And now look at you!"

skinny: very thin (used to describe a whole body or parts of the body)
skinny legs/arms
I've always been skinny.

Strong

burly: strong and heavy (used to describe a whole body)
They were rugby players; burly, with broken noses and arms the size of tree trunks.

stocky: short, heavy and strong (used to describe a whole body)
One man was tall and well-built, the other was shorter and stockier.

strapping: big, tall and strong (used to describe a whole body)
He was a small child, puny even, but he grew up into a handsome, strapping young man.

Practice

1. Group the adjectives into the following categories: HAIR (H), FAT (F), THIN (T), WEAK (W), STRONG (S), writing the appropriate category letter next to each word.

unkempt	....	glossy	....	chubby	....	skinny	....
stocky	....	lanky	....	tubby	....	permed	....
greasy	....	frail	....	tangled	....	plump	....
scrawny	....	strapping	....	burly	....	lacklustre	....
puny	....	lank	....	flabby	....	bony	....

2. Read the text and decide whether the statements below are true (T), or false (F).

Mrs Jones watched as Jimmy, her son, got to his feet. He stood out like an unsightly and unexpected weed on a neatly tended lawn. He was painfully thin and improbably tall. He had outgrown his suit, bought the summer before, and he looked like a badly dressed clown. With his jacket straining at the shoulders and the bottom of his trousers flapping well above his ankles, he made his ungainly way to the stage, flicking his lank, greasy hair out of his eyes. Mrs Jones smiled at the plump woman next to her. She hadn't seen Mrs Jolly for some time. "Still on that diet, Phyllis?" she asked. Mrs Jolly blushed and twirled a strand of greying hair around one of her short chubby fingers. "I gave up," she said. "Oh," said Mrs Jones, as she turned to look at her son, who was warily negotiating the stairs to the stage. Mr Jones, who was sitting on the other side of her, took his glasses off and continued picking at a wayward thread that was working its way loose from one of the many holes in his ancient suit.

Mrs Jones was getting emotional; her handkerchief was out, ready for the tears that would doubtless come and she had placed it on one of Mr Jones' bony knees. Mr Jones looked at her. Running his fingers through his unkempt hair, he shifted uncomfortably in his already uncomfortable chair. The boy before Jimmy Jones received his prize from the headmaster, a short frail man with thinning grey hair who, stooped in his black gown, looked like a caricature from a Gothic novel. The boy taking his prize, Mrs Jolly's son – strapping, burly, big like his mother – dwarfed the headmaster. Jimmy Jones approached. Mr Jones yawned and Mrs Jones burst into snivelling tears, her big, flabby body shaking from the top of her neatly permed hair to the bottom of her thick ankles. Jimmy Jones stepped forward, took his prize, shook hands with his headmaster and wondered why he couldn't have been given a computer game. An unruly swathe of hair dropped into his eyes. He left it. He could just about see the other end of the stage and, in any case, his jacket restricted upper body movement to such an extent that any attempt to remove the offending hair would have been futile and painful, to say the least. He could hear a murmur from the audience, which he took to be adulation. The murmurs grew louder with each step he took. He could just make out his mother. She was crying, of course, and waving her hands. "What's she doing by the stairs?" he thought, as he stepped into nothing and fell head first off the stage!

1 Jimmy Jones is lanky. ....
2 Jimmy Jones has thick curly hair. ....
3 Jimmy Jones probably didn't wash his hair before the ceremony. ....
4 Mrs Jolly is overweight. ....
5 Mr Jones is skinny. ....
6 Mr Jones has neat and tidy hair. ....
7 The headmaster is a burly man. ....
8 The headmaster is going bald. ....
9 Mrs Jolly's son is a little puny. ....
10 Mrs Jones is overweight. ....
11 Mrs Jones' hair is a tangled mess. ....

3. Circle the correct item.

1 A group of **flabby / chubby** little children were playing in the park.
2 Martin may look small and **puny / stocky** but he has a black belt in karate.
3 What can be done to improve **lacklustre / glossy** hair?
4 You're getting a bit **skinny / tubby**; your trousers won't do up.
5 At the back of the bus sat three **bony / strapping** great lads from the countryside.
6 Comb your hair every day so that it doesn't get **tangled / unkempt**.
7 The man at the door was big and **burly / scrawny** - built like a wardrobe.

4. Describe the people's hair and body using verbs from this unit.

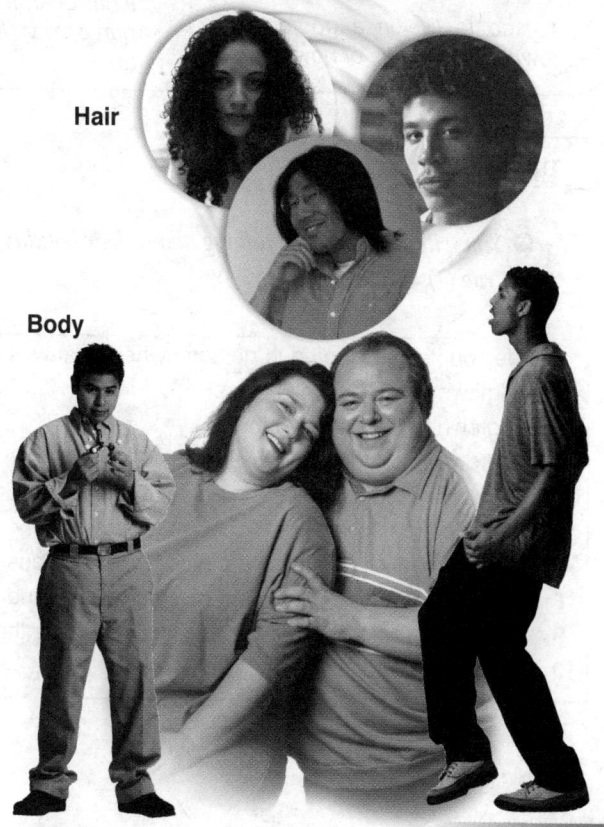

Hair

Body

105

52 Place (Adjectives)

> **Note:** * generally used before a noun ** only used after a noun, generally with the verb *to be*
> *** can be used before or after a noun

bustling: * full of activity and noise

A vibrant, bustling little town, full of local colour.

dark and dingy: *** dark and depressing (for rooms)

She showed me into her office, which was dark and dingy.

drab: *** grey and depressing

Malibrovich is nothing but a collection of drab tower blocks and dreary municipal buildings.

draughty: *** cold because cold currents of air continually enter it (under the door, through cracks in the window, etc)

A crumbling mansion full of large draughty rooms.

dreary: *** boring and depressing

Simon grew up in a dreary little town in the North.

gloomy: *** dark and depressing

You ought to do something about this room. It's so gloomy in here.

godforsaken: * horrible, boring and depressing (for towns/cities)

I used to live in a godforsaken town in the middle of nowhere.

musty: *** old and damp-smelling

We looked into the room. It was musty and huge cobwebs covered the walls and furniture.

picturesque: *** very pretty (for buildings/towns/villages)

She lives in a small, picturesque cottage near the sea.

plush: *** very comfortable and expensively decorated (for rooms/hotels/restaurants)

Hers was a life of luxury, of expensive holidays, five-star hotels and plush restaurants.

pok(e)y: *** uncomfortably small

There was only space for a bed and one chair. It was the pokiest room he had ever seen.

remote: *** far away from other towns/villages/people

We lived in a remote cottage in the middle of nowhere.

seedy: *** dirty and untidy and generally connected with illegal/immoral activities

It has changed from being a seedy part of town to a vibrant, upmarket area.

It is best to avoid the seedy side streets and stick to the main roads.

sleepy: * a very quiet place where very little happens

She lives in a sleepy little village about twenty miles south of Dublin.

spacious: *** very large

The rooms upstairs are pretty small but the downstairs rooms are really quite spacious.

stuffy: *** lacking fresh air and unpleasant as a result

It's very stuffy in here. Do you mind if I open a window?

touristy: *** designed to attract tourists (with big hotels, nightclubs, shopping centres, etc) and lacking any local colour as a result

I don't like that side of the island. It's too touristy.

unspoiled: *** has not lost its local character because of tourist developments

Further on down the coast, is Mar del Oro, an unspoiled fishing village.

Practice

1. 🎧 You will hear someone talking about their holiday. Listen to the recording and decide whether the statements below are true (T), or false (F).

		T	F
1	The couple had wanted to go somewhere that was quite touristy.		
2	Kingtown was a beautiful town.		
3	Kingtown was a colourful town.		
4	Kingtown was a remote town.		
5	The couple had expected their hotel to be plush.		
6	The hotel was situated in a good part of town.		
7	The first room the couple were given was spacious.		
8	The first room the couple were given smelt old and damp.		
9	The second room the couple was given was better than the first room.		
10	The couple liked Kingtown.		

2. *Look at the adjectives in bold below. When used to describe a room or a place, are they positive or negative in meaning? If you think an adjective is positive, write a P next to it. If you think it is negative, write an N. If you think an adjective has neither a positive nor negative connotation write an O. An example has been done for you.*

0 a **stuffy** room .....N.....
1 a **plush** room/hotel ....
2 a **picturesque** town/village ....
3 a **bustling** town/village ....
4 a **drab** room/town ....
5 a **remote** village/country ....
6 a **draughty** room ....
7 a **spacious** room ....
8 a **godforsaken** place ....
9 a **gloomy** room ....
10 a **dreary** room/town ....
11 a **pok(e)y** room ....
12 a **touristy** town ....
13 a **sleepy** town/village ....
14 a **seedy** disco/part of town ....
15 a dark and **dingy** room ....
16 a **musty** room ....
17 an **unspoiled** village ....

3. *Now complete the following sentences with one of the adjectives above.*

1 Resort towns like Blackpool are far too .... for my liking.
2 Open the window and let some fresh air in. It is very .... in here.
3 With the gas works in the background and the High Street dominated by ugly high-rise buildings and multi-storey car parks, it's hardly what you would call a .... town.
4 It's a nice room but it's a bit .... I was really looking for something a bit bigger.
5 They had painted everything grey. I had never seen such a .... room in my life.
6 Santa Clara is a(n) .... fishing village on the Atlantic coast of Costa Rica. No high-rise hotels, no tourists, no fast food restaurants.
7 We couldn't afford one of those big .... hotels in the city centre, so we stayed in a bed and breakfast on the outskirts of town.
8 Our next stop was San Pedro de las Almas, a small, ... town which straddled the Brazil - Paraguay border.
9 Grey, boring, ..., cheerless Dullstead. Of all the places they could have chosen to live in, why on earth did they pick Dullstead?
10 It was a beautiful room with oak-panelled walls. Its only drawback was that it was very .... Cold air used to whistle in under the door.
11 We were miles from anywhere, in a .... mountain village called Attawanga.
12 Norman's Nosh Bar was a dark and .... café on the Seven Sisters Road. Despite the greasy walls and the overpowering smell of cooking fat, it was the most popular café in town.
13 With the heavy velvet curtains drawn and the dark mahogany furniture, the room looked very ....
14 The château is a delightful residence, with ...., light-filled rooms.
15 It was a .... cheerless northern industrial town, full of factories and terraced houses.
16 They didn't feel safe in that ill-lit and .... part of the city.
17 It was a small, ... fishing village on the Mediterranean coast, full of colour and noise.

4. a. *Fill in the gaps in the descriptions using the words in the list below.*

sleepy – touristy – picturesque – remote – bustling – unspoiled

Well, it's a bit **1)** ...., not the kind of **2)** ...., **3)** .... place that some people like for their holidays. No, the houses there are **4)** .... and the village has a **5)** ...., **6)** .... air about it. We loved it.

b. *Using the paragraph as a model, describe a place you have visited and liked/didn't like.*

52

107

53 Problems

Politics

a ballot paper: a piece of paper you write your vote on

Spoiled ballot papers will not be included in the vote.

ballot box: the box you put your ballot paper in, once you have written you vote on it

*Ballot boxes were distributed to all the polling stations. (**polling station:** place where votes are cast)*

to cast a vote: to vote

Not all the votes have been cast.

a close-run election: an election where a number of parties win a similar number of constituencies/ votes

It was a close-run election, with the victor winning by 100 votes.

a constituency: an area/town represented in parliament by one politician

I vote in this constituency.

a constituent: sb who lives in a particular constituency

He is not a local constituent; he votes in the town where he was born.

a coup attempt: an attempt (often violent) by citizens/the military to take control of the government
[Note: **a coup (d'état):** the take-over (often violent) of the government by rebels/citizens/ the military]

A number of high-ranking army officers were involved in the coup attempt.

Supporters of the ousted president have been scrambling to leave the country following last week's coup.

the electorate: all the people entitled to vote in an election

The electorate includes everybody over the age of 18.

a gamble pays off: a risk one takes which has positive results

Holding the general election at a time of high unemployment was a gamble, but it paid off and we won.

to go to the polls: to hold an election
[Note: if a politician/ party **polls** a certain number of votes, it receives that number/percentages of votes]

The Gold Party polled only 11% of the vote in the last election.

a landslide victory: a victory in an election where one party wins many more votes than the other parties
[Note: to win by an **overwhelming majority**; to win by a **slim**/**narrow** majority]

Most political commentators predict a landslide victory for the Social Progress Party.

an opinion poll: the collected result of asking people what their opinions are

If the opinion polls are anything to go by, the present government stands to win the election.

to overthrow the government: to remove a government illegally and by force

The government was overthrown in a bloodless coup.

rampant/galloping inflation: inflation that is out of control

Rampant inflation led to massive discontent.

a staunch ...(e.g.: Republican): very loyal to, and a strong believer in (e.g.: the Republican Party)

He was a staunch Conservative.

a survey: a set of questions asking large numbers of people about their opinions/behaviour

The university did/conducted/ carried out a survey into people's voting habits.

to tackle a problem: to deal with/ solve a problem

Measures have been introduced to tackle the growing problem of unemployment.

to tarnish sb's/sth's reputation: to spoil the good opinion that people have of sb/sth

A scandal like this is bound to tarnish his reputation.

Business

to drum up business: to get business (by doing more advertising and promotional work)

We are not going to drum up more business by just sitting here. We've got to start advertising in the local newspapers.

a gap in the market for sth: an opportunity to sell a particular product/service because nobody else is selling that product/ service

We saw a gap in the market and set up our school as nobody else was offering English courses for professional sportsmen.

to be overdrawn (at the bank): to have spent more money than you have in your bank account
[Note: **overdraft** (n)]

No, we can't buy it. We're already £400 overdrawn at the bank.

I've got a huge overdraft. I must owe the bank at least £5,000.

to run into difficulties/problems: to have problems

The first problem we ran into was that we could not find spare parts for our Land Rover.

to run up a debt: to keep borrowing money so that you make your debts bigger

During the six months it took us to set up the business, we ran up huge debts.

to sort (sth) out: to deal with sth and solve it

Don't worry about the computer not working. John will sort it out.

to sue sb: to take sb to court in order to get money from them because they have harmed you in some way

He sued his employers for wrongful dismissal.

teething troubles: small problems that sb experiences when first starting a business/project

We still have some teething troubles with product development.

53

thriving: doing well, healthy
Thanks to increased investments, industry is thriving.

(to be) at one's wits' end: so worried and exhausted by problems and difficulties that one doesn't know what to do next

I'm at my wits' end with all these bills.

Practice

1. Choose the correct item.

1 After the vote of no-confidence, the government decided to go to the ....
 A constituents   C polls
 B ballot boxes   D elections

2 The price of bread has just doubled, but with .... inflation what can you expect?
 A rampant   C steadfast
 B profuse   D staunch

3 Even a suspicion of wrongdoing can .... a politician's reputation.
 A stain   C tarnish
 B impair   D smudge

4 It is people who are of voting age who make up the .... of a country.
 A constituency   C ballot papers
 B electorate   D electors

5 A(n) .... attempt by the army was quickly foiled.
 A coup   C overtake
 B overthrow   D mutiny

6 According to a recent opinion ...., the government is likely to lose the next election.
 A survey   C interview
 B inquest   D poll

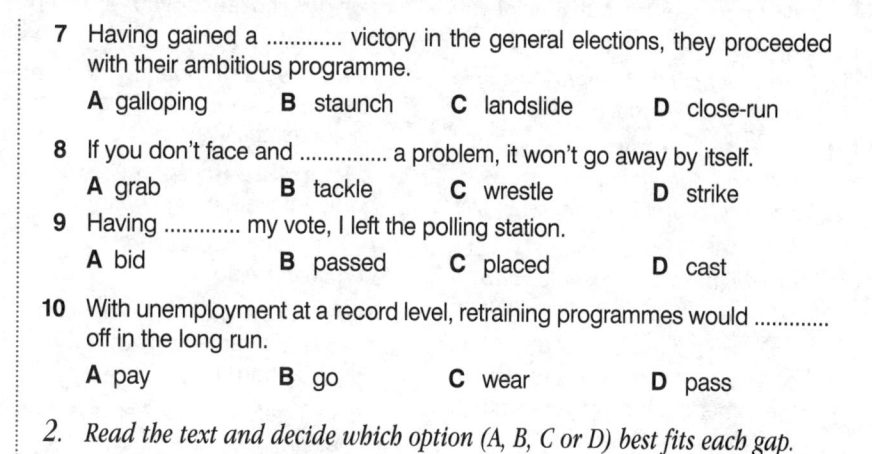

7 Having gained a .... victory in the general elections, they proceeded with their ambitious programme.
 A galloping   B staunch   C landslide   D close-run

8 If you don't face and .... a problem, it won't go away by itself.
 A grab   B tackle   C wrestle   D strike

9 Having .... my vote, I left the polling station.
 A bid   B passed   C placed   D cast

10 With unemployment at a record level, retraining programmes would .... off in the long run.
 A pay   B go   C wear   D pass

2. Read the text and decide which option (A, B, C or D) best fits each gap.

Business was bad. Sales were non-existent, I was 1) .... at the bank, I'd 2) .... up huge debts and the man who sold me the shop was threatening to 3) .... me because I hadn't paid him. I had expected 4) .... troubles when I took over the shop – all new businesses have problems in the beginning – but in the eleven months I had been open I had never had a customer. I'd tried everything to 5) .... up business – ads in the local newspaper, mid-season sales, sponsoring the local football team – but nothing I'd tried had worked. I was at my 6) .... end. A friend suggested I seek professional advice. He reassured me that his friend, Mr Stott, would help me 7) .... the problem of disappointing sales. So there I was in the city, sitting across from Mr Stott, a management consultant. "Now you live here in Willonga, a desert town, and you bought the local bakery, but you didn't keep it on as a bakery," he said. "No, I saw a 8) .... in the market and changed the focus of the business." I replied. "And things aren't going as well as they could be," he continued, sitting back in his chair. "Don't worry, Mr Redston, it's not unusual to 9) .... into difficulties on first setting up a business. I'm sure we'll be able to 10) .... everything out." He put on his glasses. "So what is it that you sell?" he asked. "Sand," I replied. "I sell sand."

1	A overspent	B overtaken	C overdrawn	D overdone
2	A put	B run	C stepped	D eaten
3	A sue	B condemn	C claim	D charge
4	A balancing	B teething	C growing	D opening
5	A draw	B work	C drum	D bring
6	A brain's	B wits'	C nerves'	D mind's
7	A tarnish	B tackle	C sort	D drum up
8	A gap	B space	C opening	D opportunity
9	A walk	B come	C bump	D run
10	A bring	B iron	C smooth	D sort

109

54 Reactions - Short and Long

Note: All the words that appear under *Reactions* are adjectives

Reactions

to be adamant: (i) to be determined not to change your mind about sth (ii) to be convinced that what you are saying is true

He was adamant that he had said nothing of the sort.

to be baffled: to find it impossible to explain/understand/solve (a mystery, a problem, a puzzle, etc)

Why, when one person yawns, does it make other people yawn? It is a mystery that has baffled scientists for years.

to be blasé: not to worry about sth that other people get very worried or excited about

We were all incredibly excited and nervous about appearing on TV but Chris, who had been on television before, was quite blasé about it.

to be devastated: to be extremely upset or disappointed

I'd set my heart on buying that house and I was devastated when they sold it to someone else.

We were devastated when we found out that she had died.

to be/feel drowsy: to be/feel half asleep

Don't drive while you are taking these tablets. They make you feel very drowsy.

to be enthralled: to be so interested in sth that it has completely captured your attention

The Sultan was enthralled by Scheherazade's stories.

to be/feel flattered: to feel very pleased because sb has said sth nice about you/has done sth special for you

He felt flattered by Einstein's comment, of course.

to be flummoxed: to have no idea what the answer to a problem/question is

I was absolutely flummoxed. I didn't even understand the question.

to be/get flustered: to be/get very nervous because you are very short of time

She has a tendency to get flustered in exams and that's why she underachieves.

to be impressed (by sb/sth): to have great admiration (for sb/sth)

I was very impressed by your curriculum vitae.

to be/feel lethargic: to feel that you have little or no energy
[Note: **lethargy** (n)]

When it gets very hot I always feel so lethargic.

to be livid: to be extremely angry

When he found out that she had lost his golf clubs, he was livid.

to be off-hand: to treat sb in a way that suggests that you are not interested in what they are saying

His off-hand manner told me he didn't want to know.

to be stunned: to be extremely surprised

We were stunned by the news.

to be/feel uptight: to be tense and nervous about sth

I don't understand why you get so uptight about exams. I mean, you've sat so many.

Short and Long

as long as: if (and only if)

You can borrow my pen as long as you give it back.

to go to any lengths to do sth: to be determined to do anything to get/achieve what you want (even if it means doing sth dishonest/cruel/dangerous)
[Note: **to go to great lengths to do sth:** to try very hard/to spend a lot of time trying to get/achieve sth (but not doing anything dishonest or cruel)]

Some people will go to any lengths to avoid paying their taxes.

I went to great lengths to get that book and all she could say was that it wasn't in very good condition!

to have (got) a long face: to look sad and/or depressed

He sat there with a long face and tears welling up in his eyes.

how long ago ...?: when ..?

How long ago did he emigrate?

it won't be long before (sth happens): sth will soon happen

It won't be long before schools close for the summer.

to speak at length about sth: to speak for a long time about sth

When I interviewed him, he spoke at length about his family.

the length and breadth of: everywhere in a place

He's travelled the length and breadth of Africa in search of fossils.

to be in short supply: to be very difficult to find or buy

Milk was in such short supply that we used to put water on our cornflakes.

to be short for sth: to be a shorter way of saying a particular name/word/phrase

Bob is short for Robert.

EFL is short for English as a Foreign Language.

to be short with sb: to speak to sb using very few words in a rude/aggressive/unfriendly way

I'm sorry I was so short with you yesterday. I was in a bad mood.

to run short of sth: to no longer have enough of sth

We're running short of coffee. Can you remember to buy some at the supermarket?

Practice

1. For questions 1 to 11, complete the second sentence so that it has a similar meaning to the first sentence, using 3 to 8 words. You must include the word given in bold, which cannot be changed in any way, and one of the following: SHORT, LONG, LENGTH or LENGTHS.

1. He is the kind of man who will do anything to crush the competition.
   go   He is the kind of man .... crush the competition.
2. The letters BBC mean British Broadcasting Corporation.
   for   BBC .... British Broadcasting Corporation.
3. "Why are you looking so unhappy?" she asked.
   face   "Why have you ....?" she asked.
4. Food was so scarce that the government had to ration it.
   supply Food was .... that the government was forced to ration it.
5. We don't have much time left.
   running We're .... time.
6. He spoke for a long time about the social implications of the plan.
   at   He spoke .... social implications of the plan.
7. Martin has travelled all over India.
   of   Martin has travelled .... India.
8. When did you send that application?
   ago   How .... that application?
9. He said he was sorry that he'd been so rude to her.
   with   He apologised .... her.
10. Soon we'll all be on holiday.
    before It won't .... on holiday.
11. If you do your revision, you should pass the exam.
    as   You should .... your revision.

2. a. Read the situation outlines (1 to 15) and match them with an appropriate **reaction** adjective from this unit. Try to use each adjective only once.

1. He is very pleased. She thinks he looks like a movie star and she told him so. It was a wonderful compliment.
2. Her plane leaves in two hours and she hasn't packed yet. She is running around, panicking.
3. Her goldfish meant the world to her. She arrives home to find it floating upside down in the fish tank. She is shocked and incredibly upset.
4. He is so angry! He had lent his car to his daughter on condition that she didn't damage it. When he next uses the car, he finds it dented in three places.
5. Her son, seventeen, and an A grade student, has just told her that he is dropping out of school. She's speechless.
6. It's hot. Where's his energy? He can't be bothered to do anything. He'll stay in his chair and do nothing.
7. When he went to the kitchen his glass was full. When he came back – five minutes later – his glass was empty. No one else is in the house. There doesn't seem to be any explanation at all.
8. All the other teachers are frantic. They're living on their nerves. There's an inspection. Everyone is panicking – except Peter, that is. He's been observed many times before. It's no big deal.
9. She hangs on his every word. Everything he says is fascinating. She has never met such an interesting man.
10. He had a splitting headache, so he took three extra-strong painkillers. The headache has gone but he can hardly keep his eyes open. All he wants to do is sleep.
11. Normally she is so nice. Always joking, always chatty. Not today. She's ignoring everyone. If someone says something, she sneers and says, " So what?"
12. He won't believe me. He says he saw me in the mall yesterday. I tell him I wasn't in the mall. I was playing golf. He still says it was me.
13. She hasn't got a clue. She just stands there, helpless. What is the answer? She doesn't know.
14. He's worried, nervous and in a bad mood. His boss is coming to dinner and he has to cook. Cooking is not his strong point. He finds it difficult to make toast.
15. She hasn't seen her sister for a long time. They meet and go to a Chinese restaurant. Her sister orders in Chinese. Wow! Her sister can speak Chinese!

b. *Can you match the pictures to any of the **reaction** adjectives?*

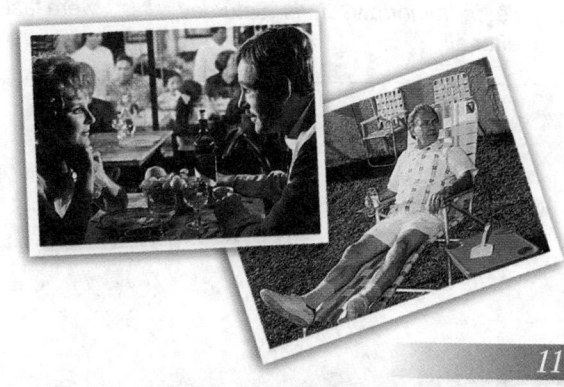

55 Sleep and Bed

to crash out: (informal) to go to bed

I'm tired. I'm going to crash out.

to doze off: to unintentionally fall asleep for a short time

It was so warm in there and the lecturer was so boring that I kept dozing off.

to drift off: to gradually and gently fall asleep

I was just starting to drift off when Chuli - my cat - jumped on to my bed and bit one of my toes.

to flake out: to fall asleep because you are very tired

I flaked out in front of the television.

to go off: (for an alarm clock) to ring

My alarm clock didn't go off this morning.

to go out like a light/to go to sleep as soon as your head hits/touches the pillow: to go to sleep very quickly, almost as soon as you get into bed

I was shattered last night. I got into bed and I went out like a light.

to have/get a good night's sleep: to sleep well and for the whole night

"I've been feeling a bit run down lately." "That's because you don't sleep enough. What you need is a good night's sleep."

to hit the sack: (informal) to go to bed; generally used in the first person

I think I'm going to hit the sack. I've got to get up very early tomorrow morning.

to lie in/to have a lie-in: to intentionally stay in bed and get up at a later time than normal

You look very tired. Why don't you lie in tomorrow? It is Saturday, after all.

to nod off: to fall asleep, often when you are sitting down (on a train, for example, or in an armchair)

I don't know what the score was. Unfortunately, I nodded off halfway through the match.

to oversleep: to wake up later than you intended to, often with the result that you are late for sth (for work or for an appointment, etc)

He woke up and looked at his alarm clock. It hadn't gone off and he had overslept.

to set the alarm: to adjust the alarm clock so that it rings at a particular time

Have you set the alarm?

Can you set the alarm for half past seven, please?

to be shattered: to be exhausted [Note: other adjectives meaning very tired: (informal) **bushed**, **beat**;

I'm going to bed. I'm absolutely shattered.

to sleep in: to intentionally stay in bed and get up at a later time than normal

On weekdays we get up at half past six. At the weekend, however, we like to sleep in.

to sleep over (at sb's house): to sleep the night at another person's house

Mum, can I sleep over at Sophie's house tonight?

to be sound/fast asleep: to be sleeping deeply [Note: **to be dead to the world**: to be so deeply asleep that almost nothing will wake you]

By the time we got home, the kids were fast asleep in the back of the car.

Apparently, it was one of the worst storms we've ever had, but I was dead to the world. I didn't hear a thing.

to toss and turn all night: to spend the night moving and changing position in bed and trying to get to sleep

She spent the whole night tossing and turning - she couldn't get what he had said off her mind.

to tuck sb in: to make sb comfortable in bed by arranging the sheets and blankets around them

Every night my mother would tuck us in, give us a goodnight kiss and then turn the lights off.

to turn in: to go to bed

Good night, everyone. I'm turning in for the night.

an unmade bed: if a bed is unmade, the sheets, blankets or the duvet have not been arranged and tidied since sb last slept in it

It was the worst hotel we had ever been to. The lift was out of order, the tap leaked and the beds were unmade.

to be wide awake: to be completely awake

It was three o'clock in the morning. I'd gone to bed at half past twelve and I was still wide awake.

not to get a wink of sleep/not to sleep a wink: not to sleep at all, especially used for not sleeping all night

What with the baby crying and Stephen snoring like a steam train, I didn't get a wink of sleep last night.

Practice

1. Read the text below and decide which option (A, B, C or D) best fits each gap.

He was tired. He was 1) .... His body felt as if it belonged to someone else. A long day's work and not a 2) .... of sleep the night before. Flat life. The neighbour above stomping on his floor. A litany of thumps, punctuated by scrapes and crashes. Next door, World War Three (battle number forty-one), and a string of explosive movies below. All night, no let up - from the moment he had crawled into bed until the moment the alarm clock 3) .... off.

So there he was. Headache, tired, 4) .... off in front of the TV. Heavy-headed, eyes closing. The voice behind his eyelids was being contaminated by the insanity of sleep - *this chair is nice*, it said, *Why bother with your bed?* Foggy reason got the upper hand. It was time to 5) .... in. He shuffled into the bedroom.

The real world. In his face. An 6) .... bed. What had he expected? Crisp, clean sheets, the smell of freshly laundered linen? Someone to 7) .... him in? Forget it. What he had, what was staring him defiantly in the face, was a lumpy mattress and a tangle of sheets. He sighed and 8) .... the alarm, a reflex action — half past six. He fell into bed and went out like a 9) ...., the keen anticipation of endless waves of sleep gently washing over him.

Two minutes had passed and he was sitting bolt upright, staring at the wall. Downstairs had bought a kareoke machine. Head under pillow, fingers in ears, feeble protest - none of it worked. Rod Stewart's Greatest Hits before dawn. Five o' clock. It was five o'clock and he was 10) .... awake. All he had wanted was a 11) .... night's sleep. He spent the next hour 12) .... and turning, thinking about not thinking. Finally, he 13) .... off into a fretful sleep. But it was sleep. Sweet sleep, sweet drea... BE... BE... BE... BEEP... BE... BE... BE... BEEP. Go away! Leave me alone, he thought, suddenly overtaken by a virulent hatred for all things with hands and cogs. Sleep logic took over. *"You can have another fifteen minutes. You don't need the alarm. You'll wake up,"* it whispered temptingly.

He woke up two hours later. He'd 14) .... No breakfast, no shower, no nothing. Five minutes and he was out the door. Taxi. Where were the taxis? No taxis. And where were the people? No people. No noise. No nothing. Crumpled, dishevelled, bleary-eyed, he paused, he thought – It was Saturday! He didn't work on Saturdays. Perhaps he could go back to bed...

	A	B	C	D
1	shattered	crumbled	broken	fractured
2	dash	wink	stroke	blink
3	called	sounded	tripped	went
4	nodding	flaking	sinking	falling
5	turn	hit	crash	fold
6	untouched	undone	unravelled	unmade
7	wrap	roll	pack	tuck
8	fiddled	set	determined	put
9	flame	bulb	light	lamp
10	wide	fully	sound	bolt
11	good	quality	positive	thorough
12	rolling	tossing	dozing	flipping
13	set	slumbered	drifted	fell
14	lain in	slept over	slept in	overslept

2. The phrases in bold in the sentences below have not been used correctly. Explain why they are incorrect and replace them with an appropriate word/phrase related to sleep from this unit.

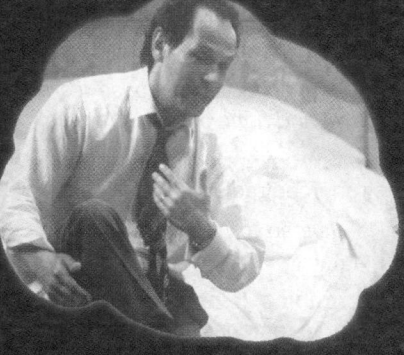

1 Goodness, is that the time? I must have **slept over**!
2 I'm going to **have a lie-in**. I've got a plane to catch first thing tomorrow morning.
3 Henry decided not to go out with his friends that night, as he was **flaked out**.
4 Grandad **went out like a light** in the armchair.
5 The shrill sound which hit Julie's ears was her alarm clock **nodding off**.
6 If you **tuck in** all night, you feel terrible in the morning.
7 She lay there, **sound asleep** all night, wondering what to do.

56 Something, Anything, Nothing - Speaking and Communicating I

Something, Anything, Nothing

not to look anything like: not to look at all like [Note: **not sound/feel/taste/smell anything like**]

George Bush! I don't look anything like George Bush.

(to be) none of sb's business: used when we tell sb that sth does not concern them

I'm not telling you because it's a secret and none of your business.

nothing of the sort: certainly not (as strong contradiction of sth said)

He claimed to be a famous actor, but he is nothing of the sort.

to be nothing if not + adjective: used to emphasise a particular quality that sb has (generally a positive quality)

She is nothing if not thorough.

to do nothing but: the only thing sb does is ... (+ bare infinitive)

I don't know why he came on holiday. He did nothing but complain the whole time.

to like nothing better than to + verb: to really enjoy

After a hard day at work he likes nothing better than to put his feet up and watch television.

to spend next to nothing on sth: to spend very little money on sth

We spent next to nothing on food, as Bob and Tania insisted on cooking for us every night.

to stop at nothing to + verb: to do anything (even if it is cruel, immoral, illegal or dishonest) to get what you want

He wants power and he'll stop at nothing to get it.

there's nothing I wouldn't do: I would do anything

There's nothing I wouldn't do to pass this exam.

sb/sth is/was nowhere to be found: you can/could not find sb/sth

We searched high and low for her passport that night, but it was nowhere to be found.

something like: approximately (followed by a number)

Something like 12,000 people attended his funeral.

to be something of a ...: to be quite/rather a ...

The play proved to be something of a disappointment.

there is something wrong with sth: sth is not working properly

There is something wrong with this computer. Every time I press the 'enter' key, the screen goes blank.

Speaking and Communicating I

to brag: to boast (in an annoying or distasteful way)

I wish he would stop bragging about how much money he earns.

to brief: to give a politician or businessman detailed information that they do not have but which they need to know (often for a meeting, conference, etc)

The Prime Minister was briefed on the latest developments in the Camp David peace talks.

to clam up: to suddenly stop talking because you are very nervous or you suddenly feel very shy

Although she did well in the written exam, she clammed up in the interview.

to insinuate: to accuse sb of sth in an indirect way

What do you mean? Are you insinuating that I took the money?

to intimate: to hint

They intimated that he would be next in line for promotion.

to mutter: to say sth in a low, quiet voice which is difficult to hear

He leaned towards me and muttered something in my ear. I had no idea what he said so I smiled and nodded.

reel off: to repeat information (generally a list of names) quickly, without having to stop and think about it

He reeled off the names of every book dealer in New York.

to waffle: to talk and talk without saying anything important or sensible

The worst thing you can do in an interview is to waffle when you are asked a question.

to whinge: to keep complaining about sth in an annoying way

First the car was too hot, then she was tired; all she did was whinge the whole way there.

to yell: to shout

Next to me was a mother yelling at her kids.

Practice

1. *Complete the second sentence so that it has a similar meaning to the first sentence, using 3 to 8 words. You must include the word given in bold, which cannot be changed in any way.*

    1 What I get up to in my spare time has nothing to do with you, you know.

    none What I get up to in my spare time ...., you know.

    2 The only thing he does is watch television all day.

    nothing He .... all day.

    3 I couldn't find my keys anywhere.

    nowhere My keys .... found.

    4 He's prepared to do anything to get what he wants.

    nothing He'll .... get what he wants.

    5 He's certainly very persistent.

    nothing He is .... persistent.

114

6 Tim and Tom? They don't look alike at all.
   anything   Tim .... Tom.
7 What he enjoys doing most on Saturdays is pottering about in his garden.
   nothing   He likes ....
                  potter about in his garden on Saturdays.
8 I'd do anything to see her face when you tell her.
   nothing   There's ....
                  .... her face when you tell her.
9 Poverty is endemic. Around ninety per cent of the population are living below the breadline.
   something Poverty is endemic. ....
                  of the population are living below the breadline.
10 Our last electricity bill came to £1.45.
   nothing   We spend next .... electricity.
11 He is quite a celebrity in this part of the country.
   something He ....
                  .... in this part of the country.
12 He says it's gold but I don't think it is.
   nothing   He says it's gold but ....
                  ...., in my opinion.
13 The computer isn't working properly.
   something There's ....
                  .... the computer.

4 Steve stood up and **reeled off** the names of all the Cup Final winners for the last fifty years.
   • Steve often had to stop and think.   ....
   • Steve has a good memory.   ....
5 "He just wouldn't stop **yelling** at me," she said.
   • He was shouting.   ....
   • He was angry.   ....
6 The meeting was in an hour. "Klein can **brief** me in the car," she said.
   • Klein knows nothing about the meeting.   ....
   • She needs to know things about the meeting.   ....
7 Barbara brushed past me, **muttering** about my father and his appalling manners.
   • Barbara was shouting.   ....
   • Barbara was happy.   ....
8 Bob paused and then went on. "Then the prosecuting attorney **insinuated** that she had stolen the money."
   • The attorney directly accused her of theft.   ....
   • Bob approved of what the attorney did.   ....
9 Whenever I give them some writing to do in the class they **whinge**.
   • They don't mind being given writing to do.   ....
   • The teacher finds the students' reaction annoying.   ....

2. *Sentences 1 to 9 contain a **speaking** verb. Based on the sentence, decide whether the statements which follow them are true or false.*

1 Whenever he meets Sally, Bernard just **clams up**.
   • Bernard is probably shy.   ....
   • Bernard is suddenly lost for words whenever he meets Sally.   ....
2 We all know Steve's won a scholarship to Cambridge, but does he have to **brag** about it all the time?
   • Steve annoys people when he talks about Cambridge.   ....
   • Steve is modest about his achievements.   ....
3 She shifted nervously in her chair. She was **waffling**, and the interviewer knew it.
   • She knew what she was talking about.   ....
   • The interviewer was impressed.   ....

3. *Listen and match. In which extract (1–5) is somebody ...*

A ... briefing some people on details?
B ... reeling off facts with surprising ease?   Extract 1 ☐
C ... whining and moaning constantly?   Extract 2 ☐
D ... clamming up with embarrassment?   Extract 3 ☐
E ... yelling angrily at somebody?
F ... muttering something indistinctly?   Extract 4 ☐
G ... waffling to hide lack of knowledge?   Extract 5 ☐
H ... bragging about his collection of paintings?

115

57 Speaking and Communicating II - Sport

Speaking and Communicating II

to bicker: to argue about unimportant things

They were bickering about/over which TV programme to watch.

to butt in (or into + obj): to interrupt when sb else is speaking or when two people are talking

I wish you wouldn't keep butting into our conversations.

Could I butt in for a moment?

to confide in sb: to tell sb a secret

If you confide in someone and get it off your chest, you'll feel better.

to gossip about sb/sth: to talk about other people's private lives [Note: **a gossip:** a person who likes gossiping]

She loves to gossip about the other teachers.

to implore sb (not) to do sth: (formal) to beg

He implored his father not to tell anyone.

to let slip that ...: to accidentally tell sb sth that you did not want them to know

The minister let slip that the government was preparing a new budget.

to nag sb (about sth): to constantly tell sb what to do and what not to do

He's always nagging me about the state of my room.

to natter (about sth): (informal) to chat about unimportant things

The two old ladies spent the entire journey nattering about their families.

to scold sb for doing sth: to tell sb off (quite formal)

I was always scolded at school for being late.

to tease sb (about sth): to make fun of sb in a cruel or playful way

The other children would tease me mercilessly about my weight.

I was always teasing her about her funny little walk.

Sport

to be all square: to have equal points. [Note: **two all:** two goals, two sets each]

After eighteen holes, Irons and Eastwood were all square.

to award a team a penalty: to give a team the possibility to score a goal, try, etc

Everton went ahead after twenty minutes, when they were awarded a penalty.

to clinch: to succeed in winning sth (a championship, the title, etc), having first had to fight long and hard for it

United clinched the title in the last match of the season.

a course: you play **golf** at a **golf course**/you watch **horse racing** at a **race course**

St Andrews in Scotland is the most famous golf course in the world.

a court: you play **volleyball/squash/ badminton/tennis/basketball** on a **court**

The hotel had two swimming pools and four tennis courts.

a field: the area of grass on which you play rugby/hockey

The school has a rugby field.

the first/second half: the period of play before/after the break in the middle of a game (**half-time**)

All the goals were scored in the second half.

to be the hot/firm favourite: to be the person/team that everyone believes and expects will win a race, match, etc

With Barcelona out of the competition, Arsenal are now hot favourites to win the cup.

nil: zero, primarily used in football [Note: **love:** zero, in tennis]

We beat them four - nil.

Strakis won the match six - love, six - love.

a pitch: the area of grass on which you play football/rugby/hockey

When the final whistle blew, hundreds of fans ran onto the pitch.

the runner(s)-up: the person or team who come(s) second in a race/tournament/championship

Who wants to come second? No one remembers the runner-up.

a scrappy match: a match which is not very good because neither team is playing well

City lost 1-0 to United in a boring and scrappy match.

to send (sb) off: to order sb to leave the field during a football /rugby/ hockey match because they have done sth seriously wrong, e.g. committed a foul

He was sent off for threatening the referee.

to shatter a record: to break a record by a large margin

His performance shattered all previous records.

to thrash: to beat sb/another team, etc very convincingly

Twelve goals to one! We didn't just beat them, we thrashed them!

an upset: a surprising result in which the person or team that everyone expects to lose beats the person or team that everyone expects to win [Note: **outsider**: one not thought likely to win]

In one of the biggest tennis upsets of the year, world number one Flavio Capurro was beaten in straight sets by fourteen-year-old Jan Kovic in yesterday's opening round of the Australian Open.

a winnning streak: a continuous series of successes

Chelsea's winning streak continued last night when they beat Liverpool 2-0 at home. Chelsea have now won nine matches in a row.

Practice

1. Match each situation outline with a **communication and speaking** verb from this unit.

   1. A person interrupting two people who are having a chat. ....
   2. A friend telling another friend about a personal problem. ....
   3. Two friends having a chat. ....
   4. Somebody begging somebody else not to drive at high speed on the icy road. ....
   5. A wife annoying her husband by continually telling him to put the top back on the toothpaste tube. ....
   6. Two bored housewives talking over the fence about the blonde woman who lives across the road from them. ....
   7. Children making fun of one of their classmates who has just had a particularly silly haircut. ....
   8. A mother telling her son off for losing his school bag. ....
   9. Two children arguing about whose turn it is to use the computer, driving their parents crazy in the process. ....
   10. A waitress accidentally telling her boss that one of her workmates is looking for another job. ....

2. Read the two texts below and decide which answer (A, B, C, or D) best fits each gap.

   A He was playing for his country now. He stood on the tee and looked down the first fairway. His caddy passed him a club. He told himself that this was an easy **1)** .... , and that England, his team, were **2)** .... favourites to win the match. He had to be mentally strong, and he reminded himself that the last time he had played here he had **3)** .... the course record by an amazing six strokes, that the last time England had played Listonia, England had **4)** .... them 18 - 2. The scoreboard behind him read England 3, Listonia 3. They were all **5)** .... He had to stay focused. He had won the Australian Open and been the runner- **6)** .... behind Tiger Irons in the US Masters. He was far better than his opponent. There would be no **7)** .... in this game. He was going to win. He walked up to his ball. One practice swing and swoosh. His club cut through the air. He heard the crowd gasp and he looked up .... He had missed the ball. Completely.

1	A court	B course	C pitch	D field
2	A hot	B heavy	C rank	D full
3	A burst	B cracked	C shattered	D splintered
4	A slapped	B smacked	C bashed	D thrashed
5	A equal	B balanced	C tied	D square
6	A over	B down	C up	D through
7	A upturns	B upstarts	C upstages	D upsets

   B It was the last match of the season between the top two teams in the division. The winner would **1)** .... the first division title. The loser would walk away with nothing. But, as so often happens, it turned out to be a **2)** .... and disappointing match. The occasion got the better of both teams, and the game was marred by a succession of ugly and unnecessary fouls. And it was one such foul that decided the game. City were **3)** .... a penalty in the closing minutes of the second **4)** ...., when United's Paul Peckham brought down Dean Chuli in the penalty area. Peckham was **5)** .... off and had to watch from the sidelines as Chuli scored the only goal of the game. One- **6)** .... So ended United's twelve-game winning **7)** .... and with it their dreams of their first championship in 25 years.

1	A reach	B seize	C clinch	D grasp
2	A scrappy	B grubby	C shabby	D scruffy
3	A appointed	B allowed	C awarded	D rewarded
4	A part	B half	C time	D act
5	A sent	B thrown	C given	D turned
6	A love	B nought	C zero	D nil
7	A stretch	B trot	C streak	D bounce

58 Talking (Reporting verbs)

to accuse: accused sb of doing sth
She accused him of stealing her pen.

to advise: advised sb (not) to do sth
Her lawyer advised her not to say anything.

to agree: agreed (not) to do sth
After hours of persuasion, she finally agreed to see a doctor.

to announce: announced that + change of tense
The company announced that it would be making 500 people redundant.

to assure: assured sb that + change of tense [Note: **to assure**: to tell sb sth will (not) happen and that therefore they should not worry]
The police assured me that he would be found guilty.

to beg: begged sb (not) to do sth
He begged her to marry him.

to blame: blamed sb/sth for sth/sth else **or** blamed sth on sb **or** sb/sth is/was to blame for sth/sth else [Note: **you have only (got) yourself to blame for...**: it is your fault and only your fault that sth bad happened to you]
He blamed the economic recession for the company's failure.
He blamed the company's failure on the economic recession.
He said the economic recession was to blame for the company's failure.

to claim: claimed that + change of tense **or** claim to do sth **or** (for actions that have happened) claim to have done sth
She claimed that she was related to the King.
Martin claimed to have a PhD in Physics.
The boy claimed to have seen an alien.

to complain: complained that + change of tense **or** complain about + noun or -ing form

He complained that he had too much work to do.
He complained about the food.
He complained about having to do so much work.

to compliment: complimented sb on + noun or -ing form **or** complimented sb on the way + change of tense
She complimented him on his cooking.
She complimented him on the way he had handled the situation.

to confirm: confirmed that + change of tense
The chairman confirmed that he was thinking of retiring at the end of the year.

to congratulate: congratulated sb on + noun or -ing form sth
They congratulated him on his results.
They congratulated him on passing his exam.

to demand: demanded that sb (should) do sth [Note: demand to (with the verbs **see/know** + question word/if + change of tense)]
He demanded that she give him back the money he had lent her.
He demanded to know where I had been.

to deny: denied doing/having done sth **or** that + change of tense
He denied having been/that he had been involved.

to describe: described + question word (how, what, etc) + change of tense **or** described + noun
He described how it had happened.
He described the picture.

to dissuade: dissuaded sb from doing sth
He dissuaded me from going bungee jumping.

to explain: explained that + change of tense **or** explain + question word (how, what, etc) + change of tense

He explained that he was late because he had missed the bus.
He explained how it worked.

to forgive: forgave sb for doing sth
He forgave her for denting his car.

to inform: informed sb + change of tense
They informed us that all flights had been cancelled.

to offer: offered to do sth **or** offered sb + noun
Tim offered to help Bob with his homework.
I offered him advice but he didn't want it.

to predict: predicted that + would
He predicted that the government would lose the next election.

to promise: promised sb that + would... **or** promised to do sth
He promised me that he wouldn't do it again.
He promised not to do it again.

to reveal: revealed + that + change of tense
In a statement to the press, Miss Lipski revealed that she had been married to Mr Nadel for six years.

to suggest: suggested (that) (I, he, they, etc) + past tense **or** that + (should) do sth **or** + possessive (my, his, etc) doing sth (formal)
I suggested he saw/he see/he should see/his seeing a specialist.

to threaten: threatened to do sth
He threatened to call the police if I didn't turn my music down.

to warn: warned sb not to do sth **or** about/of + noun **or** against doing sth
He warned us not to jump.
He warned us about the plug.
We were warned against going near the pool.

Practice

1. Choose the correct item.

1. She .... him not to speed but he wouldn't listen.
   A dissuaded   B promised   C begged

2. He stood up and suddenly .... that he was leaving.
   A informed   B announced   C advised

3. He .... them that he would call.
   A assured   B suggested   C offered

4. Sources .... that their manager had just resigned.
   A confirmed   B predicted   C described

5. We were .... that if we didn't pay within five days, we would be taken to court.
   A explained   B threatened   C informed

6. It was .... that the product be withdrawn from the market.
   A suggested   B revealed   C predicted

7. He .... to have won the football pools.
   A claimed   B denied   C confirmed

8. They .... me of breaking the vase.
   A forgave   B blamed   C accused

9. She .... him on passing the exam.
   A complimented   B congratulated   C complained

10. She .... that he pay her back.
    A confirmed   B demanded   C warned

2. For questions 1 to 10, complete the second sentence so that it has a similar meaning to the first sentence, using 3 to 8 words. You must include the word given in bold, which cannot be changed in any way.

1. "It's true that I've been asked to mediate in the dispute," he said.
   confirmed   He .... in the dispute.

2. "I had absolutely nothing to do with the theft of the paintings," he said.
   categorically   He .... to do with the theft of the paintings.

3. "Why don't we stay for another night?" she said.
   suggested   She .... more night.

4. "Be careful," she said to me. "The stairs are slippery."
   warned   She .... stairs.

5. "Kitty, I promise you that I will never go there again," said Tom.
   promised   Tom .... never go there again.

6. "If you don't turn your music down, I'm going to call the police," he said to me.
   threatened   He .... not turn my music down.

7. "It's your fault we missed the train," he said.
   blame   He said .... the train.

8. "If I were you, Bill, I'd keep a low profile for the next few weeks," she said.
   advised   She .... a low profile for the next few weeks.

9. "Okay, I'll go, but only if Sara goes with me," she said.
   agreed   She .... condition that Sara went with her.

10. "I'll give you a lift into town," said Paul to Jean.
    offered   Paul .... into town.

119

59 There is ... - Time I

There is ...

there's no call for sth: nobody wants (to buy/have/own) sth any more; [Note: **there is no call for sth that sb says/does:** what sb says/does is offensive and unnecessary]

We stopped selling records because there's no call for them any more. Everyone wants CDs.

There's no call for such rude behaviour.

there's no denying: everyone must/would admit that

There is no denying that, under this government, the country has made great leaps forward.

there's no harm in doing sth: you lose nothing by trying sth

He will almost certainly say no, but there is no harm in asking him, is there?

there's no need to: it is not necessary to

It's an informal meeting, so there is no need (for you) to wear a suit.

there's nothing like: nothing is better than

There's nothing like a long, hot bath to help you relax after a hard day at work.

there's no point (in) doing sth: doing sth would be a waste of time/serve no purpose

There's no point (in) asking him for more money. We both know he is going to say no.

there's no question of sth happening: sth will definitely not happen

There's no question of his being asked to resign.

there's no such thing as: sth does not exist

Some people say that there's no such thing as an honest politician.

there's no telling + question word: it is very difficult to know...
[Note: (with the same meaning): **There's no knowing ...**]

He's a very volatile man. There's no telling how he will react.

The situation is very uncertain. There's no knowing how things will turn out.

there's no way I ... : I absolutely refuse to ...

There's no way I'm going to let them get away with this.

Time I
prepositions of time

AT
3 o'clock, 10.30, etc
night
the weekend (UK)
midday, midnight
Christmas, Easter
bedtime

IN
the morning
the afternoon
May, April, July, etc
1998, 1756, 2005, etc
summer, spring, etc

ON
Monday, Tuesday, etc
Monday morning/ afternoon, etc
May 23, June 6, etc
my birthday, our anniversary
Christmas Day, New Year's Day
the weekend (USA)

at long last: finally

It seemed as if I had been waiting for ever for the letter, but at long last it came.

at times: sometimes, but not often

My degree course was very difficult. At times, I seriously thought about giving up.

day in, day out: happening every day, often with the result of becoming boring and tedious

It's the same old routine, day in day out. I really need a break.

every once in a while: occasionally

We don't go out very often. Every once in a while, we go to the cinema, but that's about it.

for (e.g. months) on end: continuously; for months/hours/days/weeks, etc

It was such an isolated place that sometimes I would go for days on end without seeing another human being.

from now on: starting from now

I've decided that from now on I'm going to do half an hour of yoga every day.

from the word go: from the very beginning of sth

This business was doomed to failure from the word go.

in the end: eventually

Everything turned out all right in the end.

in the meantime: between now and a particular time in the future

Your teacher is going to be twenty minutes late. So, in the meantime, I'd like you to do the phrasal verb exercise on page twenty.

on time: at the right time, punctually [Note: **in time:** early enough to do sth]

The train arrived on time.

"It's a miracle," she said, opening the door. "You are on time."

You're just in time for tea.

up until then: before a particular time in the past

Last year I read a book on the damage we are doing to the earth. Up until then, I really hadn't given the environment much thought.

Practice

1. *For questions 1 to 10, complete the second sentence so that it has a similar meaning to the first sentence, using 3 to 8 words. You must include the word given in bold, which cannot be changed in any way.*

1 "Nobody wants gas lamps these days," said the shopkeeper.
   call   "There .... gas lamps these days," said the shopkeeper.

2 "Phoning her now would be a waste of time," she said, looking at her watch.
   point   "There's .... her now," she said, looking at her watch.

3 He's very unpredictable and you never know what he might do next.
   telling He's very unpredictable and .... might do next.

4 "I refuse point blank to drive that," he said. "Look at it! It's a death trap!"
   way   "There is .... going to drive that," he said. "Look at it! It's a death trap!"

5 You can't beat a cup of tea to wake you up in the morning.
   like   There's .... you up in the morning.

6 Whatever you may think of him as a person, you have to admit that he is a superb football player.
   no   Whatever you may think of him as a person, there's .... a superb football player.

7 You could see if they have got your umbrella in the lost property office.
   harm   There's .... your umbrella in the lost property office.

8 "This government is not going to increase taxes - and that is final," said the Minister.
   question "There is .... up taxes," said the Minister.

9 "You don't have to shout," he said. "I'm not deaf."
   need   There's ....," he said. "I'm not deaf."

10 Flying horses do not exist!
   thing   There's .... a flying horse!

2. *Complete the following sentences with an appropriate preposition.*

1 I'm thinking of going to England .... **February**.
2 We waited and waited and still the bus didn't come. .... **the end**, we decided to walk.
3 It was incredibly difficult. .... **times**, I really thought we weren't going to make it.
4 I've just about had enough of my job. It's the same old routine, **day** .... **day** ....
5 "I'm going to get another tape-recorder. .... **the meantime**, could you read the questions to the listenings?" the teacher said.
6 When she went to university in 1947, she was confronted with the real world. .... **until then**, she had led an incredibly sheltered life.
7 "Things are going to change around here," the new manager said. "........ **now** ...., all executive decisions will come through me."
8 Her boss had had it in for her .... **the word go**.
9 After years of humiliation, it all changed. We started winning everything. .... **long last**, we had a team we could be proud of.
10 It was a great job but I would be away from home for **weeks** .... **end**.
11 My grandparents threw a big party .... their **fiftieth wedding anniversary**.
12 Every **once** .... **a while**, she throws a massive tantrum but generally she's very well-behaved.
13 You've been late for the two meetings. Please try to be .... **time** for this one.

60a Time II

all along: all the time, from the very beginning
None of it was true. He had been lying to her all along.

all day long: for the whole day
It rained all day long.

all the time: very often
I love that restaurant. I go there all the time.

any minute now: very soon, within the next few minutes
The train should be here any minute now.

every so often/every now and then: occasionally
He was reading a letter. It must have been funny, because every so often he'd burst out laughing.

for three days/the third day running: one day after another for a total of three days
He missed training for three days running.

for quite a while: for a long time
I haven't seen them for quite a while.

for yonks: (inf) for a very long time
I've known him for yonks.

from time to time: occasionally
We see them from time to time, but not as often as we used to, now that we've moved.

having: when (introduces the first of two connected actions in the past and is followed by a past participle form)
Having taken my details, the policeman told me I could go.

in the long run: over a long period of time in the future
His decision to accept the transfer will pay off in the long run.

in a row/on the trot: one after the other
They have won eight games in a row.
He has missed six classes on the trot.

in next to no time: very (and surprisingly) quickly
I thought it would take ages, but we got there in next to no time.

long-lasting: lasting for a long time
long-lasting peace/effects
It is hoped that this meeting will pave the way for long-lasting peace.

long-lost: sb or sth you haven't seen for a long time
One day her long-lost sister whom she'd last seen thirty years before, turned up out of the blue.

long-running: that has continued for many years (used only before a noun)
'Coronation Street' is the longest-running soap opera on British television.

long-standing: that has continued or existed for a long time
a long-standing agreement/ arrangement/argument, etc
They have a long-standing arrangement to go to the cinema on Saturdays.

long-winded: (for speeches, lectures, explanations, essays) lasting for a long time and using far too many words – and being boring as a result

All I got was a long-winded explanation that I couldn't understand.

on: when; + noun/-ing form
On arriving/my arrival in Chile, I was informed that my luggage had been lost.

on the dot: exactly (for time)
You must be there for your interview at 9 o'clock on the dot.

outright: complete, total
That was outright cheating, no matter what you say.

right away: immediately
I could see right away that something was wrong.

round the clock: all day and all night, without a break
We will have to work round the clock if we want to get this finished in time.

seldom: (formal) not very often
He seldom makes public appearances.
Seldom have we had such appalling weather.

shortly: very soon
This film will be over shortly, then you can switch channels.

straight away: immediately
I could tell straight away that something was wrong.

the other day: (inf) a few days ago
I saw John the other day. He sends his regards.

Practice

1. One, two or three of the options (A, B, C or D) can complete each of the sentences below. Circle them.

1 .... she would look up and smile.
  A Every so often   C Seldom
  B From time to time D Every now and then

2 He's missed four classes ....
  A in a row   C in the long run
  B on the trot   D running

122

3 We'll be there ....
   A shortly   C the other day
   B any minute now   D in next to no time

4 We have known each other for ....
   A quite a while   C yonks
   B long-standing   D all the time

5 He told me to do it ....
   A outright   C on the dot
   B right away   D straight away

6 .... hearing the news, she burst out laughing.
   A Having   B When   C With   D On

7 We'll have to work .... if we want to meet this deadline.
   A round the clock   C all along
   B in the long run   D all day long

8 He was amazed to see his long-.......................... brother after so many years.
   A running   C winded
   B lasting   D lost

9 The writer J D Salinger was .... seen in public.
   A outright   C shortly
   B right away   D seldom

10 It was the most boring, long-.......................... speech I have ever had the misfortune to hear.
   A lasting   C standing
   B winded   D running

2. Replace the phrases in bold with an appropriate *time word/phrase* from this unit.

1 Sheila's been in her new job **for a long time** now, hasn't she?
2 The play will be starting **within the next few minutes**.
3 You will find that **over a long period of time in the future** your investments will pay off.
4 I'll just pop the dish in the microwave and dinner will be ready **very quickly**.
5 The factory operates **all day and all night, without a break**, so the employees have to work shifts.
6 The train for Little Diddington leaves at 8 o'clock **exactly**.

3. Complete the following responses, using appropriate *time words/phrases* from this unit.

1 A: Have you seen Simon lately?
   B: Yes, I saw him only ....
2 A: I don't know what could have happened to him. He's never late.
   B: Don't worry. I'm sure he'll be here ....
3 A: That TV series seems to have been going on for ever.
   B: Yes, it's the .... series there is.
4 A: Waiter, could I have my bill, please?
   B: Yes, sir, I'll bring it ....
5 A: So, you knew from the beginning of the story who the murderer was?
   B: Yes, I knew ....
6 A: Hasn't the film started yet?
   B: No, but it's going to start ....

4. The words/phrases in bold have not been used properly. Correct them by replacing them with more appropriate ones.

1 She was busy working on her thesis **all along**, not even stopping to sleep.
2 The professor gave a **long-lasting** speech that nearly sent us all to sleep.
3 Don't worry, you don't have to wait. I'll deal with this **outright**.
4 **On** put on his coat, he walked out the door.
5 We still see David **in next to no time**, even though he has moved to the other end of town.
6 What an amazing athlete! He has won ten races **shortly**.

123

60b Time III

anywhere between five minutes and thirty minutes: as little as five minutes or as long as thirty minutes

Depending on the traffic, it could take you anywhere between fifty minutes and two hours.

beforehand: before sth happened/has happened

Do not attempt to change a light bulb without switching off the power beforehand.

for the best part of: for almost

I've been waiting for you for the best part of an hour.

to be cutting it fine: (informal) not to be leaving yourself much time to arrive on time

That will only give us twenty minutes to get to the theatre and that is cutting it very fine.

to ensue: to follow as a result

Having performed several fire drills, the students knew what to do in the event of a fire without panic ensuing.

give or take: approximately (perhaps a few minutes/hours more or a few minutes/hours less)

The journey should take you two hours, give or take a few minutes.

in ten minutes flat: in exactly ten minutes; (*flat* is used to emphasize the fact that you did sth very quickly)

I got ready in ten minutes flat.

get a move on: (informal) hurry up

Get a move on! We're late.

it's just gone one o'clock: it is a couple of minutes past one o'clock

What's the time? It's just gone half past three.

to be half-way through sth/doing sth: to be in the middle of doing sth

I was halfway through my dinner when the phone rang.

in the meantime: between now and a particular time in the future **or** between two events in the past

Normal service will be resumed shortly; in the meantime, here's some light music.

more often than not: very often

More often than not, he was broke.

prior to: (formal) before
Opp: subsequent to

Prior to our arrival in New York, we will be serving a light snack.

protracted: lasting for much longer than you expected

protracted negotiations/delays

There was a bitter and protracted struggle between the union and the management during the strike.

to be (a bit/rather) pushed/pressed for time: to be busy and not to have much time to spare

I'd love to stay and chat, but I'm a bit pressed for time. Why don't we meet up next week?

round/around about: approximately; used for money (esp with the verbs **cost** and **spend**) and time (with the verbs **take** and **spend**)

It takes me round about an hour to commute to work every day.

You'll need to take round about £500 for spending money on holiday. Meals will cost round about £200 on top of that.

roughly: approximately

It will take you roughly 30 minutes to get to the city centre.

to be running late: to be delayed

They were running late at the dentist's so I had to wait longer than I'd expected for my appointment.

to schedule sth: to formally arrange sth for a particular time

I've scheduled your meeting with Mr Crofts for Monday 16th May.

sharp: exactly, precisely (for time)

The bank opens at 9 o'clock sharp.

to be slow: (for a watch or clock) to show an earlier time than the correct time **Opp:** to be fast

Oh no! My watch is twenty minutes slow. I'll be late for work.

You don't need to hurry; that clock on the wall is fast.

for five solid hours: for five hours without stopping

I've been writing this for five solid hours and I still haven't finished.

in a tick: very soon

We'll be there in a tick.

The doctor will be with you in a tick.

for the time being: between now and a particular time in the future

He's looking for a full-time job in London. For the time being, he's working part-time locally.

to play for time: to try to delay sth because you don't want it to happen or need time to think about it

Being unsure about the prospective merger, the board of directors were playing for time.

124

60b

Practice

1. *Read the text below and decide which answer (A, B, C or D) best fits each gap.*

"I'll be with you in a **1)** ....," she said, turning to another customer. I was **2)** .... late; I couldn't afford to wait. "Sorry," I said, "It's just that I'm a bit **3)** .... for time." She ignored me. I looked at my watch. Had I known **4)** .... that the shop was going to be so busy, I wouldn't have gone in. But I didn't know and now I was half-**5)** .... buying a tie and the sales assistant had my credit card. My interview was in an hour's time, but it was across town. The journey would take **6)** .... fifty minutes. It was time for drastic action.

1	A beat	C stroke
	B tick	D chime
2	A pushing	C running
	B heading	D turning
3	A short	C slow
	B pressed	D pulled
4	A prior	C in anticipation
	B beforehand	D formerly
5	A way through	C in the middle of
	B way along	D through the middle of
6	A give or take	C anywhere between
	B round about	D in rough

2. *Circle the correct item.*

1 Reginald was **cutting it fine / playing for time**, with only five minutes to spare before his appointment.
2 **It had just gone / It was halfway through** 12 o'clock when Cinderella left the ball.
3 My watch is **slow / fast**. It gains five minutes every day.
4 They waited for **give or take / the best part of** an hour, then started the meeting without him.
5 He had been working **more often than not / for ten solid hours**, and was exhausted.
6 We had better **get a move on / schedule** if we want to catch that plane.
7 Don't forget that the office closes at four thirty **sharp / roughly** on Fridays.

3. *Read the text below and decide which answer (A, B, C or D) best fits each gap.*

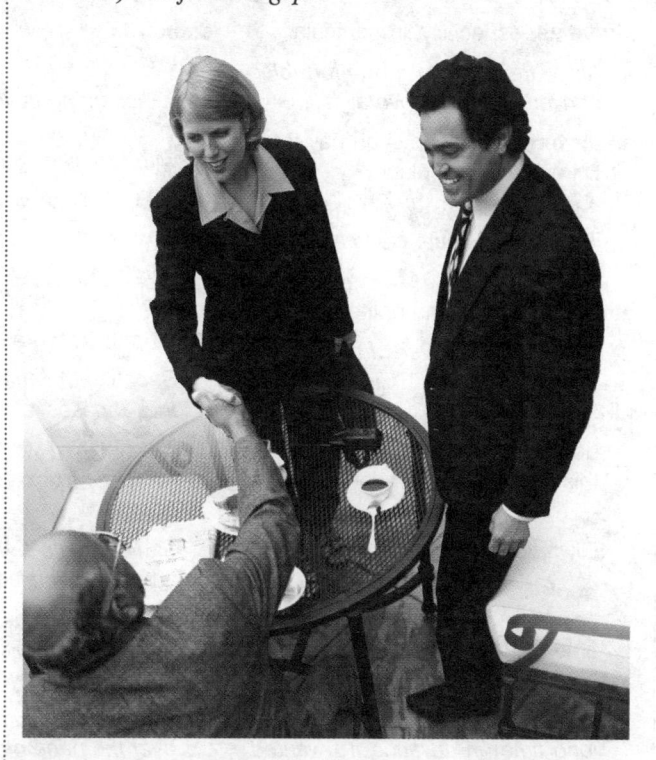

He was always late. More **1)** .... than not, it was because he had overslept – which was why she had **2)** .... the meeting for the afternoon. Where was he? She had been sitting there for five minutes, smiling like an idiot. From across the table, the two men were looking at her impatiently. Where was he? She didn't want to do it alone. She decided to **3)** .... for time. "Nice weather for the time of year," she said. "Yes," they replied in unison. A long, **4)** .... silence **5)** .... She had to start. She had no choice. "My partner has obviously been unavoidably detained, but he will be here shortly. In the **6)** ...., I'll fill you in on some of the background to this project ..."

1	A common	C usual
	B generally	D often
2	A scheduled	C agreed
	B appointed	D set
3	A wait	C delay
	B play	D hole
4	A prominent	C prolific
	B profuse	D protracted
5	A ensued	C encompassed
	B encroached	D enclosed
6	A time being	C meantime
	B interlude	D short term

125

61 Travel

above all: especially, in particular
Air travel is comfortable, convenient and above all fast.

an air fare: the money you pay for a ticket to fly on a plane
£400 for a week in Australia? That's very cheap. Does it include the air fare?

attentive: helpful and polite
The hotel staff were friendly and attentive.

to boast: if a place (a hotel, a resort) boasts a particular facility, it has this facility (brochure language)
The Grondheim Hotel boasts three Olympic-size swimming pools.

to book in advance: to reserve a ticket, a hotel room, etc, some time before you travel, stay in a hotel, etc
I was advised to book well (= a long time) in advance if I wanted to be sure of getting a good seat.

to confiscate sth: to take sth away from sb as a punishment
He confiscated all the undeclared goods they had hidden in their luggage.

to consist of: to be made up of
The Smugglers holiday resort consisted of a hotel, two luxury swimming pools and a small shop that sold newspapers.

crystal clear waters: transparent water
From our balcony we could see the crystal clear waters of the Caribbean.

a customs officer: an official who checks your bags when you go through customs
The men in uniform over there are customs officers.

direct flight: not stopping anywhere en route
Are there any direct flights to Canada?

discerning: sb who has got good taste and enjoys expensive things
A discerning traveller likes staying in expensive and tasteful hotels with excellent cuisine.

to erupt: if a volcano erupts, it explodes
When was the last time Mount Vesuvius erupted?

a five-star hotel: a luxury hotel
Because they have lots of money, the Joneses always stay in five-star hotels.

to get away from: escape from/leave behind
San Carlos is an ideal place to get away from a miserable winter.

to haggle (over the price of sth): to argue with sb over the price of sth you want to buy
He haggled with the stallkeeper over the price of the tomatoes.

high/peak season: the time of the year when most people take their holidays
Opp: low season/off season
The tickets are cheap because it is low season.

to be jet-lagged: to feel very tired and disorientated as a result of having flown somewhere
By the time I got to my hotel, I was so jet-lagged that I could hardly remember my name.

to be littered with sth: to have been made untidy and unpleasant by sth
The crowded streets were littered with rubbish.

a local speciality: if a particular kind of food or dish is a local speciality, it is common and particularly good in a certain area
The seafood here is a local speciality. Don't miss out on it!

to look onto: to have a view of
Our bedroom looked onto the beach.

to be off the beaten track: to be a long way away from the places that tourists usually visit
We hate tourist resorts. We like to go to places that are off the beaten track.

to be on offer: (i) to be available to buy or use (ii) be sold at a reduced price
The hotel has a wide range of sports facilities on offer.
Beach towels are on offer at the moment; only £3!

running water: water that comes from a tap
When we got there, we discovered that there was no electricity and no running water.

to soak up the sun: to sunbathe
While away your time soaking up the sun beside one of the hotel's three magnificent swimming pools.

a stopover: a short stay somewhere during a long plane journey
On our way back from Uruguay to France, we are going to have a two-day stopover in New York.

stretch of beach: an area of beach
Apparently, the stretch of beach between the two hotels gets very crowded at weekends.

a tariff: (formal) the price you pay for a room in a hotel
The tariff for the room must, by law, be prominently displayed.

to touch down: to land (for aircraft)
The aeroplane touched down and then taxied along the runway.

to while away the/your time: to spend time in a pleasant way doing sth that does not require too much physical activity (+ing form)
I whiled away my time in the doctor's waiting room leafing through old magazines.

126

Practice

1. *Read the text below and decide which answer (A,B,C or D) best fits each gap.*

The Brochure and the Dream - The Bay Hotel, San Leonardo

In the north-west corner of the island paradise Isla Perlita, nestling in the shadow of Mount Machu, lies the sleepy village of San Lorenzo. Off the beaten **1)** ...., there is nothing out of the ordinary about this quaint little village - nothing, that is, apart from the magnificent five – **2)** .... Bay Hotel. The Bay, as it is known locally, is a recent development catering for **3)** .... travellers who enjoy luxury holiday-making. Famous throughout the island for the outstanding quality of its accommodation and the excellence of its cuisine, the Bay **4)** .... 30 guest suites, each with a charm and character of its own. Each suite looks **5)** .... Falmer Beach, commanding breathtaking views of the four miles of white sand, which gently shelves into the **6)** .... clear waters of the Crepuscan Sea. At the heart of the Bay Hotel is personal, efficient and unobtrusive service. **7)** .... staff anticipate your every need in an atmosphere of quiet professionalism and genuine friendliness. **8)** ...., the Bay Hotel is a place to get **9)** .... from the stresses of everyday life, and whether it is **10)** .... away the hours **11)** .... up the sun or taking advantage of the wide range of recreational activities that the hotel has **12)** .... offer, you can be sure that a holiday at the Bay truly is the holiday of a lifetime. Air Perlita flies direct to Isla Perlita once a fortnight from Gatwick. It is advisable to book well in **13)** ...., especially during **14)** .... season (January through March) as flights fill up quickly. For air **15)** ...., hotel tariffs and general terms and conditions, please see pages 67 and 68 of this brochure.

1	**A** path	**B** track	**C** road	**D** way
2	**A** starred	**B** stars	**C** star	**D** starring
3	**A** disconcerting	**B** discerning	**C** distinctive	**D** discriminated
4	**A** announces	**B** claims	**C** asserts	**D** boasts
5	**A** back on	**B** onto	**C** into	**D** down
6	**A** crystal	**B** sky	**C** diamond	**D** pearl
7	**A** Preoccupied	**B** Attentive	**C** Concentrated	**D** Undivided
8	**A** All over	**B** For all	**C** Above all	**D** All along
9	**A** out	**B** over	**C** off	**D** away
10	**A** whiling	**B** wearing	**C** wending	**D** winding
11	**A** soaking	**B** drawing	**C** taking	**D** absorbing
12	**A** in	**B** for	**C** on	**D** at
13	**A** anticipation	**B** time	**C** hand	**D** advance
14	**A** high	**B** on	**C** full	**D** open
15	**A** fees	**B** rates	**C** fares	**D** tenders

2. *Circle the correct item.*

The Holiday and the Nightmare

We were jet- **1) lagged / worn** before we arrived in Isla Perlita. We had made a number of unscheduled **2) turnovers / stopovers** on our way to the island and all in **3) total / all** our journey took 36 hours. Hardly a(n) **4) express / direct** flight! It would have been quicker had we walked. Bearing in mind that this was high season, we probably should have been suspicious at being the only passengers, but it wasn't until we actually **5) touched / landed** down on the island that we began to wonder why we had believed what had been written in the brochure. The airport building was the size of a garden shed and the customs **6) officer / attendant** who searched our bags (and who, for no reason **7) confined / confiscated** our belongings) also turned out to be the island's only taxi driver and porter at the Bay Hotel. We were dropped off in San Lorenzo's main street. Or should I say its only street. San Lorenzo **8) consisted / comprised** of one dusty street, six shacks, two dogs and an empty telephone box. From there on, things went rapidly downhill. The Bay Hotel was half-built, did not have **9) flowing / running** water or electricity and was staffed by a pensioner and the taxi driver, Johnny Paraguay, who spent most of his time asleep in his bedroom. The meals lovingly prepared by the chef (Johnny Paraguay again) included such local **10) specialities / specials** as coconuts, tinned peas and coconuts with tinned peas. Falmer Beach was a long **11) stretch / sequence** of grey sand **12) littered / teeming** with rubbish. The hotel pool resembled a stagnant pond and we were unable to swim in the sea because it was full of poisonous jelly fish and man-eating sharks. Recreational activities included find the waiter, **13) handle / haggle** with Johnny Paraguay for our passports, and on our third day, run as fast as we could from San Lorenzo as Mount Machu, the supposedly extinct volcano, **14) burst / erupted** .

62 Under, Over and Out

an outburst: a sudden explosion of anger

I wanted to apologise for my outburst last night. I hope you know I didn't mean the things I said.

an outcry: an angry protest by a lot of people

The government's decision to privatise the rail network has provoked a huge public outcry.

an outfit: a set of clothes, especially women's clothes

Do you like my new outfit? I bought it for Paul's wedding.

outlandish: very strange and unusual

outlandish ideas/pair of trousers, etc

Her clothes were outlandish, as were her hair and make-up.

outlook: attitude to life and the world

My outlook on life has changed a lot since Jamie was born.

outrageous: (i) shocking and unfair (ii) unusual and amusingly shocking

Have you seen the prices they are charging in that shop? They are outrageous.

In walked Cheri wearing an outrageous hat.

Have you seen the outrageous colour they have painted their house?

from/at the outset: from/at the beginning

You must be prepared to work hard on this course from the outset.

outstanding: (i) excellent (ii) not yet paid, solved or done (of debts, problems, work)

an outstanding athlete/student

The facilities at the hotel were truly outstanding.

Most work has been handed in but there is still one project outstanding.

to outweigh: to have greater importance than

The advantages of the scheme far outweigh the disadvantages.

overgrown: if a garden is overgrown, it is covered in untidy plants

Her garden was overgrown and littered with rusty cans.

overlook: (i) to ignore and forgive sb's mistake (ii) if a building, room or window overlooks a particular place, it offers a view of it

I'll overlook your carelessness just this once.

He's got an amazing flat which overlooks the Coliseum.

overseas: outside your own country and across the seas; often used with the verbs **live** and **work**

He lives overseas.

What I would really like to do is work overseas.

overwhelming: very big and strong; used for abstract things (not people, buildings, etc)
[Note: **an overwhelming victory**: a total victory in which the opponent is completely defeated]

I suddenly felt an overwhelming desire to shout.

The support we have received for this project has been overwhelming.

the underdog: the person/team that is thought to be weaker than their opponent in a competition/game, election, etc – and therefore unlikely to win

Just because he's the underdog doesn't mean he can't win.

to underestimate: to think that sth/sb is weaker/smaller/shorter/safer/cheaper, etc than they really are

We underestimated the time it would take us to cross the mountains.

underhand: dishonest

underhand tactics/dealings

Gerald is far too honest to do anything so underhand.

to undermine: to make sb's confidence or authority weaker or less effective

By constantly questioning his decisions, she was trying to undermine his authority.

understatement: a statement which does not fully express the extent to which sth is true.

The door opened and in walked John. "It's a bit cold," he said. It was something of an understatement as it was absolutely freezing.

to be underway: (i) to have already started (ii) to start moving (for transport)

Plans to extradite the wanted men are already underway.

Food will be available in the cafeteria once the ferry gets underway.

Practice

1. *The sentences below contain a number of gaps. Each gap corresponds to one missing word. Half of each of the missing words is given at the end of each line in which a gap appears. The other half of the missing word is formed by adding either **under**, **over**, or **out**. Complete the sentences. An example has been done for you.*

0 The decision to close the local hospital caused such a public *out***cry** that the authorities decided to re-examine their options and keep it open.

1 He doesn't live in this country any more. He lives ....**seas**.

2 Westwood's clothes are nothing if not interesting, but they are so ....**landish** that no one in their right mind would actually wear them. One of her ....**fits** is made entirely out of dried banana skins.

128

14 It is yet another in a long line of failures to solve the unemployment problem and it is bound to further ....**mine** the public's confidence in this government.
15 She stormed out of the room and slammed the door behind her. Edward stood with his mouth open, astonished by this sudden, unexpected ....**burst** of emotion.
16 The prices in that restaurant are ....**rageous**. Even a glass of water costs £10!

2. *Complete the sentences below using words from this unit.*

1 It is totally unfair, ... even, that the government can get away with this new tax.
2 He was refused credit because he had so many .... debts.
3 Plans are already .... to put computers into every primary school in the country.
4 People who live and work .... are generally exempt from taxation in their country of origin.
5 Your opponent is stronger than you think, so don't .... him.
6 We bought the cottage chiefly because it .... some breathtakingly beautiful Lake District scenery.
7 Their decision to abolish the law has caused a huge public ....
8 She bought herself four pairs of shoes and three designer ....
9 This latest accident is bound to .... the public's confidence in the country's railway system.
10 The path that led to Sleeping Beauty's palace was .... with the weeds of a whole century.

3 The more we looked into it, the clearer it became that the advantages of owning a house far ....**weighed** those of renting, so we decided to buy.
4 A bit cold? That's an ....**statement** if ever I heard one. It's absolutely freezing.
5 You did not follow the instructions correctly. I'll ....**look** it this time as you are new to the company.
6 Brazil versus Canada. The World Cup. I'll be supporting Canada because they stand very little chance of winning and I always support the ....**dog**.
7 Since his accident, his ....**look** on life has changed. He no longer worries about small, inconsequential things and he now gives far greater importance to his family and friends.
8 He felt an ....**whelming** sense of relief as the train, which had been standing in the station for over twenty minutes, finally got ....**way**. He was leaving his past behind, moving on. It was a new beginning.
9 He was an ....**standing** athlete. He won the European Championship on four different occasions, he was twice world champion and won five Olympic gold medals.
10 Don't ....**estimate** Boxley United. They may only be a Second Division club, but they have got a lot of experienced players. Beating them won't be as easy as you think.
11 He cheated in the maths exam, you say? Not George. He's such an honest, decent student. I can't believe that he'd be involved in anything ....**hand**.
12 Stop worrying. Setting up and running a business isn't easy. We knew that from the ....**set**, from the very first day we opened the shop. Things will get better.
13 The gate was hanging off its hinges, but it still managed to creak as I pushed it open. The garden was ....**grown** with weeds and littered with rusty cans. I walked to the door and knocked.

63 Unhappy and Happy - Un... and In... Adjectives

◆

to burst into tears/out crying: to suddenly start crying **Opp:** to burst into laughter/out laughing

When I told her the news, she burst into tears/out crying.

cheerful: happy and positive

Everyone likes someone with a cheerful disposition.

to be desperately unhappy: to be extremely unhappy

He was desperately unhappy in that job. I'm not surprised he quit.

to be/feel despondent: to be/feel unhappy and depressed, because you have failed or you have little hope of succeeding at sth

Of course we felt despondent when we lost, but at least we know we gave it our best.

to be/feel down in the dumps: (informal) to be depressed

She was down in the dumps because of her exam results.

to be elated: to be extremely happy especially because you have just been successful (passed an exam, won sth, etc)

England had won. The manager and the players were elated.

to mope around: wander around looking and feeling unhappy

Stop moping around the house all day and go out and find yourself another job.

to be over the moon: (informal) to be very happy

I bet your parents were over the moon when you told them that you were moving back to England.

to perk up: to become/make sb happier and feel more positive

She's been a bit depressed recently, so I thought I'd take her to the Ritz for dinner. That should perk her up.

to be pleased: (i) + with + noun: to be happy and satisfied with (ii) + that clause: happy (iii) + infinitive: to be happy to

She seemed very pleased with her presents.

We are very pleased that you have decided not to emigrate.

I was very pleased to hear that you had been promoted.

to be thrilled to bits: (informal) to be very happy and excited

She was thrilled to bits when she found out she had landed a part in Spielberg's latest film.

to be on the verge of tears: to be just about to start crying

I saw she was on the verge of tears when she received the bad news.

Un... and In... Adjectives

Note: all the adjectives below can be used before or after a noun

inaccessible: impossible to reach

In winter the cabins at the top of the mountain are virtually inaccessible.

incessant: continuing without stopping

I'm fed up with your incessant complaining.

incompetent: not having the ability to do a particular job properly

The Minister of Transport was shown to be incompetent when his privatisation plans failed.

incorrigible: sb who has bad habits that you think they will not be able to break

He is an incorrigible liar.

indiscreet: sb who is careless about what they do or say

Why on earth did you tell Joanne? You know how indiscreet she is.

innocuous: harmless, not dangerous

This innocuous-looking frog is the most venomous creature on earth.

interminable: taking a very long time and being very boring as a result

interminable delays

I refuse to sit through another of his interminable speeches.

intermittent: happening often but not at regular intervals

We can expect an overcast day, with intermittent showers.

intricate: complicated and containing many small details

an intricate design/plot

intriguing: interesting (mysterious or strange)

He was an intriguing man. None of us knew anything about his past.

inviting: very attractive and tempting

The restaurant looked cosy and inviting.

uncalled-for: offensive and unnecessary

He was only trying to help. The way you reacted was totally uncalled-for.

uncanny: strange and difficult to explain; most often used with **ability/resemblance/knack**

He has this uncanny knack of being in the right place at the right time.

uneventful: a period of time during which nothing exciting happens

Until he won the lottery he had led a pretty uneventful life.

unflappable: sb who remains calm and level-headed in a crisis or in a very difficult situation

The Greek coach had chosen his most unflappable player to take their last penalty.

unforeseen: sth (problem/difficulty) one did not expect to happen

Barring any unforeseen problems, we should have the building finished by next Tuesday.

ungainly: big, awkward, clumsy

Despite his ungainly air, he is amazingly agile.

uninhabited: (of place) where nobody lives

The tiny village had for some years been uninhabited, everybody having moved to the town.

unprovoked: if an attack is unprovoked, you are attacked in some way having done nothing to deserve it or cause it to happen

He was injured in what is believed to be a totally unprovoked attack.

unruly: badly behaved, undisciplined

The children were running round and screaming in a most unruly manner.

Practice

1. Someone has already completed this multiple choice exercise. Decide whether the answers given are correct or incorrect by putting a tick (✓) or a cross (✗) in the space that appears at the end of each question. If the answer is incorrect, circle the correct item.

1 His teacher said that she was very .... with the progress that he had made.
   A cheerful   C pleased
   B glad   (D) elated   .....

2 Naturally, her parents were thrilled to .... when they found out she had passed the exam with an A.
   (A) shreds   C goodness
   B heaven   D bits   .....

3 If you are so .... unhappy, why don't you leave him?
   A wholly   C vastly
   (B) bitterly   D desperately   .....

4 There's no need to get so .... about being turned down. There are other advertising agencies out there, you know.
   A destitute   C despondent
   B descendant   (D) despicable   .....

5 I know she's a bit miserable at the moment, but she'll soon .... up when she finds out that I've booked us a two-week holiday in Barbados.
   A perk   C pump
   B look   (D) joy   .....

6 When I told her the news, she burst into ....
   A laughing   (C) tears
   B crying   D happiness   .....

7 We're over the ....! Who wouldn't be? We've just won £1 million!
   (A) moon   C stars
   B clouds   D planet   .....

8 All he has done since losing his job is .... around the house all day.
   (A) mourn   B depress
   C mope   D wallow   .....

9 She's a bit down in the .... at the moment – her husband has just lost his job.
   A world   B dumps
   (C) heart   D bottom   .....

10 I could tell from her face that she was on the .... of bursting into tears.
   A limit   C border
   (B) edge   D verge   .....

2. Match each description with one of the in... or un... adjectives from the unit.

1 A village that is difficult or impossible to reach. ....
2 Annoying noises that will not stop. ....
3 An attack for which there is no apparent cause. ....
4 A boring speech that went on and on for a very long time. ....
5 A class or a child that is very difficult to control. ....
6 A liar or cheat who is incapable of behaving decently. ....
7 An island on which nobody lives. ....
8 A remark that is unnecessarily rude or unfair and liable to offend someone or hurt their feelings. ....
9 A pattern or argument, made up of small, complicated parts and which has been expertly put together. ....
10 An idea or work of art which is very interesting because it is strange or mysterious. ....
11 Someone who carelessly gives away your secrets. ....
12 A journey on which, or a day in which, nothing interesting or unusual happens. ....
13 Something (a particular noise, rain showers, etc) which happens more than once but at irregular intervals. ....
14 A problem which wasn't expected. ....
15 A person who does not panic in stressful or difficult situations. ....
16 A person who is very bad at his or her job. ....
17 An adolescent whose movements look awkward and clumsy. ....
18 An ability or coincidence which is surprising and difficult to explain. ....
19 A thing or remark that is neither dangerous nor harmful. ....
20 An offer, smell, sight, which you find very attractive. ....

131

64 Verbs I

to double-cross: to cheat sb you have just committed a crime with

In this new novel, Pete double-crosses his partner in crime and runs off with the money.

to rig: to illegally arrange the result of an election

The Opposition leader claimed that the election was rigged.

to swindle: to get money from sb by deceiving them

He managed to swindle the shop out of £3,000 in three months.

*

to carve: to cut meat into slices

He put a huge turkey on the table. "Will you carve?" he asked.

to mow: to cut grass

Your lawn needs mowing.

to slash: to cut sth violently with a knife

He looked at his car. Someone had slashed the tyres.

to trim: to make sth neat by cutting away untidy pieces

Your hair needs trimming.

You mow the lawn and I'll trim the hedge.

*

to plummet: to fall dramatically (e.g. for prices)

The price of oil continues to plummet and has now reached an all-time low of 50 cents a barrel.

to plunge: (i) to fall dramatically (for prices and temperatures) (ii) to dive into water (iii) to move forwards and then fall a long way down

The temperature plunged to a record low.

He plunged into the sea and swam towards the shore.

The car crashed through the barrier and plunged over the cliff.

to slump: to suddenly or dramatically fall (for prices and business)

We were doing very well for the first three months of this year and then, for no discernible reason, our sales slumped.

*

to die down: to become less intense (without necessarily disappearing)

We will have to wait for the storm to die down before we attempt to rescue them.

to fizzle out: to end and disappear in a weak and disappointing way

The protest against the new tax soon fizzled out as the government would not bow to the protestors' demands.

to peter out: to gradually disappear and come to an end

The rain eventually petered out.

to wear off: to stop having an effect

You'll be fine for a couple of hours, but when the anaesthetic wears off you will be in some pain.

*

to bug: to put very small listening devices somewhere so as to listen to and/or record conversations

Be careful what you say, as the room may be bugged.

to eavesdrop: to intentionally listen to the private conversations of other people

He stood outside the room eavesdropping on their conversation.

to overhear: to unintentionally hear sb talking to sb else

As I walked past his office, I overheard him tell his secretary that he was thinking of resigning.

to tap: (a telephone): to put a very small listening device in so as to listen to telephone conversations

Suspicious noises led me to believe that my phone was being tapped.

*

to dig up: to find sth which has remained hidden for a long time

We know she had cosmetic surgery about ten years ago. See what you can dig up about that.

to stumble on: to find by chance

A man who was out walking his dog stumbled on the treasure.

*

to shadow/to tail: to follow and watch sb closely

The police have been shadowing/tailing her for a week.

to stalk: to follow and try to get near a person or animal in order to attack them

The cat was hiding in the long grass, stalking a mouse.

*

to banish: to send sb out of their native country as a punishment for sth they have done

For her part in the plot, the King banished her from England.

to evacuate: to have to/ to force sb to leave a building or area because it is dangerous

Once the hurricane warning had been given, it took the authorities three hours to evacuate the village.

to evict: to force sb to leave the flat or house they live in because they have broken a law or the contract

They were evicted when they didn't pay the rent.

to expel: to dismiss sb from school permanently because they have done sth very bad

She was expelled from school for playing practical jokes on the teacher.

*

to climb: to steadily increase (for money and temperature)

By mid-afternoon, the temperature had climbed to 37°.

to rocket: to increase dramatically (for prices)

House prices have rocketed by 65% in the last ten months.

to soar: to increase dramatically (for prices and temperatures)

Soaring inflation has made it impossible for people to manage.

*

to curb: (for inflation, the rising tide of inner-city violence, the spread of a disease, etc) to do sth to stop sth bad from continuing/getting worse

A further 100 tax inspectors have been appointed to help curb increasing instances of tax evasion.

to hamper: to make movement or progress difficult

Rescue efforts have been hampered by bad weather.

to hinder: to prevent or delay progress

He is hindered by his shyness.

*

to chuck: (informal) to throw

He screwed up the note and chucked it in the bin.

to fling: to throw sth somewhere or at sb with great force

He screwed up the letter and flung it in the fire.

to hurl: to throw sth violently and with great force, often because you are angry

He was sent off for hurling mud at the referee.

to pelt: to throw sth at sb and hit them with it [Note: **to pelt down** = to rain heavily]

They pelted each other with snowballs.

*

to comb: to search a place thoroughly or look at information carefully

The police combed the entire area for clues.

to fish around in: to look for sth using your hands and not your eyes

She fished around in her handbag for her keys.

to scour: to make a thorough search of a place or sth

I scoured the entire house looking for my watch.

to sift through: to examine sth (e.g. evidence) thoroughly

The organisers are still sifting through the competition entries.

Practice

1. The words in the groups are connected because they are similar in meaning. Label the groups using the verbs from the list below to show what their similarities are.

cut – follow – find – fall – listen – increase – stop – cheat – disappear – force to leave – throw – look for

1 .... : bug – eavesdrop – overhear – tap
2 .... : slash – trim – carve – mow
3 .... : peter out – fizzle out – wear off – die down
4 .... : evict – expel – banish – evacuate
5 .... : fling – hurl – chuck – pelt
6 .... : scour – sift through – comb – fish around in
7 .... : plummet – plunge – slump
8 .... : hamper – hinder – curb
9 .... : rig – swindle – double-cross
10 .... : stalk – tail – shadow
11 .... : stumble on – dig up
12 .... : rocket – soar – climb

2. Now complete the sentences below with an appropriate verb (in the correct tense or form) from exercise 1.

1 She was very late. She was flustered. She grabbed whatever clothes and toiletries were nearest at hand and, ... them into her suitcase, she rushed out of the door.
2 The old lady was .... out of her life savings by a man pretending to be an investment consultant.
3 We were .... from our last flat for not paying the rent.
4 Take an umbrella with you; it's .... down outside.
5 It was a schoolboy, out on a walk, who .... the prehistoric cave.
6 The price of oil .... to an all-time low yesterday when it was announced that a new engine had been developed which could run on water.
7 Driving rain and poor visibility .... rescue efforts to such an extent that the search was called off until the weather cleared up.
8 A further 100 police officers have been drafted into the high crime areas of the city in an attempt to .... the rising tide of armed robberies.
9 We can't go sailing until this storm ....
10 One of my Sunday chores was to .... the lawn.
11 Rescuers .... through the rubble looking for survivors from the earthquake.
12 In the last three years house prices have .... by an incredible 300%.
13 I was walking past John's office and I .... him saying to George that Mr Jenkins is retiring.
14 As the fire swept towards the town, thousands of people had to be .... from their homes.

65 Verbs II

to abhor: to hate something because you think it is morally wrong (formal)
I abhor blood sports.

to assess: to make a judgement about sth; consider/decide, based on testing or careful thought
Some people believe that exams are the only way of assessing people's intellectual abilities.

to bluff: to pretend to do sth that you know you will not do
He said he'd resign but I knew he was only bluffing.

to boost: to cause to increase/improve/be more successful
boost sales/confidence/morale/ego
"You're the best student I've got," he said, in a feeble attempt to boost her confidence.

to condone: to accept that sth is morally right
Whilst I cannot condone this kind of behaviour, I do understand it.
I cannot condone the use of violence under any circumstances.

to crave: to really want, especially **attention/recognition/security/acceptance/food** [Note: noun: **craving**]
He's not the kind of actor who craves media attention.

to deem: (formal) to consider
The headmaster will take whatever action deemed necessary to prevent this kind of incident from ever happening again.
If the doctor deems it advisable, then you will need to have an operation.

to dispel: to stop people believing rumours/feeling worried/having doubts
The management did everything in their power to dispel the rumours that the factory was going to close down.

to disperse: to spread over a wide area; (to make) the people in a crowd separate and go away in different directions, to scatter
The police tried to disperse the crowd.
The meeting broke up and the crowd dispersed peacefully.

to dwindle: to become less and less or fewer and fewer
[Note: adj: **dwindling**]
The number of gorillas living in the wild has dwindled to two hundred.
We had to close the shop because of soaring overheads and dwindling sales.

to exacerbate: to make a bad situation worse
I know Mary is your sister, but if you interfere in her marriage, you will only exacerbate the situation.

to feign: to pretend to have a particular feeling or illness
I feigned interest in her story, although I'd heard it before.
I feigned a headache and went home early.

to fend for yourself: to look after yourself without having to depend on other people
I was 15 when my parents died. In those days there wasn't a social services system so I was left to fend for myself.

to flaunt: to show your **wealth/success/beauty** in a very obvious way so as to obtain other people's admiration
I don't understand why he feels it necessary to always flaunt his money. We all know he's rich!

to flout: to deliberately and openly ignore **law/rules/regulations**
The countries which have decided to flout the new rules laid down by FIFA will not be invited to play in next year's qualifying rounds for the World Cup.

to glean: to find out facts or information in small amounts and with difficulty
I gleaned what information I could about him from books in the reference library.

to jeopardise: to risk losing or ruining sth that is very important or very valuable; to endanger
Your foolish remarks could jeopardise the success of these talks.
What you did has jeopardised the lives of everyone on this expedition.

to linger: (i) to stay at a place for some time, not wanting to leave (ii) **linger on:** to stay and, though probably becoming weaker, not go away
A number of people were still lingering (around) outside the theatre long after the concert had finished.
The memory of that night will forever linger on in my mind.

to lurch: to move forward suddenly and violently
He slammed on the brakes and I put out my hands as I lurched forward.

to mislead: to make sb believe sth that is not true
I did not deliberately mislead you. I told you what he told me.
You misled me into thinking that everything was included in the price. When I got to the hotel, I was told that I had to pay for all my meals and any drinks I had.

to vow: to promise yourself or sb else (infinitive/clause)
He vowed never to go there again.

to waft: to pass through the air (generally for smells)
The smell of burnt toast wafted upstairs. James was making breakfast.

Practice

1. *Complete the following sentences using an appropriate verb from the box below. You may have to change the tense or form of the verb.*

> vow – bluff – flout – exacerbate – waft – feign – crave – jeopardise – assess – boost – deem – mislead – disperse – flaunt – glean – fend – dwindle – abhor – condone – dispel – lurch – linger

1 He announced that he had no intention of stepping down, thereby .... the rumours that had been circulating in the press about his imminent resignation.
2 He said that unless we met his union's demands there would be a strike, but I think he is ....
3 After the accident, he .... never to drive a racing car again.
4 Countries that .... the rules and regulations laid down by the CITES agreement run the risk of having sanctions imposed upon them.
5 Hardly anyone was prepared to talk to us but we managed to .... a little information from his maid.
6 The smell of roast chicken .... into the living room. Dinner was on its way.
7 When their mother died, the orphaned cubs were left to .... for themselves.
8 He was too tired to listen to what she had to say about the board meeting. "Really?" he said, ... interest. "That's interesting."
9 In the past, crowds of up to ten thousand would come and watch us play. Nowadays, numbers have .... to such an extent that we're lucky if two hundred supporters manage to make it to a match.
10 One of the advantages of the new curriculum is that it helps teachers to .... their students' progress without relying too heavily on exams.
11 I cannot .... the use of violence as a means of solving problems, no matter how pressing that problem may be.
12 At the age of fifty, he finally achieved the recognition he had always secretly ....
13 I .... racism. It goes against everything I believe in.
14 In an attempt to .... sales, they decided to give away a free mug with every thirty pounds spent in their store.
15 The United Nations said that it would sanction the use of force in the dispute if the members of the Security Council .... it necessary.
16 As the limousine whisked him away, the crowd that had gathered outside the theatre quickly ....
17 In days gone by, there was a saying that went, *If you've got it,* .... *it.* Nowadays, however, it is considered vulgar to show off your wealth.
18 You deliberately .... me. You told me that there would be no risk involved when you knew full well that we could have lost everything!
19 We didn't leave with the others. We .... for a while, hoping to catch a glimpse of her.
20 He shakily let out the clutch. The car .... forward so suddenly and so violently that his driving instructor was nearly catapulted through the window.
21 Telling him you think he's in the wrong will only .... the situation. Why make a bad situation worse?
22 He knew that by leaking the document to the press he was .... not only his own political career but also the prospects of the party at the next general election.

2. *Provide a response to the following using the verbs presented in the unit.*

1 Do you think he is serious?
    ....
2 So, he didn't tell you the truth then?
    ....
3 Did you find anything that could help with the project?
    ....
4 Why don't you release the baby crocodiles into the wild?
    ....
5 So, what did the man from the insurance company do?
    ....

66 Verbs III

to aggravate: (i) to make a bad situation worse (ii) to annoy sb

Threatening him will only aggravate the situation.

If you know that comments like that aggravate her, why did you say it?

to boycott: (i) to refuse to do business with a company or country (especially by refusing to buy products from that company or country) as a way of protesting (ii) to refuse to take part in an organised event (the Olympics, the World Cup, etc) as a way of protesting

The only way to stop them experimenting on animals is to boycott their products.

Boycotting a sporting event by not participating in it is not considered an effective form of protest.

to dismantle: to separate sth into pieces

"I told you not to dismantle it," I said. "I bet you can't put it back together again, can you?"

to divulge: (formal) to give sb information (especially secret or sensitive information)

She refused to divulge the names of the candidates.

to elapse: to pass (for time)

Twenty years were to elapse before he returned to Argentina.

to endeavour: (formal) to try

We will endeavour to comply with your request.

to fray: if sb's temper frays, they get annoyed

Bob tried to smile. He reminded himself that he was on holiday, but his temper was beginning to fray.

to grant: (i) to grant **permission**: to give permission (ii) to grant sb **access** to sth: to allow sb to see sth/enter somewhere (iii) to grant a **request**: to say yes to sb's request [Note: **I grant you that ...**: I agree that sth is true]

They have been granted permission to build their new factory on a piece of wasteland next to the river.

The firm currently under investigation for tax fraud refused to grant the Inland Revenue access to its computer system.

I grant you that he is an exceptionally talented player, but I'm worried about his temperament.

to harbour: (i) to hide and offer protection to a criminal (ii) to have (a thought, emotion, secret) in your mind for a long time

Harbouring a known criminal is a punishable offence.

Even years later she still harboured feelings of jealousy towards her sister.

to heckle: to shout and interrupt sb who is speaking in public

No sooner had he stood up to speak than a number of people in the audience started heckling him.

to mar: to ruin, to spoil

It was an excellent match, which was marred by a last-minute brawl involving all the players and both managers.

to oust: to remove a person from a position of power

Attempts to oust the chairman of the board failed.

to quibble: to argue about small points/details/differences

All right, then, I won't quibble about the exact meaning of the word.

to refrain: (formal) not to do sth

Passengers are kindly requested to refrain from using mobile telephones and laptop computers during this flight.

to scrap: to decide not to continue with a plan/project because you believe it to be useless or impractical

The government decided to scrap its plan to reintroduce the tram, claiming that it would not be feasible.

Practice

1. For questions 1 to 15, complete the second sentence so that it has a similar meaning to the first sentence. The word(s) that you need to complete the second sentence can be found in the box below.

> to be scrapped – had elapsed – harbouring – dismantling
> – was ousted – boycotted – to divulge – to fray
> – was marred – heckling – to grant – to refrain – aggravate
> – would endeavour – quibbling

1 She had promised the informant complete confidentiality, which is why she didn't want to tell anyone what his name was.
- She had promised the informant complete confidentiality, hence her reluctance .... his name.

2 It took the fire brigade over twenty minutes to get to Susan's house and by then all that was left was a charred and gutted shell.
- By the time the fire brigade arrived at Susan's house, over twenty minutes .... and all that was left was a charred and gutted shell.

3 Every time a member of the planning committee stood up to talk they had decided to shout out and interrupt, thereby disrupting the meeting.
- Their aim was to disrupt the meeting by .... every time a member of the planning committee stood up to talk.

136

4 Opposition parties protested by not attending the meeting on the new measures.
   - Opposition parties .... the meeting on the new measures.

5 David managed to take the radio to pieces in ten minutes, but it took him three and a half hours to put it all back together again.
   - David spent ten minutes .... the radio, but it took him three and a half hours to put all the pieces back together again.

6 The hotter it got, the more irritable people became. Before long a fight broke out.
   - It was hot and tempers soon began .... Before long, a fight broke out.

7 It was a shame that he spoiled his essay by making appalling spelling mistakes because it was full of good ideas and excellent vocabulary.
   - His essay was full of good ideas and excellent vocabulary, but unfortunately it .... by poor spelling.

8 The police said that she had allowed a wanted criminal to hide in her house.
   - She was accused of .... a wanted criminal.

9 The government were forced to abandon their plan to abolish private schools because it was proving to be very unpopular with the electorate.
   - The government's plan to abolish private schools was proving to be so unpopular with the electorate that it had ....

10 We have approached the council in the hope that they will allow us to knock down the old town hall and put up a shopping mall in its place.
   - We have asked the council .... us permission to knock down the old town hall and put up a shopping mall in its place.

11 We will try to get the goods to you by six o'clock tomorrow.
   - He said they .... to get the goods to me by six o'clock the next day.

12 We would like to remind passengers to remain in their seats during take-off.
   - Passengers are kindly requested .... from leaving their seats during take-off.

13 The military overthrew the president in a bloodless coup.
   - The president .... in a bloodless coup.

14 The bill was wrong, but I wasn't going to argue about it; we had enjoyed our meal and she had only overcharged us by a few cents.
   - The bill was wrong, but I didn't see the point of .... over it – we had enjoyed our meal and she had only overcharged us by a few cents.

15 You'll just make a bad situation worse if you refuse to apologise.
   - Refusing to apologise will only .... the situation.

2. *Choose the correct item.*

1 It is better to forgive and forget than to .... feelings of bitterness and resentment.
   A refrain   C endeavour
   B harbour   D grant

2 Many companies have had to .... their plans for expansion due to the economic recession.
   A scrap   C refrain
   B harbour   D oust

3 I .... you that this new job is a step up the ladder, but it will mean moving to another part of the country.
   A divulge   C endeavour
   B quibble   D grant

4 The only thing that .... the race was Kaba's accident.
   A dismantled   C marred
   B scrapped   D frayed

5 OK, the soup is not boiling hot. Surely you are not going to .... over such a minor problem.
   A quibble   C fray
   B heckle   D aggravate

6 Visitors are kindly requested to .... from taking photographs inside the museum.
   A refrain   C elapse
   B endeavour   D grant

7 Fortunately, we were .... access to the institute's private files.
   A refrained   C divulged
   B boycotted   D granted

8 I asked you not to whistle and you are whistling! Are you deliberately trying to .... me?
   A mar   C oust
   B aggravate   D quibble

67 Walking and Running

to amble: to walk slowly in a relaxed manner

The cattle ambled down the country road.

to canter (across/along, etc): (for horses) to run slowly and steadily

We cantered across the fields.

to clamber: to quickly climb up a hill, slope, mountain, on your hands and knees

He clambered up the hillside.

to come tearing (out of/into/down, etc): to run very quickly

The children came tearing downstairs like greased lightning.

to crawl (into/through/along, etc): to move slowly on your hands and knees

We crawled through a hole in the fence.

to creep: to move quietly and slowly

He crept up to the window.

to dash (over to/out of/into/across, etc): to run

She dashed into the restaurant and asked to use the phone.

to elbow one's way through a crowd: to push people in crowd out of the way so that you can move forwards

She elbowed her way through the throng.

to gallop (across/along, etc): (for horses) to run very fast

We galloped across the fields at breakneck speed.

to go for a stroll: to go for a slow, pleasurable walk, without any particular destination in mind

Let's go for a stroll in the country.

to go somewhere on foot: to walk somewhere

It isn't far. Let's go on foot.

to hobble: to walk slowly and with difficulty because it is painful for you to walk

The old lady hobbled down the street.

to jog: to run slowly and steadily for a long time

He used to jog/go jogging twice a day to keep fit.

to limp (over to/out of/off/across, etc): to walk without putting pressure on one leg (because that leg is injured)

The injured player limped off the field.

to make a bolt for: to suddenly run in the direction of (a door or exit), trying to escape from sb

The dog seized the steak and made a bolt for the door.

to march (over to/out of/into/across, etc): (i) formally walk together in a group (soldiers) (ii) walk somewhere quickly and with determination

The soldiers marched smartly in the parade.

She marched into the headmaster's office and demanded to know why her son had been expelled.

to pace up and down: to walk backwards and forwards, because you're nervous or anxiously waiting for sth

He paced up and down outside the interview room.

to paddle: to walk in shallow water, often for pleasure

children paddling in the sea

to run as fast as one's legs will carry one: to run a as fast as one can

Once out in the open, he ran as fast as his legs would carry him.

to scamper (over to/out of/into, etc): to walk quickly with little steps

The puppy scampered up to me.

to shuffle (over to/out of/into, etc): to walk without lifting your feet from the ground

He shuffled slowly and painfully over to the door.

to sidle up to sb/into: to move slowly and quietly towards sb/ somewhere, trying not to attract attention

A man in a raincoat and dark glasses sidled up to me. "Agent 005?" he asked.

to skip: to move as if dancing, with little hopping movements

The children were laughing as they skipped down the road.

to skulk (around): to move around secretly, often hiding

He was fed up with having paparazzi skulking around his house.

to sprint (past/towards/for, etc): to run very fast (generally used for sb engaged in a sporting activity)

He got the ball, sprinted past two defenders and scored a goal.

to stagger: to walk very unsteadily, as if you are about to fall

He staggered forwards and fell down.

to stalk: to follow a person/animal in order to attack them

Lions stalk their prey, following them stealthily and then pouncing.

to storm out of (a room/building/meeting): to leave (a room/building/meeting) angrily, probably slamming the door behind you

Their delegation stormed out of the meeting, shouting as they went.

to stretch your legs: (informal) to go for a walk (e.g. after sitting down for a long time)

We had been driving for hours, so we stopped to stretch our legs.

to stride (into/down, etc): to walk confidently, with long steps

A tall man in an expensive suit strode into my office.

to strut (out of/into/down, etc): to walk in a proud, arrogant way, with shoulders back and chest pushed forward

The boxer strutted towards the ring.

to stumble: to catch your foot on sth and almost fall

She stumbled on the table leg, and almost fell into the wedding cake.

to swagger (over to/out of/into, etc): to walk arrogantly, swinging your shoulders as you go

He swaggered confidently into the room.

to trample: to walk on sth and crush it or destroy it as a result

Someone had got into her garden and trampled on her flowers.

to trot (across/along, etc): (for horses) to move quite quickly
The pony trotted down the lane.

to trudge: to walk wearily (because you are tired or unhappy)
The farm labourers trudged home after a hard day's work in the fields.

to wade: to walk in deep water which probably reaches your waist
He waded slowly back to shore.

to walk at a gentle pace: to walk slowly and unhurriedly
The ramblers walked at a gentle pace.

Practice

1. Complete the sentences with a verb from this unit.

1. Soldiers ....
2. Babies who haven't learned to walk ....
3. People in a daze ....
4. Injured football players ....
5. A herd of frightened elephants may well .... on anything in their way.
6. Lions .... their prey before they attack.
7. Children love to .... in the sea.
8. Someone who is late for a lecture might try to .... the lecture room unnoticed.
9. Farm animals might .... down a country lane.
10. In a busy store, a customer may have to .... a crowd to get to the sales counter.
11. Fathers-to-be .... hospital corridors.
12. People who like to keep fit often .... in the morning.

2. Choose the correct item.

1. "How dare you!" she screamed, and, picking up her bag, she .... of the room.
   A stormed out   C made a bolt
   B dashed   D sprinted

2. Looking hurriedly over his shoulder, he .... up the steep bank, cutting his hands on the broken roots embedded in the soil.
   A waded   C clambered
   B strode   D paddled

3. With a self-confidence bordering on arrogance, Francelli got out of his car and .... over to the crowd of journalists.
   A skulked   C swaggered
   B crept   D shuffled

4. Our legs ached as we .... wearily through the snow.
   A strutted   C trudged
   B scampered   D galloped

5. The student .... into the auditorium, hoping that nobody would notice that he was late.
   A sidled   C shuffled
   B stormed   D strode

6. Catching her foot, the waitress ...., dropping the tray into a customer's lap.
   A stumbled   C skipped
   B clambered   D dashed

7. Having chewed my new slippers to pieces, Toby the dog was .... under the table.
   A skulking   C clambering
   B stalking   D marching

8. She marched .... him, smiled and slapped him round the face.
   A until   C over to
   B across   D up with

9. "Let's stop," he said. "We've been driving for hours. I need to .... my legs."
   A flex   C walk
   B bend   D stretch

10. He ran off as fast as his legs could .... him.
    A transport   C bear
    B carry   D hold

11. In the afternoons we would go for a .... along the seafront.
    A stroll   C stride
    B stretch   D strut

12. Late for school again, Andy came .... out of his house and down the garden path.
    A skipping   C cantering
    B tearing   D hobbling

13. We walked at a gentle ...., stopping every hour for a rest.
    A trot   C bolt
    B bend   D pace

68 Ways of ...

Ways of walking

to edge away from: to walk backwards, taking small steps away from sth/sb that frightens you

He edged away from the approaching tiger.

to edge towards: to move slowly towards sth

She edged cautiously towards the parcel.

to pick your way through a crowd/ a cluster of tables, etc: to walk between people or objects that are in your way

He picked his way through the crowd, hoping to get to the front of the stage.

to saunter (over to/away/into, etc): to walk in a slow and lazy way

He sauntered over to the jukebox.

to scurry (over to/away/into, etc): to move quickly with little steps (insects and small animals scurry)

I lifted the stone and a beetle scurried away.

to slip into a room: to enter a room quietly, hoping not to be noticed

Gently pushing the door open, he slipped into the room.

Ways of Sitting

to lounge on the sofa/a deckchair: to be sitting in a very relaxed way

John was by the pool, lounging in a deckchair. He looked up from his book as I approached.

to be slumped in/on a chair/over the table: not be sitting straight, but leaning at an angle

He was found slumped over the steering wheel, unconscious and barely breathing.

Ways of Reading

to flick/leaf through a book/ magazine: to turn the pages of a book, etc without reading much of it

There she was, sitting by the window, leafing through a magazine.

to pore over a book: to read very carefully and for a long time

The lights of the library were still on. He could see a solitary figure near the window, poring over a book.

Ways of Looking

to gaze: to look for a long time without really seeing what you are looking at

They sat, gazing into each other's eyes.

to peer: to look with difficulty because you cannot see properly (maybe it is dark or maybe you have poor eyesight)

He peered at his watch.

He peered out of the window.

Ways of Writing

to jot (sth) down: to write notes/ telephone numbers/addresses very quickly, especially in response to what sb is saying or telling you

I remember jotting her number down on the back of one of my business cards.

to scribble: to write sth very quickly which is often unreadable as a result

She scribbled a note to her teacher.

to take (sth) down: to write long notes (at a lecture, for example) while listening to sb speak

At lectures some people record what the lecturer is saying with tape recorders but I prefer to take down notes.

Ways of Speaking

to mumble: to speak quietly and unclearly

He mumbled something about being sorry for the trouble he had caused.

to whisper: to speak very quietly

They were whispering about the teacher's new haircut.

Ways of Laughing/Smiling

to beam: to smile with happiness showing in all your face

He beamed at us. "I passed," he said.

to burst out laughing (or to burst into laughter): to suddenly begin laughing loudly

Whatever it was he had been reading, it must have been funny, because every now and then he would burst out laughing.

to giggle: to laugh in a childish way because you are embarrassed, nervous or amused

The girls were giggling in a corner of the playground, probably over a silly joke.

to grin: to smile widely (normally because you are very pleased – however a grin can also be sinister)

He grinned at me and went on working.

to snigger: to laugh quietly and disrespectfully, especially at sth rude

"What are you sniggering at?" he snapped angrily.

Ways of Looking For

to fumble about: to try and reach or hold sth in a clumsy way because you are upset or in a hurry

I dropped my purse as I was fumbling for change.

to rummage about: to look for sth in your pockets/your bag/etc using just your hands

She rummaged about in her handbag for her keys.

to scour a place/area/piece of writing for: to look very carefully and thoroughly for sth in an area, etc

The police scoured the room for fingerprints.

140

Practice

1. *Categorise the verbs below: Ways of Walking (A), Sitting (B), Laughing or Smiling (C), Writing (D), Speaking (E), Looking (F), Reading (G) and Looking For (H).*

1	to edge	10	to be slumped	19	to lounge
2	to jot down	11	to gaze	20	to flick through
3	to take down	12	to rummage about	21	to peer
4	to pore over	13	to mumble	22	to scribble
5	to fumble about	14	to giggle	23	to grin
6	to beam	15	to slip into	24	to snigger
7	to leaf through	16	to whisper	25	to scurry
8	to scour	17	to pick your way		
9	to burst out laughing	18	to saunter		

2. *Now replace the phrases in bold with one of the verbs above.*

She walked up to the window and **0)** *peered* **(looked with some difficulty)** in through the net curtains. He was there. She knew he would be. He was **1)** .... **(sitting looking tired)** in a chair, cradling a package in his hands. She **2)** .... **(entered quickly and quietly)** the café. He wouldn't be able to see her unless he turned round. The café was much as she had expected, small and spartan, though clean, with a minimum of furniture. How appropriate, she thought. She could smell coffee brewing. She watched the waiter, the only other person in the place, quickly **3)** .... **(write)** something, probably the bill, and pass it to the man. The man looked up, **4)** .... **(smiled)** at the waiter and **5)** .... **(said indistinctly)** something to him, then opened the package in his lap and **6)** .... **(read carefully)** its contents, before replacing them and turning to **7)** .... **(look abstractedly)** out of the window. She had seen that faraway look before.

Unable to stand it any longer, she **8)** .... **(walked in a slow and casual way)** over to his table, looking for all the world as if she had just happened to have been passing and, on the spur of the moment, had decided to walk in.

She didn't want to alarm him. He looked up, seeing her for the first time, a flicker of recognition in his eyes. He began to **9)** .... **(look for something)** in his coat pocket until, with hands that were now trembling, he fished out a sealed envelope. He **10)** .... **(looked with some difficulty at)** the contents of the package once again and placed them, together with the sealed envelope, on the table. Pushing them towards her, he **11)** .... **(wrote quickly and carelessly)** something and left the café. She picked up the note. It read: "These photos and this life insurance policy cheque are for my daughter, Sadie." "But father," she **12)** .... **(said quietly)** to the door that had already closed, "*I'm* Sadie."

3. *Using the paragraph as a model, write a story of your own, using verbs from exercise 1 to colour your narrative.*

4. *Complete each sentence using an appropriate verb from exercise 1.*

1. It was too hot to do anything but .... down the street and take in the scenery.
2. If you don't understand what I say, ask me to speak more clearly; I have a tendency to ....
3. Vivian .... the small print of the contract for ages, unwilling to sign until she was certain.
4. The old sailor sat .... wistfully out of the window.
5. I .... the address down so hastily that now I can't read it.
6. I never .... notes in a lecture. I record everything!
7. "Tell us all the joke, Jackson, if it's so funny," the teacher remarked to the boy who was .... at the back of the classroom.
8. The ants were .... about in all directions.
9. He sat down, picked up a magazine and having quickly .... through it, put it back on the table.
10. She .... the house looking for the ring but it was nowhere to be found.
11. "That was very clever of you," said the villain, ... evilly at the hero.
12. All Adrian ever does is .... around in front of the TV all day.

141

69 Weather I

Hot

to be baking/boiling (hot): to be very hot

It was baking (hot) all week.

It's boiling (hot) outside.

to be balmy: to be pleasantly warm, with gentle winds

a cool balmy evening

a drought: a long period of time with very little or no rain

If the drought continues, water will soon have to be rationed.

a heatwave: a period of unusally hot weather

The heatwave is expected to continue for another two weeks.

to be humid/to be muggy: hot, wet and uncomfortable

Buenos Aires is very hot and humid in the summer.

a scorcher: a very hot day

The weather couldn't have been better. Sunday was a real scorcher.

to be sweltering/stifling: to be uncomfortably hot [Note: the **sweltering heat**]

It's sweltering outside.

It's stifling in here. I'll open a window.

Cold

a blizzard: a very bad snow storm

It was foolish of the climbers to go out during a blizzard.

chilly: a little bit cold (*chilly* can also be used before a noun)

a chilly day

Wrap up warm. It's quite chilly outside.

frost: a thin layer of ice which forms on the ground (often overnight) when temperatures fall below freezing [Note: **frosty** (adj)]

There was frost on the ground. Winter was well and truly on its way.

nippy: a little bit cold

It was nice and warm during the day, but at night it was quite nippy.

sleet: a mixture of rain and snow

The rain turned to sleet. If it got any colder, it would snow.

slush: wet snow

Passing cars had turned the snow to slush.

a snowdrift: a deep mass of snow pushed together by strong winds (generally against sth like a house) to form sth that looks like the side of a hill

They had to dig the car out of the snowdrift.

Wet

to bucket/to pour down: to rain very hard

She looked out of the window. It was pouring/bucketing down.

a cloudburst: short period of very heavy rain - as if a cloud had burst

A sudden cloudburst left us all drenched.

a downpour: a short period of very heavy rain

"You're soaked!" "Yes, I got caught in that downpour."

drizzle: a very fine rain [Note: **to drizzle** (v)]

It was drizzling outside and the sky was grey and overcast.

hail: frozen rain which falls as hard balls (hailstones) of ice [Note: **to hail** (v)]

Hailstones the size of tennis balls began to fall from the sky.

to be spitting: to rain very lightly

Of course we can play. It's not as if it's pouring down. It is only spitting.

Windy

a breeze: a soft and gentle wind

The trees were swaying in the summer breeze.

a gale: very strong wind

It's blowing a gale outside.

Combinations

blustery weather: rough, wet, windy weather

It was a blustery autumn day.

a clap of thunder: the noise made by thunder

There was a sudden clap of thunder, followed by a flash of lightning.

a flurry of snow: a light snow shower which lasts for a short time

It was a very mild winter. I think we had one flurry of snow and that was it.

a gentle breeze: a soft breeze

It was a perfect day for a picnic, sunny, with a gentle breeze.

a gust of wind: a sudden strong rush of wind

A sudden gust of wind blew my hat off.

a howling gale: very strong winds

You can't go sailing in this weather. It's blowing a howling gale out there.

not a drop of rain: no rain at all.

Not a (single) drop of rain fell.

a patch of fog: an area of fog

With the exception of one or two patches of fog on higher ground, it will be a clear and mainly dry night.

a spell of bad/good weather: a period of time when there is bad/good weather

It was a typical English summer. We had one spell of good weather in July – I think it lasted for a week – and that was it.

thick fog: fog that is impossible to see through

The fog was so thick that I could see no further than one metre in front of me.

a thin veil of mist: a thin layer of mist in the morning (mist is like fog, but not as thick)

The fields were shrouded in a thin veil of mist.

torrential/driving rain: very heavy rain

It was a typical English holiday - one day of sunshine and six days of torrential/driving rain.

Practice

1. **a.** *Do the following words refer to warm* **hot, cold, wet** *or* **windy** *weather? Categorise them accordingly. Sometimes a word can belong in more than one category. When you have finished categorising the words, do the listening that appears below them.*

1	It's chilly	....	13	a blizzard	....
2	It's boiling	....	14	slush	....
3	It's humid	....	15	frost	....
4	It's spitting	....	16	balmy	....
5	It's bucketing down	....	17	a breeze	....
			18	a heatwave	....
6	It's baking	....	19	a downpour	....
7	It's sweltering	....	20	a cloudburst	....
8	It's muggy	....	21	a gale	....
9	It's stifling	....	22	a snowdrift	....
10	sleet	....	23	a drought	....
11	drizzle	....	24	It's nippy	....
12	a scorcher	....	25	hail	....

b. 🎧 *Listen and indicate whether the statements are true or false by placing a T or F at the end of each sentence. For each question, justify your answer by writing* **why** *you think the statement is true or false.*

1. It is drizzling in London. ......
   Reason: ....
2. It is going to be very windy in Cornwall. ......
   Reason: ....
3. Temperatures may well go below zero during the day in Scotland. ......
   Reason: ....
4. It will be quite a warm morning in France, Belgium and Holland. ......
   Reason: ....
5. The European Cup had to be called off because of continual rain the day before. ......
   Reason: ....
6. The Austrian Tourist Board are guilty of understatement. ......
   Reason: ....
7. It has been hot in Spain for quite some time. ......
   Reason: ....
8. It will be a humid day in Rome. ......
   Reason: ....
9. It will be very sunny in Greece. ......
   Reason: ....
10. It will be sweltering in the evening in Greece. ......
    Reason: ....

2. *Match the* **"of"** *expression or* **adjective** *in column A with its appropriate weather noun in column B.*

	A			B
1	A **gust** of	☐	a	snow
2	A **patch** of	☐	b	good weather
3	A **flurry** of	☐	c	rain
4	A **thin veil** of	☐	d	fog
5	A **spell** of	☐	e	thunder
6	A **clap** of	☐	f	mist
7	A **drop** of	☐	g	wind

1	A **howling**	☐	a	fog
2	A **gentle**	☐	b	showers
3	**thick**	☐	c	rain
4	**driving**	☐	d	gale
5	**blustery**	☐	e	breeze
6	**torrential**	☐	f	rain

3. *Describe the pictures using vocabulary from exercises 1 and 2.*

70 Weather II

(it's) bitter: it's very cold

Take a warm coat with you. It's bitter outside.

to brighten up: to become better (for weather)

Let's hope it brightens up later.

be chucking it down: (informal) to be raining very hard

Can't we wait a bit before we go out? It's chucking it down.

to clear up (of bad weather): to go away and be replaced by good weather

The rain should clear up after lunchtime, and we can expect a bright and sunny afternoon.

to die down: (of storm) to become less intense, not necessarily going away completely

We will have to wait for the storm to die down before we attempt to rescue them.

to be fog-bound: to be covered in thick fog

We couldn't land in Warsaw because the airport was fog-bound.

to be in the grips of: to be experiencing sth that cannot be controlled (an economic crisis, a famine, bad weather, etc)

Switzerland is in the grips of its worst winter on record.

to let up: to stop (for bad weather)

If this rain does not let up, we are going to have to call off the match.

to be pouring (down): to be raining very hard

It was such a nice morning, but look at it now. It's pouring down.

to set in for the day: to start and seem likely to continue (of rain)

The rain has set in for the day.

to turn cold: to become cold

Why didn't you bring a coat? I told you it would turn cold.

If the weather holds: if the good weather continues (not used for bad weather)

It's been a lovely week so far. If the weather holds, we'll go to the coast for the weekend.

It has turned out nice: contrary to your expectations, the weather is good

Although it was dull early in the morning, it turned out really nice for our picnic.

Idioms, Verbs and Expressions

it was a breeze: it was easy

"Was it a difficult exam?" "No, it was a breeze!"

to flood in: to enter/arrive in large numbers

They opened the doors to the stadium and the crowds flooded in.

I don't have the foggiest idea: I really don't know (used as a simple response or followed by a question word)

"Do you know why he said those things?"
"No, I haven't got the foggiest idea."

I haven't got the foggiest idea how this thing works.

to shower sb with sth: to give sb a lot of sth

He showered her with gifts.

The critics showered his film with praise.

to be skating on thin ice: to be doing sth which might result in sth bad happening to you

Alan had been late three times that week and now he was late again. He had been skating on thin ice as he had been warned that if he continued to show up late he would lose his job.

to storm out of a room: to leave a room angrily, probably slamming the door behind you

Seeing that she couldn't get her own way, she turned round and stormed out of the room.

a stormy meeting: a meeting (generally between a group of people – e.g. company directors) in which people shout at and argue with each other

I think we are in for a very stormy meeting tonight.

to have/sell, etc everything under the sun: to have/sell, etc a huge variety of products

I'm sure Cottonworths will have it – they sell everything under the sun.

to feel under the weather: not to feel 100% well

I've been feeling a bit under the weather recently. It's probably through lack of sleep.

to get wind of sth: to find out about sth

If the tax office gets wind of what he's doing, he could get into serious trouble.

Practice

1. 🎧 You will hear a conversation between the members of the board of directors of a company. Listen and decide whether the statements below are true (T), or false (F).

	T	F
1 The company is to blame for its problems.		
2 The country is experiencing economic problems.		
3 The shop steward angrily rejected a pay offer.		
4 The union's tactics are risky.		
5 The union members understand the severity of the crisis.		
6 The directors don't want the union to know about their plans yet.		

144

2. *Read the texts below and decide which option (A,B,C or D) best fits each gap.*

A Wednesday in June
A: It's **1)** .... really cold, hasn't it?
B: I'll say! The weatherman says we're in the **2)** .... of the coldest summer on record.
A: I wouldn't be surprised. It's **3)** .... outside. Mind you, the wind has **4)**........................ down.
B: Thank goodness! I went to get the cat in this morning and I was almost blown off my feet... and as for the rain...
A: I know. When I woke up this morning it was **5)** .... it down. You must've got soaked.
B: I did. It was raining that hard.
A: Well, thank heavens it **6)** .... up.
B: I'll say! Mind you, it's freezing out.
A: I know! Apparently, the weatherman says we're in the ...

A Wednesday in September
A: Look at it out there. It's **7)** .... !
B: I know, and I reckon it has **8)** .... in for the day.
A: Who knows? The weatherman seems to think it will **9)** .... up later today. We might even get some sun.
B: I don't know. Whenever they say it will **10)** .... up it always gets worse. I can't see this rain going away, can you? And as for the fog ...
A: I know. I suppose Tom and I should've gone to Ethel's yesterday instead of saving it for today. You know, seeing as it was so nice. But you're not to know, are you? I mean, if I had told you yesterday that today the motorway would be **11)** .... you would never have believed me, would you?
B: You're right. Well, you never know, it might turn **12)** .... nice tomorrow, and if the weather **13)** .... you could go to Ethel's on Saturday. Make a weekend of it.
A: Well, let's hope so.
B: I hate being stuck indoors, don't you? But look at it out there. It's bucketing down.
A: I know, and I reckon it has ...

1	A changed	B turned	C reverted	D transformed
2	A grips	B clutch	C grasps	D clench
3	A bitter	B stifling	C piercing	D crisp
4	A died	B fallen	C dropped	D turned
5	A flinging	B casting	C pitching	D chucking
6	A finished	B cleared	C gave	D drew
7	A chucking	B spilling	C pouring	D oozing
8	A put	B taken	C set	D brought
9	A let	B hold	C draw	D end
10	A lighten	B brighten	C straighten	D soften
11	A fog-covered	B fog-thickened	C fog-bound	D fog-shrouded
12	A over	B out	C along	D through
13	A remains	B maintains	C holds	D preserves

3. *Complete the sentences with an appropriate word from the box below.*

| weather – flooded – wind – sun – foggiest – stormed – stormiest – breeze – showered – ice |

1. It was easy. It was a .... I knew all the answers and I finished with half an hour to spare.
2. We're completely lost. I haven't got the .... idea where we are.
3. It was an extremely distasteful programme and for the next week letters of complaint .... in.
4. "I hate you!" she cried. And with that she .... out of the room, slamming the door behind her.
5. I don't need to see a doctor. It's just that I feel a bit under the .... I've probably got a slight cold.
6. It was the .... meeting I'd ever been to. Three people walked out and towards the end, the CEO sacked the Director of Finance.
7. Patsy's friends really spoiled her on her birthday. They .... her with presents.
8. Whatever it is you need, Munns have got it. They sell everything under the ....
9. He's skating on thin .... If he makes one more mistake, they will fire him.
10. No one must know because, if my mother ever gets .... of what we're doing, there will be trouble.

71 Wishing, Wanting, Requests, Permission and Preferences

Permission

The most common ways of asking permission are:

can I + bare infinitive

Can I borrow your bicycle?

may/could I + bare infinitive (more formal)

May I open the window?

do you mind if I + Simple Present (more polite)

Do you mind if I borrow your camera?

would you mind if I + Simple Past (the most polite)

Would you mind if I invited Paul, too?

*

General Preferences

Prefer and **would rather** can be used to express the fact that, **in general**, you like one thing more than another thing.

prefer + noun + to + noun

I prefer tea to coffee.

prefer + ing form + to + ing form

I prefer playing cricket to watching it.

prefer + full infinitive + rather than + bare infinitive

I prefer to read rather than watch TV.

would rather + bare infinitive + than

I'd rather go by train than drive.

would rather cannot be followed by a noun

~~I'd rather tea than coffee~~

*

Specific Preferences

Would prefer and **would rather** can be used to express a preference made **on one occasion**, generally in response to a question.

would prefer + noun

"Tea or coffee?" "I'd prefer tea, please."

would prefer + full infinitive

"Do you want to stay in or go out?" "I'd prefer to stay in."

would rather + bare infinitive

"Shall I tell you?" "I would (I'd) rather not know."

*

Requests

The most common ways of making requests are:

could you + bare infinitive

Could you shut that window?

would you mind + ing form

Would you mind shutting that window?

imperative + question tag (less formal)

Shut that window, will you?

You can also use **would prefer**, **would rather** and **would sooner** to make requests. They are used as polite ways of saying *please do sth/please don't do sth*. These structures are used in the following ways:

I would prefer you + full infinitive

I'd prefer you not to speak Greek in class.

I would prefer it if you + Simple Past

I'd prefer it if you didn't speak Greek in class.

I would rather you + Simple Past

I'd rather you didn't speak Greek in class.

I would sooner you + Simple Past

I'd sooner you didn't speak Greek in class.

*

Wanting

do you fancy + ing form (informal): would you like to... ?

Do you fancy going to eat out tonight?

would like + full infinitive: want

Sue would like to join us.

would like: the past tense of **would like** is used to communicate the idea that you wish you had done sth in the past

I would like to have gone to your party.

I would have liked to have gone to your party. (informal)

*

Wishing

wish + Simple Past: used to communicate the idea that you would like your circumstances (e.g. the way you look, the place you live, etc) to be different from what they are **now**.
[Note: **I wish I was – I wish I were:** both are possible and acceptable, *I wish I were* is more formal]

I wish I lived in a hotter country.

wish + could: used to communicate the idea that you would like to be able to do sth but you **can't**.

I wish I could write like you.

wish + Past Perfect: used to express regret for sth you did or did not do in the **past**.

I wish I hadn't shouted at her.

I wish I had gone to her party.

wish + sb + would: used when you want sb to do sth, when you want sb to stop doing sth or when you are complaining about sth annoying [Note: you can never say, ~~I wish I would~~]

I wish he would stop talking.

if only: it can be used instead of **I wish** and follows the same rules but it makes wishes more emphatic; in spoken English, **only** is often heavily stressed

If only I'd taken them up on their offer.

146

Practice

1. *For questions 1 to 16, complete the second sentence so that it has a similar meaning to the first sentence, using 3 to 8 words. You must include the word given in bold, which cannot be changed in any way.*

1. I'd love a holiday in the Caribbean, but I can't afford it.
   enough I wish .... to the Caribbean.
2. I regret lying to her.
   wish I .... the truth.
3. It's a pity that there isn't any way of contacting them.
   only If .... of contacting them.
4. Mrs Jones will insist on playing her radio full blast and it's driving me up the wall.
   wish I .... down.
5. It was stupid of me not to take him up on his offer.
   regret I .... up on his offer.
6. Please don't wear such informal clothes to the office.
   to I'd .... such informal clothes to the office.
7. Would you mind not eating in class?
   it I'd .... in class.
8. Please don't mention this to anyone.
   rather I'd .... anyone about this.
9. Please don't say such things in front of the children.
   sooner I'd .... in front of the children.
10. I don't like playing football as much as I like watching it.
    prefer I .... it.
11. Given the choice, I would like to work from home as opposed to going into the office every day.
    prefer I'd much .... to the office every day.
12. The minister said that he didn't want to say anything about it.
    rather The minister said that he .... on it.
13. A cruise or a touring holiday? Give me a cruise any day!
    rather I'd much .... a touring holiday.
14. "May I open the window?" he asked.
    mind "Would ....?" he asked.
15. Would you like to go to the cinema tonight?
    fancy Do .... cinema tonight?
16. I really wanted to go to the concert but I couldn't.
    like I .... but I couldn't.

2. *Complete the sentences using the words in the box. Each gap in a sentence corresponds to a word. You should have used all the words when the sentences are complete.*

> not – it – kept – wash – to – had – to – would – could – it – mention – entered – play

1. It's a secret, so I'd prefer you .... to anyone.
2. It's a secret, so I'd rather you .... yourself.
3. Apparently Tim won £1000. Don't you wish you .... that competition?
4. I wish you .... up after you have cooked!
5. I wish I .... the guitar.

3. *Write an appropriate sentence for each situation, using the structures presented in this unit.*

1. Your flatmate never does the cooking. You find that irritating.
   ....
2. You had the opportunity of taking a free computer course but didn't and now you regret this.
   ....
3. You like motorbikes more than cars.
   ....
4. A friend has got tickets for the cinema but you like the theatre more.
   ....
5. A friend is going shopping and you would like her to get you some milk.
   ....
6. You are lonely because you don't have many friends.
   ....

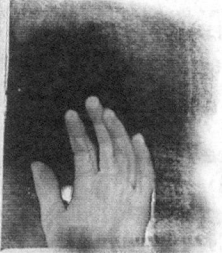

147

72 Work and Earning a Living

to apply in writing: to write a letter/e-mail to apply for sth
If you are interested in this post, apply in writing to Mark Keninsky, Munns Ltd.

career prospects: chances of promotion and future success
This job offers excellent career prospects.

a competitive salary: a good salary for the job that you are doing
Do you want a rewarding job in advertising, with a competitive salary and excellent career prospects?

a (full) curriculum vitae (CV): a (detailed) summary of your life (personal details, education, work experience)
Please enclose a full curriculum vitae with your application.

a deadline: the time by which sth must be done or finished [Note: **to work to tight deadlines**: to be given work to do which must be finished in very little time]
We'll never meet that deadline!

to do/work overtime: to work extra hours [Note: **to be paid overtime**: to be paid extra money for overtime]

She will have to work overtime to get this finished in time.

to have previous experience/to have a track record in sth: to have done that kind of work before
No previous experience necessary as we will give first-class training.
Applicants must have a proven track record in sales.

a mundane job: a job that is boring and ordinary
Lion taming is hardly what you would call a mundane job.

to be numerate: to have mathematical skills
Candidates for this job must be numerate.

a rewarding job: a job that satisfies you because you feel that you are doing sth important or useful
Not only do I earn a fortune but it is a very rewarding job.

a shift: in places which operate 24 hours a day (hospitals, some factories, etc) the working day is divided into a number of shifts, i.e. set periods during which there is always a group of people working
He can't join us tonight because he is working the night shift.

sick leave: time away from work because you are ill
[Note: **maternity leave**: time away from work for a woman who has just had a baby]
She is away on sick leave at the moment.

a sound working knowledge of: to know sth (a language, a computer program, an area of business) very well
A sound working knowledge of Quark is essential.

to take over sth from sb: to replace sb who has left their job (permanently or temporarily)
David has resigned. I wonder who will take over from him.

a telephone manner: the way you speak on the telephone
The new operator has got an excellent telephone manner.

£10K = ten thousand pounds (often used in job advertisements with reference to salaries)
Salaries of £50K are not unusual in management positions.

a vacancy has arisen: a job has become available
A vacancy arose in a publishing department so I applied for it.

Practice

1. Read the text below. Use the word given in capitals at the end of some of the lines to form a word that fits the space in the same line.

I knew the last 1) ……………… that walked through my door. He didn't recognise me but I most certainly recognised him. His name was Simon Hogwash. I looked at his 2) ……………… form and curriculum vitae. According to his CV, he had been working as a senior 3) ……………… at a 4) ……………… bank in the city of London. Up until a month ago, that is, when he had handed in his 5) ……………… . He claimed that he had resigned because he no longer found his job challenging. Now, Mr Hogwash and I had been to school together and I knew for a fact that his brain was the size of a pea. It was not inconceivable that he had gained the 6) ……………… he claimed he had, but the 7) ……………… was that his CV was a tissue of lies. My suspicions were 8) ……………… out by his poor performance during our interview. We said our goodbyes and I immediately rang one of the 9) ……………… he had named at the end of his curriculum. I was sure that this person would tell me the truth about Mr Hogwash's track record. Mr Hogwash had indeed worked for a big city bank, not as part of their 10) ……………… team but rather as the person who made the tea in the morning. I then rang up the bank and found out that he had not resigned - he had in fact been fired. I was told that he was lazy, rude, and permanently late; that his 11) ……………… was legendary and that he was completely lacking in any 12) ……………… skills – and bear in mind that all he had to do was make tea. So what did I do? Did I give him the benefit of the doubt and employ him? I'll let you be the judge of that.

INTERVIEW
APPLY
ECONOMY
PRESTIGE
RESIGN

QUALIFY
LIKELY
BEAR
REFERENCE

MANAGE

COMPETENT
ORGANISE

2. Read the job advertisements below and decide which option (A, B, C, or D) best fits each gap.

Stuck in a 0) *mundane* job? Fed up with eking out a living behind a desk? Want to spice up your life? Looking for something more 1) .... ? If you are enthusiastic, mature and ready for anything, then this is for you. We are looking for a new lion tamer to take 2) .... from the Mighty Simba after his tragic accident during a

LION TAMER
Big Bob's Travelling Circus

performance in Moscow last month. No 3) .... experience necessary. Must be willing to travel and must like animals.

If you are interested, please contact Bob Travis on (01645) 485739

HAMPSHIRE COUNTY COUNCIL

- Care Assistant
- £3.95 per hour

Due to long-term sick 14) .... of one of the members of our support staff a vacancy has 15) .... in the Southampton area for a temporary Care Assistant.

This is a fixed-term contract of four months and is an ideal position for someone who enjoys working with people who have problems.

The successful applicant should have a caring and flexible approach and should be able to work in a team. Strength and fitness are essential. The successful applicant will be working alternate 16) .... (three nights, two days).

Application forms are available from Fiona Simms, The Southampton Criminal Care Centre, Kent Road, Southampton

Personnel Assistant

Due to our continuing dynamic growth we are looking to recruit a personnel assistant for our London outlets. We offer: * A 4) .... basic salary * A monthly bonus scheme * Paid 5) .... * A first-class pension scheme * Excellent career

The Pizza Company

6) ....
In return, we would expect you to be: * Highly motivated and hard-working * Willing to take risks * Able to work under pressure * Educated to degree level. No previous experience necessary.

☏ Andrew Smith on (0181) 4857223

ADMINISTRATIVE ASSISTANT

We are looking for an energetic and flexible admin. assistant to provide general office support to our Oxford management team. Duties include filing, case paper retrieval and data input. The suitable applicant should have good organisational and communication skills, be 8) ...., should have a 9) .... working knowledge of software applications and

£15 - 19 7) ....Oxford should possess a pleasant telephone 10) .... Previous experience of working in an office environment is essential. Please apply 11) .... writing, enclosing a 12) .... curriculum vitae, to Carol Roaux, 34, Headley Street, Oxford, OX4 2DN 13) .... for applications: September 26

0	A	rut	B	mundane	C	rusty	D	immobile
1	A	rewarding	B	rekindling	C	reverberating	D	regarding
2	A	on	B	along	C	in	D	over
3	A	post	B	former	C	previous	D	past
4	A	competent	B	competitive	C	comparable	D	compelling
5	A	extra-hours	B	overhours	C	extra-time	D	overtime
6	A	prospects	B	probabilities	C	prognosis	D	promise
7	A	K	B	C	C	L	D	M
8	A	numerated	B	numerous	C	numerable	D	numerate
9	A	wide	B	deep	C	sound	D	total
10	A	capacity	B	manner	C	method	D	capability
11	A	with	B	by	C	in	D	for
12	A	comprehensive	B	total	C	full	D	broad
13	A	Limit	B	Closure	C	Deadline	D	Stoppage
14	A	licence	B	leave	C	absence	D	vacation
15	A	raised	B	aroused	C	arose	D	arisen
16	A	shifts	B	stints	C	rotas	D	stretches

149

73 Compound Adjectives - Adverb Combinations I

an action-packed movie: a film full of action (explosions, stunts, etc)
If you like action-packed movies, then you have got to see Total Explosion 3.

all-out war: total war
Desperate negotiations were taking place in an effort to avoid all-out war.

badly-run: badly and inefficiently managed and organised
It's a mystery how such a badly-run company could have made so much money.

a close-knit community: a community in which everyone knows each other
In such a close-knit community everyone knew what you had said five minutes after you had said it.

far-fetched: unlikely to be true or practical
far-fetched idea/story/excuse
That a crocodile ate your homework is a far-fetched excuse.

far-reaching: having a big impact on a large number of people, with effects that will last for a long time
far-reaching actions/events/consequences

last-minute: happening at the very latest moment
last-minute attempt/cancellation
We did some last minute shopping before the dinner party.

long-winded: a long-winded speech/explanation/account/answer/report continues for too long and is boring as a result
The bride's father gave the most long-winded speech I have ever heard in my entire life.

nerve-(w)racking: making you feel very tense and worried
Appearing on television can be a nerve-wracking experience.

the odds-on favourite: the person, team, political party, athlete, etc that everyone thinks will win a race, competition, election, etc
He is the odds-on favourite to win the tournament.

so-called: who is supposed to be
This so-called expert didn't know the first thing about computers.

well-earned: well-deserved
a well-earned holiday/ rest/break
After working flat out on the project, he took a well-earned rest.

Adverb Combinations I

to categorically deny sth/doing sth: to completely and strongly deny sth
He categorically denied being involved.

to clean forget to do sth: to completely forget to do sth (usually used in the phrase **I'm sorry, I clean forgot**, which is used in response to the question **Did you remember to...**)
I clean forgot to post the letter.

to distinctly remember sth/doing sth: to clearly recollect sth/doing sth
I distinctly remember telling you...

to drive flat out: to drive as fast as possible
We'll have to drive flat out if we want to get there by midday.

to fully expect sth to happen/that sth will happen: (formal) to confidently believe that sth will happen
The government fully expects the new train system to be operational by the end of next year.

to be highly critical of sb/sth: to criticise sb/sth very strongly
The report was highly critical of the new bill.

to be well worth doing: to be a very good thing to do because you will get some benefit from it
His new book is well worth reading.

to know full/perfectly well: to know exactly what you are doing/to understand perfectly what the consequences of your actions are/will be
You knew full well that you were breaking the rules.

to laugh out loud: to suddenly laugh loudly
He suddenly laughed out loud and everybody looked at him.

to refuse point blank to do sth: to firmly refuse to do sth
He refused point blank to hand over the document.

to be relatively inexpensive: to be quite cheap, considering the quality of the thing you are buying/paying for
It is relatively inexpensive to rent a small flat in the city centre.

to rely heavily on sth/sb: to depend greatly on
This university relies heavily on donations from ex-students to finance research projects.

to start sth afresh: to start sth again, from the beginning and in a new way
He decided to start the novel afresh, with different characters and a less complicated plot.

to be strictly confidential: to be top secret (for reports, records, information, etc)
What I've told you is strictly confidential and off-the-record.

to strongly object to sth/to doing sth: to be strongly against sth (a plan, a decision, etc) because you think it is unfair or wrong
I strongly object to the government's plans to ...

to travel light: to travel without much luggage
I travel light, whereas my wife takes at least 90 kilos of luggage with her.

to be vitally important: to be very important (often used in the phrase: **it is vitally important that..**)
It is vitally important that the press do not get wind of this.

to win hands down: to beat your competitors very easily
Thinking he was better than Liz at table football, he challenged her to a game. She won hands down!

Practice

1. *Match each compound adjective (1-12) with an appropriate noun (a-l).*

1 far-reaching	....	a favourite
2 the odds-on	....	b cancellation
3 a far-fetched	....	c holiday
4 long-winded	....	d movies
5 a badly-run	....	e consequences
6 all-out	....	f speeches
7 a well-earned	....	g company
8 a last-minute	....	h experts
9 action-packed	....	i excuse
10 so-called	....	j war
11 a nerve-(w)racking	....	k community
12 a close-knit	....	l experience

2. *Complete the sentences below with suitable combinations from exercise 1.*

1. Speaking in public can be a ....
2. "It's fully booked," she said. "The only way you'll get a seat is if there is a ...."
3. Nobody there knows what they're doing. It is such a ....
4. Sylvester Stallone is famous for his ....
5. A scandal like this is bound to have ....
6. It was a surprise that he lost because he was the .... to win.
7. None of their .... knew the first thing about developments in fibre optics.
8. After a long year of hard work, he took a ....
9. Do I have to go? I can't think of anything worse than having to sit through yet another of his painfully .... on declining family values.
10. The increasing frequency of border clashes and the accompanying government rhetoric made it clear that the country was on the verge of ....
11. Moving to London came as something of a shock to me. I grew up in a small, ..., where everybody knew everybody. In London I knew nobody.
12. Road works, a street demonstration and a circus parade made him three hours late for work! Only Henry could come up with such a ridiculously ....

3. *Complete the sentences using an appropriate adjective or verb from the vocabulary presented in this list.*

1. Never take too much luggage when you go on holiday. It's always best to .... light.
2. I strongly .... to being treated in such an off-hand way.
3. "We fully .... her to make a complete recovery," said the doctor, putting all our minds at rest.
4. He .... point blank to have anything to do with it.
5. I don't understand. Why did you say it? You .... full well she'd be offended.
6. If you found a letter with 'strictly .... emblazoned across it, would you open it?
7. The president categorically .... having had anything to do with the vote-rigging scandal.
8. I distinctly .... telling you not to post the letter until I got back. So why did you post it?
9. The press have been highly .... of the minister's failure to come up with a viable solution to the problem of spiralling unemployment.
10. I saw the latest Polanski film last night. It's excellent and is certainly well .... seeing.
11. "Did you remember to ask him about the car?" "Oh! Sorry, John, I clean ...."
12. We were late and we were going to miss the ferry, so we took the toll road and .... flat out all the way from St Omer to Calais.
13. They may look as though they cost a fortune but in fact they were relatively ....
14. Most of the world's poorer nations .... heavily on the richer countries for economic support.
15. After two days of writing, he decided to scrap everything and .... afresh.
16. Should the two teams meet in the final, there is no doubt in my mind that South Africa will .... hands down.
17. It is vitally .... that this letter should get to the General. It's a matter of life and death.
18. Her excuse was so ridiculous that I couldn't help .... out loud.

74 Adverb Combinations II

to apologise profusely: (formal) to apologise a lot [Note: please accept our **profuse apologies** (formal)]

She apologised profusely for having made such a terrible mistake.

to be bitterly disappointed: to be very disappointed

I was bitterly disappointed when I found out I hadn't got the job.

to borrow heavily: to borrow a great deal of money [Note: **to be heavily in debt**: to owe a lot of money]

We'll have to borrow heavily if we are to get this project off the ground.

Why are we so heavily in debt?

to be deadly serious (about sth): to be very serious

I think he was deadly serious when he said he was taking us to court.

to be deeply divided: not to be united, in strong disagreement (for members of a group)

The members of the committee were deeply divided over whether or not to call a strike.

to deeply regret: to regret very much

I deeply regret telling him.

to desperately need: to need very much

Julie quit, so we desperately need a new secretary.

to be excruciatingly painful: to be extremely painful

It was excruciatingly painful. Did you see the size of the needle?

to fail miserably: to fail totally [Note: it was a **miserable failure**]

He tried to stop eating chocolate but he failed miserably.

to freely admit: to be willing to admit (a bad thing)

I freely admit that I made a mistake when I invested the company's money in stocks.

to be fully booked/booked solid: used to describe a theatre, restaurant, hotel, etc where all the seats, tables, rooms, etc are occupied

All the flights to Prague are fully booked/booked solid for the next two weeks.

to be highly thought of: to be greatly admired and respected [Note: **to think/speak highly of sb/sth**: to greatly admire and respect sb/sth]

He/His book is very highly thought of abroad.

Mike thinks very highly of you.

He spoke very highly of your work.

to be hysterically funny: to be extremely funny (for jokes, films, comedians, books, etc)

Read it. It's hysterically funny.

sth is long overdue: sth (e.g. a **change**/a **reform**/a **promotion**, etc) should have happened a long time ago

His promotion came as no surprise. Actually, it had been long overdue.

to be painfully thin: to be extremely thin (for people or animals)

You need to eat more. You're painfully thin.

to be patently obvious: to be clearly obvious

It was patently obvious that he was lying. His story was full of inconsistencies.

to be perfectly willing to do sth: to be happy to do sth

I'd rather not talk about it now, but I'm perfectly willing to discuss it at the press conference tomorrow.

to be prohibitively expensive: to be too expensive for most people to afford

It's an excellent restaurant but it is prohibitively expensive.

sth is readily available: sth can be easily bought or obtained

Cheap accommodation is readily available in the city centre.

to richly deserve: to very much deserve (often used in passive)

His promotion/punishment was richly deserved.

to be scrupulously honest: to be very honest

You can trust him. He is scrupulously honest.

to be sorely tempted to do sth: to really feel like doing sth, even though you know doing it is wrong, stupid or unnecessary

I was sorely tempted to tell her the truth but I didn't want to hurt her.

to be sparsely populated: if an area/region is sparsely populated, very few people live there
Opp: densely populated

Of all continents, Oceania is the most sparsely populated.

to be spotlessly clean: to be very clean (for rooms, furniture, hands, clothes)

"GO" soap leaves your clothes spotlessly clean.

to be stunningly beautiful: to be extremely beautiful (for women, places, etc)

It's a stunningly beautiful country.

vastly improved: much better [Note: **to be a vast improvement on** is used when comparing two things mentioned; if the two things are not mentioned, the preposition that is used is **in**]

a new, vastly improved formula

There has been a vast improvement in their service.

to be vastly overrated: if sth (a book, film, product, etc) or sb (usually a performer) is vastly overrated, people have a higher opinion of it/them than it is/they are worth

I think Elvis Presley was vastly overrated.

very nearly: very close to happening [Note: **very nearly the same as**: almost the same as]

He was involved in a car crash and very nearly died.

to be (only too) well aware of/that: to know very well

I'm only too well aware of the truth!

74

Practice

1. a. *Match the adverbs with the adjectives. An example has been done for you.*

0	stunningly	k	a	booked
1	bitterly	......	b	painful
2	hysterically	......	c	serious
3	fully	......	d	funny
4	spotlessly	......	e	disappointed
5	vastly	......	f	tempted
6	patently	......	g	obvious
7	excruciatingly	......	h	overrated
8	painfully	......	i	willing
9	sorely	......	j	thin
10	perfectly	......	k	beautiful
11	deeply	......	l	divided
12	deadly	......	m	clean

b. *Now use the combinations to complete the sentences below.*

0 In addition to being *stunningly beautiful*, she is also a very talented actress.
1 She polished the crystal goblets until they were ....
2 I'm .... to walk the dog for you at weekends. I just can't do it during the week.
3 She was .... to speak her mind but held her tongue instead.
4 The restaurant we wanted to eat at was .... , so we went elsewhere.
5 The sequel is .... , even better than the first film.
6 Jeremy was .... to find out that he hadn't won the scholarship.
7 Greg isn't joking. He's .... about emigrating to Australia.
8 The committee members couldn't agree and were .... on the subject of how to use the extra funds.
9 If your employer constantly overlooks you for promotion despite your good work, it is .... that he undervalues you.
10 Although the book is a best-seller, I think it is .... and not particularly well-written.

2. *Order the speech. The beginning and ending have been done for you.*

[1] As you know, I am looking to take over from Sir Richard Cookson as this company's chairman. Sir Richard has publicly stated that he has no intention of standing down and challenged me to come before you and state my case. So here I am. I think you all know who I am. I was chairman of this company fifteen years ago. I freely

[ ] honest leader but also a consummate and skilful businessman. Indeed he is so highly

[ ] aware that Sir Richard has done a grand job since I was forced to resign. This company is in great shape and for the last six years has made record profits. Thanks to a vastly

[ ] admit that during my brief time at the helm of this company I failed

[ ] available even in the most isolated and sparsely

[ ] regret many of the decisions that I made. I should never have sacked the company accountant and taken charge of the financial side of things myself. You may remember that under my leadership this company borrowed so

[ ] expensive that we sold next to nothing for a period of eighteen months. I can but apologise

[ ] miserably as both a businessman and a leader. I was young and now, looking back, I deeply

[ ] improved distribution system, its products are readily

[ ] heavily that we had to sell off all of our assets to pay off our debts. I'm sure you will remember that we very

[ ] thought of that he has won businessman of the year on three separate occasions and was knighted last year. There can be no denying that he richly

[ ] profusely for the pain and torment shareholders must have suffered when their shares plummeted to such an extent that they were almost worthless. But, gentlemen that is the past. I am no longer the naive young man I used to be. I am back and I have returned with a vision of change. Change, gentlemen. Radical, magnificent change. Change that, as I am sure you all agree, is long overdue. The first change is to say goodbye to Sir Richard. I am of course well

[ ] needed saving. I recognise that Sir Richard is not only a scrupulously

[ ] nearly went bankrupt when I decided to double the price of all our products. It pains me to recall the days when our products were so prohibitively

[ ] populated corners of this island. I know that all this is down to Sir Richard Cookson, the man who came to this company's rescue when it so desperately

[17] deserves the praise that has been heaped upon him. But I can do better. I can take this company further than Sir Richard. I have learnt, gentlemen, learnt valuable lessons while I have been away. Sir Richard lacks vision, lacks drive. Under my leadership this company could double, no, triple its profits. How? you may ask. The answer is simple. Very simple. All we have to do is double our prices and borrow some money from the bank.

153

75 Noun Combinations I

a broad accent: a very strong regional accent

Despite living in England for over twenty years, she still speaks with a broad Irish accent.

a broad grin: a very big smile

"I'm getting married," she said, with a broad grin on her face.

a close friend: a good friend

I don't know him that well; we're not close friends.

a close shave: (sb had a close shave/ sth was a close shave) sb very nearly had an accident/got into serious trouble

It was a close shave. Had the fire brigade arrived two minutes later, we might have died in the fire.

to take a close look at sth: to examine sth very closely

If you take a close look at the signature, you can see that it is not Picasso's.

to be thrown in at the deep end: to be given a very difficult job

It was my first day on patrol and they threw me in at the deep end.

to be in deep trouble: to be in a lot of trouble

If the teacher finds out about her, we could be in deep trouble.

a deep voice: a very low-sounding voice

He has a very deep voice for a boy of his age.

at full blast: at maximum volume

They had their radio on at full blast.

full responsibility: all the blame for sth bad that has happened

I will take full responsibility if we do not succeed in getting the contract.

a party is in full swing: the party has reached its highest level of activity

It was late when we arrived and the party was in full swing.

to be in sb's good books: sb (your boss, your teacher, your parents, etc) is pleased with you
Opp.: to be in sb's bad books

Paul may not be the teacher's pet but he's certainly in her good books.

it's a good job that: it's fortunate that

It's a good job that you were wearing your seatbelt. Otherwise, you could have been seriously injured.

I've a good mind to do sth: used to introduce a threat that one will not carry out, but it shows that one is annoyed

Listen to the noise they are making. I've a good mind to call the police.

a heavy cold: a very bad cold

My youngest son is in bed with a heavy cold.

heavy traffic: lots of traffic

We were held up in heavy traffic.

a heavy week: a very busy and/or tiring week

I had had such a heavy week that all I wanted to do was stay at home and do nothing.

to have high hopes of sth happening: to think that there is a good chance that sth you have been working hard to achieve will happen

She has high hopes of becoming the next President.

it's high time: you really should [Note: **it's high time you/he/she, etc + past tense**]

It's high time you got a job.

high unemployment: a high percentage of the population do not have a job

It's time the government did something about the high unemployment rate

as a last resort: if nothing else works

I'll get the money somehow. As a last resort, I could sell my car.

the last straw: the final bad thing that happens to you – coming after a number of other bad things

He'd been moved into a smaller office and he'd lost his secretary. Reducing his salary was the last straw. He quit.

to be the last word in: to be the latest, newest and best

The X34J is the last word in laptop computers.

loose change: coins

He fished about in his pocket for some loose change.

to be at a loose end: to have nothing to do

If you're at a loose end while in Paris, go and visit my brother.

to tie up loose ends: to complete sth (a business deal, a plan, etc) that is almost finished

The deal is almost complete. We just have to tie up one or two loose ends.

a mixed blessing: sth that happens to you is in some ways good but in other ways bad

Winning the lottery was a mixed blessing for them. On the one hand, they would never have to work again, but on the other they lost a lot of friends.

to have mixed feelings about sth: part of you thinks sth is a good idea while the other part of you thinks it is a bad idea

I've got very mixed feelings about becoming self-employed.

the small hours: after midnight and in the very early morning

It's difficult to get used to working during the small hours, when everyone else is sleeping.

a tight match: a match in which both players/teams are equally good

It will be a tight match; both players are playing the best squash of their careers at the moment.

a tight squeeze: only just enough space for peope/things to fit in a particular place

It was a tight squeeze, but we managed to get all the boxes into the back of the car.

Practice

1. The words in bold have been jumbled. Swap them around to make correct collocations.

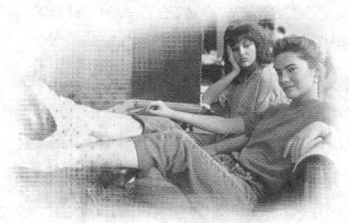

1. These exams are important and I think it's **good** time you got down to some serious revision.
2. I've got very **tight** feelings about moving to New Zealand. Part of me wants to go and part of me wants to stay here.
3. "We can all go in my car," she said. "It'll be a bit of a **last** squeeze, but it's only a short trip."
4. He speaks with such a **close** Scottish accent that even I find him difficult to understand - and I'm English!
5. We can get the money. We can try the bank, you could ask your father and I suppose as a **mixed** resort we could always sell the car.
6. I was certainly thrown in at the **good** end when I started teaching as I was given the biggest and most badly behaved class in the school.
7. I'm going to ask my boss for a day off on Friday. I'm in her **high** books at the moment so I'm sure she'll say yes.
8. It was a **broad** shave. If the teacher had arrived five minutes earlier, we'd have been caught red-handed.

2. Circle the correct item.

1. I'd love to come out tonight, but I can't. I'm too tired. I've had a very **heavy / loaded** week.
2. Brian's losing his job was a **full / mixed** blessing as it forced him to think about his future and set up what is now a very successful business.
3. As it says in the advertisement, the Omicron Zoom is the **final / last** word in digital cameras.
4. I've known him for donkey's years. He's like a brother to me. He's a very **close / near** friend.
5. He's not noisy?! Are you joking? He's got the radio on at **full / high** blast and he's singing at the top of his voice.
6. If your parents find out what you have done, you will be in **high / deep** trouble.
7. The traffic was so **heavy / deep** in the city centre that it took me two hours to get to the office.
8. There he stood with a **broad / full** grin on his face. "I've passed," he said.
9. Nobody ever finds themselves at a **dead / loose** end in New York. There's too much going on.
10. Don't worry. I will take **great / full** responsibility if anything goes wrong.
11. She had such a **deep / full** voice that when she first spoke to me over the phone I thought she was a man.
12. Can you hear the noise they are making next door? I've got a **full / good** mind to report them to the police.
13. Rising inflation, **deep / high** unemployment, an enormous trade deficit. How can you say that this government is anything but incompetent?
14. He has **high / full** hopes of winning the gold medal at next year's Olympic Games.
15. It was a **near / tight** match, with neither player ever getting the upper hand. Balkov finally won 7-6, 6-7, 7-6.
16. Last week I was the only one who didn't get a holiday. Now everyone is getting a bonus except me? Well, that's the **last / final** straw.
17. I'm afraid Roberta is not very well. She's in bed with a **deep / heavy** cold.
18. In general, he was happy with the contract, but there were still a few **loose / undone** ends that needed tying up before he would sign.
19. The party started at 7:30 and when we got there it was in **good / full** swing.
20. She needed to make a phone call but she didn't have any **little / loose** change.

3. Choose the correct item.

1. He gave his father back the keys, knowing that to have taken the car would have landed him in .... trouble.
   A full   B deep   C close   D loose
2. With the present .... rate of unemployment, the government stands little chance of being re-elected.
   A mixed   B broad   C tight   D high
3. She was burning the midnight oil, working into the .... hours to finish her thesis.
   A high   B heavy   C small   D broad
4. He decided to take a .... look at the contract before signing it.
   A full   B close   C tight   D small
5. Look, it's started raining. It's a .... job we brought an umbrella.
   A heavy   B broad   C great   D good

155

76 Noun Combinations II

at breakneck speed: extremely fast (generally for driving)

He took the corner at breakneck speed, lost control, and his car shot off the road.

sb comes from a broken home: sb's parents have got divorced (often used to suggest that the child's home life is/was unhappy)

Many of these young offenders come from broken homes.

a bumpy flight: a journey on a plane in which the plane moves about a lot because of air turbulence

It was quite a bumpy flight, which was a bit frightening for the more nervous passengers.

a capacity crowd: a crowd or audience that fills all of the seats in the room/hall/stadium

McCartney played to a capacity crowd wherever he went.

a catchy tune: a tune that is easy to remember [Note: **a catchy slogan/song**]

It will sell because it's got a catchy tune.

to have a clean driving licence: never to have been convicted of a driving offence

Applicants must have a clean driving licence.

common knowledge: sth everybody knows

It's common knowledge that they pulled strings to be where they are today.

a compulsive liar: a person who lies all the time and cannot stop himself from doing so [Note: If a book is **compulsive reading**, you can't stop reading it; if a TV programme is **compulsive viewing**, it is so interesting that you can't stop watching it]

Not only is he an inveterate cheat but he is also a compulsive liar.

a condemned building: a building that is going to be pulled down

She lived in a condemned block of flats in a run-down part of town.

a cushy job: a very easy job that does not take up too much of your time and usually pays well

She's got an incredibly cushy job. No wonder she gets out so often!

cutting-edge technology: the latest and most advanced technology

Using cutting-edge technology, we have designed a car that will outperform any other in its class.

a foregone conclusion: a result that you can predict with absolute certainty

Of course Benning will win. It's a foregone conclusion.

a mobile home: a large caravan, parked in a particular place and used as permanent accommodation [Note: **a mobile phone:** a portable telephone]

They bought a mobile home to spend their holidays in.

a non-stop flight: a flight which does not stop on the way to its destination

"Are we stopping in Frankfurt?" "No, it is a non-stop flight."

to be in the public eye: to be continually appearing on TV, in newspapers and magazines

Constantly being in the public eye is one of the drawbacks of being famous.

a remote possibility/chance (that sth will/ could happen): very little possibility of sth happening

There is, I suppose, a remote chance that you'll get your money back, but I wouldn't bank on it.

a resounding success: a complete success

His seminars were a resounding success. There was never an empty seat.

small talk: conversation about unimportant things that people usually make at social occasions

I hate those parties where you don't know anyone and you just make silly small talk.

the sole survivor: the only person to survive an accident

It was a terrible accident. John Smith, the sole survivor, says the only thing he remembers was hearing a massive crash.

strong language: bad and offensive language

The film was given an 18 certificate because it contained a lot of strong language.

a total/complete stranger: sb you have never met before

I thought I knew him but when he turned round I saw that he was a total stranger.

a vicious circle: a difficult problem which creates new problems which cause the original problem to reoccur

She couldn't get a visa because she couldn't get a job, but she couldn't get a job because she couldn't get a visa. It was a vicious circle.

to have had a wasted journey: to arrive somewhere only to find out that you cannot do/get what you planned to do/get there

I'm sorry you have had a wasted journey, but we sold every ticket we had within half an hour.

Practice

1. *Collocate the adjectives below with the correct noun. Two of the nouns should be used twice. Completing the sentences in exercise 2 using the nouns below (a-u) will help.*

1	a non-stop	......	a	conclusion
2	a cushy	......	b	job
3	a wasted	......	c	tune
4	a foregone	......	d	crowd
5	a catchy	......	e	flight
6	a compulsive	......	f	speed
7	the public	......	g	driving licence
8	a condemned	......	h	liar
9	a broken	......	i	journey
10	strong	......	j	building
11	a total	......	k	home
12	the sole	......	l	knowledge
13	a capacity	......	m	survivor
14	a vicious	......	n	language
15	a resounding	......	o	possibility
16	a clean	......	p	stranger
17	common	......	q	success
18	a bumpy	......	r	circle
19	breakneck	......	s	eye
20	a remote	......	t	technology
21	cutting-edge	......	u	talk
22	a mobile	......		
23	small	......		

2. *Complete the sentences using the nouns from exercise 1.*

1. No other passenger got out of the crash alive. She was the **sole** ....
2. He's got such a **cushy** .... He gets to work at eleven, does nothing and leaves at four.
3. He is incapable of telling the truth. He's a **compulsive** ....
4. They played to a **capacity** .... wherever they went. No matter how big the venue, not a seat remained empty.
5. They want someone with a **clean** .... , which counts me out as I was fined for speeding.
6. It was **common** .... that Sandra was planning to leave the company.
7. His last film was hardly what you'd call a **resounding** .... The critics hated it and it lost over ten million dollars.
8. He is living in a **condemned** .... on the Bays Road. I wonder where he'll go when they pull it down.
9. Not only was the film extremely violent but it also contained a lot of **strong** ....
10. Buenos Aires to London in twelve hours? It must have been a **non-stop** ....
11. I'd never met her before. She was a **total** ....
12. It's very unlikely that he'll win. There's a **remote** .... , I suppose. But it would take a miracle.
13. It's one of those songs with a really **catchy** .... It sticks in your mind.
14. You've travelled 200 miles to see him? But he moved last year. I'm sorry, it looks like you've had a **wasted** ....
15. The pilot said that there was a lot of turbulence en route and that we should expect a bit of a **bumpy** ....
16. He was driving around these narrow, winding mountain roads at **breakneck** .... in a powerful sports car. I was terrified.
17. She had a terrible childhood. Her father left home when she was five and, like most kids from a **broken** .... , she grew up feeling insecure about relationships.
18. Manchester United are playing the Women's Institute third team in the first round of the cup. That Manchester United will win is a **foregone** ....
19. This really is **cutting-edge** .... You won't find a more advanced scanner anywhere on the market.
20. It was a **vicious** .... We were losing customers so our sales were down. As a result, we had to put up our prices to cover costs. However, because we had put up our prices we lost more customers.
21. John is hopeless at **small** .... He gives one-word answers to anything you ask him!
22. Rather than live in a conventional house, he chose to live in a **mobile** ....
23. He says that he hates being on the front page of all the tabloids every other day, which is rubbish because we all know that he loves being in the .... **eye**.

77 Noun Combinations III

bare feet: without shoes or socks on
I've told you not to walk in the garden in bare feet. You could tread on a thorn.

full marks: to get everything right in an exam/test and be given maximum points
I got full marks on the Listening Comprehension paper.

a gaping hole: a very big hole
I've got to go to the dentist. A filling fell out of one of my back teeth and now I have got a gaping hole in it.

a ghost town: a town that has been abandoned by most of its inhabitants and is empty and very quiet as a result
This place used to be thriving but, since that explosion at the nuclear waste factory, it's been a ghost town.

a golden opportunity: a very good chance (to get sth valuable or be successful)
Being offered a part in the most popular soap opera on American television was a golden opportunity for a young actor like him.

the gutter press: newspapers that concentrate on gossip and scandals rather than serious news
I wouldn't trust anything I read in the gutter press.

a heated argument: an argument which is very passionate and probably involves a lot of shouting
The two drivers got out, looked at the damage to their vehicles and a heated argument ensued.

a hefty fine: (informal) a big fine
If you get caught, you will have to pay a hefty fine.

the hot favourite: the one that everyone expects to win (the race, match, etc)
He is the hot favourite to win the title.

a household name: a name of a person or product that everyone knows
Pear Computers was launched in 1997, and within two years it was a household name throughout the world.

a husky voice: a deep, rough sounding but attractive voice
She had a deep husky voice that I found oddly attractive.

irreparable damage: damage that cannot be put right
The scandal was likely to do irreparable damage to his reputation.
The virus had done irreparable damage to their computers.

juicy gossip: very interesting, scandalous gossip
I've got a really juicy piece of gossip to tell you.

a nail-biting finish: a very exciting and dramatic end (to a sports match, book, film, etc)
It was a nail-biting finish to what had been a rather dull film.

the not-too-distant future: the near future
He claims that there will be a natural disaster of devastating proportions in the not-too-distant future.

a package holiday: a holiday in which everything (flights, hotels, meals, excursions, etc) is organised for you
He's far too independent to want to go on a package holiday.

rampant/galloping/spiralling inflation: inflation that is out of control
Rampant inflation was destroying the country's economy.

a recurrent/recurring dream: a dream that you have again and again
If you have a recurring dream, it means that you are worried about something.

a straight answer: a direct answer
I want a straight answer. Did you or did you not tell John that I hated him?

to get a/the wrong number: to make a mistake when you are dialling and get through to the wrong person
"Hello, is Derek there?" "No, I'm sorry, you have (got) the wrong number."

Practice

1. The words in bold below have been jumbled. Swap them around so that the sentences make sense.

   1. Although 'Nosia' was only founded four years ago, it has become a household **dream**.
   2. The gutter **gossip** got hold of the story and distorted it out of all recognition.
   3. A recurring **future** about falling bothered him so much that he made an appointment with a psychologist.
   4. I read this column in the Daily Herald because it's always full of juicy **press**.
   5. In the not-too-distant **finish**, fossil fuels will have run out and we'll have to use alternative sources of energy
   6. They were shouting and waving their arms, clearly in the middle of a heated **name**.
   7. Spiralling **damage** is making life increasingly difficult
   8. The fans were on the edge of their seats as they watched the nail-biting **argument**.
   9. The flood did irreparable **inflation** to many of the city's oldest buildings.

2. a. Complete the noun combinations by providing the missing noun in column B. The first letter of the missing word is given and the spaces that follow indicate the number of missing letters. The **Association Words** box will provide clues for the missing Column B word. The meaning of the adjective half of the combination (A) is given in the **Meaning of A column**.

	A	B	Meaning of A	Association Words
1	a heated	A _ _ _ _ _ _ _	angry, passionate	anger, words
2	a recurrent/recurring	D _ _ _ _	happening repeatedly	sleep, nightmare
3	the not-too-distant	F _ _ _ _ _	close, near	past, present
4	a golden	O _ _ _ _ _ _ _ _ _ _	good, not-to-be-missed	chance, possibility
5	irreparable	D _ _ _ _ _	cannot be fixed	destruction, repair
6	juicy	G _ _ _ _ _	scandalous	rumours, private life
7	a husky	V _ _ _ _	deep, hoarse	sound, speak
8	a straight	A _ _ _ _ _	honest and truthful	question, reply
9	a hefty	F _ _ _	large	money, punishment
10	full	M _ _ _ S	maximum	exam, points
11	a gaping	H _ _ _	very big	cavity, dig, leak
12	bare	F _ _ _	without shoes and socks	toes, inches
13	rampant	I _ _ _ _ _ _ _ _	rapidly increasing	economics, prices
14	the hot	F _ _ _ _ _ _ _	most people's	popular, winner
15	a/the wrong	N _ _ _ _ _	incorrect	six, four, nine
16	a ghost	T _ _ _	empty, abandoned	city, village
17	a package	H _ _ _ _ _ _	with everything organised	sun, rest, brochure
18	a nail-biting	F _ _ _ _ _	tense, exciting	end
19	a household	N _ _ _	very well-known	first, John
20	the gutter	P _ _ _ _	tabloid, sensationalist	paper, squeeze

b. Now complete each of the sentences below with one of the above noun combinations.

1 Hello. Hello. Is Tim there? ... Tim Ford... Is that 37465? ... Sorry, I must have got the ....

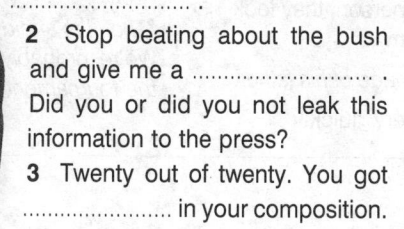

2 Stop beating about the bush and give me a .... Did you or did you not leak this information to the press?

3 Twenty out of twenty. You got .... in your composition. Wow!

4 I'd never go on a .... I like my independence too much and I hate huge resorts.

5 You shouldn't walk around the garden in .... You could tread on a wasp.

6 I'm not surprised it sank. There's a .... in the bottom of it.

7 If you are caught driving without insurance, not only will you lose your licence but you will also have to pay a ....

8 Newells Old Boys are the .... to win this year's championship, and with the likes of Arano, Jansen and Copani in their side who would bet against them?

9 .... was crippling the country's economy.

10 When I spoke to his secretary for the first time, it was on the phone. She had such a .... that I thought I was talking to a man.

11 It wasn't so much a blazing row as a ....

12 At night, once the temperatures had dropped there were people everywhere, but during the day it was a ....

13 A scholarship to study at Cambridge! It was a .... that she just had to take.

14 We believe that these pesticides are doing .... to the environment, which is why we want them banned - before it is too late.

15 There was a .... to the World Cup last night, when, after thirty minutes of extra time, the game went to a penalty shoot-out.

78 Noun Combinations IV

a bank holiday: an official public holiday when most banks and businesses are closed
Tomorrow is a bank holiday, so the shops will be closed.

a crushing blow: if sth (a plan, peace talks, etc) is/are dealt a crushing blow, sth happens that has a terrible effect on it/them
The peace talks were dealt a crushing blow when one of the delegations walked out.

a narrow margin: if you win sth (generally an election) by a narrow margin, you only just beat your opponent(s)
The party won the election by a very narrow margin.

a nervous wreck: tired and unhealthy as a result of being constantly worried and nervous
After her divorce she was a nervous wreck.

a niggling doubt: a small doubt that keeps worrying sb and will not go away
It was a niggling doubt that refused to go away.

to be an only child: to have no brothers or sisters
I am an only child.

poetic justice: a deserved punishment (often used when sb who continually does bad things is punished for sth they didn't do)
It was the first time she had told the truth but the jury did not believe her. That indeed was poetic justice.

a regular customer: a person who goes to the same shop/restaurant, etc on a regular basis
[Note: **a regular listener/viewer:** a person who listens to a radio programme/watches the same television programme on a regular basis]
I have been a regular customer at this shop for over thirty years.
As regular listeners will know, tonight's programme is the last in the series.

a rough guess: a very approximate guess
At a rough guess, I'd say there were about 300 people there.

scrap of paper: a small piece of paper often used for writing notes on
She handed me a scrap of paper with her telephone number on it.

small print: the minor details of a legal document (a contract, an entry form for a competition, etc) often written in very small letters
It says here in the small print that employees of the company cannot enter the competition.

the spitting image: if sb is the spitting image of another person, they look very similar to them
He's the spitting image of his father.

in a split second: very quickly
I took my eyes off my bag for a split second and it was gone!

a steady job: a regular, stable and serious job which you are likely to have for some time
As a student, I don't have a steady job.

a sweeping generalisation: to say that sth is true in every case and in every situation
He makes these sweeping generalisations just to see my reactions.

to have a sweet tooth: to love eating sweet things
Both my children have got a sweet tooth and love cakes and sweets.

sth is an uphill struggle: sth is very difficult to do, and in order to succeed you have to fight very hard all the time
Our first year in business was a real uphill struggle.

beyond one's wildest dreams: more than one could ever have imagined or hoped for
Now that they had won the lottery, they were rich beyond their wildest dreams.

wishful thinking: a false belief that sth positive will happen
"Maybe we will win this year." "That, I'm afraid, is wishful thinking. We're probably the worst team in the tournament."

Practice

1. The sentences below are definitions of noun combinations. Choose the correct **noun combination** for each definition by matching an adjective from column A with a noun from column B on page 161.

   1 If you go to one particular shop all the time, then the shopkeeper would consider you to be one of these. ....

   2 Nobody works on one of these nowadays. ....

   3 If it happens in this amount of time, then it happens very quickly indeed. ....

   4 You sometimes need some of this in an exam. You might need it to make notes on. ....

   5 'All football fans are hooligans' is an example of one of these. ....

   6 It's only approximate. You don't know for sure. ....

7 If you have got one of these, uncertainty just won't go away. ....
8 If you are one of these, you should take a holiday and try to relax. Worrying all the time will only make you ill. ....
9 If someone who cheats at a sport without being caught is later disqualified for something he/she didn't do, you could say it was this. ....
10 If you work at the same place for a long time and it is probable that you will continue doing so, then you have this. ....
11 If you are this of your mother, then you look just like her. ....
12 If the X party beats Y party in an election, but only wins by one of these, then the Y party only needed a few more votes and they would have won the election. ....
13 If you have got one of these, then you almost certainly love chocolate. ....
14 If a plan you have is dealt one of these, then something has happened that means your plan will probably have to be abandoned. ....
15 You have bought a lottery ticket. You want to believe that you are going to win but you know what this is. ....
16 It's at the bottom of a contract and you should always read it before signing anything. ....
17 The economy is a total disaster. Getting the country back on its feet again will be very difficult and will take a lot of time. This is what it will be. ....
18 Of course you are amazed that you won the lottery. You never thought it would happen to you, not even in these. ....
19 He/She has not got any brothers or sisters. ....

	Column A		Column B		
1	bank	a	guess	......	......
2	a steady	b	child	......	......
3	scrap	c	generalisation	......	......
4	the spitting	d	justice	......	......
5	poetic	e	second	......	......
6	a niggling	f	wreck	......	......
7	wildest	g	doubt	......	......
8	a regular	h	thinking	......	......
9	small	i	customer	......	......
10	an only	j	margin	......	......
11	an uphill	k	struggle	......	......
12	a split	l	holiday	......	......
13	a rough	m	paper	......	......
14	a nervous	n	tooth	......	......
15	wishful	o	print	......	......
16	a sweeping	p	image	......	......
17	a crushing	q	job	......	......
18	a narrow	r	dreams	......	......
19	a sweet	s	blow	......	......

2. *Answer/Respond to the following using **noun combinations** from exercise 1.*

1 I've just eaten two cream cakes and a bar of chocolate.
 ....
2 I'm just going to the bank to get some money.
 ....
3 How many people attended the concert, then?
 ....
4 Is this pile of paper part of the economy drive at your office?
 ....
5 I didn't know that the guarantee covered my computer for replacement of parts but not for labour.
 ....
6 When I was young, my parents had to encourage me to make friends to stop me being lonely.
 ....
7 Do you always shop at Brightways Supermarket?
 ....
8 He looks so much like his grandfather, doesn't he?
 ....
9 I would love to be on holiday on an exotic island rather than being stuck in a stuffy office.
 ....

79 Verb Combinations I

to cut a long story short: a phrase used when you want to quickly finish a story

... so, to cut a long story short, they fell in love and got married.

to cut corners: to do sth (especially sth connected with building) in the easiest, quickest, cheapest way you can - (often ignoring rules and regulations and often with the result that what is produced is badly made)

I want this to be the best and most impressive building in the city, so do not cut corners.

to cut short: to stop sth (e.g. a holiday) earlier than planned

On hearing that war had broken out, the Prime Minister cut short his holiday and returned home.

to draw sb's attention to sth: (formal) to make sb notice sth

I'd like to draw your attention to clause 34 in the contract.

to draw a crowd: to attract a crowd

The street performers drew a large crowd.

to draw the curtains: to close the curtains

It was dark. She got up and drew the curtains.

to hold a meeting: to have a meeting

Our last staff meeting of the year will be held on December 18.

to hold a number of: (for place/ thing) to have enough space for a number of people

The new Mega cinema can hold up to 700 people.

to hold sb responsible (for) sth: to consider sb responsible for sth

If we don't get this contract, I'll hold you personally responsible.

to jump on the bandwagon: to do what other people are doing because it is fashionable/likely to be successful

Why jump on the bandwagon just because other people dye their hair pink?

to jump the queue: to go to the front of a queue without waiting your turn

He was surprised that no one said anything about the man who had just jumped the queue.

to jump to the conclusion that: to decide that sth is true before you are in possession of all the facts

Don't jump to the conclusion that he is unfriendly, just because he is on the quiet side.

to keep abreast of: to keep informed about the latest ideas/news/developments

I buy the Daily Trader magazine to keep abreast of the latest developments in the stock market.

to keep sth at bay: to keep sth away to stop it from bothering you

Keeping yourself occupied will keep boredom at bay.

to keep sb in the dark: to deliberately not tell sb about sth

I would rather know than be kept in the dark.

to lose touch: to stop visiting/writing/speaking to sb

We used to see each other fairly regularly, but after he moved we lost touch.

to lose track of time: to forget what time it is

He couldn't believe it was 10 o'clock; he had been so engrossed in the film that he had totally lost track of time.

to lose your way: to get lost

He would never get there on time. He was late when he left home and now he had lost his way.

to meet one's death: to die

He met his death in a duel.

to meet sb's demands: to do what sb wants

I have no intention of meeting such unreasonable demands.

to meet with sb's approval/disapproval: (formal) to be approved of/disapproved of

[Note: **to meet with little/no success**: to be unsuccessful]

The Minister's plan to abolish the tax met with widespread approval.

to raise the alarm: to warn people about danger/to contact the fire services/the police

An old lady saw the bag, thought it looked suspicious and raised the alarm.

to raise one's voice to sb: to shout at sb because one is angry

Don't raise your voice to me.

to raise public awareness of sth: to improve people's knowledge about/of sth

We must raise public awareness of the problems facing refugees.

to run a temperature: to have a high temperature

You don't look very well. Are you running a temperature?

sth runs in the family: if a particular characteristic, skill, disease, etc runs in a family, many members of that family have it

Asthma runs in our family. My grandfather, my father and both my brothers suffer from it.

to run rings (a)round sb: to beat an opponent very easily

They'll run rings round such a poor team.

to stand empty: to be vacant (for buildings)

The castle stood empty for centuries.

to stand to do sth: to be in a position where you are likely to do sth, (e.g. to win, earn or lose money)

If this deal comes off, we stand to make a lot of money.

to throw a party: to have a party

The college is throwing a party next Friday to mark the end of term.

to throw a punch: to punch (hit) sb

So who threw the first punch, then?

Practice

1. Complete the sentences using the verbs in the list in the appropriate form.

> stand – draw – hold – jump – lose – keep – meet – cut – run – raise – throw

1 It is important to .... abreast of the latest developments in teaching methodology.
2 .... the curtains, will you? It's too bright in here.
3 Julius Caesar .... a violent death at the hands of some of his most trusted friends.
4 We're .... a party next Saturday. Why don't you come?
5 He's just as awkward as his father. Being stubborn .... in the family.
6 Anyway, to .... a long story short, he ended up in Hawaii.
7 He lost his temper and started to shout at her. "Don't .... your voice to me," she said.
8 Tomorrow's meeting has been postponed and will now be .... at ten o'clock on Thursday morning.
9 The old lady walked to the front of the line and struck up a conversation with the man nearest the counter. I bet she was trying to .... the queue!
10 She blushed when she said it, so he immediately .... to the conclusion that she was lying.
11 Clearly the company had not wanted us to know about the merger, so we were .... in the dark until the very last moment.
12 We invested heavily in that company, and if it goes bankrupt we .... to lose a lot of money.
13 Glastonbury is Britain's biggest music festival. Every year it .... crowds well in excess of 100,000.
14 When the management said that it had no intention of .... the union's demands, the union leader called for immediate strike action.
15 I used to see Derek fairly regularly, but when he joined the army we .... touch.
16 I didn't start it. He did. He .... the first punch!

2. Circle the correct item.

1 I don't feel at all well. I must be **keeping / running** a temperature.
2 "I'd like to **draw / throw** your attention to rule number 24a, on page six of your booklet," he said.
3 I'm sorry I'm late. I was reading this amazing book and I completely **kept / lost** track of time.
4 The Minister's plan to abolish compulsory military service **met / ran** with widespread approval.
5 Use this liquid repellent. It will help **stand / keep** the mosquitoes at bay.
6 Domestic problems forced the President to **keep / cut** short his holiday and return home early.
7 Why did you say that you would ensure that everything ran smoothly? Now they will **hold / keep** you responsible if anything goes wrong.
8 They are not interested in the environment. They've just **run / jumped** on the environmental bandwagon. They know green issues are popular and they think these policies will win them votes.
9 In an attempt to **draw / raise** public awareness of the problems facing blind people, the Blind Association launched a massive public information campaign.
10 She's a much better player than he is. Of course she'll win, she'll **throw / run** rings round him.
11 They are the kind of company that don't believe in **jumping / cutting** corners. They take their time, they use the best materials available and they make sure that their work is properly done.
12 It's a big room. It can **keep / hold** up to 3,000 people.
13 If his next door neighbours hadn't **raised / jumped** the alarm when they did, his house would have burnt to the ground.
14 If you had remembered to bring a map, we wouldn't have **lost / met** our way.
15 If he wins this round, he **keeps / stands** to win the competition.
16 I don't care who **threw / raised** the first punch. I just want you to stop fighting.
17 The mansion had **stood / kept** empty for many years and was said to be haunted.

80 Verb Combinations II

- **to arouse suspicion:** to make sb suspicious

  What first aroused my suspicion was that every time he came into the shop he was too friendly.

- **to beat about the bush:** to avoid or delay talking about sth embarrassing or unpleasant

  Oh, come on, stop beating about the bush and tell me what you think.

- **to broach the subject:** to start talking about sth which the person you are talking to might find embarrassing, offensive or annoying

  He decided to broach the subject of promotion.

- **to damage sb's reputation:** to have a bad effect on sb's (good) reputation

  A scandal like this is bound to damage his reputation.

- **to dash sb's hopes:** to do or say sth that makes sb feel that they cannot achieve what they were hoping to

  Their rejection of his manuscript dashed his hopes of becoming a best-selling novelist.

- **to declare war on:** to officially announce that a war will begin

  Negotiations having failed, they declared war on the neighbouring country.

- **to derive pleasure from/out of sth:** to get pleasure from sth
  [Note: **to derive (some/any kind of) benefit from sth:** (formal) to get some kind of benefit from sth]

  Martin derives a lot of pleasure out of his stamp collection.

  The only people who will derive any benefit from this new law are the rich.

- **to devote one's time/life to sth:** to spend most of one's time/life doing sth

  She devoted her life to looking after the sick and needy.

- **to dissolve into tears:** to start crying

  She looked into his expressionless eyes and dissolved into tears.

- **to draw the line at sth:** to refuse to do sth or to disapprove of sth because it crosses a limit that one thinks should not be crossed

  Most people would draw the line at such unethical behaviour.

- **to draw up a chair:** to bring a chair to a table so as to join people already sitting at the table

  "Draw up a chair," he said. "We were talking about tomorrow's game."

- **to drop a hint:** to say sth indirectly

  I was too embarrassed to say I liked her. Anyway, I've dropped enough hints.

- **to earn a living:** to work and make money in order to live

  Before becoming famous, Granger earned a living as a waiter in a burger bar.

- **to express an interest in sth:** to say or show that you are interested in sth
  [Note: **to express your concern/your doubts about sth:** (formal) to say that you are concerned/have doubts about]

  He suddenly expressed an interest in going on the trip with us.

  They expressed their concern about whether planning permission would be granted.

- **to fight back the tears:** to try and stop yourself from crying

  Determined to be strong, she fought back the tears.

- **to find fault with sb/sth:** to criticise sb/sth

  What is it with you, Sarah? Why is it that you have to find fault with everything I say and do?

- **to follow in sb's footsteps:** to do the same job as sb (e.g. a parent/grandparent, an elder brother or sister)

  My father was a doctor, as was my grandfather before him. Both my brother and I were expected to follow in their footsteps.

Practice

1. Complete the gaps in the text with a verb from the box in the appropriate form. There are some extra verbs that you do not need to use.

   > fight – damage – draw – express – declare – devote – draw – beat – earn – dissolve – follow – drop – dash – derive – arouse – broach – find

The parlour door creaked as I pushed it open and walked into the uncomfortable silence. Mother sat, stony-faced, at a large, bulky desk and peered disapprovingly over her glasses as I **1)** .... up a chair to face her. She said nothing. I smiled and searched for a few empty words that might bring some warmth to the proceedings. Warmth, however, was never my mother's strong suit so I stopped after 'hello'.

"I'm sure you **2)** .... some kind of bizarre pleasure out of this," she said. She knew. How did she know? "There are rules, Giles", she continued. "Strict rules. Our rules." She paused. She shook her head and fumbled for a handkerchief. She was struggling to **3)** .... back the tears. "You will **4)** .... this family's reputation beyond repair." She allowed the words to hang in the air. An inner voice told me to deny everything.

"What are you talking about, mother?" I asked.

"You know full well."

I'd been keeping odd hours, because of rehearsals. I knew it would 5) .... suspicion. I'd obviously been seen. I'd probably been followed.

"Your father, poor man, is devastated. Shocked. Thirteen generations, Giles. Thirteen! Each Babbington son 6) .... in his father's footsteps ... until now. All of them accountants. Then you become ... you become"- she could hardly find the words to say it - "an actor!"

She 7) .... into tears. I had never seen my mother cry before but I knew that these were not tears of sadness, grief or disappointment. They were tears of indignation. Something stirred in me. Not pity, not contrition. It was resolve. My silence spoke volumes. "You don't deny it then?" she asked.

The blood drained from my mother's face. The one hope that she had been clinging to – that her informant had somehow misheard or misunderstood – had been 8) .... It was as if I had 9) .... war on thirteen generations of Babbingtons.

"This shouldn't come as a surprise," I said. "I may not have said it in as many words, but goodness knows I've 10) .... enough hints." I was lying. I hadn't said anything, directly or indirectly. The truth was that I had been far too frightened to 11) .... the subject. The consequences didn't bear thinking about. My mother stood up and, brushing past me, left without saying a word.

2. The words in bold have been used incorrectly. Replace each word with a correct one to make reasonable combinations.

1 The man in the mac and dark glasses immediately **expressed** my suspicion.
2 True or not, these accusations are bound to **beat about** his reputation.
3 I had hurt her feelings and I could see that she was trying to **express** the tears.
4 All hopes of finding survivors were **earned** by the news.
5 It's cold outside, so **drop** a chair and come and sit by the fire.
6 Our boss **declares war on** everything we do.

3. Complete the sentences using the verbs from the box in exercise 1. You may have to change the form of some of the verbs.

1 The sports injury .... all Keith's hopes of a career in the armed forces.
2 An overcritical individual .... fault with whatever other people do.
3 In the novel, Scotland .... war on Wales.
4 Is sitting there with your coat on your way of .... a hint that it's cold?
5 Clara .... all her spare time to helping charitable organisations.
6 Clive tried to .... the subject of a pay rise but was unable to.
7 He .... his concern about the proposed by-pass.
8 In times of recession, it is difficult to .... a decent living.
9 I don't mind high spirits, but I .... the line at this kind of behaviour.
10 I won't .... about the bush. I'll come straight to the point.

4. Make up appropriate questions for these responses.

1 A: .... ?
   B: He didn't want to arouse suspicion.
2 A: .... ?
   B: No, I think he would draw the line at fraud.
3 A: .... ?
   B: Well, she dropped a hint.
4 A: .... ?
   B: You don't like beating about the bush, eh?
5 A: .... ?
   B: She simply dissolved into tears.

81 Verb Combinations III

to bend the rules: to change the rules slightly on one particular occasion

The man behind the counter told us that, although it was past midnight, he would bend the rules and give us something to eat.

to bow to sb's demands: (for a government/company) to finally and reluctantly agree to do sth

After months of strikes and failed negotiations, the management finally bowed to the union's demands.

to cost a bomb: to be very expensive

You can't afford a car like that. They cost a bomb.

to hail a taxi/cab: to signal to a taxi (so that it stops and picks you up) while you are standing in the street

He stood in the street, trying to hail a taxi.

to issue (sb with) a ticket or permit/licence: to give sb a ticket or permit/licence that they have paid for

They told me that they would issue me with a new parking permit.

to jog sb's memory: to help sb remember sth

Perhaps this letter will jog your memory.

to level an accusation/a criticism: to accuse/criticise

Accusations of mismanagement were levelled against the board.

to owe sb an apology: to feel that you need to apologise to sb

"I owe you an apology," she said.

to pin the blame on sb: to say that an innocent person is to blame for sth bad that has happened

They pinned the blame for the crash on him.

to rack one's brains: to try very hard to think of sth or remember sth

He racked his brains, trying to remember the caller's name.

to run rings round sb: to be much better than sb and beat them very easily (generally used for sport)

You think City will beat United? Are you mad? United will run rings round City.

to seek advice: to ask (and probably pay) sb (a doctor, a lawyer) for professional advice

If the symptoms persist, you should seek medical advice.

to settle a bill: to pay a bill

He called the waiter over and settled the bill.

to swallow your pride: to decide to do sth even though you think it will cause you to lose some respect

He would have to swallow his pride and admit his mistake.

to tackle a problem: to deal with and try to solve a problem

The government has introduced these measures to tackle the growing problem of unemployment.

to try sb's patience: to make sb feel impatient/annoyed

He had been waiting to be served for over twenty minutes and it was beginning to try his patience.

to undermine sb's confidence: to make sb feel less confident

It is his first ever performance. Don't be too critical; it will undermine his confidence.

to wear thin: (i) an **excuse** or **explanation** that is beginning to wear thin has been used so often that you are beginning not to believe it (ii) if sb's **patience** is wearing thin, they are beginning to feel impatient/annoyed

He was late again; it was the same old excuse and it was wearing thin.

He'd been waiting for hours and his patience was wearing thin.

Practice

1. 🎧 You will hear five people talking about some rather unpleasant experiences. Listen to the recording and decide which of the speakers (1-5) is talking about ...

   A ... somebody who tried his/her patience?
   B ... settling a bill?
   C ... somebody who undermined his/her self-confidence?
   D ... having to bow to some people's demands?
   E .... racking his/her brains trying to remember something
   F ... ordering something that cost a bomb?
   G ... somebody who bent the rules?
   H ... jogging somebody's memory?

   Speaker 1 ☐
   Speaker 2 ☐
   Speaker 3 ☐
   Speaker 4 ☐
   Speaker 5 ☐

166

2. Fill in the word puzzle by completing the gapped sentences below.

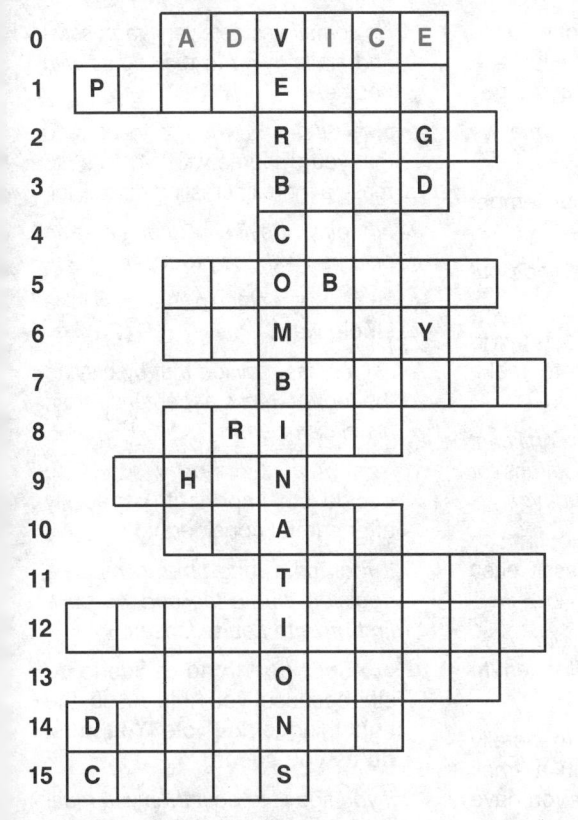

0		A	D	V	I	C	E		
1	P			E					
2				R		G			
3				B		D			
4				C					
5				O	B				
6				M		Y			
7				B					
8			R	I					
9		H		N					
10				A					
11				T					
12				I					
13				O					
14	D			N					
15	C			S					

0 If the symptoms do not go away within 3 days, you should seek medical ...advice... .
1 The deafening noise from next door was enough to try the .... of a saint.
2 She's a much better player than he is. Of course she'll win. She'll run .... round him.
3 I know children are not allowed, but my son is desperate to see the final and you are the only café in the area that has satellite TV. Surely you can .... the rules just this once?
4 She stood outside her hotel in the pouring rain, trying to hail a .... They were all full.
5 The government has introduced new legislation which it hopes will tackle the .... of spiralling unemployment.
6 She says she doesn't have any recollection of the meeting. If we show her the photo, perhaps it will jog her ....
7 No matter how hard I racked my ...., I just couldn't come up with the answer.
8 You are going to have to swallow your .... and admit that you were wrong.
9 He was late again, for the fourth time. He couldn't use the old excuse again – it was wearing a bit ....
10 They needed a scapegoat and he was insignificant enough to be the right candidate. So they pinned the .... on him.
11 I rang the airline to see if they would change my booking and issue me with a .... for the next day.
12 This latest scandal is bound to further undermine the public's .... in the government.
13 I owe you an .... I thought you had misled me. I was wrong. I'm sorry. 
14 The workers threatened to go on strike if they didn't get a pay rise. So, the management had no alternative but to bow to their ....
15 It's a great outfit, but how are you going to afford it? It .... a bomb!

3. Circle the correct item.

1 The children are being so noisy that they are really trying my **demand / patience** today.
2 You had better swallow your **pride / advice** and apologise, seeing that you were in the wrong.
3 I racked my **memory / brains** in search of an answer, but was unable to find one.
4 I suggest you seek legal **rules / advice** .
5 He levelled bitter **criticism / blame** against our company's environmental policies.
6 The doorman will **tackle / hail** a taxi for you.
7 If you shout at him all the time, you'll only **undermine / swallow** his confidence.
8 Our supplier's excuses for not delivering goods on time are beginning to **bow / wear thin** .
9 Where was this ticket **owed / issued** ?
10 A house in the suburbs would **cost a bomb / wear thin**.
11 The suspect tried to pin the **blame / accusation** on his accomplice saying it was all her idea.

82 Verb Combinations IV

to bear a resemblance to: to look like [Note: (i) to bear **a strong/striking** resemblance to: to be very similar to (ii) to bear **little** resemblance to: to be quite different from (iii) to bear **no** resemblance to: to be completely different from]

He bears a striking resemblance to his grandfather.

to bear the brunt of sth: to receive the main force or impact of sth

The town nearest the epicentre bore the brunt of the earthquake.

to carry weight: if a person's opinions or views carry (a lot of) weight, then other people respect and pay a lot of attention to them, probably because the person is respected and influential

Try to get Mr Harris to support your idea. His opinion carries a lot of weight in this company.

to clear your throat: to cough in order to speak more clearly

He stood up, cleared his throat and began his lecture.

to clear your debts: to get rid of all your debts by paying back all the money you owe

Once we have cleared all our debts, we'll take a holiday.

to deliver a speech: to make a speech in front of a lot of people

He was the only minister at the conference not to deliver a speech.

to drive sb crazy: to really annoy sb

The noise they are making next door is driving me crazy.

to drive a hard bargain: to argue aggressively and be unwilling to make concessions so that you get the best price for sth

As a businessman, he has a reputation for driving a hard bargain.

to grab sb's attention: to make sb notice you

Can you grab the waiter's attention? I want to order.

to hit the road: (informal) often used when you are about to leave a place and make your way home

John looked at Jill. "It's time we hit the road," he said.

to hit the roof: to lose your temper and become very angry

She'll hit the roof if she finds out what you've done.

to lay the foundations for sth: to provide the conditions to make sth successful in the future

The treaty, considered insignificant at the time, laid the foundations for the unification of the country.

to lay oneself open to criticism: to do/say sth which makes it easy for sb to criticise one

By being careless with your work, you are laying yourself open to criticism.

to leave a tip: to leave sb (generally a waiter in a restaurant) a small amount of money, after you have paid your bill

We don't have to leave a tip. It says on the bill that service is included.

to leave a deposit: to pay part of the price of a product in order to reserve it

Would it be all right if I left a deposit of £30 on it now and you put it aside for me?

to pay sb a compliment: to say nice things to sb

She blushes whenever somebody pays her a compliment.

to pay sb a visit: to visit sb

I'll pay him a visit next time I'm passing through.

to pick sb's brains: to ask sb questions in order to get some information/help

You know a lot about computers. Do you mind if I pick your brains about one or two things?

to pick a fight: to deliberately try to start a fight with sb by acting aggressively towards them

He sometimes gets very aggressive and starts trying to pick fights with people.

to play devil's advocate: to pretend that you disagree with sth so as to make a more interesting discussion

I'll play devil's advocate and disagree with the proposal.

to play the fool: to behave in a stupid way

James has realised that by playing the fool he gains acceptance from his classmates.

to reach a decision/verdict: to decide sth important, especially after careful consideration

It took us a long time to reach a decision, but in the end we gave first prize to Laura Jansen.

to see fit to do sth: to decide to do sth because you think it is the right thing to do [Note: **You must do as you see fit**]

If you see fit to do it then you must do it, but I think it is a bad idea.

"You must do as you see fit. But you might find that the law is on their side," she said.

to settle an argument: to do sth which will end an argument by showing which side is right

Look, the only way to settle this argument is to check the spelling in a dictionary.

to steer (well) clear of sb/sth: to avoid a place or a person because it is/they are dangerous

The cafés in this city are generally friendly places, but I would steer well clear of those near the bus station.

Practice

1. Match the verbs in Section A with their appropriate combinations in Section B. Then, complete the sentences in Section C with (an) appropriate word(s) from Section B. An example has been done for you.

Section A

0	to steer	l
1	to play	......
2	to see	......
3	to pay	......
4	to pick	......
5	to settle	......
6	to deliver	......
7	to leave	......
8	to reach	......
9	to grab	......
10	to carry	......
11	to lay	......
12	to drive	......
13	to hit	......
14	to clear	......
15	to bear	......

Section B

- a   an **argument**
- b   someone's **brains**, a **fight**
- c   the **foundations for**, yourself **open to criticism**
- d   **devil's advocate**, the **fool**
- e   someone **crazy**, a **hard bargain**
- f   the **brunt of**, **little resemblance** to
- g   the **road**, the **roof**
- h   **fit**
- i   a **deposit**, (someone) a **tip**
- j   your **throat**, your **debts**
- k   **weight**
- l   (well) **clear of** someone/something
- m   someone a **visit**, someone a **compliment**
- n   someone's **attention**
- o   a **speech**
- p   a **decision**

Section C

0   The guide says that the neighbourhoods around the docks are pretty dangerous and it advises travellers to steer well *clear of* them – especially at night.
1   The waiter had been rude and inattentive all night. No way was I going to leave a ....
2   He stood up, shuffled his papers, cleared his .... and started to speak.
3   Look, why don't you just ask her how old she is and settle the .... ?
4   Can I pick your .... for a moment? I have to teach the third conditional next class and I need an activity to practise it. Have you got any ideas?
5   Is that the time? We ought to hit the .... We've got a long journey home.
6   I couldn't put up with it, living right next to a main road. All that noise would drive me ....
7   He was pushing me and insulting me. He was obviously trying to pick a ....
8   If Dad finds out you have been driving his car, he'll hit the ....
9   I've been asked to deliver a .... to the Women's Guild on Thursday. I've never spoken in public before and I'm terrified.
10 It is hoped that these talks will lay the .... for long-lasting peace in the region.
11 He wanted £500 for it but I told him £200 was my last offer. "You drive a ....," he said and sold the chair to me for £200.
12 We're going to Scotland for our holidays. My sister lives in Edinburgh, so we are going to pay her a ....
13 We all agree that fox-hunting is wrong. However, this is a debate, so half the class will have to play ....
14 We should get Jones to support us. He's an influential man and his opinions carry a lot of .... around here.
15 I've been trying to grab the waiter's .... for the last ten minutes. Surely he must have seen me waving!
16 My students paid me a really nice .... today. They said I was the best teacher they had ever had.
17 I didn't have enough money with me to pay for it, so I left a .... of £25 and went back the next day to pay the remainder.
18 We can only buy a new car once we have cleared all our ....
19 I know they are twins but they bear very .... to one another.
20 He said he had no intention of interfering in the day-to-day management of the team. That was my job and I should do things as I saw ....
21 It took the jury six hours to reach a .... and in the end they all agreed - Gandolfo was guilty as charged.

83 Verb Combinations V

to allay concerns/fears: to make sb feel less concerned/afraid

The manufacturer's reassurances have done little to allay people's fears about the product's safety.

to claim responsibility: to officially say that you are responsible for sth bad that has happened

A political group claimed responsibility for the damage.

to conduct a survey: to ask people a set of questions in order to find out their opinions on sth

In a survey conducted recently, 85% of people said they preferred free-range to battery farm eggs.

to cut class: to deliberately miss a class at school or university

There's a free concert in the park this afternoon. Why don't we cut class and go to it?

to hazard a guess: to guess

I don't know the answer but I'll hazard a guess and say it's answer C.

to hurl abuse at sb: to shout insults at sb

The player was thrown out of the team for hurling abuse at his coach.

to hurt sb's feelings: to upset or offend sb

You know how proud she is of her cooking. If you don't eat it, you will hurt her feelings.

to launch a new product: to make a new product available for the public to buy

Our new range of cosmetics, launched last month, is already selling well.

to let out a scream: to scream

On seeing the mouse, she let out a scream.

to level an accusation against sb: (formal) to accuse sb of (doing) sth

Of the many accusations that have been levelled against him, this is by far the most damaging.

to mount a search: to organise and start a search

A thousand people combed the area in one of the biggest searches ever mounted by the police.

to pluck up (the) courage to do sth: to make an effort to be brave enough to do sth

I've always wanted to leave my job and travel around the world. I just haven't been able to pluck up the courage to do it.

(not) to pull your weight: (not) to do your fair share of the work

If you don't start pulling your weight in this office, you will be asked to resign.

to push your luck: to take a big risk (because you have taken the same risk before and nothing bad has happened to you)

You had a pay rise six months ago, It's pushing your luck to ask for another so soon.

to realise an ambition: to achieve an ambition

He realised his life-long ambition when he won a medal in the Sydney 2000 Olympic Games.

not to ring true: if an excuse, explanation, etc doesn't ring true, you find it difficult to believe

His story about the dog eating his homework just doesn't ring true.

to stay put: not to move

Jimmy was lost. He had two options, to stay put and hope that his mother would come back or to start running around crying.

to stem the flow of sth: to stop sth from spreading/developing/increasing

These new measures have been introduced to stem the flow of illegal goods entering the country.

He tied a tourniquet round the wound to stem the flow of blood.

to talk shop: to talk about work in your time off and especially during a social occasion (a party, etc)

The problem with Bob is that, whenever we go out socially, all he does is talk shop.

to wear a hole in sth: to make holes in sth you use or wear

If you don't wear slippers in the house, you'll wear a hole in your socks.

to wield power: to have a lot of power and influence

The unions no longer wield the power that they used to.

to win a scholarship: to get a scholarship by performing well in an exam or an interview

He won a scholarship to Yale.

to wreak havoc: to cause chaos and/or a lot of damage

Last night's heavy snowfall has wreaked havoc throughout the south of England.

Practice

1. *Fill in the crossword by answering the clues that appear below the grid. Each clue is followed by the word you need, however, the letters are jumbled up.*

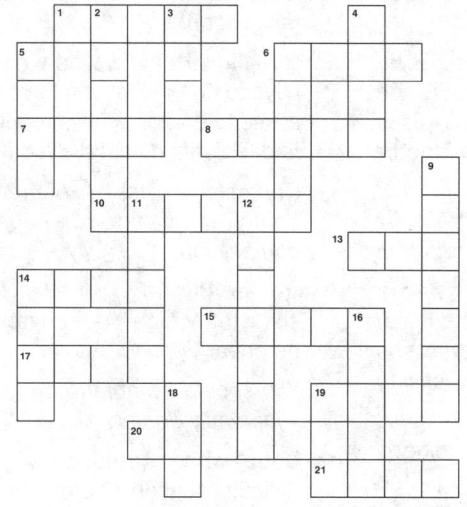

Across

1. to ...... **up courage** = to make yourself do sth you are afraid of doing *(UKLPC)*
6. to ...... **a hole in sth** = to use sth so much that you make holes in it *(ARWE)*
7. not to ...... **true** = when an excuse, explanation, etc is difficult to believe *(GIRN)*
8. to ...... **havoc** = to cause chaos and/or damage *(AKRWE)*
10. to ...... **a guess** = to guess *(AZRHDA)*
13. to ...... **a scholarship** = to get a grant by performing well in an exam or an interview *(NIW)*
14. not to ...... **your weight** = not to do your fair share of the work *(LPLU)*
15. to ...... **responsibility** = to officially say that you are responsible for sth bad that has happened *(ALCIM)*
17. to ...... **put** = not to move *(ASYT)*
19. to ...... **sb's feelings** = to say or do sth which makes sb feel upset and offended *(TRUH)*
20. to ...... **an accusation against sb** = to accuse sb of sth *(LLEEV)*
21. to ...... **the flow of sth** = to stop sth from spreading or developing *(ESTM)*

Down

2. to ...... **a new product** = to make a new product available on the market *(HLNUCA)*
3. to ...... **class** = to deliberately miss a class at school or university *(UTC)*
4. to ...... **shop** = to discuss your work - especially on a social occasion *(KLTA)*
5. to ...... **abuse at sb** = to shout insults at sb *(LHRU)*
6. to ...... **power** = to have a lot of power and influence *(LEDIW)*
9. to ...... **a survey** = to ask people a set of questions in order to find out their opinions about sth *(DOCNTUC)*
11. to ...... **concerns/fears** = to make sb feel less concerned/afraid *(YLALA)*
12. to ...... **an ambition** = to achieve an ambition *(SAIERLE)*
14. to ...... **your luck** = to take a risk that may lead to trouble *(SHPU)*
16. to ...... **a search** = to organise and start a search *(NUTOM)*
18. to ...... **out a scream** = to scream *(TLE)*

2. *Now complete the following sentences with a suitable verb, noun or verb and noun. You may have to change the form of the verb.*

1. It's a wonderful university, but I won't be able to go there unless I .... a ....
2. The President denied all the .... that had been .... against him.
3. It was the biggest manhunt ever .... by the police.
4. I'm not a very brave person, so how did I .... to ring her? I got my mum to do it!
5. In most countries the President .... a great deal of power.
6. Nobody .... for the attacks.
7. The French 2CV was loved and loathed in equal measure from the day it was .... in 1948.
8. I've already asked for one day off this week. I'd be .... my .... if I asked for another one.
9. I don't believe her. That pathetic story about her bag being stolen just doesn't ....
10. The home supporters were livid and spent the rest of the match .... at the referee.
11. In a survey .... by the Statistics Bureau, 90% of those interviewed said they intended to vote.
12. On seeing the spider, she .... a ....
13. Two people were killed and hundreds were made homeless as hurricane force winds .... along the South Florida coastline last night.

84 A, B and C Prepositions

to abide by sth: to accept and/or obey sth – (the) law/rules/regulations/a decision/an agreement [Note: **a law-abiding citizen:** a person who obeys the law]

You may not agree with him, but he is the referee, and you must abide by whatever decision he makes.

to be absorbed in sth: to be very interested in sth (a book/a film/your work/a video game, etc) and give all your attention to it [Note: **an absorbing book, film,** etc: a very interesting film, book, etc]

I was so absorbed in my work that I missed lunch.

to account for sth/the fact that...: to explain (often used in academic essay titles)

The fact that she's been under a lot of pressure may well account for her strange behaviour.

'Account for the fall of the Roman Empire.'

in the aftermath of sth: in the period of time following a disaster (earthquake, bomb explosion, etc), tragedy or a war

The President declared a state of emergency in the aftermath of the earthquake.

aside from sth/sb: except for/apart from, + noun or -ing form

Aside from one or two spelling mistakes, this really is an excellent composition.

an asset to sth: very valuable to sth (company or institution)

Bill has been an asset to this company. Without his drive and creativity, we would not be the successful company that we are today.

a ban on sth/doing sth: an official prohibition

The government intends to introduce a ban on unregulated building.

to be barred from somewhere/doing sth: (i) to officially be prevented from entering a place (ii) to officially prevent a **doctor** from practising medicine or a **lawyer** from practising law

After the fight, he was barred from ever entering the restaurant again.

She was found guilty of professional misconduct, so she was barred from ever practising medicine again.

to be based on sth: if one thing is based on another thing, the former is developed from/is founded on the latter.

The film "Apocalypse Now" is based on a novel by Joseph Conrad.

to bombard sb with questions: to ask sb a lot of questions

The minister was met by a wave of reporters who bombarded her with questions.

to brag about sth: to proudly talk about sth in such a way that other people find it annoying.

I wish he would stop bragging about how much money he earns.

to cater for: to provide things/a service that sb needs or wants [Note: **to cater for all tastes:** to satisfy and provide for all likes/interests]

Our holiday company mainly caters for young professionals in search of adventure.

to collide with sth/sb: to crash into

The London train collided with the Canterbury train as they were both pulling into Ashford station.

to comment on sth/sb: to give an opinion about sth/sb

The minister's wife was asked to comment on her husband's resignation.

to comply with sth: to do what you have to do or what you have been asked to do (for a rule/a regulation/a decision/a demand/a request)

Contestants are expected to comply with the rules of the competition.

to confide in sb (about sth): to tell sb sth which is private or personal

You should be able to confide in your family doctor.

to cope with sth: to deal with a difficult situation or problem

It's a lot of work but I'm sure she will cope with it.

She couldn't cope with a nine-to-five job and raising a family at the same time.

to be credited with sth/doing sth: to be considered responsible for sth good/important

Lipsin has always been credited with the invention of the turbo charger, but it now appears that it was his partner, Evans, who came up with the idea.

to be cruel to sb/sth: to do/say sth that hurts (physically or mentally) a person/animal

I think that being cruel to animals in the name of scientific research is completely unacceptable.

a cutback in sth: a reduction in the numbers of sth or the amount of money spent on sth

Cutbacks in staff have meant that on average there are now 34 pupils in a class.

84

Practice

1. In each of the sentences below there is a word and preposition in bold. Some of the prepositions are correct, some of them are not. Put a tick (for those prepositions that are right) or a cross (for those prepositions that are wrong) in the space provided at the end of each sentence. If the preposition is incorrect, supply the correct one.

1 The film was loosely **based in** Charles Dickens' novel "Hard Times". ....
2 I can't **cope with** all this work. There's too much of it. We're going to have to take on a secretary. ....
3 When does the **ban on** parking in the city centre come into effect? ....
4 He was really late as he had been so **absorbed on** his book that he had lost track of time. ....
5 As he left the court, the minister was surrounded by journalists who **bombarded** him **in** questions. ....
6 Evita Peron is widely **credited with** bringing the vote to women in Argentina. ....
7 **Aside of** Josefina, we all had an excellent time. ....
8 **In the aftermath of** the Second World War many families emigrated to South America in search of a better life. ....
9 Having been found guilty of gross negligence in a court of law, the doctor was **barred from** ever practising medicine again. ....
10 I hate it when people are **cruel with** animals. ....
11 If we don't **comply on** the rules, then anarchy will prevail. ....
12 Richard has been an **asset with** this school. He is an excellent and dedicated teacher and we shall be very sorry to see him go. ....
13 The Prime Minister refused to **comment on** the rumours that were flying around regarding the business deal. ....
14 "Simba" is a record store that **caters for** all tastes in music. You can be sure that, whatever it is you are interested in, they will have it in stock. ....
15 Why does Colin have to constantly **brag with** his big house in the country? ....
16 Digby had been lucky. It's not often that you **collide into** an articulated lorry at a hundred kilometres an hour and walk out unscathed. ....
17 It was difficult for me to talk about my problems and when I **confided in** you about them I foolishly believed that you would keep what I said to yourself. ....
18 Rules are rules, and if you don't **abide with** them, you get disqualified. ....
19 How can the government justify the recent **cutbacks on** public spending when it has just spent £50 million on defence? ....
20 "How do you **account on** the fact that in the two weeks you were left in charge of the shop profits fell by forty percent?" Mr Higgins asked. ....

2. Now use the correct combinations from exercise 1 to complete the sentences.

1 I wish you would stop .... your exam results.
2 A partial withdrawal of government subsidies has led to a(n) .... public transport services.
3 Craig sat at the back of the class, ... his private daydreams.
4 Although we will be sorry to lose Mr Perkins, we feel certain that he will be a(n) .... any potential employer.
5 What is the point of playing a game if you have no intention of .... its rules?
6 Hurrying towards one another from opposite directions, the two men .... each other and fell over.
7 The finalist in the quiz show was .... questions in quickfire succession.
8 You say that you were in Warsaw on Monday. How, then, do you .... the fact that you were seen in Chicago on Monday afternoon?
9 What is not generally known is that, ... being a brilliant mathematician, he is also a gifted linguist.
10 The film, although presented as fiction, is .... a true story.

173

85 D to J Prepositions

to disapprove of sb/sth: to dislike sb/sth, not to approve of sb/sth

I strongly disapprove of the way advertisers control the commercial TV channels.

to dissuade sb from doing sth: to persuade sb not to do sth

We tried to dissuade him from joining the army.

to be disqualified from sth: to be prevented from taking any further part in a competition/sporting event because you have broken a rule

He was disqualified from the tournament because they found traces of a banned substance in his blood.

to have an effect on sb/sth: to affect or influence sb/sth

I don't care what you do in your spare time as long as it does not have an adverse effect on your work.

to elaborate on sth: to explain sth in more detail

Would you care to elaborate on that statement?

to embark on a journey: to start a long journey

In 1778 he embarked on a journey that was to take him halfway round the world.

to endeavour to do sth: (formal) to try to do sth

I shall endeavour to do my best.

to excel at sth: to be very good at sth

At school she excelled at everything except maths.

an excerpt/extract from sth: a short passage taken from a book/film/piece of music

An extract from his latest novel was printed in the local newspaper.

an expert in/on: sb who knows a great deal about sth

Doctor Jansen is an expert in ancient Greek philosophy.

to be familiar with sth: to know sth or understand it well

Are you familiar with the works of Chester Himes?

to fish for compliments: to say/do sth so that sb pays you a compliment

"Do you think I'm getting fat." She said. She knew she wasn't. She was fishing for compliments.

to have a flair for sth: to have a natural ability to do sth well

She has a flair for languages.

a flaw in sth: an imperfection or weakness, especially in an argument

You say that Marlowe wrote Shakespeare's plays. There's just one flaw in your argument: Marlowe died before most of Shakespeare's plays were written.

fluctuations in sth: sudden changes in sth (price or temperature)

Fluctuations in prices are more usual in times of recession.

to be fraught with: if a situation is fraught with problems or danger, it involves a lot of them

The life of a war correspondent is fraught with danger.

to be glued to the television: to watch the television with great interest and all your attention

During the World Cup final, millions of people around the world will be glued to their televisions.

to haggle over the price of sth: to argue with sb over the price of sth in order to get a better price

That seems a good price to me, so I shan't haggle over it.

to be hopeless at sth: to be very bad at sth

Don't ask me. I'm hopeless at geography.

to be identical to sth/sb: to look exactly the same as sth/sb

She's identical to her sister.

to have an impact on sb/sth: to have a big effect on sb/sth

The discovery of Mad Cow Disease had a massive and immediate impact on the British meat industry.

to be impressed by/with sth: to think that sth is exceptionally good and to admire and respect it as a result

We have been impressed with the progress you have made since you joined this company.

to be indicative of sth: to clearly show sth

The fact that he does so little is indicative of his lack of interest in his work.

to have/be a good/bad influence on sb/sth: to affect/have a positive/negative effect on sb/sth

James is a very bad influence on Mark. That is why I have sat them at opposite ends of the class.

information on/about: information regarding

I'd like some information on your Spanish courses.

to ingratiate yourself with sb: to try and make sb (generally a person in a postition of power) like you

It's no good trying to ingratiate yourself with me by using flattery.

to be intent on doing sth: to be determined to do sth (often sth that other people think you should not do)

He seems to be intent on joining the army.

to invest in sth: to give or lend money for a useful or profitable purpose

Would you like to invest in my company?

judging by sth: based on what I can see/have seen/have heard, this is my opinion

Judging by the look on his face, I'd say that he has just received some very good news.

to be justified in doing sth: to have a good reason for doing sth

The local council were perfectly justified in evicting them – they hadn't paid their rent for months.

Practice

1. Complete the sentences by filling in the gaps with one of the words below.

> disqualified – disapprove – flair – elaborate – expert – flaw – fraught – familiar – embark – dissuade – fishing – endeavour – impressed – effect – fluctuations – extracts – excelled

1. He'll know if it is genuine or not. He is a(n) .... **on** eighteenth-century pottery.
2. Should we .... **on** a journey so .... **with** danger that we are likely to get killed?
3. He was .... **from** the tournament when it was found out that he had lied about his age.
4. Try as we might, we couldn't .... him **from** dropping out of college.
5. He has a(n) .... **for** languages and plans to study Spanish and French at Oxford.
6. "I'm not looking my best today, am I?" she asked, obviously .... **for** compliments.
7. The alarm they had fitted was extremely sensitive to .... **in** room temperature. Any increase in temperature would trigger it off.
8. There is an obvious .... **in** your argument. You say that the Xinxu tribe had no concept of the future, and yet the words 'tomorrow' and 'later' both occur in their language.
9. The author was supposed to talk about her life and her writing techniques, but all she did was read a number of .... **from** her latest novel.
10. He stood up and looked at the jury. "The Prosecution will .... **to** show that the accused did wilfully set fire to Rochester Public Library."
11. Being constantly ill was bound to have an adverse .... **on** his school work.
12. Not only was he a very gifted student but he also .... **at** sports.
13. The other directors might .... **of** my methods but they know that I get results."
14. You mentioned in your book that you had a difficult childhood. Would you care to .... **on** that?
15. Chad? I'm not .... **with** this part of the world. It's in Africa, isn't it?
16. "I am most .... **by** the progress you have made in your schoolwork this term," said the headmaster.

2. Complete the sentences below with an appropriate preposition.

1. They don't look like twins?! You can't be serious! They are **identical** .... one another.
2. It would be unwise to **invest** .... gold at the moment as the market is currently very unstable.
3. **Judging** .... his accent, I'd say he was Spanish.
4. Their music has had, and will continue to have, a huge **influence** .... generations of musicians.
5. Mother in the kitchen, children **glued** .... the television, father at work. Domestic harmony – 1950's style.
6. If you would like further **information** .... any of our courses, please do not hesitate to call us.
7. I am **hopeless** .... maths. I can add and subtract, but that's about it.
8. He never did any work and he was always causing trouble. As far as I'm concerned, they were perfectly **justified** .... giving him the sack.
9. He wanted £80 for it. I couldn't afford £80, so we **haggled** .... the price and he eventually sold it to me for £65.
10. The **impact** that this project is likely to have .... local communities is not to be underestimated.
11. There are many **flaws** and inconsistencies .... the voting system.
12. He was forever trying to **ingratiate** himself .... his superiors, so he was popular with the company directors, but none of his co-workers could stand him.
13. The present government seems **intent** .... destroying everything good about this country. It's latest decision to do away with free medical care for the needy is **indicative** .... its callousness towards those who need its help the most.
14. Remember that if you express an opinion during the interview, you may be expected to **elaborate** .... it.
15. Sean has a **flair** .... business, and I don't doubt that he will be a millionaire before he is thirty.

86 K to P Prepositions

to be kind to: to treat sb/sth in a gentle and friendly way
He was always very kind to me.

to be lacking in sth: not to have enough of sth
His problems stem from the fact that he is lacking in confidence.

to lapse into another language: to start speaking in a different language (especially your mother tongue)
When she got excited she had a tendency to lapse into Italian.

to lavish praise on sb/sth: to say that sth (particularly a book or film) is very good
"You can't expect the critics to lavish praise on everything you write," she said.

to be licensed to do sth: to have official permission to do sth, or to sell sth
We are not licensed to sell fireworks.

to liken sb/sth to sb/sth else: to say or write that sth/sb is similar to sth/sb else
The poet likens the lady to a summer's day.

to long for sth: (literary) to really want sth
She longed for him to take her dancing.

to marvel at: to be very surprised by sth (because it is very good, very clever, etc) and to admire it as a result
He marvelled at the way she dealt with the problem.

to meddle in sb's life/affairs: to interfere in a situation which does not concern you, causing other people problems
Now she hates you. That's what you get for meddling in her affairs.

to meet with little/no success: (formal) to be unsuccessful

The minister tried to persuade the union to call off the strike, but met with little success.

to merge with: to join together to form one (company)
If BMY merges with Vectron, the resulting company will become the biggest automobile manufacturer in the world.

to model sth on sth else: to design a particular system (educational, legal, electoral, transport, etc) so that it is a copy of another system
They've modelled their electoral system on ours.

to be a newcomer to: to have recently started/arrived
We're newcomers to this area.

to be noted for: to be well known and admired for [Note: **to be notorious for:** to be well known for having a bad quality]
This region of Chile is noted for its beautiful mountain scenery.
Chanta Air is notorious for its appalling in-flight service.

to be obsessed with: not to be able to stop thinking about sth
He is obsessed with football.

It never occurred to me that/to do sth: at no time did I think that/of doing sth [Note: for questions **Didn't it ever occur to you that...** (criticism is implied), **Did it ever occur to you that...** (no criticism is implied)
It never occurred to him that she might/would be offended by what he said.
Didn't it ever occur to you that I might be worried?
Did it ever occur to you that your book would become the biggest selling novel of all time?

to be opposed to: to disagree with and disapprove of sth
I'm not coming with you. I'm (totally) opposed to bullfighting.

to persist in: to continue to do sth even though you have previously been warned or told not to
If you persist in being late, you will be expelled.

a place is plunged into darkness: the lights suddenly go off in a place and it becomes very dark
An electrical fault plunged the area into darkness.

to be popular with: to be liked by
This kind of music is popular with teenagers.

to be powerless to do sth: to be unable to do sth because you lack legal power / authority / enough strength
Heavily outnumbered, the police were powerless to prevent the rioters from entering the palace.

to pretend to/that: to behave as if you did or felt sth when in fact you didn't
He pretended to be surprised.
He pretended that he hadn't heard.

to be pressed/pushed for time: to be in a hurry and hence have very little time to do sth
I think I'm going to take a cab. I'm a bit pressed for time.

to prevent sb/sth from doing sth: to stop sb from doing sth
The government has introduced price controls in order to prevent the economy from spinning out of control.

to pride yourself on sth/the fact that: to be proud of
The Venice Film Festival prides itself on being the arty alternative to the more commercially orientated Cannes Film Festival.

prior to: (formal) before
Opp: subsequent to
We did a lot of market research prior to launching this product.

Practice

1. Complete the sentences below with an appropriate preposition.

1 She opened the letter in anticipation. "You don't know how much I've **longed** .... this day!" she said. "Now I'll find out the truth."

2 If you are **kind** .... others, they will be **kind** .... you.

3 Accidents are more likely to happen when a ferry carries more people than it is **licensed** ....

4 His attempts to persuade her to accept the promotion **met** .... little success.

5 I couldn't help but **marvel** .... the way the trapeze artists flew through the air with such ease and grace.

6 The opposition may be **lacking** .... experience, but they more than make up for it with intelligence and skill.

7 If this company **merges** .... Acme and Sons, we could all lose our jobs.

8 The Prince **likened** the museum's new extension .... an ugly scar on the face of an old friend.

9 Neither of us felt that the film deserved quite as much praise as the jury had **lavished** .... it.

10 His mother was Spanish. Her English was excellent, except for a tendency to **lapse** .... Spanish whenever she got excited.

11 Many countries around the world have **modelled** their systems of government .... that of the USA.

12 When will you learn that nothing good ever comes of **meddling** .... other people's affairs?

2. For questions 1 to 14, complete the second sentence so that it has a similar meaning to the first sentence, using 3 to 8 words. You must include the word given in bold, which cannot be changed in any way.

1 There was nothing we could do to stop him.
   powerless   We were .... him.

2 She's proud of her cooking.
   prides   She .... her cooking.

3 If you continue to cause trouble, we shall have no alternative but to dismiss you.
   persist   If you ....
   .... forced to dismiss you.

4 All his students liked him.
   popular   He .... students.

5 I never thought for one moment that Harry might be involved.
   occurred   It never ....
   Harry might be involved.

6 I strongly disagree with any kind of hunting.
   opposed   I'm ....
   any kind of hunting.

7 As I have only just started teaching, I rely a lot on my colleagues for help and advice.
   newcomer   As I am ...., I rely a lot on my colleagues for help and advice.

8 His generosity was well known to everyone.
   noted   He was .... generosity.

9 Suddenly, the lights went off.
   plunged   Suddenly, the room ....
   .... darkness.

10 Only sign a contract after you have read the small print.
   prior   Always read ....
   .... any contract.

11 He's not really hurt. He's putting it on.
   pretending   He's only .... hurt.

12 He couldn't participate in the tournament because he was injured.
   prevented   His ....
   .... part in the tournament.

13 I'd love to stop and chat, but I can't. I'm running rather late.
   pressed   I'd love to stop and chat, but I can't. I'm a .... time.

14 All he ever thinks about is making money.
   obsessed   He is .... money.

177

87 R and S Prepositions

to be racked with (guilt/pain): to feel very guilty about sth/be in great pain

I was racked with guilt over what I had said to him.

He was racked with pain from his toothache.

to reconcile oneself to sth: to accept an unpleasant situation

She never managed to reconcile herself to her father's death.

a reduction in: a decrease in
Opp: an increase in

Over the past ten years there has been (a dramatic/a gradual/only a slight/a significant/a steady/an unprecedented) reduction in the number of robberies in the United Kingdom.

a (sad) reflection on: if sth is a (sad) reflection on a person or thing, it gives a bad impression of them/it

It is a (sad) reflection on the society we live in that a film that glorifies war has been nominated for eleven Oscars.

to refrain from: to deliberately not do sth

Please refrain from leaving your seats during the performance.

to be related to sb: to be members of the same family

We look alike, but we are not related to each other.

a report on: a report describing

The ecology agency have produced a report on the devastating effect insecticides are having on the environment.

to have a reputation for: to be well known for

Mr Simpson has a reputation for being a fair-minded teacher.

restrictions on: limits on

There are no restrictions on the amount of perfume that you can bring into this country.

to revel in sth: to enjoy sth, especially sth that other people would not expect you to enjoy

He revelled in the notoriety that the scandal gave him.

to be rude to sb: to be impolite to sb

He was sent to the headmaster for being rude to his teacher.

to be scathing about sth/sb: to be very critical of sb/sth

Lord Boxley, the author of the report, is scathing about the way the police handled the case.

a solution to: an answer to

We need to find a solution to this problem as soon as possible.

to specialise in: to give particular attention to

I sell all kinds of books, but I specialise in crime fiction from the 1940s and 1950s.

a stance on: a government's/organisation's official opinion/attitude towards sth

The government has adopted a tough/uncompromising stance on fox-hunting and is currently pushing legislation through parliament to make it illegal.

a stickler for sth: if sb is a stickler for sth (e.g. cleanliness) they always demand or require it
[Note: stickler for **rules/accuracy/punctuality,** etc]

Don't be late. Mr Thompson is a stickler for punctuality.

to stoop to sth: to lower or completely ignore one's moral standards in order to get what one wants

I might be desperate to pass the exam, but you don't honestly think I would stoop to cheating, do you?

to stray from a path: to leave a path

There's only one path through the forest. Don't stray from it or you will get totally lost.

to be strewn with sth: to be covered in sth

His bedroom floor was strewn with odd socks, dirty shirts and crumpled pieces of paper.

a struggle for: a long and difficult attempt to achieve sth
[Note: (i) **to struggle to do sth**: to find it very difficult to do sth (ii) **to struggle with sb**: to fight sb who is attacking you]

The small country's struggle for independence was really admirable.

We are only a small company and in the present economic climate we are really struggling to survive.

He's not really struggling with an attacker. It's a martial arts contest.

to substitute for sb/sth: to take the place of sb/use sth instead of sth else

If you suffer from insomnia try substituting camomile tea for coffee.

to succumb to pressure/temptation: to find it impossible not to do what sb is trying very hard to persuade you to do/the temptation is so strong that you finally do what you have been trying not to do

The government is unlikely to succumb to public pressure to abolish the voting tax.

She knew that if she succumbed to the temptation to buy the dress, she'd be broke for the rest of the month.

to survive on (an amount of money): to have enough money to pay one's bills and buy the things one needs to survive

I don't know how she can survive on such a low salary.

to be susceptible to sth/sb: to be very likely to be affected/influenced by sth/sb

Don't be too harsh on him; he's very susceptible to criticism.

87

Practice

1. Complete the following sentences with an appropriate preposition.

1. If you **stray** .... the path, you will get lost.
2. Patrons are kindly requested to **refrain** .... using mobile phones during the performance.
3. The latest government **report** .... inner city crime makes horrifying reading.
4. Sue is very **susceptible** .... flattery.
5. I could have helped her but I didn't, and I have been **racked** .... guilt ever since.
6. That he was never charged with any crime is a sad **reflection** .... our criminal justice system.
7. I think most people would hate all this publicity, but not Tom – he's positively **revelling** .... it.
8. There should be tougher **restrictions** .... the sale of fireworks in this country.
9. Ms Jones is **substituting** .... our teacher tomorrow.
10. He resigned because he vehemently disagreed with the party's **stance** .... education.
11. How Bob and Sally manage to **survive** .... £45 a week I just don't know.
12. This is a serious problem and if we don't find a **solution** .... it fast, we're going to be in deep trouble.
13. He might be in a very difficult position but I doubt whether he would **stoop** .... that kind of behaviour.
14. He was highly critical of the government in his report. He was particularly **scathing** .... its proposed cutbacks in social services.
15. Finally, the government **succumbed** .... public pressure and abolished the poll tax.
16. Sharon had to **reconcile herself** .... the fact that her best friend had betrayed her.
17. As a lawyer, I am prepared to support you in your **struggle** .... justice.
18. The pavement outside the Princess' house was **strewn** .... wreaths, flowers and messages of condolence.
19. Mr Jenkins, our headmaster, was a fair man but he was a **stickler** .... the rules.

2. Complete the second sentence so that it has a similar meaning to the first sentence, using 3 to 8 words. You must include the word given, which cannot be changed in any way.

1. It was wrong of me to have insulted her.
   rude   I shouldn't .... her.
2. His honesty was well known.
   reputation   He .... honest.
3. What is the President's position with regard to nuclear weapons?
   stance   What is the .... nuclear weapons?
4. I don't think I could make ends meet on a salary like his.
   survive   I doubt .... salary like his.
5. Even though they are not relatives, they have the same surname.
   related   They might .... have the same surname.
6. The economy is in better shape because the price of oil has dropped.
   reduction   The economy is in better shape thanks .... oil.
7. I'm going to concentrate on contract law once I have graduated.
   specialise   After I .... contract law.
8. Taking out a bank loan will solve your problems, but only temporarily.
   solution   Taking out a bank loan will only .... your problems.
9. There were empty lemonade bottles and half-eaten sandwiches all over his floor.
   strewn   His floor .... half-eaten sandwiches.
10. We would appreciate it if passengers did not use their mobile phones during take-off.
    refrain   We would kindly remind passengers .... mobile phones during take-off.

179

88 T to W Prepositions/At... Prepositional Phrases

sth (a course, a holiday, etc) is tailored to one's needs: sth has been designed to provide the things that sb specifically needs

At Fogey's holidays we have tailored our tours to meet the specific needs of older holidaymakers.

to talk sense into sb: to persuade sb to stop doing sth foolish

He wants to give up his job and become a rock star. Someone has to talk some sense into him!

to have (bad/good) taste in sth: to have bad/good aesthetic sense when it comes to choosing things, relationships, places, etc

He's got really good/bad/poor taste in clothes.

to be teeming with people/animals: to be crowded with people or to be full of animals (conveys the idea of a lot of movement)

The plains below us were teeming with wildlife.

to think nothing of doing sth: to think that sth is normal and not be bothered about it (whereas most people would find it unusual/difficult)

A lot of people in Japan think nothing of travelling for three hours to get to work.

to thrive on sth: to enjoy and be stimulated by sth that most people would find unenjoyable, difficult and unpleasant

He thrives on working under pressure.

to be translated into another language: to be said/written in another language

Most of his books have been translated into Chinese.

to be unique to one thing/person/place: to belong to or concern only that thing/person/place

"That is the Windrush tree. It is unique to this island," she said proudly.

to update sb on sth: to give sb the most recent news about sth [Note: **an update on**]

The President said that he wanted to be updated every hour on the progress of the peace talks.

to venture out: to leave a place (and in doing so taking a risk because it might be dangerous outside)

If you do decide to venture out, please remember to steer clear of the poorly lit streets.

to vie for sth: to compete with sb for sth

Three construction companies are vying for the contract to build the new town hall.

to be wary of sb/sth/doing sth: not to trust sb because you think they might harm/trick you in some way/to be cautious about (doing) sth because you think it's dangerous

I'm very wary of opening my door to strangers.

to withdraw money from a bank: to take money from your bank account

I'd like to withdraw £30 from my current account, please.

At... Prepositional phrases

keep sth at bay: (keep sth) away from you so that it does not hurt or trouble you

We installed an electric fence around the house in the hope that it would keep the bears at bay.

at all costs: whatever happens, used with the verbs **avoid** and **prevent**

Drinking the tap water should be avoided at all costs.

to be/put at a disadvantage: to have a disadvantage/sth gives you a disadvantage

Obviously, the fact that they had 10 players and we had only 9 put us at a disadvantage.

to be at sb's disposal: to be available for sb to use

During your stay, all the hotel's facilities will be at your disposal.

at gunpoint: with sb pointing a gun at you

He was robbed at gunpoint.

to be at large: to have escaped and not yet have been caught

It is reported that the remaining convict, who was still at large last night, has been recaptured.

at the latest: no later than (used with a time or a date)

Entry forms must reach this office by May 3 at the latest.

at length: for a long time (used for speaking/talking)

In the interview, Clapton spoke at length about his childhood.

not to be at liberty: (formal) not to have permission or the authority to say/do sth

I'm afraid I am not at liberty to answer that question.

at long last: finally

At long last, the local council have put new street lights along Canal Avenue.

at a loss to explain: unable to explain [Note: **to be at a loss for words**: not to know what to say]

Her parents were at a loss to explain why she had done such a thing.

When she told me what had happened, I was at a loss for words.

at the most: the maximum (for money and time)

It won't be expensive. It will cost £4 at the most.

at (such) short notice: with (so) little advance warning

He apologised for telling us about the meeting at such short notice.

at a push: with difficulty

I can be there by 5 o'clock at a push, but no earlier than that.

at random: not according to a particular system/pattern/method

Students were chosen at random to fill in a questionnaire.

at this rate: if we continue like this

We're losing £100 a day. At this rate, we are going to go bankrupt in six weeks.

to be at stake: to be at risk

You can't give up on the expedition now. Too much is at stake!

Practice

1. Complete the sentences with an appropriate preposition.

1 This particular species of parrot is **unique** .... this island.
2 We were told that, if we wanted to **venture** .... at night, we should stick to the area around the hotel.
3 For a man who edits a fashion magazine, he has appalling **taste** .... clothes.
4 Our one-to-one courses are **tailored** .... the individual needs of each and every one of our students.
5 It was three o'clock in the morning and the streets were still **teeming** .... people.
6 I hate **withdrawing** money .... cash point machines. I'm always worried that I'll put my card in and I won't get it back.
7 Most people would hate the kind of attention he gets from the media. But not Jan. He **thrives** .... it.
8 She'd been on holiday, so I **updated** her .... what had been going on while she had been away.
9 You should always be **wary** .... people selling electrical goods at dramatically reduced prices. They often fall to pieces within two days of your buying them.
10 Her last novel was **translated** .... 25 different languages.
11 Now he says he wants to leave university. See if you can **talk some sense** .... him. He won't listen to me.
12 With four games to go, Manchester United have already won the championship. Behind them and **vying** .... second place are three other teams.
13 Elvis Presley would **think nothing** .... getting on a plane and flying 2000 km just to buy his favourite kind of sandwich.

2 He looked at the speedometer, which read 30 miles per hour. "We'll never get there **at** .... Can't we go a bit faster?"
3 "When's the deadline?" "I was told that everything had to be handed in by Tuesday **at** ...."
4 Hello, Karen, it's Mark. Look, I'm sorry to ask you this **at** ...., but could you take Claudia's classes tomorrow morning?
5 **At** ...., the council has decided to do something about the appalling state of the roads around here.
6 "We can't risk it," he said. "It's too dangerous. There are too many lives **at** ...."
7 She was **at** .... to explain her son's behaviour. He liked school, so why on earth would he want to drop out?
8 It's not at all expensive. It will cost you £20 **at** ....
9 On being asked who had supplied her with the information, she told the reporters that she was not **at** .... to divulge her source's name.
10 It's eight o'clock and it is already very hot. This is where the Northern Europeans are **at** .... The Southern Europeans are used to playing in these temperatures, while we are not.
11 It's a highly infectious disease, so contact with people who have been infected with it should be avoided **at** ....
12 Police have warned the public that two of the escaped leopards are still **at** ....
13 The people who were interviewed for this survey were chosen **at** ....
14 On our way to the ranch, we'll be stopping off at the Buenos Rios hotel, where the swimming pool will be **at** ....
15 "We don't need to take three cars," she said. "We can get five people in mine. Maybe even six **at** ...."
16 In a particularly exciting scene in the film, the hero is robbed **at** ....
17 He spoke **at** .... about the financial benefits of the project, its social implications, and even its effect on the environment.

2. Complete the sentences with an appropriate word/phrase from the box below.

> long last – random – the most – a push – all costs – the latest –
> a disadvantage – stake – large – bay – liberty – this rate –
> our disposal – length – such short notice – gunpoint – a loss

1 We managed to keep the mosquitoes **at** .... by burning one of those all-night mosquito coils.

89 In ... Prepositional Phrases

to be in agony: to be in a lot of pain

"Did it hurt?" "Of course it hurt! I was in agony!"

to be in arrears: not to have paid sth you have to pay on a regular basis

He was horribly overdrawn at the bank and his rent was five months in arrears.

to be in bloom: if a plant or tree is in bloom, the flowers on that plant or tree are open

It was summer and all the flowers were in bloom.

in disarray: if sth (e.g. your clothes, your life, a country, etc) is in disarray, it is very untidy, disorganised or in a state of confusion

The strikes have left the country in complete disarray.

in (very) good condition: in a good state

We buy second-hand books, but only if they are in good condition.

to be in a foul mood: to be bad-tempered and easily annoyed

He was in a foul mood that morning.

to be in full swing: if a party is in full swing, all the guests have arrived and the party has reached its highest level of activity

It was late when we arrived and the party was in full swing.

in the heat of the moment: without thinking, rashly or impulsively

I didn't mean to quit. It was done in the heat of the moment.

in moderation: not to excess

She is not the kind of person who does things in moderation.

to be in order: if an official document (a passport, an export licence, etc) is in order, it is complete, legal and correct

I wasn't allowed to enter the US because the immigration officers said my passport wasn't in order.

(to be) in (very) poor taste: to be unacceptable and/or offensive

I thought his comments about her father were in very poor taste.

in short supply: when there is very little available

Basic foodstuffs were in such short supply that the government had to introduce a system of rationing.

in stock: if a shop has (got) sth in stock, they have it in the shop and it is available to buy

We do not have that size in stock, but we can order it for you.

in store (for sb): if sb has got a surprise in store (for them), they are going to get an unpleasant surprise

He thinks that he'll find it easy to get a job. Well, he has got a few surprises in store for him.

In the ... Prepositional Phrases

to see/meet sb in the flesh: to see/meet sb in real life (having previously only seen them in pictures/on television/in a film)

You met Brad Pitt?! In the flesh? What was he like?

to be in the limelight: to receive a lot of attention from the media

Even though he says he hates being in the limelight, you'll notice that he never actively shuns it.

in the long run: at some time in the distant future

These floors are okay for the time being. But in the long run we will have to replace them.

in the meantime: between now and a particular time in the future

Your teacher will be here in twenty minutes. So in the meantime, do the exercises on page twenty of your textbooks.

to be in the minority: to form less than 50% of a larger group

It is difficult to make your wishes heard when you are in the minority.

to be in the open: if a secret is in the open, everybody knows about it

The news about her promotion was finally in the open.

sth is in the pipeline: sth (a new law, an event, a change) is being prepared or discussed and will happen or be completed soon

The minister said that plans to build a new road were in the pipeline.

in the same breath: to say sth which directly contradicts sth you have just said

She said she was a vegetarian and then in the same breath she told me she had had steak for lunch!

in the same vein: similar in style and content

[Note: if sth written or spoken continues **in the same vein/in a similar vein**: it starts in a particular way and continues in that way]

"The Sabo" is not in the same vein as his other novels – it is much darker and far more political.

The letter starts with a torrent of abuse and continues in the same vein until the last paragraph.

to be in the wash: if clothes are in the wash, they are being washed

"Where are my new jeans?" "They are in the wash."

to be in the way: to be stopping you from moving/seeing sth

Could you move that vase of flowers, please? I'm watching TV and it's in the way.

in the wild: if an animal lives in the wild, it lives in its natural environment (i.e. not in a zoo or an environment controlled by human beings)

It is virtually impossible to see gorillas in the wild nowadays.

to be in the wrong: if you are in the wrong, you are to blame for an accident that has taken place, a mistake that has been made, etc

Seeing that he was in the wrong, he apologised immediately.

Practice

1. Complete the sentence beginnings in section A with an appropriate ending from section B. Write the number of the section A beginning in the space next to its corresponding ending in section B.

Section A

1 When we arrived, the party was
2 It isn't worth very much because it isn't
3 He said those hurtful things
4 I'm sorry. We sold the last red cardigan ten minutes ago and we don't have any more
5 I'm not surprised she was offended. Your last remark was
6 This garden is particularly beautiful when the roses are
7 It won't do you any harm as long as you do it
8 If she thinks it is going to be easy, then she's got a few surprises
9 Before you travel, make sure that all your documents are
10 I wouldn't talk to him at the moment. He'll bite your head off. He's
11 The actual extraction didn't hurt, but when the anaesthetic wore off I was
12 His wife had left him, he'd just lost his job and he was being evicted from his flat. His life was
13 They are being evicted from their home because their rent is six months
14 You could get hold of basic foodstuffs, but so-called luxury goods – caviar, chocolate, etc – were

Section B

in bloom. ....
in stock. ....
in a foul mood. ....
in very good condition. ....
in moderation. ....
in very poor taste. ....
in order. ....
in agony. ....
in full swing. ....
in disarray. ....
in short supply. ....
in the heat of the moment. ....
in store. ....
in arrears. ....

2. Complete the sentences with an appropriate word or phrase from the box below.

> limelight – pipeline – meantime – way – wild –
> long run – minority – wrong – wash –
> same breath – same vein – open – flesh

1 I saw Robert de Niro yesterday **in the** .... I was sitting next to him in the theatre.
2 "Mum, have you seen my tennis shoes?" "They are **in the** .... They were filthy".
3 He pretends that he doesn't like all this media attention, when in fact he likes nothing better than to be **in the** ....
4 No, it wasn't my fault. It was the other driver who was **in the** .... He was the one who pulled out without looking.
5 I'm very happy here in Italy, but I think, **in the** ...., I'd like to return to England and settle down there.
6 I can't see a thing. Your head is **in the** ....
7 For some reason, these animals only live for ten years in captivity. **In the** ...., however, they can live for as long as twenty-five years.
8 With the publication of his letters by a major newspaper, his secrets were well and truly out **in the** ....
9 Some of the shareholders want to close down our Latin American subsidiaries, but they are **in the** .... as most of us would never hear of such a thing.
10 We've run out of coffee and the supermarket doesn't open for another hour. **In the** ...., you'll have to make do with tea.
11 There are many other changes **in the** .... These changes will transform this once ailing company into Europe's leading car manufacturer.
12 You're not making sense. You say that voting should be made compulsory and yet, **in the** ...., you say that you would refuse to vote. You are contradicting yourself.
13 If you liked his first film, then you'll like his second, because it is very much **in the** ....

90 On ... Prepositional Phrases

(to win) on aggregate: (to have) a higher total score in a game/competition with more than one round/stage

With more points than anyone else, Ricky Crowther wins on aggregate.

on alert: ready to deal with anything (used for the police, the army, etc)

After the recent spate of forest fires, the fire brigade has been put on alert.

on arrival: when one arrives (e.g. at an airport)

The President was greeted on arrival by a brass band.

on balance: all things considered

The government's record is, on balance, good.

on behalf of: as a representative of

On behalf of the committee, I'd like to thank you for all your hard work.

on condition that: (formal) if, and only if

I will lend you my car on condition that you return it by ten o'clock.

on offer: available to be bought or used

There are far too many medical schemes on offer; I can't tell which one's the best.

on paper: theoretically

It is a wonderful plan on paper, but will it work in practice?

(to refuse to do sth) on principle: to refuse to do sth because of a moral code one believes in

I will not buy any of their products on principle. They import from countries that use child labour.

on purpose: intentionally

He says it was an accident, but I'm sure he did it on purpose.

on second thoughts: a phrase used to say that you have changed your mind about sth

A cheese and tomato sandwich, please ... No, on second thoughts, I'll have egg mayonnaise.

(to be) on tenterhooks: to be very excited and a little nervous while waiting for sth to happen [Note: **to keep sb on tenterhooks:** to make sb excited and nervous keeping them waiting for sth]

Howard had been on tenterhooks all day, waiting for his exam results.

(to be) on good terms with sb: to have a good relationship with sb

I'm not on very good terms with him.

On the ... Prepositional Phrases

on the air: being broadcast on TV or radio **Opp:** off the air

Are we on the air?

to live on the breadline: to be extremely poor

Over half the population of the country live on the breadline.

to be on the brink of: to be very close to

on the brink of collapse/war/a breakthrough/a successful career

Negotiations between the two countries are on the brink of collapse.

to be on the cards: it looks as if sth is likely to happen [Note: sth has been **on the cards for ages:** sth is no surprise because it always seemed likely that it would happen]

With three goals to one, it looks like another United victory is on the cards.

on the contrary: no, the opposite is true

"... but you hate modern art, don't you?"
"No, on the contrary. I love it."

on the dot: exactly; at an exact time, punctually

The performance will begin at 8 o'clock on the dot.

on the grounds that: (formal) because [Note: **on what grounds ...?:** for what reason ... ?]

He was refused entry into the US on the grounds that his visa had expired.

on the house: if food or drinks are on the house, they cost you nothing because they are given to you by the owner/manager of the restaurant that serves them

Coffee's on the house tonight!

on the line: at risk [Note: **to put your job on the line:** to risk losing your job]

one's job/life/career/reputation can be on the line

I'm putting my job on the line by giving you this information.

on the market: that you can buy; available

It's the cheapest sports car on the market.

on the outskirts of: in the parts of the town/city that are furthest away from the centre [Note: (with the same meaning) **in the suburbs**]

I live on the outskirts of Paris, not in the centre.

to be on the point of (doing sth): to be about to do sth

We were on the point of signing the contract when he said he had changed his mind.

on the ... side: a little bit too ... [Note: **to be a bit on the short/heavy/long/thin/cold, etc side:** to be a little too short/heavy/long/thin/cold, etc]

This essay is thought-provoking and well-written. However, I think it is a little bit on the short side.

on the trot: one after the other in succession

He has missed six classes on the trot.

to be on the verge of: to be very close to

on the verge of tears/extinction/a nervous breakdown

Seeing she was on the verge of tears, I changed the subject.

Practice

1. Complete the sentences with an appropriate word/phrase from the box below.

> dot – market – short side – paper – trot – brink/verge – cards – grounds – contrary – condition – principle – very good terms – tenterhooks – breadline – outskirts – line – second thoughts – purpose – behalf

1 That's twenty-five defeats **on the** ....! Face it, Frank! Your team are rubbish!
2 There are so many computers **on the** .... nowadays that I really don't know which one to buy.
3 They always close at six o'clock **on the** ...., not one minute earlier and not one minute later.
4 City beat United 3 – 1, and I have to say that I'm a little bit surprised. **On** ...., United are a much stronger team than City.
5 I live in Birmingham, not in the very centre, but **on the** ....
6 **On** .... of the college, I'd like to thank you for your fund-raising efforts.
7 With 25% of this city's inhabitants living **on the** ...., isn't it time we faced up to the fact that we've got a major problem on our hands?
8 You can't be surprised that they're calling a general election. It has been **on the** .... for ages.
9 I'll have a soda... no... hang on, **on** ...., I'll have a glass of mineral water.
10 We were **on the** .... of a major scientific discovery when the government took away our funding.
11 "So, what you are saying is that doing a course like that is a waste of time." "No, **on the** .... Courses like that can be very useful indeed."
12 The reader is kept **on** .... until the last chapter, anxiously waiting to find out who killed the unfortunate movie star.
13 Of course I did it **on** .... I only pretended to trip. Well, it made them laugh, didn't it?
14 She was refused a visa **on the** .... that she didn't meet the requirements.
15 All our jobs are **on the** .... so the important thing is that we all stick together and try to do something to stop the closure.
16 You can borrow my car, but only **on** .... that you promise to look after it.
17 I don't think Simon will lend us his van. We're not **on** .... at the moment.
18 I won't shop there **on** .... They sell products that have been tested on animals and animal testing is something that I strongly disagree with.
19 The play was a bit **on the** ...., more of a sketch than a proper play, really.

2. The phrases in bold have been jumbled. Swap them around so as to make sense.

1 The court room was **on tenterhooks**, with everybody pushing and shouting. ....
2 Your composition is a bit **on the outskirts**, but otherwise it is very good. ....
3 He prefers to live **on the verge of chaos** of the city and travel into work. ....
4 If you intend to upgrade your computer, look for the best deal **on the short side**. ....
5 It looks as if a devaluation of the dollar is **on the market**. ....
6 She is **on the cards**, waiting to see whether she has passed the interview. ....

3. Circle the correct item.

1 I went to the sales to see what was on **arrival / on offer**.
2 With more stormy weather being forecast, the coastguard is **on the air / on alert**.
3 **On what grounds / On the contrary** is he being prosecuted?
4 We paid for our main course but our puddings were **on the house / on the air**.
5 **On aggregate / On balance**, I think it was a very productive meeting.
6 That's the third match **on the trot / on the line** United has lost.

185

91 Prepositional Phrases/Prepostition... Preposition I

(to be) at cross purposes: to be working towards/talking about different things without realising it

He was talking about buying and his friend about renting. They were obviously at cross purposes.

beyond repair: too badly damaged to be repaired

The car was an insurance write-off after the accident, having been damaged beyond repair.

beyond a shadow of a doubt: an expression used to emphasise the fact that sth is true

England are beyond a shadow of a doubt the best team in the tournament.

by all accounts: according to what everyone says

It is, by all accounts, one of the most beautiful beaches on the island.

by any/no stretch of the imagination: an expression used to emphasise the fact that sth is not true [Note: By no stretch of the imagination can start a sentence, in which case it is followed by an inversion]

By no stretch of the imagination could you call it a cosy room.

for safekeeping: so that it will not get lost, broken or stolen

I left my passport with the hotel reception desk for safekeeping.

(to be) in demand: to be very popular and wanted by a lot of people

Tickets for the concert were in such demand that they were sold out within half an hour of going on sale.

(to be) of your own making: to have been caused by you and not by anybody else

Don't blame me for what has happened. Your problems with Jan are entirely of your own making.

(sth is) to one's advantage: sth gives you an advantage (i.e. it helps you to be better/more successful than others)

The fact that Johnson had been with the company for six years was obviously to his advantage.

to such an extent that...: so much that...

Poor visibility hampered rescue efforts to such an extent that the search for the fishing boat had to be called off.

to the touch: when you touch it

Be careful when using a microwave oven as the plate may be cold to the touch but the food will be very hot.

under no circumstances: a phrase which emphasises the fact that sb must not do sth (generally, under no circumstances begins a sentence and is followed by an inversion)

Under no circumstances must photographs be taken inside the museum.

(to say/mutter sth) under your breath: to say sth very quietly so that nobody can hear what you said

He was sure she hadn't heard him. He had said it under his breath.

(to be) under the impression that: to wrongly believe that sth is true, permissible or a fact

I was under the impression that the concert started at 7:30, not at 7:00.

(to be) within easy reach of: to be near

The beach is within easy reach of the hotel.

Preposition... Preposition I

for fear of sth: if you do not do sth for fear of sth else (normally a bad thing) happening, you do not do it because you are frightened or worried that this bad thing might happen

I said nothing for fear of hurting their feelings.

in connection with + noun: (formal) about [Note: to be wanted in connection with a particular crime: the police want to talk to that person because they think they are connected in some way with that crime]

I'm writing in connection with last night's programme about the rainforests.

He is wanted in connection with the theft of several paintings from the National Gallery.

in keeping with sth: suitable in relation to sth

This new tax is very much in keeping with the revenue policies outlined in our election manifesto.

in the event of: if there is

In the event of a decrease in cabin pressure, oxygen masks will fall from a compartment above your heads.

(to be) in the middle of (doing) sth: to be halfway through doing sth

I'm sorry I didn't answer the phone when you rang. I was in the middle of having a bath.

(to cost/be charged) in the region/neighbourhood of: to cost/to be charged approximately (followed by an amount of money)

They'll probably charge you in the region of £200 to have it fixed.

The scheme cost in the neighbourhood of one million pounds.

in return for: in exchange for or as a payment for

I offered to buy him dinner in return for some advice.

with a view to: hoping to

He bought the land with a view to building on it when he retired.

with the exception of: except for

With the exception of Agnes, everyone passed the exam.

Practice

1. *Complete the sentences using an appropriate phrase from the box below.*

> any stretch of the imagination – a shadow of a doubt – no circumstances – such an extent – the touch – safekeeping – your advantage – all accounts – your breath – cross purposes – easy reach – demand – repair – own making – the impression

1. Michael Jordan is, **beyond** ...., the best basketball player there has ever been.
2. Oxford is a beautiful city and **within** .... of London.
3. Unemployment has risen **to** .... that twenty or more people are competing for every vacancy.
4. The fire gutted the tiny gallery, and while all the paintings being exhibited were rescued, the gallery itself was damaged **beyond** ....
5. He was, **by** ...., a very kind and gentle man. No one ever spoke badly of him.
6. Thrusting an envelope into my hands, he told me that **under** .... was I to discuss the information it contained with anyone but a colleague.
7. I was **under** .... that we were allowed to take as many photocopies as we liked.
8. Don't worry. He can't have heard you. You said it **under** ....
9. He was a remarkable artist and nowadays his paintings are greatly **in** ....
10. I gave the money to my father **for** .... because I knew that if I had it I'd probably lose it.
11. Not **by** .... could you call Featon a beautiful town, but I suppose it's got its own peculiar charm.
12. He knew he couldn't blame anybody else for his money problems. They were entirely **of** his ....
13. It would be very much **to** .... to accept the promotion, even though it would mean moving to head office.
14. Since I changed washing powders, my clothes have looked whiter and felt softer **to** ....
15. I was talking about water skiing but Dan thought I was talking about diving. We didn't realise we were talking **at** .... until he started telling me about the time a small fish got into his snorkel.

2. 🎧 *Listen to the extracts and write a sentence about them using the prepositional phrase in bold. The sentences have been started for you.*

A for fear of
Harry kept ....
....

B in the neighbourhood of
Relocating the lions ....
....

C in the middle of
The minister was ....
....

D with the exception of
All our family ....
....

E with a view to
Stan and Ivy bought ....
....

F in keeping with
Paolo thought ....
....

G in connection with
Two men are wanted ....
....

H in the event of
The notice said that ....
....

I in return for
The gorillas eventually ....
....

187

92 Preposition ... Preposition II

Note: all the structures below are relatively formal

(to go something) along the lines of: an expression used if you repeat or recite sth but do not know the exact words

It goes something along the lines of "Your writing is both good and original. But the part that is original is not good and the part that is good is not original."

(to be) at odds with: to be different from/disagree with

Richard was at odds with his colleagues over the decision.

(to be) at pains to do sth: to make an obvious and special effort to do sth (followed by verbs such as: deny, disassociate, distance, avoid, stress, play down, emphasise)

Gunnerssen was at pains to emphasise that he had acted alone and not on behalf of his company.

(to be) at the mercy of: not to have the power to protect yourself from

No shelter was in sight and they were at the mercy of the storm.

by the looks of: judging from appearances

By the looks of it, I'd say that the play has already started.

for the sake of/in the interest(s) of + noun: in order to help or improve

She had to give up competing professionally for the sake of her health.

Both leaders made great efforts in the interests of peace.

in addition to + ing/noun: as well as

In addition to winning the Pulitzer Prize, she was awarded the Nobel Prize for Literature.

in common with + noun: like, similar to (generally used at the beginning of a sentence)

In common with most politicians, she is incapable of giving a straightforward answer.

in lieu of: instead of

We used to give our landlord vegetables from our garden in lieu of the rent.

(to be) in need of: to need

My car is in desperate need of a service.

in response to: as an answer to

These measures were taken in response to the government's failure to comply with the United Nations' ban on CFCs.

(to be) in search of: to search for

They went in search of the treasure.

(to work) in tandem with: to work together

The Arts Council is working in tandem with the local corporation on this project.

(to be) in the grips of: to be experiencing sth bad (weather, famine, etc) and not be able to control or stop it

Switzerland is in the grips of its worst winter on record.

in the hope of + ing form: hoping that

They waited outside the theatre in the hope of catching a glimpse of the King.

(to be) in the throes of: to be experiencing a difficult or unpleasant situation which probably lasts for a long time

The country was in the throes of its worst economic crisis on record.

(to follow/come) in the wake of + noun: to happen after and as a result of

A new interest in Egyptology was generated in the wake of the opening of the Tomb of Tutenkhamen.

in view of sth/the fact that: taking sth into consideration

In view of the fact that it is such a good offer, you'd be foolish to turn them down.

on account of + noun: because of (often used to give the reason for sth bad that has happened)

We were delayed on account of the appalling weather.

on the strength of + noun: if you do sth (normally a good thing) on the strength of a particular piece of information or a particular characteristic or quality (when dealing with people), you do it because that information or quality has persuaded you to do it

He was given the job on the strength of his previous experience.

Practice

1. Complete the preposition... preposition combinations in A, B and C with an appropriate word from each box.

interests – pains – hope – search – view – account

   A
   1. in .... of
   2. on .... of
   3. in the .... of
   4. in .... of
   5. at .... to
   6. in the .... of

throes – tandem – wake – strength – common – response – looks – lines – mercy – lieu

   B
   7. in .... with
   8. at the .... of
   9. in .... to
   10. on the .... of
   11. along the .... of
   12. in the .... of
   13. by the .... of
   14. in .... of
   15. in .... with
   16. in the .... of

grips – odds – sake – need – addition

C 17 in .... of
18 in .... to
19 at .... with
20 for the .... of
21 in the .... of

2. Complete the sentences with an appropriate phrase from exercise 1, using each phrase only once.

1 He's always been .... his father, ever since he was a child. They've never been able to see eye to eye on anything.
2 His written work is .... improvement. If it doesn't get better, he could fail the exam.
3 I would say that, ... it, it's going to rain.
4 .... most children of his age, he's liable to throw a tantrum when he doesn't get his way.
5 The government is going to work .... the United Nations in an attempt to solve this problem.
6 I can't remember the exact words, but I think it goes something .... *I will start my song to the rhythm of the viguella.*
7 The knights of the Round Table went .... the Holy Grail.
8 The police combed the area .... finding some clues to the whereabouts of the missing child.
9 Zimbabwe is .... its worst drought on record. Not a drop of rain has fallen anywhere in the country for the last five months.
10 The union decided to press for a pay rise .... the increase in the rate of inflation.
11 .... public safety, authorities have decided to ban swimming in the River Gunk.
12 Her CV was very impressive indeed but he felt that it would be foolish to give someone a job .... their CV alone, so he wanted her to come to an interview.
13 .... offering a translation service, they also provide interpreters.

14 .... the present economic crisis that is crippling Redland, we would recommend that you do not invest in this region until the situation has been brought under control.
15 All flights will be delayed .... adverse weather conditions in and around Gatwick.
16 The minister's admission of involvement in the so-called Bathwater Affair has caused considerable embarrassment, especially as it comes at a time when the government has been .... distance itself from the scandal.
17 With our sails ripped to pieces and our engine broken, we were .... the sea.
18 The forest fires which followed .... the drought caused massive destruction to the environment.

3. The phrases in bold have been jumbled. Swap them around to make correct sentences.

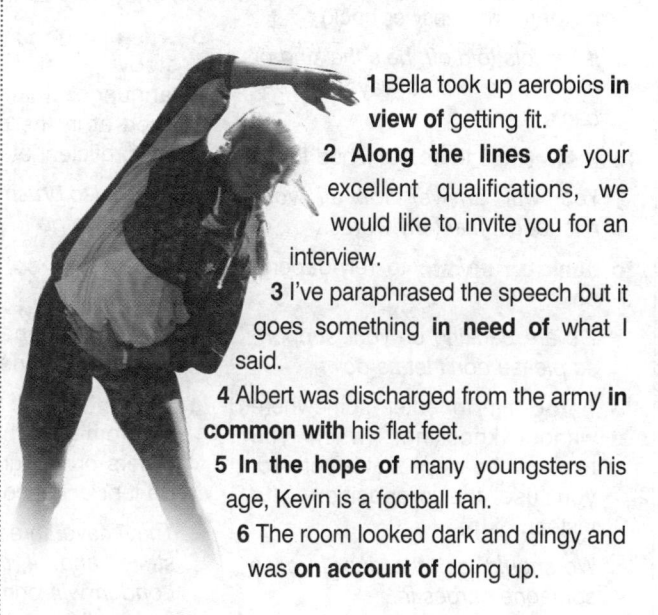

1 Bella took up aerobics **in view of** getting fit.
2 **Along the lines of** your excellent qualifications, we would like to invite you for an interview.
3 I've paraphrased the speech but it goes something **in need of** what I said.
4 Albert was discharged from the army **in common with** his flat feet.
5 **In the hope of** many youngsters his age, Kevin is a football fan.
6 The room looked dark and dingy and was **on account of** doing up.

4. Circle the correct item.

1 It is unfair when somebody gets a good job **in addition to / on account of** his or her connections.
2 Some employees work and are paid double time **in lieu of / on the strength of** taking holidays.
3 After the torrential rain, the country was **at odds with / in the grips of** floods.
4 He agreed to go to the wedding **for the sake of / in response to** his daughter's happiness.
5 The country was **in tandem with / in the throes of** a civil war.

189

93 A, B and C Phrasal Verbs

to account for: to cause/explain

I don't know how to account for the fact that my best student failed his exams.

to act for sb: to represent sb in a legal or financial matter

Please contact our lawyer. He will be acting for the company in this matter.

to act up: to behave badly/malfunction

What's that noise? Are the twins acting up?

The washing machine was acting up again.

to answer sb back: to reply in a rude way to sb in authority who has told you off (generally, it is children who answer back)

If he gets told off, he's the kind of child who will always answer back.

to answer for: to be punished for

You will answer for all your misdeeds, mark my words.

to bank on sb/sth: to rely/depend on

We are banking on your support, so please don't let us down.

to barge in: to enter somewhere without knocking; (when you mention the place that is entered, you use the preposition **into** instead of **in**)

We should lock the door in case someone barges in.

Suddenly, a woman barged into the office and demanded to see the manager.

to be barking up the wrong tree: (informal) (i) to wrongly accuse another person of sth (ii) to mistakenly believe that sb will help you

You're barking up the wrong tree if you think Vince will help you out.

to block sth off: to completely close a road/street/exit/path, etc so that nothing can move along it

The police blocked off all the side streets that led onto the main thoroughfare.

to bottle sth up: to keep strong feelings and emotions inside you without expressing them

You should have a good cry. Bottling things up will only make you feel worse.

to branch out (into): do sth different from your normal activities or work.

In order to be competitive, we decided to branch out and teach Portuguese as well as English.

to brush up on sth: to practise and study a skill (particularly a language) that you were very good at in the past, so that you are proficient at it once again

I'll need to brush up on my French before we go to Paris.

to bump into sb: to meet sb by chance

I was in the supermarket the other day and I bumped into Rob.

to carry sth out: if you carry out sth (a promise/a threat/a task, sb's orders or instructions/a test) you do it or act according to it

They have threatened to go on strike, and, if they carry it out, London will come to a complete standstill.

If I give an order, I expect it to be carried out.

We can't tell you what's wrong with him until we carry out more tests.

to catch on: to become popular or fashionable

I doubt whether this new fashion for ankle socks and high heels will catch on.

to catch up (with sb/sth): (i)to reach sb (walking/in a car) that is ahead of you (ii) to reach the same intellectual level as sb

They are miles ahead of us, and he's driving really fast. We'll never catch up with them.

I've missed a lot of lessons so I have to work hard in order to catch up with the others in the class.

to churn sth out: to produce sth in great quantities

At one point, the factory was churning out a million plastic dolls a week.

to clamp down on sb/sth: to take firm official action to stop sb/sth (a criminal/an illegal activity)

The authorities need to clamp down on this kind of behaviour.

to conjure up (images of): to bring (a picture or image) to mind

The name of the hotel conjured up images of the faded splendour of the Raj.

to be cooped up (in a place): to be in a place (a room, office, house, etc) which is too small so that you feel uncomfortable and you want to get out

I hate being cooped up indoors when it is sunny outside.

to crop up (at work): to happen/appear suddenly and unexpectedly (often used in excuses for not doing things or for breaking arrangements)

I'm afraid I can't come. Something has just cropped up at work.

Practice

1. Choose the correct item.

1. Listen, I can't make it for dinner tonight. Something has **cropped** .... at work and it looks like I'm going to be stuck at the office all night.
   A out   B up   C in   D through

2. Polynesia. The very name **conjures** .... images of sundrenched beaches and warm turquoise seas.
   A out   B up   C over   D in

3. Never **bottle** things .... If you have a problem, you should get it off your chest and share it with someone.
   A over   B up   C in   D along

4. She is a prolific writer. She **churns** .... at least five novels a year.
   A over   B off   C away   D out

5. She hasn't spoken German for over a year and I think she wants to **brush** .... a few things.
   A out in   B on with   C up on   D over on

6. I'd been **cooped** .... in my office all morning so I went out for a walk and a spot of fresh air.
   A over   B by   C down   D up

7. The door burst open and his mother **barged** .... "I thought so," she said. "You're not doing your homework."
   A into   B in   C on   D along

8. I know he said he would help but I wouldn't **bank** .... it. You know how unreliable he is.
   A for   B with   C to   D on

9. His refusal to **carry** .... his superior's orders resulted in his being court-martialled.
   A out   B through   C off   D on

10. As their bookshop wasn't doing very well, they decided to **branch** .... and sell compact discs and cassettes as well.
    A out   B over   C down on   D out for

11. The government are strongly committed to **clamping** .... unregulated parking.
    A out on   B over   C down on   D out for

12. She looked at her son. "You must not **answer** .... when your teacher tells you off," she said.
    A down   B off   C over   D back

13. If they think Jan did it, they are **barking** .... the wrong tree. He was with me when it supposedly happened.
    A by   B up   C down   D back

14. "I was in Oxford last weekend and you'll never guess who I **bumped** ....," he said.
    A for   B along   C into   D through

15. As part of their demonstration, the students **blocked** .... several roads that ran through the city centre.
    A down   B out   C back   D off

16. They were very fashionable on the Continent, but for some reason they never really **caught** .... in England.
    A in   B by   C on   D over

17. You'll have to study hard if you want to **catch** .... with the rest of the class.
    A up   B through   C on   D upon

2. Rewrite the following sentences using a phrasal verb from this unit.

1. We've decided to expand our business by selling second-hand books.
   ....
   ....

2. Something is wrong with the computer.
   ....
   ....

3. Before I go to the interview I ought to study and improve my Italian.
   ....
   ....

4. The fact that she is under a lot of pressure might explain why she is behaving so strangely.
   ....
   ....

5. Someone will have to pay for this terrible mistake.
   ....
   ....

6. The government has promised to take strong measures to stop vandalism in inner city areas.
   ....
   ....

7. The lawyers representing him asked the judge to dismiss the case.
   ....
   ....

8. He might be able to give you some extra work but I wouldn't rely on it.
   ....
   ....

94 D, E and F Phrasal Verbs

sth dawns on sb: sb realises the truth/ a particular fact for the first time, although it should have been apparent before

After he had waited for a bus for over an hour, it suddenly dawned on him that there was a bus strike.

to dig sth up: to find sth that was well hidden or that you thought was lost

"I've managed to dig up some very interesting information on the case," she said.

(could) do with sth: would like sth/ need sth

I don't know about you, but I could do with a cola.

to drag on: to continue for longer than necessary

The months turned into years, and the war dragged on.

to draw up: (for documents) to prepare and write out

The lawyer was busy drawing up the agreement.

to dream sth up: to invent or create a story, an excuse, a plot, a plan, etc which is often very complicated or fanciful

Whoever dreamt up such a ridiculous slogan?

to dredge up: to find and bring to people's attention an unpleasant or embarrassing fact or incident that had been forgotten

This old scandal they have dredged up could be very damaging for the government.

to dress up: to put on special clothes (particularly formal wear) for a particular occasion (a ball, a party, a company dinner) [Note: **to dress up as sth/sb** (a clown, a cowboy, Robin Hood, etc): to put on and wear unusual clothes that make you look like sb else]

One of the reasons I hate going to these company dinners is that I have to dress up.

Whenever there is a fancy dress party, I dress up as Cleopatra.

to drown (a sound/noise) out: to be so loud that another sound/noise cannot be heard

Our conversation was suddenly drowned out by the ear-splitting sound of a pneumatic drill.

to ease up: to reduce in degree, speed or intensity

After a while, the rain eased up and they were able to resume play.

to eat into: to use part of (especially a sum of money/time)

Dealing with other people's problems is eating into his time.

to edge out: to just manage to beat sb or get in front of them

The company has edged out others in the same field.

to egg sb on: to encourage sb to do sth dangerous or foolish

His friends were egging him on to jump into the river.

to eke out a living: to manage to earn just enough to live on

For ten years he eked out a meagre living cleaning tables at a local fast food restaurant.

to fish for: to try and get information or praise in an indirect way

He's not as modest as you think; he's just fishing for compliments.

(not to be able) to fathom sth out: to find it very difficult to explain/ understand sth

We couldn't fathom out why she would want to leave such an excellent job.

to fill sb in (on sth): to give sb up-to-date information which they need but don't have

Jim will fill you in on what's been happening while you've been away.

to fit sb in: to find time in a schedule for an appointment (used in connection with doctors, dentists, hairdressers and other people who work with the public on an appointment basis)

I know it's urgent, Mr Thomas, but I'm afraid the only time I can fit you in is at six thirty.

to fizzle out: if sth (enthusiasm, a protest, an attempt to do sth, a romance, etc) fizzles out, it gradually decreases and finally disappears

Student politics - passion, protest, righteous indignation; it soon fizzles out when exam time comes around.

to fob sb off (with sth): to try and stop sb complaining by giving them excuses, stories or explanations that are obviously untrue

I've rung up six times and I'm fed up with being fobbed off with your pathetic excuses.

to frown upon/on sth: to disapprove of sth (not sb)

In this company, failing to recycle paper is frowned upon.

Practice

1. *Fill in the gaps with one of the phrasal verbs in this unit. The definitions (a-p) will help you.*

1. His enthusiasm for work soon .... when he realised he would be spending the next thirty-five years of his life behind a desk.
2. As I had been unable to go to the meeting, I asked Laima to .... what had been discussed.
3. Wearing casual clothes to the office is not prohibited, but it is most definitely ....
4. "I'm sorry, Mrs Richards," said the doctor's receptionist, "I can't .... today. How about four o'clock tomorrow?"
5. The lecturer's voice was suddenly .... by the noise of an aeroplane directly overhead.
6. "I found a picture of us when we were at school. Look." "Good grief! Where did you .... that .... ?"
7. When I complained that I had not received my order, the woman on the phone tried to .... with the unlikely story that it had probably got lost in the post.
8. It's not that she's inquisitive; she was just .... some indication as to how Josh is doing.
9. No one could .... why she would want to drop out of college and get a job with no prospects.
10. Before he became famous, he .... a meagre living working as a cashier.
11. The hall was empty and the lights were off. The only sound came from a vacuum cleaner. Gradually, it .... him: the lecture had been cancelled!
12. Had it not been for the government's intervention, the strike would have .... for months.
13. The children were busy .... for the carnival parade.
14. Every year inventors .... new kitchen gadgets to make our lives easier.
15. If you .... the contract ...., I'll sign it.
16. Why do you keep .... that stupid mistake? I said I was sorry!

a to disappear
b to give sb information that they need
c to disapprove of
d to find time for
e to make one noise impossible to hear by covering it with another noise
f to find - usually something that was hidden or that you thought was lost
g to give poor excuses to stop someone complaining
h to try and get information in an indirect way
i to understand
j to earn money (but not very much) to live on
k to realise
l to continue for too long, becoming annoying/boring as a result
m to put on formal or fancy clothes
n to invent/think of
o to prepare and write out
p to remind

2. *Make up appropriate questions for the following answers.*

1. A: ....
   ....
   B: Yes, the high rate of inflation is making it difficult for us to manage.
2. A: ....
   ....
   B: No, I think it has set in for the day.
3. A: ....
   ....
   B: No, I think it is wrong to encourage people to do such foolish things.
4. A: ....
   ....
   B: Yes, that sort of negative criticism is very damaging for someone's self-confidence.
5. A: ....
   ....
   B: Yes, he only just beat his opponent.
6. A: ....
   ....
   B: Yes, they tried to make me take a replacement.

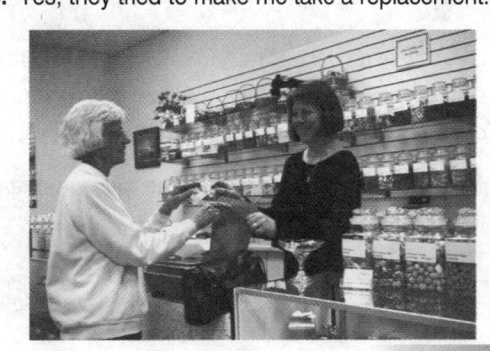

95 G to M Phrasal Verbs

to gang up on: to join together and form a group, often in order to harm or frighten sb

The bigger boys at my school would often gang up on the smaller boys.

to glaze over: (for eyes) to become dull and lose expression

Her eyes glazed over with boredom during the speech.

to gloss over: to ignore or deal very quietly with a problem, mistake, etc

The government spokesman glossed over the administration's policy mistakes.

to grow on sb: to gradually start liking sth/sb, even though you probably started out hating it/them

I hated London at first. However, the longer I lived there the more it grew on me.

to hang about/around: to wait and stay in a place doing nothing in particular

I'm not going to hang around waiting for them any longer.

to hang onto sth: to keep sth (and not sell it or give it away)

That record collection of yours is worth hanging onto. It could be valuable one day.

to be held up: (i) to be delayed (ii) to be robbed by sb with a gun

I'm sorry we are late. We were held up in traffic.

In Chapter 1, the hero is held up at gunpoint.

to hit it off: if two people hit it off, they really like one another (generally used when two people meet for the first time)

We hit it off immediately.

to hit back at sb: to reply, forcefully, to sb who has criticised you for sth

The minister hit back at his critics, saying that his privatisation of the mines had saved them from closure.

to hush (sth) up: to stop people from finding out about sth that might cause you embarrassment/ damage your reputation

The government did its best to hush up the scandal.

to jot (sth) down: to write notes / telephone numbers/ addresses very quickly, especially in response to what sb is saying or telling you

I'll just jot that address down.

to knock off (work): to finish working for the day

What time do you normally knock off work?

to lay (sb) off: to dismiss sb from their job because the company they work for can no longer afford to employ them/no longer has work for them to do

Last year the company made a loss of £56 million. As a result, it has announced that it is going to lay off 25% of its workforce.

to leave (sth) out: not to include sth

We've decided to leave questions 3 and 5 out of the exam because we think they are too difficult.

to line (sth) up: to arrange for sth to take place during a special event, a concert, a holiday, etc

I've lined up a magician for Petra's party.

to liven (sth) up: (i) to make sth (a party, a lesson, etc) more exciting (ii) to become more exciting and entertaining

Your lessons are boring. They need livening up.

It always takes a couple of hours for a party to liven up.

to be/get mixed up in sth: to be/get involved in an illegal or dishonest activity [Note: **to be/get mixed up with sb:** to become involved with/associated with bad people]

They must have made a mistake. Peter would never get mixed up in something like that.

to mope about/around: to wander around a place feeling sorry for yourself, without making any effort to be cheerful

There's no point in moping around, just because you've failed your exams.

to mull (sth) over: to think long and hard about sth (an offer, a suggestion, etc) so as to be able to make a decision about it

It was a good offer, but he would need time to mull it over.

Practice

1. For each of the sentences below, write a new sentence as similar as possible to the original sentence, using an appropriate phrasal verb from above.

   1 Two armed men robbed them as they were leaving their hotel.
   They ....
   ....

   2 "It's a good speech, but I don't think you should include the part about tax cuts," he said.
   He said that it was a good speech, but he suggested ....

   3 "What time do you finish work tonight?" she asked.
   She wanted to know ....

   4 All he does is stay at home all day, feeling sorry for himself.
   He does nothing ....

5 I hated it at first, but the more I listened to it, the more I liked it.
   I hated it at first, but the more ....

6 We will have to make 25 of our employees redundant if we want to reduce our costs.
   Reducing our costs will mean ....

7 The party was pretty boring until the band came on.
   Only when ....

2. For questions 1 to 19, complete the second sentence so that it has a similar meaning to the first sentence. The word(s) that you need to complete the second sentence can be found in the box below.

> being left – mulled – livening – to jot – gangs –
> had got mixed – hit – will grow – to bang – glazed –
> to have lined – didn't hit – of banging – were held –
> in bushing – to lay – mope – knock – glossed

1 I've heard that they have arranged for a celebrity speaker to come to tonight's meeting.
   They are supposed .... up a celebrity speaker for tonight's meeting.

2 After careful consideration, we decided to take him up on his offer.
   Having carefully .... it over, we decided to take him up on his offer.

3 Rather than staying here doing nothing, why don't you go out and look for a job?
   Why don't you go out and look for a job instead .... about here all day?

4 You might not like his music at first but the more you listen to it the more you will get to like it.
   You might not like his music at first, but if you listen to it enough times it .... on you.

5 "Could you quickly write down your telephone number on this piece of scrap paper?" she asked.
   She asked me .... down my telephone number on a piece of scrap paper.

6 How on earth did Paul get involved with such people?
   I wondered how on earth Paul .... up with such people.

7 I don't know why everybody is against me.
   I don't know why everybody .... up on me.

8 It would be a good idea to keep those books your grandfather gave you – they could be valuable some day.
   You ought .... onto those books your grandfather gave you – they could be valuable some day.

9 The government thought that they had managed to keep the scandal a secret from the public.
   The government thought they had succeeded .... up the scandal.

10 Since he lost his job he has done nothing but wander aimlessly around the house, depressed and feeling sorry for himself.
   Since losing his job, all he does is .... about the house all day.

11 You need to make your act more exciting.
   Your act needs .... up.

12 If we can't get a bank loan, we'll have no alternative but to make half our workforce redundant.
   If the bank doesn't lend us the money, we'll be forced .... off half our workforce.

13 Sorry we're late. We were stuck in a traffic jam on the M30.
   Sorry we're late. We .... up on the M30.

14 He was very disappointed when he found out that the manager had not included him in the team.
   He was bitterly disappointed at .... out of the team.

15 Seldom do we leave work before seven o'clock on a Monday.
   We rarely .... off before seven o'clock on a Monday.

16 It's odd that you and Delia took an instant dislike to each other. You seem to have so much in common.
   I'm surprised you two .... it off. You seem to have so much in common.

17 The Prime Minister responded angrily to those who had accused him of losing touch with the ordinary man in the street.
   The Prime Minister .... back at those who had accused him of losing touch with the grass roots.

18 They ignored the glaring errors in the report.
   They .... over the glaring errors in the report.

19 They play was halfway through when his eyes became dull and expressionless.
   Halfway through the play his eyes .... over. He had lost interest.

96 N, O and P Phrasal Verbs

to name after: to give sb/sth the same name as sb/sth else

George was named after his grandfather.

to narrow sth down to: to reduce/limit sth or the range of sth

The police have narrowed the search for the missing child down to ten streets in the East End of the city.

to nod off: to fall asleep often while sitting down

He nodded off in front of the TV.

to nose around: to look around somewhere curiously to see if you can see sth interesting; to snoop

The cat was nosing around in the cupboards, looking for things to play with or eat.

to notch up: to achieve a score or total

That's the tenth medal he has notched up so far.

to opt out: to choose not to participate in sth

Those who wish to do so may opt out of the pension plan.

to own up: to confess

The little boy owned up to breaking the window.

to part with sth: to sell / give sth to sb

I love that painting. If I offered him £3,000, do you think he would part with it?

This furniture has been in our family for five generations and there's no way I would part with it.

to pass away: to die

He passed away peacefully in his sleep, at the age of ninety-two.

to pass yourself off as: to pretend to be sb you are not

She managed to pass herself off as a cousin to the Queen.

to pass up: not to take (an opportunity)

Everything was half-price, so it was too good an opportunity to pass up.

to patch things up/patch up sth (a relationship, etc): to make friends again after a bad argument

I know they are not talking to each other now, but I'm sure they will patch things up.

to pay sb back for sth: (i) to return money that is owed to sb (ii) to get revenge on sb

Can you lend me £50? I'll pay you back tomorrow, I promise.

Gabriella decided that she was going to pay Alan back for what he had done to her family.

to phone in sick: to telephone sb at work to tell them that you are not coming in because you are ill

I'm not feeling well. I am going to phone in sick.

to pick on: to victimise

When I was a child, the older boys in my village always used to pick on me.

to pick up: to learn or acquire (e.g. new skill, language)

Greg had no formal training in using a computer, but he soon picked it up.

to piece sth together: to put together different (but connected) facts to make a whole story/ to get a complete picture of sth

Having pieced together all the clues and evidence, the police felt they had a strong case.

to pipe up: to start to speak, especially when you have been silent for some time [Note: (i) **to pipe up with an/the answer:** to tell sb the answer to a question (ii) **Pipe down!:** (informal) be quiet]

The teacher had just about given up when suddenly Billy piped up with the answer.

Suddenly, a small voice piped up from the back seat, "Are we almost there?"

Will you two pipe down? I'm trying to work!

to play sth down: to make sth seem less important than it really is

Although the workforce were on the verge of calling a strike, the management played the crisis down.

to ply sb with sth: to give sb a constant supply of sth (especially used about food and drink)

Auntie Edith plied us with so much food that I could hardly walk when it came time to leave.

to point out (sb) that: to explain sth/tell sb sth that they did not know

My lawyer then pointed out to me that, if I refused to pay the fine, I could be sent to prison.

to potter about: to spend time doing small unimportant things that require little effort

He likes nothing better than to spend his Sunday mornings pottering about in the garden.

to pull yourself together: to take control of your emotions and feelings when you are very nervous / frightened / upset (especially) because you are not behaving sensibly)

She was sobbing and refused to get into the car. "Pull yourself together" I said. "It's only an exam."

to pull up a chair: to move a chair nearer to sth (often used as an invitation)

Why don't you pull up a chair?

to pull it off: to succeed

I never thought I'd pass the audition, but I pulled it off.

to push sb around: to give sb orders in a rude and aggressive way

I never liked him. He pushed me around and he took me for granted.

to push (the door) to: to close/nearly close

It's cold in here. Could you push the door to?

Practice

1. Complete the gaps in the text below with an appropriate verb from the box below in the correct form.

pay – patch – push – own – part – pull – point – potter – phone – pipe

It was ten thirty in the morning. The Serious Crime Strategy and Feedback Meeting was about to begin. Someone should have **1)** .... out to Calls that Bletchley, was not New York. But they hadn't, and Calls carried on regardless. PC Elk looked over at PC Flint. He didn't like Flint. Not one bit. Flint was lazy and arrogant and Elk was tired of being **2)** .... around. Well now Elk was going to **3)** .... Flint back for the years of continual bullying and snide remarks. He would show Flint up for what he really was and prove himself to be much more capable.
Calls entered the room, **4)** .... up a chair and sat down. He quickly handed Elk and Flint the SCSFM agenda, and launched into the day's proceedings.
As you can see there are three items on today's Agenda. They have been arranged in alphabetical order. In addition, they have been numerically arranged into sections for ... for what, Elk?
Future cataloguing purposes, Sir.
Future cataloguing purposes. Exactly. Good... Section One: The Carstairs Incident. Feedback: P.C. Elk.
Elk was going for the double whammy. He pulled out his note book and cleared his throat.
Case closed, sir. I talked to Mr Steven's, Mr Carstairs' neighbour, and he **5)** .... *up to everything. He has promised to pay for the damage he caused to Mr Carstairs' window and assures me that nothing like this will ever happen again.*
Does Mr Carstairs wish to press charges?
No, Sir. It would seem that the two men have now **6)** .... *things up.*
Calls nodded. It was an appreciative nod and Elk made a mental note to remember this moment. Calls moved on to Section Two: Mrs George and the Lawn Mower Dispute. He was in full flow.
Mrs Timms who lent the mower to Mrs George last month saw Mrs George **7)** .... *about in her garden with the said mower. Mrs George now admits that she does indeed have Mrs Timms' mower but she refuses to* **8)** .... *with it. I'd like you, Flint to pay a visit to Mrs George's and retrieve the mower.*
Use... what Flint?
Use the car, Sir?
Elk could hardly contain himself and **9)** .... up with, Use tact, reason and diplomacy, Sir. Calls nodded and glared at Flint. Flint was beginning to wish he had **10)** .... in sick. Elk smiled. Everything was going to plan.

2. Match the phrasal verbs in bold with their definitions (a to j).

1 This street is **named after** a Roman emperor. .....
2 He yawned. The room was warm and his chair was comfortable. It wasn't long before he **nodded off**. .....
3 I'm afraid Mr Simpkins doesn't work here any more. He **passed away** last year. It was his heart, you know. .....
4 He got the part in the play by **passing himself off** as a friend of a well known actor. .....
5 It's a lovely book, but he is offering me £3,000 for it. Much as I'd love to keep it, I just can't afford to **pass up** that kind of money. .....
6 None of us did our homework, yet only I got punished. Why does he always **pick on** me? .....
7 It sounds and looks like a difficult language to learn, but I promise you it isn't. You'll **pick it up** in no time. .....
8 The government will, of course, do everything in their power to **play down** this crisis – any government would. But it is time to face the facts. .....
9 Could you **push** the door **to**? .....
10 It's too risky and complicated. We'd never **pull it off**. .....

a to victimise
b to ignore
c to succeed
d to die
e to fall asleep
f to close/nearly close
g to learn/acquire
h to pretend that you are sb that you are not
i to give sb/sth the same name as sb/ sth else
j to make sth seem less important than it really is

3. Complete the sentences using a verb from this unit in the correct form.

1 I know it's an important interview but try to .... yourself together and go in looking calm and confident.
2 After the meal, they .... us with chocolate cake and sweets.
3 It was a difficult choice but the judges .... down the contestants to three before selecting the winner.
4 Having .... together all the clues, I was able to guess the ending of the whodunnit before I'd finished reading it.
5 What a sportsman! He has .... up more golf tournament victories than any of his competitors.
6 If you don't like this new pension scheme, you can .... out whenever you like.
7 Who do you think you are .... around like that, a private eye?

97 R to S Phrasal Verbs

- **to rave about/over/on about sth:** to talk very enthusiastically about sth

    Everybody is raving about his new book/this new restaurant.

- **to rule (sth) out:** to say that sth is not possible.

    They ruled out the possibility of a retrial.

    We can't rule out the possibility that she will call an early election.

- **to rustle (sth) up:** to quickly cook sth, often when not expecting to cook

    She rustled us up an omelette.

- **to scrape by (on):** to manage to live on very little money

    Somehow we managed to scrape by on £4 a day.

- **to scrape through:** to only just pass an exam/test

    Somehow I managed to scrape through my maths exam.

- **to shake a cold off:** to get rid of a cold

    I've been on antibiotics for a week but I can't seem to shake this cold off.

- **to show (sb) in, into/out (of):** to lead sb into/out of a place/room/building

    Goodbye, Mr Johnson. My secretary will show you out.

- **to show up:** to arrive, especially at a place where sb is expecting you [Note: **to show up sth:** to make it possible to see/notice bad things]

    Do you think Tom will show up?

    His questions showed up the flaws in her argument.

- **sth sinks in:** to slowly understand very important (good or bad) news/ideas/suggestions

    It took a moment or two for the news to sink in – I was going to be a father!

- **to sit (for) an exam:** to take an exam

    I sat for the FCE exam in June 1999.

- **to sit through sth:** if you sit through a lecture/meeting/speech, you stay until it is finished, even though you are not enjoying it

    I refuse to sit through another one of his lectures.

- **to slip (sth) off:** to quickly take off an article of clothing

    "Slip off your shirt and I'll look at your shoulder," said the doctor.

- **to slip over:** to quickly put an article of clothing over (your head/shoulders/arms)

    As it was getting chilly, I slipped a cardigan over my shoulders.

- **to slip through:** to pass through sth which is intended to stop such a movement [Note: **to slip through someone's fingers:** to escape from sb just when they think they have caught you]

    He slipped through the barrier without being seen.

    You let him slip through your fingers again! We had him surrounded.

- **to slip up:** to make a mistake

    I must have slipped up and told them the wrong date.

- **to snuff (a candle) out:** to extinguish a candle by blowing it out

    Don't forget to snuff out the candles when you leave.

- **to stick by sb:** to support sb who is in a difficult situation

    The minister's wife stuck by him, despite the allegations.

- **to stick to a path:** to stay on a path [Note: (i) **to stick to the rules:** to follow the rules; not break them, (ii) **to stick to the point/subject/facts:** to talk about only what you are supposed to talk about]

    Stick to the path or you'll get lost.

    If you had stuck to the rules, you wouldn't have been disqualified.

    Spare me the details and stick to the point, will you?

- **to be stuck for sth:** (words/an answer/reply) not to be able to find (the necessary words/answer, etc)

    When asked about the scandal, the minister was clearly stuck for an answer.

Practice

1. Using the cues, make up questions for the following answers.

1. No, but I can rustle something up.
2. It hasn't sunk in yet.
3. It's a little complicated. My secretary will show you out.
4. I don't know. Someone must have slipped up.
5. Because I've just had to sit through a six-hour meeting on boosting sales.
6. Because he has always stuck by me.
7. Well, I don't think we can rule it out, can we?
8. Because everyone has been raving on about it.

Have you got ...?
What does it feel like to ...?
Where's ...?
Why ...?
Why are you ...?
Why are you ...?
Do you think that ...?
Why did you ...?

2. *Someone has already done the following multiple choice exercise. Decide whether the circled answers are correct or incorrect. If you think the answer is correct, put a tick in the space. If you think the answer is incorrect, put a cross in the space and circle the correct answer.*

1 "It looks as if it will be a fine day," he said, "but I don't think we should **rule** .... the possibility of rain later on."
   A away   B over
   C off   (D) out   ....

2 I saw that film everyone's been **raving** .... Maybe I'm missing something, but I thought it was fairly ordinary.
   (A) on   B about
   C up   D for   ....

3 "How do you feel about winning the lottery?" "To be honest, it hasn't **sunk** .... yet. I keep pinching myself to make sure I'm not dreaming."
   A down   B in
   (C) through D up   ....

4 "You make yourself at home," she said, "and I'll see if I can **rustle** us .... something to eat."
   A on   B over
   (C) up   D in   ....

5 It's one o'clock and, if he were coming, he'd have **shown** .... by now.
   A up   B out
   C by   (D) in   ....

6 You won't get lost as long as you **stick** .... the path.
   A along B to
   C by   (D) for   ....

7 "I'm off to bed, then," he said, **snuffing** the candle .... and closing the door.
   (A) out B over
   C off   D away   ....

8 Somehow I managed to **scrape** .... my physics exam. The pass mark was 55 and I got 56.
   A by   (B) along
   C out of D through ....

9 Well, someone's **slipped** .... somewhere along the line, because it is humanly impossible to use that much electricity.
   (A) up   B over
   C through D down   ....

10 I've had this cold for a month. I just can't seem to **shake** it ....
   A out   (B) down
   C off   D away   ....

11 A good friend is somebody who will **stick** .... you through thick and thin.
   A on   (B) by
   C to   D with   ....

12 I'm **stuck** .... ideas for a composition title. Can you help?
   A with (B) in
   C for   D at   ....

13 He **showed** them .... of the dark and dingy building.
   (A) out B down
   C in   D up   ....

14 "Yes, I'm tetchy," she said. "So would you be if you'd had to **sit** .... seven hours of meetings today."
   (A) for B over
   C through D on   ....

3. *Circle the correct item.*

1 "It's hot," he said, slipping **off** / **through** his jumper.
2 As a student, she had to scrape **through** / **by** on very little money.
3 The main problem with your composition is that you don't stick **by** / **to** the point.
4 Slipping an anorak **over** / **off** her cardigan, she went out into the snow.
5 The jeweller's eyeglass showed **in** / **up** the flaws in the diamond.
6 He'll be sitting **for** / **through** the exam this summer.

98 T and W Phrasal Verbs

to tag along: to join sb and go with them to a particular place

Sally said you were going to the football game later. Do you mind if I tag along?

to talk sb into doing sth: to persuade sb to do sth

There is no way you are going to talk me into going to that party.

to talk sth over with sb: to discuss sth in detail with sb

If I took the job it would mean moving to Australia, so I'd have to talk it over with my wife and children first.

to be able to tell things/people apart: to be able to tell the difference between two or more people/things

She can't tell butter and margarine apart.

to think (sth) over: to carefully consider sth (an offer, a suggestion, etc) so as to be able to make a decision about it

When they offered me a job in their Athens office, I said I would think it over.

to throw sb out (of a place): to make sb leave a place because they have behaved badly

He was thrown out of the restaurant for insulting one of the waiters.

to tone sth down: to make sth written (a speech, a letter of complaint, etc) less aggressive and/or less offensive

I know it is a letter of complaint, but don't you think you should tone it down a bit?

to touch on sth: to briefly mention sth

In last week's lecture, I briefly touched on Plato's vision of the ideal state.

to toy with the idea of doing sth: to think about doing sth (but not very seriously)

We've been toying with the idea of selling this house and moving to Spain for years.

to trigger (sth) off: to cause sth (normally involving violence – a riot, a fight, etc) to happen

The government's decision to increase taxes triggered off widespread protests throughout the country.

to trot out (ideas/information/opinions/reasons/excuses): to give answers, opinions, reasons, excuses that everyone has heard before so that people get fed up with hearing them and no longer believe them

Every time he's late, he trots out the same excuse.

to turn (sb) away: not to allow sb to enter a place (a nightclub, disco, etc)

I was turned away at the door because I was wearing jeans.

to turn to sb: to go to sb for help, advice or comfort

When he lost his job, he had nobody to turn to.

to wait up for sb: not to go to bed because you are waiting for sb to return home

I'm not going to be back until really late, so don't wait up for me.

to wear off: to gradually stop having an effect (for medicine, feelings, sensations, etc)

When we first got the dog, everyone wanted to take him for a walk. Of course, the novelty soon wore off and now I have to do it.

This kind of anaesthetic wears off fairly quickly.

to weigh (sth) up: to consider your options or the advantages and disadvantages of doing sth so that you can make some kind of choice or decision

Having weighed up the various merits of each school, we decided to send our daughter to Vinters.

to while away the/one's time: to spend time in a pleasant way doing sth that does not require too much physical activity

while away the day / morning / afternoon / evening / the entire summer / etc

He would while away the afternoons doing crosswords by the pool.

to whip up: to do sth (make a speech/launch an advertising campaign/make an appearance on television, etc) in order to get more support for sth

He gave speeches all over the country to whip up support for his 'Help the Homeless' campaign.

to wind down: to relax

There's nothing like a long hot bath to help you wind down after a stressful day at work.

to work (sth) out: (i) to find an answer to a mathematical problem (ii) to understand or find an explanation for sth
[Note: (i) **I've got it all worked out:** I have a perfect plan for how to do sth] (ii) **sth work(s) out:** sth develops smoothly and reaches a successful conclusion]

124 multiplied by 76. I'll need a calculator to work that out.

There were wires and plugs everywhere. I couldn't work out where anything went.

We need to save £1,000 by Christmas. I've been thinking about it and I've got it all worked out.

Unfortunately, things didn't work out (as planned) and we were forced to close the company down.

Practice

1. Complete the sentences using an appropriate verb from the box below. You may have to change the tense or the form of the verb.

> talk – tone – trigger – wind – turn – trot – work –
> throw – talk – while – weigh – think – wait – wear –
> turn – touch – toy – tell – whip – tag

1. I go straight to the pool when I come back from work. I'm normally quite stressed and a swim helps me .... **down**
2. You talked right through the performance! No wonder they .... you **out!**
3. It's very good, but I think a lot of people will find it very offensive. You should .... it **down** a bit if you want to get it published.
4. It gets so crowded at the weekend that after nine they start .... people **away.**
5. It's a good offer, but before I accept it I'll have to .... it **over** with my business partner.
6. "These sales people can be very persuasive, so don't let them .... you **into** buying anything," she said.
7. "Hello, guys," he said. "I heard you were going to the cinema. Do you mind if I .... **along**?"
8. The kids loved their new bikes at first and were riding them all day, every day. However, the novelty soon .... **off** and within two months the bikes were rusting away in the garage.
9. "It's certainly an excellent offer, gentlemen," he said, "but give me a few days to .... it **over** and then I'll give you an answer."
10. The twins looked so alike that nobody except their mother could .... them **apart**.
11. In my last lecture I briefly .... **on** Frankel's theory of inverse inversion. Today I would like to discuss this theory in more detail.
12. "I'm going to be late," he said, "so don't .... **up for** me."
13. Whenever government representatives are called on to defend cutbacks in essential social services, they .... **out** the same old nonsense about it being in the country's best interests.
14. Having .... **up** the pros and cons of owning a house, we decided that it would be better for us to rent.
15. It would be a terrible shame if they split up. Let's hope they manage to .... things **out**.
16. She would .... **away** the hot summer evenings sitting on her balcony, watching the world go by.
17. We've been .... **with** the idea of emigrating for ages and, what with Peter being made redundant and everything, now seems as good a time as any.
18. The advertising campaign was designed to .... **up** support for the government's crusade to encourage blood donation.
19. It was a huge fight. Everyone on the pitch was involved. I don't know what .... it **off**.
20. A good friend is someone you can always .... **to** for support and advice.

2. The phrasal verbs in bold in the sentence below have not been used correctly. Replace them with appropriate ones from this unit.

1. You'll find that the side-effects of the tablets are mild and should **trigger off** in a few days.
2. Although Professor Foster **toyed with** the subject of perspective in art in his lecture, he didn't go into it in any detail.
3. She's **waiting up for** the pros and cons of going freelance.
4. You know we are going to the swimming pool this afternoon, would you mind if my brother **trotted out**?
5. Sitting in a comfortable armchair reading a good book is an ideal way to **work out** after a hectic day at work.
6. Everybody needs someone to **turn away** when they have problems they can't solve alone.
7. Knowing that they would be home late from the concert, she decided not to **think over** for them.
8. I really can't **throw** these two pictures **out**, as they look exactly the same to me.
9. The management's decision **toned down** a wave of strikes throughout the industry.
10. He finally **weighed up** how to complete his taxation form.

99 Phrasal Verbs I

to back down: to accept that the person you are arguing with is right and that you are wrong

He knew I was right, but he refused to back down.

to back on to: when the back of a building faces sth (a motorway, a river, a park, etc), it backs on to it

Our old house backed on to the river Ouse.

to back sb up: to say that sb's telling the truth, to support sb

I was at home all day. Just ask Perla. She'll back me up.

to call in sick: to contact your place of employment and say that you are ill and that you are going to stay at home

Both David and Ben have just called in sick and we haven't got anyone to cover their classes.

to call for sth: to demand sth (an inquiry / an inquest / patience / change / reforms, etc)

The Liberal Party have repeatedly called for reforms in the current electoral system.

to call sth off: to cancel a meeting/search/match, etc

We've decided to call the search off.

Unfortunately, the match had to be called off because of the appalling weather.

to cut down on (the number/amount of) sth: to reduce consumption of

The doctor advised me to cut down on fatty foods.

to cut sb off: (for a service company: electricity/gas/telephone) no longer provide sb with electricity, gas, etc – generally because they haven't paid their bill [Note: **to be cut off** (during a telephone conversation): the line suddenly goes dead, maybe because of a fault on the line]

The line's dead. We've been cut off.

No, I didn't tell her in the end. We were cut off!

to be cut out for sth/to do sth: to have the right character/qualities for sth

I soon realised I wasn't cut out to be a teacher.

She wasn't cut out for this kind of work.

to hold down a job: to stay in one job for a reasonable period of time (generally used in the negative with **can't** or **couldn't**)

Why is it that she can't hold down a job for more than a couple of weeks?

to hold off: (for bad weather): to stay away

The sky was heavy with black clouds. We hurried, hoping the rain would hold off until we got the tents up.

to hold out for: to refuse to accept sth which you do not think is good/large enough and continue to demand more

In the end, the miners agreed to a 10% pay rise, despite the fact that union leaders had promised that they would hold out for at least 20%.

to let sb down: to disappoint/fail sb

I know you are counting on me. I won't let you down, I promise.

to let yourself in for: if you don't know what you are letting yourself in for, you have agreed or decided to do sth without realising that it is going to cause you a lot of problems

You agreed to work with Mackinnon? You do know what you are letting yourself in for, don't you?

to let sb in on a secret: to tell sb a secret

I'll let you in on a little secret.

(not) to live it down: (not) to be allowed to forget

If they beat us, we'll never live it down.

to live off sth/sb: to get your money or food from sth/sb

He's never worked. He just lives off his parents.

If I won two million pounds, I'd put it all in the bank and live off the interest.

to live up to sth: to be as good as sth; live up to sb's expectations/its reputation [Note: **to live up to your promise:** to fulfil your potential]

The holiday didn't live up to our expectations.

to see sb off: to say goodbye to sb at an airport, train, bus station, etc

No one came to see her off.

to see sb out (of a building/room): to lead/show sb to the exit of a room or building
[Note: **I'll see myself out:** it is not necessary for sb to show me/lead me to the exit]

The receptionist will see you out.

to see to sb/sth: to attend or help sb (espesially in a shop) [Note: **I'll see to it that ...:** I'll make sure that ...]

George, could you see to that lady in the red dress, please?

I'll see to it that you are not disturbed.

to step forward: to contact an organisation (the police, a rescue organisation, etc) in order to volunteer information or help

Several members of the public stepped forward with information pertaining to the incident.

to step in (to...): to intervene and give financial or moral help

If the union had not stepped in, the strike would have dragged on for months.

202

to step up sth: to increase production/efforts or intensify a campaign/publicity drive, etc
The firm is stepping up its economy drive.

to work on sb: to try for some time to persuade sb to do/agree to sth
I'm sure we can persuade them. You work on mum, and I'll work on dad.

to work out: to develop smoothly and reach a successful conclusion (for a relationship, a plan, etc.)
Her plans to become a concert pianist didn't work out.

to work out at: to be equal to (used with reference to money)
They won 12% of £354,000. So how much does that work out at?

Practice

1. Circle the correct item.

1 Whenever I have to go abroad for a long time on an assignment, everyone in my family, including the dog, comes to the airport to **back / see** me off.
2 We need to **work / step** up production if we are to meet the new targets set by the management.
3 The rent will be £160 a week. There will be four of us, so it will **work / cut** out at £160 each per month.
4 He had **let / called** in sick, saying he had a bad cold when in fact he had just wanted a day off work.
5 It didn't take me long to discover that I wasn't **held / cut** out for teaching and I gave it up after a year.
6 Knowing that his assistant was busy, he said that he would **see / call** to the customer that had just walked through the door.
7 New Zealand came to England with the reputation of being the best rugby team in the world, a reputation which they have so far managed to **back / live** up to.
8 He told them he had been with his girlfriend, hoping that she would **back / hold** him up and tell them he had been with her at the cinema.
9 I don't know what's wrong with him; he doesn't seem to be able to **hold / call** down a job for more than a couple of months.
10 Now that he had won the lottery he would never have to work again. He could **live / cut** off his winnings for the rest of his life.
11 "I'm counting on you," she said, "so please don't **let / step** me down."

2. Read the following sentences and decide if the phrasal verbs in bold have been used correctly. If they have, give a synonymous verb or phrase. If not, correct them, supplying the appropriate verb.

1 There was no way he was ever going to find the exit, so he asked the secretary to **let him out**.
2 As the rail company was now in private hands, the government said that it was not in any position to **step in** and settle the dispute.
3 Tom said he'd take the job in the Middle East. "If it doesn't **work out**, I can always leave and come back home," he said.
4 It was clear to everyone involved that the strike was going nowhere, so the union leaders **let it off**.
5 The doctor told me that I had to **cut down on the number of** cups of coffee I drank as it was starting to affect my health.
6 "I don't think you know what you've **stepped yourself in for**, do you?" she said. She was right.
7 He was the number one chess player in the world. He knew that, if he lost, the press would never let him **hold it down**.
8 Tom is the kind of person who adopts a certain position in an argument and won't **back down**, even if he knows he is wrong.
9 Despite the heavy clouds, the rain **let off** and the match went ahead as scheduled.
10 The police are asking anyone who witnessed the robbery to **call forward** with whatever information they may have.
11 Mother will be easy to persuade, but we'll have to **see on** father. I'm not sure he's going to like the idea of our having a party while they're away.
12 When the details of the scandal came to light, the opposition **held for** a public enquiry, which it hoped would acutely embarrass the government.
13 If we don't pay our electricity bill, the electricity company will **let us off**.
14 "It's a secret," he said, "I'll **call you in on** it, provided you promise never to tell anyone."
15 They are horrible houses. They are small, in poor condition and they **back down** the local rubbish dump.
16 The 5% pay rise we've been offered is an insult and we intend to **call out for** the 15% we originally asked for.

100 Phrasal Verbs II

to blow (sth) out: to extinguish a fire/candle/flame/match by blowing

She lit the gas fire and blew out the match.

a storm blows over: a storm comes to an end [Note: **a scandal blows over:** a scandal comes to an end and is forgotten]

We weren't able to play until the storm had blown over.

There's no point hoping that this scandal will just blow over. It's here to stay, I'm afraid.

to blow (sth) up: (i) to destroy using explosives or a bomb (ii) to enlarge a photograph

Guy Fawkes is remembered for trying to blow up the Houses of Parliament.

If you blow the photo up, you'll see the details.

to drop in/by: to pay a casual visit to sb's house

Alan said he would drop in/by tomorrow evening.

to drop sb off (somewhere): to give sb a lift somewhere

If you're going into town, could you drop me off at the cinema?

to drop out (of somewhere): to leave school/ college / university without finishing your studies

I wouldn't have met Meg if I hadn't dropped out of university.

to grow apart: to gradually become less and less intimate with sb (a close friend/partner/parents, etc)

Although close as children, we later grew apart.

to grow into sth/sb: to become a particular kind of person as an adult

It's difficult to believe that such an obnoxious child should grow into such a charming young man.

to grow out of: to become too big for (clothes)

Sheila has grown out of last year's uniform.

to keep on (at sb about sth): to be continually telling sb to do sth in an annoying way

I said I would fix the fence, so why do you have to keep on at me about it?

to keep to sth: (i) **to keep to a path**: not to leave a path (ii) **to keep to the rules**: not to break the rules (iii) **to keep to an agreement**: to do what you agreed to do

There's only one path through the forest. Keep to it or you will get lost.

If you do not keep to the rules, you'll be disqualified.

We made an agreement and they did not keep to it. That's why I do not trust them.

to keep up with sb/sth: to go at the same speed/pace as sth/sb

I found it impossible to keep up with his fast serve.

He'll need extra lessons to keep up with the others in his class.

to move in: to enter a new house/ to start sharing a house with sb

Someone has moved in next door.

to move on (to sth): to start talking about a new subject in a discussion

I'd like to move on to the subject of conservation.

to move over: to move so as to make room for sb

If you move over, we'll both be able to sit on the sofa.

to settle down: to get married and lead a routine and stable life

You are 43. Isn't it time you settled down?

to settle for sth: to accept sth, especially sth that is less than what you want

The unions made it clear that they would not settle for anything less than a 20% increase in salaries.

to settle up (with sb): to pay the bill at a restaurant or hotel

You settle up with the waiter, while I fetch the coats.

to stand for sth: (i) to represent / be an abbreviation of (ii) to tolerate (used in the negative)

V.A.T. stands for value added tax.

I won't stand for his impertinence any longer.

to stand in for sb: to temporarily replace sb (in their job/at a meeting/ at a ceremony)

Mrs Jones will not be able to chair tomorrow's meeting so Mrs Appleton has kindly agreed to stand in for her.

to stand up for sth/sb: to defend sth/sb in situations where they are being threatened

Learn to stand up for yourself, or people will always bully you.

to turn sb down: to refuse/reject sb (applying for a job/offering sth/sb proposing marriage)

I asked her to marry me but she turned me down.

to turn out: to happen in a way you are / were probably not expecting

Although the match promised much, it turned out to be scrappy, boring and very ordinary.

to turn over: to change from one television channel to another

This is rubbish. Do you mind if I turn over?

to tie (sb) down: to limit sb's freedom

"I'm not having children," he said. "They tie you down too much."

to be tied up: to be so busy (generally at work) that you have no time to do anything but work

I'd love to have lunch with you tomorrow, but I can't. I'm tied up all day.

to be tied up in sth: to have money invested in sth (only used in passive voice)

All my money is tied up in property.

Practice

1. *Fill in the gaps using the verbs in the box below in the appropriate form.*

> keep – stand – move – drop – settle – tie – blow – turn – grow

1. You shouldn't let them treat you like that. You should .... up for your rights.
2. We're a one-car family, so I always .... my wife off at the railway station on my way to work.
3. "Can you believe it?" he said. "I was clearly the best man for the job and yet they .... me down."
4. You must be tired after driving for such a long time. .... over and let me drive.
5. We were best friends at university. When we graduated, however, our lives went in different directions and we gradually .... apart.
6. "I can't see you tomorrow," she said. "I'm .... up all day."
7. "This is my treat," he said, "so you fetch the coats while I .... up."
8. "If this scandal doesn't .... over in the next few days, I'm afraid I will have to ask for your resignation," she said.
9. I was driving an old jeep and Sadie was driving a brand new sports car. She was driving flat out so I found it impossible to .... up with her.
10. If we .... to the path, we won't get lost.
11. As all our money was .... up in stocks, when the bottom fell out of the market we lost everything.
12. I bought the cottage last month and I'm hoping to .... in next week.
13. He did not take the job because he did not want to be .... down by even more responsibilities.
14. TS Eliot. His first name was Thomas, but what did the S .... for?
15. She says she hates university and that she wants to .... out.
16. All he wanted was to .... down and raise a family.
17. Never forget to make three wishes when you .... out the candles on your birthday cake!
18. She couldn't do her last class because she had to go to the doctor's so she asked me to .... in for her.
19. Dan and Sue live in Dover and we don't see them very often. As we were catching a ferry from Dover, we decided to .... in on them and say hello.
20. The demolition men .... up the condemned building using dynamite.
21. Haven't you .... out of taking your teddy bear to bed yet?
22. We thought it would be an appalling party, but it .... out to be quite good fun.
23. She quickly took the remote control and .... over to another channel.
24. I told them that I wanted a salary of £3,500 a month and that I wouldn't .... for anything less.
25. He was an ugly duckling as a child, but he .... into a very handsome man.
26. I think we have just about covered everything regarding the environmental impact of this project, so I'd like to .... on and discuss its social implications.
27. My wife .... on at me all the time about my doing the washing up.

2. *The phrasal verbs in bold have the wrong particles. Swap them around so as to make sense.*

1. We thought it would rain but it turned **down** to be fine after all.
2. Donald hated being tied **up** by the responsibilities of a nine-to-five job.
3. I won't settle **up** less than the best.
4. The ugly duckling, as everybody knows, grew **out of** a lovely swan.
5. Could you stand **up** for me while I am on holiday?
6. I'll drop you **in** on the corner, shall I?
7. Slow down a bit. I can't keep **on at** you.
8. Paul moved **on**, to make room on the bench.
9. The ship couldn't leave the harbour until the storm had blown **out**.

101 Phrasal Nouns

a breakdown: a failure or ending of sth e.g. a relationship, system, plan etc

The breakdown of trade talks between the two countries led to financial instability.

a break-in: a burglary

The story begins with a break-in at the firm's headquarters.

a breakthrough: (i) an important new discovery, often made after years of research (ii) a new and important development
[Note: **sth has been hailed as a breakthrough:** people are saying sth is a breakthrough]

The discovery of a vaccine for smallpox was rightly hailed as one of the biggest breakthroughs in medical history.

(to make/stage) a comeback: to become popular or important again, having been unpopular or unimportant for some time (generally, sports people or entertainers make comebacks)

After a long period in the wilderness, they made a comeback with a new CD.

a cover-up: an attempt by a government or large organisation to stop the public from finding out the truth about sth

The President denied having had anything to do with the cover-up.

a downfall: a fall from position of power/a complete loss of money/social position. [Note: **sth was sb's downfall:** sth was someone's weakness and it caused them to lose everything (money, power, social position, etc)]

His refusal to deny the allegations against him was instrumental in bringing about his downfall.

His inability to say no proved to be his downfall.

a drawback: a disadvantage

One of the biggest drawbacks of living in Australia was that I was so far away from Europe.

(to make) a getaway: to escape after committing a crime

They made their getaway in a stolen van.

a hold-up: (i) a delay (ii) an armed robbery

There has been a pile-up on the main London-Ipswich road, so you should expect long hold-ups.

After the hold-up, the thieves made their getaway in a stolen transit van.

an income: the amount of money that sb earns

Whether or not they will give you a mortgage depends on your income.

the layout: the arrangement of pictures and/or writing on a page or letter

We are going to have to change the layout of this page. It looks very untidy and unattractive.

a let-down: sth (a book, film, restaurant, football match, etc) which is not as good as you expected it to be

The match promised to be exciting but proved to be a let-down.

a let-up: a reduction or pause in sth (fighting, bad weather, the amount of work that you have to do, etc)

There was no sign of any let-up in the rain.

a mix-up: a mistake that causes confusion

"I think there has been a mix-up," he said. "I was given seat 13A but there is already someone sitting there."

an outbreak: the sudden start of a war or a disease

There has been an outbreak of yellow fever in the southern provinces of the country.

an outcome: the final result (of a meeting, election, discussion, war, etc)

We will not know the outcome of the election until tomorrow morning.

(from/at) the outset: from/at the beginning

You were warned at the outset that you had to train every day if you wanted to get into the team.

a pile-up: an accident involving a lot of cars

A pile-up on the A1 has made diversions necessary.

a setback: sth that delays progress/upsets sb's plans [Note: **to suffer a (major/minor) setback:** to be delayed/have one's plans upset]

The President's plan to introduce a tax on pets suffered a major setback when the Supreme Court ruled that it was unconstitutional.

a takeaway: a meal prepared in a restaurant and which you take home to eat

Why don't we get a Chinese takeaway instead of cooking tonight?

a turnout: the number of people who go to a meeting or vote in an election [Note: **high turnout:** a lot of people attend a meeting or vote in an election **Opp.:** a low turnout]

The turnout for last night's meeting was disappointingly low.

a write-up: a review written in a newspaper or magazine

It should be good. It was given (it has received/it got) excellent write-ups in the press.

206

Practice

1. Fill in the gaps in the sentences below. Each gap corresponds to one phrasal noun. The verb half of each of the missing words is given at the end of each line in which a gap appears. The other half of the missing word is formed by adding a preposition to the beginning or end of the verb. Hyphens have been given where they are required.

1. It is difficult to predict what the .... of this latest meeting will be as neither the management nor the unions are willing to make concessions.   **COME**
2. We had vaccinations before visiting that area, as there had recently been a(n) .... of cholera.   **BREAK**
3. There was no sign of the van that they had made their .... in.   **GET**
4. We knew from the .... that we were taking a massive risk investing our money in such an unstable industry.   **SET**
5. It started raining the minute we set foot on the island, and - with the exception of two hours last Tuesday - there was no .... in the bad weather until the day we left.   **LET-**
6. "Including that picture will mean changing the .... of the page," said the editor.   **LAY**
7. I know George said it was the worst film he had seen in ages, but it got an excellent .... in the press. I think we should go and see it.   **WRITE-**
8. With the setting up of the welfare state, people without a(n) .... received financial support in the form of a monthly social security cheque.   **COME**
9. Drivers travelling south on the M2 can expect long .... this morning as there has been a seven-car .... on the motorway near junction five.   **HOLD- PILE-**
10. Perhaps the biggest .... of being famous is that you have to say goodbye to your private life and be prepared to live forever in the public eye.   **DRAW**
11. Why has information about the shady deal only come out now? Obviously there was a(n) .... What government wouldn't try to hide such politically damaging information?   **COVER-**
12. The government's plan to implement a new electoral system suffered a major .... when the Supreme Court judged it to be unconstitutional.   **SET**
13. Somewhat surprisingly, what led to the government's .... was not military defeat but rather their inability to manage the post-war economy.   **FALL**
14. The .... occurred round about midnight.   **BREAK-**
15. "I think there has been some kind of ....," he said, handing his bill to the receptionist. "This must be someone else's bill."   **MIX-**
16. Is there any news about the .... at the central bank this morning?   **HOLD-**

2. Complete the passages using phrasal nouns from this unit.

A He should never have done it. He was too old to make a **1)** .... We weren't to know, though, and we couldn't wait to see him sing. What a **2)** ....! His voice had all but disappeared and he had lost all of his once magnificent stage presence. Some people walked out. We stayed. He must have read the same dreadful **3)** .... that we read the morning after, because he never sang in public again.

B I enjoy **1)** .... meals, but ordering them over the phone can have its **2)** .... Take the other day, for instance. I ordered a meal from a local restaurant and was told that I would have to wait no longer than twenty minutes. I waited, and waited and after forty five minutes I phoned up the restaurant and asked them what the **3)** .... was. They apologised and said that there had been a **4)** .... and that my meal had been delivered to an address on the other side of town. They then asked me if I would care to go and get it!

C It is a pity that scientists face many a(n) **1)** .... in their research, due to lack of proper government funding. It is to them, after all, that we owe the progress made after each medical **2)** .... in the fight against diseases. We forget that, even half a century ago, a(n) **3)** .... of any infectious disease would kill hundreds or perhaps thousands of people. The **4)** .... of starving science of funds for medical research purposes can only be guessed at, but underfunding is bound to have tragic consequences.

102 Be (Phrases)

to be after sb: (i) if the police are after sb, they are looking for that person, generally to arrest them (ii) if sb is after sth (a book, a record, etc) they are looking for it because they want to buy it

Interpol have been after him for years.

Bob will be so pleased that I managed to find this book. He's been after it for ages.

to be against sth: not to be in favour of sth/to think that sth is wrong [Note: **to be all for sth:** to strongly support sth]

I'm totally against fox-hunting. I think it should be banned.

I'm all for the government privatising the railways.

a computer is down: a computer is not working properly; often because it is part of a big network (e.g. in a travel agency) and the central source of that network is not working [Note: **to be/look/feel down:** to be/look/feel depressed]

I can't get you the dates of the flights because my computer is down.

Jim looks really down. What is the matter with him?

to be in for sth: to be likely to experience/have sth (bad)

If he thinks getting into university is going to be easy, then he's in for a big surprise.

sb is in for it: sb is going to be in trouble

"Now I'm in for it," he thought. He'd forgotten to get her the library books.

to be into sth: to like, to be very interested in and enthusiastic about sth [Note: **I'm not into sth:** I don't particularly like sth]

My son is into thrash metal at the moment.

I'm not really into classical music.

I'm off: I'm leaving (usually only used with the pronouns **I** and **we**)

Right, I'm off. Thanks for the coffee.

to be off: if meat, fish or a dairy product (milk, cream, yoghurt, etc) is/smells off, it is/smells bad or rotten [Note: if a **sports match** or **meeting** is off, it has been cancelled]

Don't use the milk. It smells off.

Tomorrow's staff meeting is off. Mr Hudson is ill.

to be off to: if sb is off to a particular place, they are going there

I'm off to Rome on Saturday.

sth is not on: (the way sb behaved/the way sb treated you) is not acceptable or reasonable

She expects me to work for four more hours a week without any extra pay. It's not on, is it?

to be on about sth: to talk about sth, often for a long time or in a boring/annoying way

[Note: **what are you on about?** is sometimes used in response to an accusation introducing your denial; alternatively, if the word **are** is stressed in the question, it shows that you do not understand what sb is talking about]

She's been on about getting a new car again. I reckon she thinks we're made of money.

What are you on about? Of course I didn't take it.

to be out of sth: to no longer have any left

The car shuddered and stopped. "I think we're out of petrol," she said.

to be over: to have finished

I can't believe our holiday is over already. It seems like only yesterday that we arrived.

to be up against sb: to be facing a competitor (in a sports match, an election or for a business deal)

The government will be up against some strong competition in the next election.

to be up to: to be doing, most commonly used in question form

What have you been up to (recently/since I last saw you)?

what's up with sb?: what is wrong with sb?

What's up with Simone? It looks as if she has been crying.

Practice

1. Fill in the gaps with the preposition(s) from the box below. Definitions of the **be** phrasal verbs follow each sentence.

after – up – to – off – over – out – of – in – for – into – in – for – off – off – on – against – down – up – about – up – against – on – with – to

1. What have you been .... since I last saw you? **(doing)**
2. We're .... sugar. **(don't have any left)**
3. The police are .... him. **(looking for)**
4. I think this milk is .... **(bad)**
5. We're .... Spain tomorrow. **(going to)**
6. I'm totally .... any form of censorship **(opposed to)**
7. I think you're .... a shock. **(going to get)**
8. Is that the time? I'm .... ! **(leaving)**

9 What's .... John? He looks really upset. (wrong with)
10 Oh no! It's your mum. Now we're .... it! (going to be in trouble)
11 I'm not .... horror films. (interested in)
12 Thank goodness that's .... ! (finished)
13 That kind of behaviour is simply not .... (acceptable)
14 He's been .... buying a new car for months. (continually talking about)
15 I'm sorry but I can't give you that information. All our computers are .... at the moment. (not working)
16 If you make it to the final, you will be .... some of the best sprinters in the world. (competing with)

8 The train now .... from platform 9 will be calling at ...
9 Help! The computer .... What should I do?
10 Hey, where did you get that fantastic jacket? I .... one like that for ages.
11 Certain members of the opposition have .... that the minister had brokered the deal behind the President's back.
12 His teacher is a stickler for formality and .... to being called by his first name.
13 These wild allegations .... and may even constitute defamation.
14 He's training hard for the marathon because he'll .... some stiff competition.

3. *Answer/Respond to the questions using appropriate **be** phrasal verbs.*

0 A: So why don't you want to come to "La Bohème" with us?
   B: *Well, I'm not really into opera.*
1 A: This yoghurt smells funny.
   B: ....
2 A: Stop writing, please. That's the end of the test.
   B: ....
3 A: Are you going anywhere nice?
   B: ....
4 A: Leave me alone!
   B: ....
5 A: It's 7 o'clock now and your meeting is at 7.30. Shouldn't you be going?
   B: ....
6 A: Why won't you answer the questions in our opinion poll?
   B: ....
7 A: Could I have some biscuits?
   B: ....
8 A: Why did you pull out of the chess tournament?
   B: ....
9 A: Why can't you find the information? Isn't it all stored on the computer?
   B: ....

2. a. *Match the following **be** phrasal verbs with their formal verb equivalents.*

1	be down	......	a	insinuate
2	be against	......	b	pursue
3	be up against	......	c	be unacceptable
4	be off	......	d	object
5	be on about	......	e	malfunction
6	be after	......	f	confront
7	be not on	......	g	depart

b. *Now use either a formal or a phrasal verb to fill in the gaps below.*

1 "I really don't know what you are ...., Julia, but I don't like the sound of it," said the woman.
2 Radiation is assumed to damage computers, causing them to ....
3 "The secret," continued the psychiatrist, "is to .... your fears and conquer them, so as to regain control over your life."
4 It ...., the way you answer me back, Jason.
5 In view of your client's willingness to settle out of court, our clients will not be .... the matter and have agreed not to press charges.
6 I .... really .... pop stars being paid so much. What about you?
7 It's getting late. I'd better ....

103 Break – Bring – Catch (Phrases)

Break

a boy's voice breaks: a boy's voice becomes lower and he begins to sound like a man

My voice broke when I was 12.

to break down: to lose control of one's feelings and start crying (often used in the phrase *sb broke down and cried/wept*)

[Note: if a **large machine** (especially a car) breaks down, it stops working]

When she saw the damage the storm had done to her house, she broke down and wept.

Our car broke down on the way over there.

to break even: to make neither a profit nor a loss

At the end of our first year of trading, we broke even.

to break a habit: to stop a habit

In order to lose weight, she had to break the habit of snacking in between meals.

to break for lunch: to stop working and have lunch

Let's break for lunch, shall we?

sth breaks one's fall: sth (e.g. a tree) stops one from falling directly to the ground

He would almost certainly have been killed if a tree had not broken his fall.

it breaks/broke my heart to/when: it makes/made me very sad to/when

I loved that house and it broke my heart to sell it.

It broke my heart when I sold that old car.

to break new ground: (i) to be completely new and different (ii) to do sth that nobody has ever done before

[Note: (i) **ground-breaking work/ research:** research or work in which a lot of discoveries are made (ii) a **ground-breaking film/play/ book:** a film/play/book which is innovative and different from any other]

This model of computer breaks new ground.

Donald broke new ground when he staged this experimental play.

He was awarded the Nobel Prize for Physics for his ground-breaking work on black holes.

to break the news to sb: to give sb bad news

I was the manager, so it was my job to break the news to him that he was not going to be in the team.

to break off one's engagement: to end one's engagement

Have you heard about Sally and Harold? They have broken off their engagement.

to break up a fight: to stop a fight

It took three teachers to break up the fight.

Bring

to bring sth to sb's attention: (formal) to tell sb (normally a person in a position of authority) about a problem or sth bad that is happening

I'm sorry, Sir Geoffrey, I was under the impression that Mr Smithers had brought it to your attention.

to bring back memories: to remind sb of sth (usually happy)

Hearing that song brought back memories of his university days.

to bring sb out in spots/a rash: to give sb spots or a rash

I love chocolate milk, but I can't drink it. It brings me out in spots.

to bring pressure to bear on sb/sth: to use one's power and influence to try to get what one wants from another group/organisation/person

The only way the unions could bring pressure to bear on the government was to organise a strike.

to bring sb up to date: to give sb up-to-date information which they need but don't have

He asked his assistant to bring him up to date on the Manhattan deal.

Catch

to catch your breath: to stop after a lot of physical exercise because you are finding it difficult to breathe

I had to stop in order to catch my breath.

you wouldn't catch me (doing sth): (informal) I would never (do sth)

You wouldn't catch me wearing something like that.

to catch yourself (doing sth): to realise that you are doing sth that irritates you when other people do it

Suddenly, I caught myself cracking my knuckles.

to catch sb off-guard/to catch sb unawares/to catch sb on the hop: to do sth/to ask a question which sb was not expecting and was unprepared for.

The security men were caught unawares. They were sitting having coffee when he burst in.

Her question on our agricultural policy caught me completely off-guard. I did not know what to say.

She really caught Mr Martin on the hop when she asked him to solve the equation on the board.

Practice

1. The verb **break** cannot be used in four of the short sentences in Section A below. Which are the incorrect sentences? Completing the sentences in Section B with an appropriate word or phrase in bold from Section A will help you. An example has been done for you.

A

1 He broke **up the fight**.
2 I broke my **brains** over it.
3 It broke my **fall**.
4 Let's break **for lunch**.
5 He broke his **chances**.
6 I've heard they've broken **off their engagement**.
7 It breaks my **heart**.
8 His **voice** hasn't broken yet.
9 He broke his **opinion**.
10 His mother broke **the news** to him.
11 You have to break this **habit**.
12 At least we broke **even**.
13 She broke **down and cried**.
14 His theories broke **new ground**.
15 He broke the **car to a halt**.

B

1 Let's break ...., shall we? We've been working all morning and I'm starving.
2 Biting your nails is a difficult .... to break.
3 I don't want to make a profit, but I don't want to lose money either. I just want to break ....
4 Naturally we were somewhat taken aback when we found out that they had broken off .... They seemed so happy together.
5 He wouldn't have survived if the trees outside his window hadn't broken his ....
6 When she found out that her dog had died, Jill .... and cried.
7 Poor girl! It broke her .... when her pet died.
8 She was on holiday and I had been chosen to break .... to her. What do you say to someone whose house has just burnt down?
9 This film breaks .... It is the first animated film for which all the voices and all the animation were done by computer.
10 They started fighting and scuffling in the amphitheatre. In the end, the police had to be called to break ....
11 I loved singing in the local choir but had to leave when my .... broke. I must have been twelve at the time.

2. Match the beginning of a sentence in Section A with an appropriate ending from Section B.

A

1 I can't eat cheese because it brings ....
2 Look, we have to stop. We've been running for half an hour. I need to catch ....
3 You know how much I hate the kids whistling when they are in the house. Well, the other day I caught ....
4 Seeing those old family videos brought ....
5 I didn't have an answer. I really wasn't expecting her question. She caught ....
6 I'd been away for quite a while so my assistant had to bring ....
7 He worked over the weekend non-stop. You wouldn't catch ....
8 I'm not surprised the government gave in when you consider the pressure that was brought ....
9 No, Jonathan, I didn't know that. Thank you very much for bringing it ....

B

1 my breath.
2 to my attention.
3 me doing a thing like that.
4 me out in spots.
5 me up to date.
6 to bear on it.
7 myself doing it.
8 back a lot of memories.
9 me completely off-guard.

104 Come (Expressions/Phrasal Verbs)

Come Expressions

to come to blows: to argue and hit one another

We nearly came to blows over the money.

to come in for criticism: to be criticised

The government has come in for (severe/heavy/a lot of/harsh/savage) criticism over its new education policies.

to come into effect/operation: to officially start to happen/to be used

The new law/rule/system will come into effect on September 26.

to come to a head: to reach a critical stage

The argument came to a head when neither side would admit that they had made a mistake.

to come to light: to become known

If the truth/this information/this story ever comes to light, it will bring down the government.

to come onto the market: to become available for people to buy

The new product should come onto the market next month.

to come to sb's rescue/to come to the rescue of sb: to save sb from a dangerous/difficult situation

Firemen had to come to the stranded woman's rescue.

to come to a (complete) standstill/halt: to stop moving [Note: if a **city/factory/airport/production comes to a complete standstill**, there is no longer any activity]

All of a sudden, the train came to a standstill/halt.

The airport came to a complete standstill as a result of the air traffic controllers' strike.

to come as a surprise: to be surprising [Note: (i) to come as **no** surprise: not to be surprising (ii) to come as **something of** a surprise: to be a little surprising

It came as a surprise to John to find out that Bill had resigned.

Her promotion came as no surprise. She's extremely hardworking and diligent.

I know he's a free spirit, but his sudden decision to drop out of university and travel all over the world came as something of a surprise.

to come to terms with: to learn to accept a bad / new thing

She couldn't come to terms with her husband's death.

that's (pretty) rich, coming from sb: a spoken phrase used when sb has accused you of sth bad that they themselves are guilty of

He said I was aggressive, which is pretty rich, coming from him.

Come Phrasal Verbs

to come across sth: to find by chance (not used in passive)

"I came across these letters while I was tidying up your cupboard," she said.

to come at sb: to attack sb especially with a knife (not used in passive)

... and then he came at the hero with a knife.

to come by sth: to find or to get; often used in the phrase: **sth is/are hard to come by**: to be difficult to get or find

Twenty years ago you could find these records everywhere, but nowadays they are very hard to come by.

to come off: if a plan comes off, it succeeds (not used in passive)

It's an ingenious plan, but I doubt whether it will come off.

to come out: (i) to be published; for newspapers and magazines (ii) to be available to buy; for books, CDs and records (iii) to appear (for the sun, the stars and the moon)

'The Book Collector' magazine comes out every Friday.

His new LP comes out next week.

The clouds disappeared and the sun came out.

to come out with: to suddenly say sth that the person listening to you was not expecting to hear (not used in passive)

I asked him why he hadn't turned up for the meeting and he suddenly came out with some story about being stuck in a lift for two days.

to come over: (i) to pay a visit to someone's house (ii) **I don't know what has come over sb:** I don't know what has happened to sb (implying they are behaving strangely and out of character)

Why don't you come over and we can watch the match together?

I'm sorry for that outburst last night. I don't know what came over me.

to come to/(a)round: to regain consciousness after you have fainted, been given an anaesthetic, or lost consciousness

I don't know what happened, I just fainted. When I came to/(a)round, I was in an ambulance.

to come up: (i) to appear; for questions in an exam (ii) if sth (sb's name, the problem of, the issue of, etc) comes up in a conversation, meeting or discussion, it is mentioned or discussed [Note: **something has come up:** sth (normally a problem) has happened unexpectedly and I have to deal with it]

That question about 'Hamlet' comes up every year.

We're talking about putting a three-lane highway through the middle of the village. For a start, the question of noise is bound to come up.

Hello. Listen, something has come up so I'm going to be late tonight.

to come up with: to think of an idea, excuse, an answer to a question/ a solution to a problem

He was late again. He had to come up with a convincing excuse.

Who came up with that idea?

Practice

1. 🎧 *Listen and indicate if the statements are true or false by placing a T or an F in the space provided.*

1. The Minister of Education's resignation was unexpected. ....
2. The new measures aimed at improving education are already in operation. ....
3. Not much was said about insufficient educational funding. ....
4. We do not know the reasons for the Chancellor of the Exchequer's actions. ....
5. The public transport strike is expected to have little effect on the capital. ....
6. The proposed axing of an underground line particularly upset the transport workers' union. ....
7. Had it not been for a court ruling, an animal shelter would have been closed. ....
8. Cindy Topman believed that her husband had no talent. ....
9. Nono Farrago was not affected by his wife's success. ....
10. Topman and Farrago had often fought. ....
11. You can't buy the new Harriet Porter novel yet. ....

2. *For questions 1 to 8, complete the second sentence so that it has a similar meaning to the first sentence, using 3 to 8 words. You must include the word given in bold, which cannot be changed in any way.*

1. It was difficult for him to accept that the company no longer needed him.
   terms   He found .... the fact that the company no longer needed him.
2. Neither of us was surprised by the news that he had got the job.
   came   It .... to learn that he had got the job.
3. Cars are no longer being produced as a result of the strike.
   standstill   Car production .... because of the strike.
4. The new pills will be available for people to buy as from May 3rd.
   market   The new pills .... from May 3rd.
5. "If anyone ever finds out about this, we will be in serious trouble," he said.
   light   "If this .... we will be in serious trouble", he said.
6. In the end it was Harry's father who saved us by lending us US $ 5,000.
   rescue   Finally, Harry's father .... US $5,000.
7. The new law becomes operational at the end of September.
   effect   The new .... September.
8. The police were strongly criticised for the way they handled the case.
   for   The police .... of the case.

3. *Substitute the phrasal verb in bold with a verb or phrase from the box below.*

> was mentioned – is successful – think of – happened to – obtain – will be published – say – found – attacked – regained consciousness

1. If this plan **comes off**, we'll both be rich.
2. His new novel **comes out** next month.
3. Your dog ate it! Couldn't you **come up with** a better excuse than that?
4. We were talking about possible candidates for the managing director's job in Japan and your name **came up** in the conversation.
5. It's very unlike Dave to **come out with** something as tactless as that.
6. I remember falling, but that's about it. When I **came to**, I was in a hospital bed with my wife at my side.
7. "I **came across** this while I was tidying your desk," she said, handing him the memo. "It should have been acted on yesterday."
8. He's been so cheerful lately, so happy. I don't know what has **come over** him. He's normally so miserable.
9. "You're lucky to get this – especially in this condition," he said, picking up the book and examining its cover. "They are difficult to **come by** these days."
10. Of course I ran away. The dog **came at** me with teeth bared.

105 Do or Make

Do

to do away with sth: to get rid of sth (a rule/law/tax/institution) so that it no longer exists

Following a public outcry, the government decided to do away with the poll tax.

to do your best: to try as hard as you can to do or achieve sth

We might have lost, but we did our best - and you can't ask more than that.

to do likewise: to do the same (used at the end of a sentence)

James joined the army, and his brother did likewise.

sth does more harm than good: sth causes more problems than it solves

To raise wages in line with inflation would do more harm than good.

to do sb a power of good: to be beneficial to sb

Getting away from the stresses of work would do you a power of good.

to do some revision: to look at and study your books and notes before you take an exam

I don't need to do any revision. I know everything already.

to do a roaring trade in sth: to sell lots of sth

During the heatwave, we did a roaring trade in electric fans.

that should/will do the trick: (informal) that should/will solve a small problem that we have

"That should do the trick," he said, putting some oil on the squeaky hinge.

to do one's utmost (to do sth): to try as hard as one can to do or achieve sth

We will do our utmost to see that this never happens again.

Make

to make no attempt to do sth: not to try to do sth (especially in a situation where you should have tried)

He made no attempt to help.

to make do with sth: to satisfy yourself with what you have, as opposed to what you want

If there's no butter, I'll make do with margarine.

to make an effort (to do sth): to try hard to do sth

[Note: **every effort has been made to...**: sb has/have done their very best to ....]

Tired as he was, he made an effort to be pleasant at the party.

Every effort has been made to make each room as unique and as comfortable as possible.

to make a habit of doing sth: to keep doing sth bad or wrong

He won't be angry that you are late; it's not as if you make a habit of it.

to make the most of sth: to use an opportunity or situation so that you get the maximum possible benefit you can from it

I made the most of my time in England and learned as much English as I possibly could.

to make a point of doing sth/to make it a point to do sth: to be very careful to do sth because you believe it is important; often when you want other people to see that you are doing it

He made a (special) point of being sociable.

I make it a point to remember all my students' first names.

Practice

1. Complete the collocations by putting either **do** or **make** in the spaces provided.

....	away with
....	your best
....	more harm than good
....	do with
....	a habit of
....	the trick
....	some revision
....	a roaring trade in
....	your utmost
....	an effort
....	you a power of good
....	likewise
....	no attempt to
....	a point of
....	the most of

2. For questions 1 to 11, complete the second sentence so that it has a similar meaning to the first sentence, using 3 to 8 words. You must include the word given in bold, which cannot be changed in any way.

1 He tried as hard as he could to break the world record.
   did He ....
   .... to break the world record.

2 Whenever there is a power cut, we sell a lot of candles.
   do Whenever there is a power cut, we ......
   .... candles.

3 I am quite sure I double-locked the door.
   made I ....
   .... when I left.

4 "A long, lazy holiday would make you feel very much better," she said
   do   "A long, lazy holiday would ....," she said.
5 "I'll forgive you this time, provided you promise not to keep doing it," he said.
   make   "I'll forgive you this time, provided you promise not to ....," he said.
6 Her contempt for him and his family was more than obvious.
   made   She .... hide her contempt for him and his family.
7 When we first moved into our house we didn't have a bed, so we had to manage without and sleep on a mattress on the floor.
   make   When we first moved into our house we didn't have a bed, so we had to .... a mattress on the floor.
8 The government had decided to abolish compulsory military service.
   do   The government had decided to .... compulsory military service.
9 We took full advantage of our stop-over and spent the day exploring the city.
   made   We .... our stop-over and spent the day exploring the city.
10 Have you revised for this exam?
   done   Have you .... for this exam?
11 I agree he ought to know but don't you think telling him will only make the situation worse?
   do   I agree he ought to know, but telling him ...., don't you think?

3. *Respond to the following, using expressions with **make** or **do**.*

0 Isn't it gorgeous weather today?
   Yes, let's make the most of it and have a picnic.
1 What did he do when his brother emigrated to Australia?
   ....
2 Why shouldn't I water the plants again?
   ....
3 Why don't you think I should try and help?
   ....
4 Try as hard as you can in the tennis tournament tomorrow.
   ....
5 It's your history exam on Monday.
   ....
6 I think it's terrible that blood sports are still allowed.
   ....
7 There's no cake, I'm afraid, only biscuits.
   ....
8 But do you think it will help to just bang a nail in it?
   ....
9 Sorry I'm late, sir.
   ....
10 Timmy isn't trying very hard at maths, is he?
   ....
11 Don't forget to check the time on the tickets.
   ....

4. *Complete the sentences using **one** word in each space.*

1 Liz didn't have a new dress for the party so she had to make .... with her old one.
2 He made a .... of checking that all electrical appliances were unplugged before leaving the house.
3 She ordered the most expensive dish on the menu and her friend did ....
4 Take this tonic; it will do you a .... of good.
5 The street was full of people and the market was doing a .... trade that day.
6 Soak that stained T-shirt before putting it in the washing machine; that should do the ....
7 Young people today have so many choices; you should make the .... of your opportunities.

106 Fall (Expressions/Phrasal Verbs)

- **to fall:** (i) move quickly (from an upright position) towards the ground

  fall off a ladder/down (the stairs)/ to the ground/into the water/out of a tree

  (ii) decrease in amount, value or strength [Note: **a fall in** (the number of sth)] (iii) pass into a state

  fall asleep/ill/prey/victim/into disrepair/ into disrepute

  There was a fall in the number of road accidents last month.

  Many of the city's once prized buildings have fallen into disrepair.

- **to fall flat on your face:** to fall and land on the front of your body with your face towards the ground

  It was so embarrassing. I was ready to receive my prize when I tripped and fell flat on my face.

- **to fall on:** to take place on a certain day or date

  January 1 falls on a Sunday this year.

Fall - Phrasal Verbs

- **to fall back on:** to use in an emergency or as a last resort when there is nothing else

  The workers always had the strike option to fall back on.

- **to fall behind with (your rent, etc):** to be late paying (a bill, etc)

  They had fallen so far behind with their instalments that the TV was repossessed.

- **to fall for sb:** to fall in love with sb

  I fell for her the minute I saw her.

- **to fall for a lie:** to believe a lie

  I'm not gullible enough to fall for that old story.

- **to fall in with:** to become friends and start spending a lot of time with people who are a bad influence on you

  Ever since she had fallen in with Tommy Jones and his gang, her school work had gone downhill.

- **to fall out with sb:** to quarrel with sb and stop being friends with them

  We fell out with him when he criticised my sister.

- **to fall over:** to fall while walking/ running/moving, etc

  She fell over and hurt herself.

- **to fall through:** not to be successfully completed (used for **plans, projects, arrangements**)

  Our project to set up an English school fell through when we found out how much we would need to invest.

Fall - Expressions

- **to fall about laughing:** to laugh uncontrollably

  When I told them the story, they fell about laughing.

- **sth is falling apart at the seams:** lots of things are going wrong with sth (a country/a company/sb's life)

  Although once successful, the company is now falling apart at the seams.

- **to fall by the wayside:** (i) to fail to continue or be competitive; often used for sport (ii) to be considered no longer important (and to be forgotten or ignored as a result) (iii) to be considered impossible; generally used for promises, ideas and plans

  After 30 laps, both the Fettucci drivers had fallen by the wayside.

  Whenever a political party gets into office, most of its pre-election promises fall by the wayside.

  Our plan to set up a book business soon fell by the wayside as it would cost us too much.

- **to fall foul of sb:** to do sth to annoy sb with the result that they want to punish or hurt you [Note: to fall foul of **the law/the authorities:** to do sth illegal with the result that you are punished for what you have done]

  He soon fell foul of the manager, who then demanded that he be sold to another team.

  It wasn't long before he fell foul of the authorities and was taken to court for tax evasion.

- **to fall from power:** to lose one's position of power; generally used for leaders (presidents, prime ministers, etc) and governments of countries

  He fell from power in a bloodless coup.

- **to fall into place:** if different (but connected) facts or events fall into place, they come together and make sense, when before they had been confusing because you could not see the connection between them

  A few pages before the end of the story, everything fell into place and I knew who the murderer was.

- **to fall into the trap of doing sth:** to make a mistake that many people make

  Just because it looks like an easy job, don't fall into the trap of thinking that it is.

- **to fall into the wrong hands:** if sth (information, a photograph, a document, etc) falls into the wrong hands, sb (an enemy, a competitor, a rival, the press, etc) gets it and will probably use it to hurt you or cause you trouble

  These plans are top secret, so I wouldn't want them to fall into the wrong hands.

- **to fall on deaf ears:** to be ignored by the person being spoken to

  A plea/ a request/an appeal for help or money/a demand falls on deaf ears.

  They asked his parents for help, but their appeal fell on deaf ears.

- **to fall (all) over oneself to do sth:** to do sth very eagerly

  When we introduced a commission on sales, our assistants were suddenly falling all over themselves to serve the customers.

- **to be falling to pieces:** to be old and in poor condition, with bits missing from it

  This car is falling to pieces. It's time we got a new one.

Practice

1. Complete the sentences with the correct preposition(s).

1. He fell .... his bike.
2. He fell .... the stairs.
3. The kite fell .... the sea.
4. It rolled off the table and fell .... the floor.
5. She fell .... the window.
6. There has been a fall .... the number of participants.
7. She fell flat .... her face.
8. What day does your birthday fall .... ?

2. Complete the following sentences with the appropriate preposition(s) from the box below.

> in with – out with – back on – for – for – over – behind with – through

1. She tripped and **fell** ...., knocking herself out on the kerb.
2. We **fell** .... each other over money. It happened last year and I haven't talked to him since.
3. Our plans to travel around Asia for six months **fell** .... when Sid was rushed to hospital with acute appendicitis.
4. He told you he wanted the money for a sick relative and you **fell** .... it? How can you have been so gullible?
5. When we **fell** .... our mortgage repayments, we had to take out another loan.
6. She was worried about not having enough holiday money. He smiled. "If we run out of cash, we've always got our credit card to **fall** ...."
7. He's changed completely, ever since he **fell** .... that arty crowd.
8. It was love at first sight. I **fell** .... Chris the minute I set eyes on him.

3. Complete the sentences with an appropriate word from the box below.

> hands – ears – seams – trap – place – over – about – bits – face – prey – wayside – power – foul

1. "Don't fall into the .... of believing that, the longer your composition is, the more marks you'll get," said the teacher.
2. Should these documents fall into the wrong ...., the scandal that would ensue would very likely bring down the government.
3. They were rather off-hand with me at first, but when they found out that I was famous they were falling .... themselves to be of help.
4. Unemployment, corruption, inflation and violence. This country is falling apart at the ....
5. He couldn't understand why his son was always so secretive and why he was never at home. Then he found the letters. Suddenly, everything fell into ....
6. The child pleaded with her mother for more chocolate but her cries fell on deaf ....
7. As soon as I walked into the room, everyone fell .... laughing. What was so funny? What had I done?
8. On the second day, most of the field had fallen by the .... Only the serious athletes were left.
9. We've got to get rid of this furniture. It's falling to ....
10. The new teacher was careful not to fall .... of the headmaster, a notoriously difficult and tetchy individual.
11. The President fell from .... when he was forced to resign, following a number of crushing defeats in the Senate.
12. She fell .... to stage-fright and was unable to utter a single word.
13. To trip up and fall flat on your .... on the catwalk is an embarrassing experience for a model.

107 Get (Expressions I)

let's get something/one thing clear/straight: an expression used to tell sb that they must understand and have no doubts about what you are going to say

"Let's get one thing clear," I said. "You must not, under any circumstances, reveal your sources."

not to be able to get a word in edgeways: not to get a chance to speak because the person you are with is talking too much

She went on and on talking ... I tried to say something but I couldn't get a word in edgeways.

not to be able to get your tongue round: to find a word or phrase very difficult to pronounce

I gave up learning German because I found it impossible to get my tongue round even the simplest of words.

this is getting us nowhere: this is not helping us in any way

Talking about setting up a business instead of doing it is getting us nowhere.

to get away from it all: to have a holiday and escape the routine and stress of daily life

Exhausted and overworked, he decided to get away from it all for a few days.

to get carried away: to become so excited/interested/angry/emotional, etc that you lose control of what you are saying or doing

When they gave him the microphone, he got carried away and began singing Sinatra songs!

to get hold of the wrong end of the stick: (informal) to misunderstand sth that sb says

When I talked about Canada, Gerald got hold of the wrong end of the stick and thought I was emigrating.

to get off to a good/bad start: to begin well/badly (often used for sporting events)

We got off to a bad start on our holiday when we forgot to take our passports.

to get out of bed on the wrong side: to be bad tempered from the moment you get up

Pat's very irritable today; I suppose she got out of bed on the wrong side!

to get on sb's nerves: to annoy sb

Her constant need to be the centre of attention got on his nerves.

to get rid of sth: (i) to sell or throw away sth (ii) to do sth to remove or take away an unpleasant thing (pain, a cough, a stain on your clothes) which is bothering you

Why don't we get rid of it and buy a new one?

Take two of these tablets. They will get rid of the pain.

to get sth off the ground: to put sth (an idea or plan) into practice so that it starts to be successful

It was a wonderful idea but, to get it off the ground, we would have had to invest £20,000 each.

to get sth over with/to get sth over and done with: to do sth unpleasant and finish it so that you no longer have to think or worry about it

I know you don't want to have the operation but it's better to get it over with now.

to get the hang of sth: to learn how to do sth or use sth

I know using it can be a bit tricky at the start, but you'll soon get the hang of it.

to get the shock of your life: to be very surprised by sth

I opened the door and got the shock of my life. There was my brother, whom I hadn't seen for over twenty-five years.

to get to grips with: to take action and deal with a problem

The government hasn't yet got to grips with the unemployment problem.

to get to the bottom of sth: to solve a mystery or to find the real cause of a problem

Inspector Morts was determined to get to the bottom of the mystery.

get to the point: to talk about a particular subject, instead of avoiding it or talking about other, less important things

He went on and on about how he appreciated my help. "Please get to the point," I said.

to get the point of sth: to understand the reason for

I don't get the point of putting those papers in alphabetical order before binning them.

to get underway: (i) to start happening (ii) to start moving (for transport)

Work on the new underground line has yet to get underway.

Food will be served in the cafeteria and will be available once the ferry gets underway.

to get wind of sth: to find out about sth

If anyone gets wind of what I am doing, I could get into serious trouble.

to get your hands on sb: to catch or find sb who has done sth to you

(often used in the expression: "If I get my hands on the person who/that..., I'll...")

If I get my hands on the person responsible, I'll make him sorry.

to get your own way: to do what you want to do even though sb else wants you to do sth different

If he doesn't get his own way, he sulks.

Practice

1. Complete the words in the boxes below. The words, which form part of a **get** expression, must be written horizontally. The numbers that appear before each horizontal column correspond to the example sentences below the grid.

6. No, he didn't mean that. You **got the wrong end of the** ....
7. "Let's **get it over** ....," he said and, taking a deep breath, he went into the dentist's surgery.
8. Teaching beginners was difficult at first, but I soon **got the** .... **of it**.
9. If our competitors **get** .... of this, they'll bring out their own version.
10. All this waiting around is **getting on my** ....
11. We **got the** .... **of our lives** when we heard that he had dropped out of college.
12. They never **got to the** .... of who the subject of the portrait really was. It remains a mystery to this day.
13. The television was so old that we had to **get** .... **of** it.
14. He is a very spoilt child. If he doesn't **get his own** ...., he throws a tantrum.
15. There is no need to **get** .... **away**. It's only a football match.
16. As a Chinese student of English, he has difficulty in **getting his** .... **round** words that contain the letters r or l.
17. Arguing about it instead of solving it will **get us** ....
18. England **got off to a good** ...., scoring two goals in the first ten minutes.

2. Complete the sentences with appropriate **get** phrases from the box below.

the hang of – to grips with – the point of – away from it all – on the wrong side – one thing clear

1. "You'll soon get .... fishing," he said.
2. It's time the government got .... the ailing economy.
3. For a perfect way to get ...., take a Sunway Cruise.
4. Let's get ....; you are not to eat sweets between meals.
5. The main problem with the exercise is that the students didn't get .... it.
6. Why are you shouting at me? Did you get out of bed .... again?

0. Let's **get one thing** clear. If you do that again, you'll be in trouble.
1. Preparations for the festival **got** .... last week.
2. **Get to the** ...., will you? I haven't got all day!
3. When I **get my** .... on him, I'll show him!
4. It took a while for the business to **get off the** ....
5. She spoke so much that I **couldn't get a word in** ....

108 Get (Expressions II/Phrasal Verbs)

Get Expressions II

I don't get it: I don't understand

I don't get it. Why would he want to sell that beautiful cottage?

I don't get it. Was that supposed to be funny?

don't get me wrong: do not misunderstand me and be offended by what I am going to say/have just said

Don't get me wrong, I liked your acting. I just didn't think much of the film.

to get a kick out of doing sth: to really enjoy doing sth or be excited about it (often for short time)

He got a kick out of seeing himself on TV, and videoed it for all his friends.

to get back together again: if two people get back together again, they re-establish their relationship

They split up two months ago and I doubt whether they will get back together again.

to get one's comeuppance: to finally get the punishment one deserves

It was good to see the villain get his comeuppance at the end of the story.

to get sb down: make sb feel depressed

The routine of a dead-end job was getting him down, driving him almost to despair.

to get hold of sb/sth: to contact sb/ to find/buy/borrow sth

I've been trying to get hold of Nigel, but he is never in and no one is answering the phone.

I've been trying to get hold of that new CD but I can't find it in any of the shops.

to get your own back: to do sth bad to sb who has previously done sth bad to you; get revenge

When you consider how his friends had betrayed him, you can't blame him for wanting to get his own back on them.

what gets me (about sth): what annoys me about sth

What gets me about this government is the way they say they are going to do one thing and then do exactly the opposite.

Get Phrasal Verbs

to get at: to insinuate; most commonly found in the question **What are you getting at?**; What are you trying to say? (I don't understand) Are you indirectly criticising me or accusing me of sth?

I can't see what you're getting at, so could you put it more simply?

What are you getting at, saying that you do all of the work around here?

to get behind with: to be late in paying sth (especially rent) [Note: to **get behind with your work**: not to have done as much work as you should have]

If you get behind with your rent, you might find yourself in trouble.

I've got so behind with all my paperwork, that I'll have to work all weekend to catch up with it.

to get by: to have enough money to pay your bills and buy the things you need to survive (food and clothes, etc)

She earns only £75 a week. I don't know how she can get by on a salary like that.

to get down to sth: to start giving serious attention to sth/ to start working seriously on sth

It was time I got down to some serious work on my thesis.

to be getting on for: to be nearly (used for time/age)

"What time do you think it is?" "I have no idea, but it must be getting on for 3 o'clock."

He must be getting on for 50, though he looks much younger.

to get on to: (i) to start talking about (ii) to contact sb for help/information

He then got on to the subject of his wartime exploits.

The lights suddenly went off for no apparent reason so I got on to the electricity board.

to get out of (doing sth): to avoid doing sth you are supposed to do or you have previously arranged to do

I am not really in the mood but I said I'd go to Mick's party and I don't think I can get out of it.

You are not getting out of doing the supermarket shopping this time.

I can't get over how: I can't believe how (used to express surprise)

I can't get over how expensive everything is in this country these days.

to get round sb: to persuade sb to do sth by being nice to them

I could always get round my mother by buying her chocolates.

to get round to doing sth: to finally find time to do sth

I received the letter on Monday and finally got round to answering it on Friday.

to get through to sb: to contact and talk to sb by telephone

I can't get through to him. Every time I ring, I get his answering machine.

to get up to: to do; most commonly found in the question **What did you get up to...?**

"What did you get up to this weekend?" "Not much."

They boys are very quiet at the moment. I wonder what they are getting up to.

what's got into sb: what has happened to sb (surprise because sb is behaving very differently from the way they normally do)

I don't know what's got into Laszlo. He's rude, aggressive and always in a foul mood these days.

220

Practice

1. In Passage A, a man is talking to his psychologist. Passage B is a summary of what the man (Andy) says. Using Passage A as a guideline, complete Passage B.

Passage A

It's almost as if she **gets a kick out of** being a success while I'm a failure, and I'm not surprised. Now **don't get me wrong**, I'm not bitter about her success - well, all right, I am - but I know I **got my comeuppance** and fair enough. After all, I was the one who left the band. I guess I thought the whole band would split up but then **she gets hold of** another bass guitarist. **What really gets me** is that I'm always seeing them on TV and that she's always sending me complimentary tickets for a gig. Talk about **getting your own back**! Talk about rubbing it in! I've often toyed with the idea of asking her if we could **get back together** again, but then there's the new bass guitarist, as I say. Now I'm out in the cold, as far as professional music is concerned. I **don't get it**. I'm every bit as talented as the rest of the group, but here I am selling fruit and vegetables in the market instead of being up there in front of an audience, my name in lights and everything. I try not to let it **get me down**, but it's hard.

Passage B

Andy believes that his ex-partner in the group is 1) .... his discomfort. He 2) .... that he 3) .... to be treated badly by her, which, of course, is positive. He had assumed that the band would no longer stay together. However, she 4) .... another musician to replace him. What really 5) .... him is not only that he continually sees them on the television but that his ex-partner repeatedly sends him complimentary tickets for concerts. He feels very strongly that this is done from sheer vindictiveness, from a desire to 6) .... on him. Andy has frequently considered asking his ex-partner if they could 7) .... the group, although he realises that this is unlikely given the presence of the new bass player. Andy's future as a professional guitarist looks bleak. Andy 8) .... why this should be the case as he considers himself to be a gifted and talented musician. Andy feels frustrated and 9) .... that he now sells fruit and vegetables at a local market instead of playing in a band. This is something that Andy has to come to terms with.

2. Complete the sentences with (an) appropriate preposition(s) from the box below. You can use some of the prepositions more than once.

> on – for – to – up – out – by – with – down – into – through – round – behind – of – at – over

1. What do you mean by what you just said? What are you getting .... ?
2. They must be out. I've been trying to get .... to them all evening, but no one is answering the phone.
3. It must have been getting .... two o'clock when we left the club.
4. He thinks that flowers will persuade me, but he won't get .... me that easily.
5. I managed to get .... doing the washing-up by telling him I was allergic to soapy water.
6. He hasn't done any revision yet. He really must get .... some serious work.
7. I don't know how she makes ends meet. I couldn't get .... on a salary like hers.
8. I don't know when I'll get .... answering all these letters.
9. What's got .... Howard? He never washes up and then suddenly today he's done it twice.
10. What did I get .... this weekend? Nothing really. I just watched TV.
11. What with losing my job and having to pay outstanding debts, I got seriously .... my rent and had to move out.
12. I can't get .... how much she has grown. She was a child the last time I saw her.
13. You had better get .... the post office to see what happened to that parcel.
14. Wake me up when he gets .... something more interesting.

109 Give (Expressions/Phrasal Verbs)

Give Expressions

to give as good as you get: (i) to be as aggressive or forceful as the person you are arguing with (ii) to hurt the person you are fighting as much as he or she hurts you

She may look small and timid, but, when she argues, she most certainly gives as good as she gets.

to give of your best: to do sth as well as you possibly can or try as hard as you can to do sth

He was disappointed, but he had given of his best and that is what really counts.

to give priority to sth/sb: to consider sb/sth more important than other things/people and therefore pay more attention to it/them or deal with it/them first

Priority is being given to couples with three or more children.

to give sb a hand (with sth): to help sb to do sth

Don't worry about moving the fridge. I'm sure Tim would be more than happy to give you a hand (with it).

to give sb a hard time: (i) to criticise sb a lot (ii) to cause sb a lot of trouble or make them feel uncomfortable (iii) to ask sb a lot of difficult questions

My wife is giving me a really hard time at the moment. I can't seem to do anything right.

When I first got the job, the people in my office gave me a really hard time because I was very young.

It was the worst interview I have ever had. They gave me a really hard time.

to give sb credit for sth: to praise sb for the effort they have made or the good work they have done (often used in passive voice)

The credit for our recent success should be given to our manager.

to give sb the lowdown on sth: to give sb the most important facts about sth/sb

She asked me to give her the lowdown on the meeting.

to give sb your word: to promise

You must give me your word that you will not repeat what I tell you to anyone.

to give sth a go: to try doing sth especially because it is unusual or you have never done it before

If they offered me the chance to go parachuting, I would definitely give it a go.

Give Phrasal Verbs

to give (sth) away: to give sth to sb without charging them money for it

Munns Stores is giving away a free T-shirt with every pair of trousers that you buy.

to give yourself/sb away: if sth gives you away, it shows others who or what you really are

Although he denied having anything to do with it, his nervousness gave him away.

to give in to sth: (i) to finally (after a lot of argument and/or discussion) and unwillingly do what sb wants you to do (ii) to allow sth (an emotion or desire) to take hold of you

The government gave in to public pressure and abolished all its new parking laws.

She wanted to eat chocolate but was determined not to give in to temptation as she was on a diet.

to give off: to produce (a particular sound, smell or kind of light)

This lamp doesn't give off much light, does it?

The fruit of the bandando tree gives off an unpleasant smell.

to give out: to distribute sth (a leaflet, homework, a form to fill in, etc)

At the end of the seminar we will be giving out a feedback form which we would like you to fill in.

to be given out: (i) (for information, facts, etc) to be officially announced (ii) to be distributed

[Note: **It was given out that...**: it was announced that...]

As yet, this year's trade figures have not been given out.

At the press conference it was given out that the president intended to resign.

Leaflets with information about how to recycle were being given out.

to be given over to: if part of your time is given over to a particular activity, you spend your time doing that activity; [Note: if part or all of a newspaper/magazine/TV or radio programme is given over to an interview/a story, it is especially used for that interview/story, etc]

Most of his time is given over to lecturing and promoting his books.

His whole life was given over to helping the poor and needy.

This week's programme is given over to a profile of an eminent scientist.

to give up: (i) to stop doing sth/trying to answer] (ii) to resign (from one's job) [Note: **I give up:** I don't know the answer]

He used to be a heavy smoker but he's long given up.

I've never thought of giving up teaching.

"Who wrote the 'Oresteian Trilogy'?" "I give up. Who wrote it?"

to give yourself up: to allow yourself to be arrested by the police

Robin Hood refused to give himself up to the Sheriff of Nottingham.

to give up on sb/sth: to stop hoping/believing that you can change or improve sb/sth

Don't give up on her just yet; you've only been her coach for two months and you know she has the makings of a first class sprinter.

He's given up on getting that novel of his published.

Practice

1. *Choose the option (a, b or c) which best completes each of the **if** sentences below.*

1 If you give someone a hand, you
   a hit them.
   b help them.
   c forgive them for something bad they have done to you.
2 If you give priority to something over something else, you consider
   a the latter to be more important than the former.
   b the former to be more important than the latter.
   c them to be equally important.
3 If you give someone the lowdown on something, you
   a describe something in a very negative way.
   b provide them with information that they need.
   c hit them because they have insulted you.
4 If you give someone a hard time, you
   a criticise them.
   b feel sorry for them.
   c are a judge and you have just sentenced them to twenty years in prison.
5 If you give someone credit for something, you
   a give them more time so that they can meet a deadline.
   b lend them some money so that they can buy something.
   c praise them for what they have done.
6 If you give of your best, you
   a wish someone luck.
   b try as hard as you can to do something.
   c give someone some very good advice.
7 If you give someone your word, you
   a write to them.
   b promise them that you will do something.
   c criticise them.
8 If you are the kind of person who gives as good as you get, you
   a are very generous.
   b keep your promises.
   c are not afraid to fight or argue back.
9 If you give something a go, you
   a complain about something.
   b give your permission for something to take place.
   c try to do something despite thinking you are unlikely to succeed.

2. *Replace the words in capital letters with an appropriate form of the verb **give** and the correct preposition(s).*

1 He swore he was English but his French accent **betrayed him**. ....
2 After three weeks on the run, the villain of the story **surrendered** to the police. ....
3 I **don't know the answer**. What were Napoleon's last words? ....
4 When I opened the packet, the cheese **produced and sent out** a particularly nasty smell. ....
5 He stood on the street corner **distributing** leaflets. ....
6 I've **abandoned all hope of** ever seeing that money again. ....
7 He refused to **submit** to media pressure and take back what he had said. ....
8 It was **announced** that the minister had resigned in order to pursue a career in journalism. ....
9 The editor obviously liked your article. The whole of page two was **used for** it. ....
10 They are **giving for free** a set of six stickers with every burger you buy. ....

3. *Choose the correct item.*

1 Will this candle give .... enough light for us to see by?
   A up   B off
   C out   D away
2 Drivers have to give .... to traffic already on the roundabout.
   A credit B way
   C a go   D priority
3 Could you give me .... with this window? It's stuck.
   A the lowdown   C a hard time
   B a hand   D of your best
4 Oscar Wilde once remarked that the only way to remove temptation was to give .... it.
   A over to   B up on   C credit for   D in to
5 The debate went on for hours, with each side giving ....
   A as good as it got   C the lowdown
   B a go   D a hard time
6 After so many rejections, he had given .... getting a good job.
   A over to   B up on   C in to   D off
7 A mean-spirited person will refuse to give .... where it is due.
   A his word   C credit
   B priority   D a hard time

223

110 Go (Expressions)

bang go/goes sth: (informal) the chances of sth happening have been ruined

And then they discovered that I was tone-deaf, and bang went my chances of becoming a concert pianist.

to go behind sb's back: to say/do sth without telling or consulting the person it directly concerns

So instead of complaining to me – her teacher – she went behind my back and told the director.

to go berserk: to become uncontrollably violent

This is the scene where Hamlet goes berserk and kills Polonius.

sth will go down in history as... : sth will be remembered and recorded in history books as...

Today will go down in history as one of the blackest and saddest days in King Bostok's short and troubled reign.

sth goes downhill: sth is no longer as good as it was and is continuing to get worse (generally used with the present perfect or past tense)

Sammy and Elise's restaurant has gone downhill since they sold it to the present owners.

to go easy on sb: not to be too strict with sb (especially because they probably behaved badly because of special circumstances)

I know what she did was inexcusable, but go easy on her. She's been having a very difficult time since her parents split up.

to go easy on sth: not to use too much of sth (probably because you do not have much left)

Go easy on the matches. We've only got one box left.

to go far/a long way: to be successful in one's career

He'll go a long way if he is ambitious enough.

She's really talented; I'm sure she'll go far.

to go to great lengths: to try very hard to achieve sth

She went to great lengths to bring herself up to competition standards.

to go to a lot of trouble to do sth: to spend a lot of your time and to put a lot of effort into doing sth [Note: (with the same meaning) **to go to a lot of time and trouble to do sth**]

In those days the Hollywood studios went to a lot of trouble to protect their stars from the prying eyes of the media.

my mind went blank: I was temporarily unable to remember anything

The questions were easy, but my nerves got the better of me and my mind went blank. I couldn't remember a thing.

to go over the top: to do or say sth that other people consider to be too extreme

To say it is the best novel written in the last twenty years is going a bit over the top, isn't it?

to go to rack and ruin/to go to the dogs: to have been neglected to the point of being in very poor condition (a building) or in a state of complete disorganisation

They have let the castle go to rack and ruin.

Under his management the company went to rack and ruin.

it just goes to show that: it proves that...

He seemed to be such an ordinary man. We found out, however, that he was a tycoon. It just goes to show that appearances can be deceptive.

to go on a (massive) spending spree: to spend a lot of money in a short period of time [Note: to go on a **shopping spree**: to buy a lot of things in a short period]

The first thing they did when they received their winnings was to go on a massive spending spree.

sth goes (straight) to sb's head: sth (power, fame, money, etc) makes sb excessively proud and confident

It is all too easy, as a child star, to let fame go straight to your head.

to go through a bad/sticky patch: to experience difficulties and problems for an extended period of time

We went through quite a bad patch in January and February when we hardly sold anything.

to go unpunished: if sth (generally a crime or bad behaviour) goes unpunished, the person who commits the crime or who behaves badly is not punished

Unlike the present government, we will not turn a blind eye to tax evasion. This must not, and will not, go unpunished.

it goes without saying that...: a phrase meaning that what you are about to say is so obvious that you do not really need to say it – but nevertheless you will

"Your behaviour is totally unacceptable," Mr Jones said. "It goes without saying that I will be asking for your immediate resignation," he continued.

Practice

1. Complete the sentences with an appropriate word from the box below.

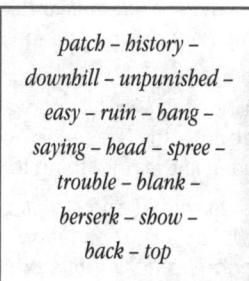

> patch – history – downhill – unpunished – easy – ruin – bang – saying – head – spree – trouble – blank – berserk – show – back – top

1. Hey, Tom, **go** .... **on** the pizza, will you? You've already polished off three slices.
2. Her early success as a novelist **went straight** to her .... She began seeing herself as a genius.
3. United are **going through a bad** .... at the moment. They've lost five out of their last six matches.
4. **I went to a lot of** .... **to** get her that book and all she could say was, "Is that all you bought me?"
5. It was horrible. The examiner asked me to outline Weber's theories on capitalism and **my mind went** .... I wasn't able to say a thing.
6. He won his first two matches but from then on things **went** .... He hasn't won a match since.
7. His parents **went** .... when he told them he was dropping out of college. His father started shouting and his mother collapsed in anguished sobs.
8. Everyone thought he was just an insignificant clerk and then he went and won the Nobel Prize for Physics. **It just goes to** .... **that** you can't judge a book by its cover.
9. "I think Walt Disney was the greatest film director who ever lived." "You're **going a bit over the** ...., aren't you?"
10. The first thing she did when she collected her winnings was to **go on a massive spending** ....
11. We've just received a medical bill for three thousand pounds, so .... **goes** our holiday.
12. The 1980s will probably **go down in** .... as the last century's tackiest decade.
13. "You have tirelessly served this community for nigh on thirty years and **it goes without** .... **that** you will be sorely missed", he said.
14. It offends people's sense of justice to see a crime **go** ....
15. It must once have been such a beautiful house, but the people who owned it had let it **go to rack and** ....
16. **Going behind** her supervisor's .... and telling the managing director about the lack of team spirit among the workers was bound to cause trouble.

2. Match the incomplete sentences (1-8) with the appropriate endings (a-h)

1. Going behind my back .....
2. We had gone to a lot of trouble .....
3. The economy had gone to rack and ruin .....
4. The critic went over the top .....
5. The leading actor's mind went blank .....
6. Ambitious people will go to great lengths .....
7. He'll go far .....
8. Bang went the sprinter's chances of a medal .....

a. to reach the top of their profession.
b. providing he works hard.
c. in lavishing praise on the new Broadway musical.
d. when he injured a tendon.
e. was a mean thing to do.
f. to arrange Beth's surprise birthday party.
g. when he was about to say his opening lines.
h. because of the government's incompetence.

3. Using the expressions presented in this unit, answer the following questions in as many ways as you can.

1. Why shouldn't he be punished?
   ....
   ....
2. You had an argument. Why?
   ....
   ....
3. What is your opinion of your country's leading entertainer?
   ....
   ....
4. Why did she resign?
   ....
   ....
5. How do you think people will remember the 1990s?
   ....
   ....
6. President Shaw was a terrible president. Why?
   ....
   ....

225

111 Go (Phrasal Verbs) Have (Expressions)

Go

to go about sth/doing sth: to make a start at doing sth difficult; often prefaced by **I don't know how I/I don't know how to/How do I ...**

I'd love to set up my own business, but I just don't know how to go about it.

to go along with sth: to agree to participate in sth (a plan/scheme/idea)

If you knew you were going to get into trouble, why did you go along with his plan?

to go by sth: to use a book/guide book, etc to form an opinion, for information or to make a judgement; most commonly used in the negative with **wouldn't**

Di Sallio wrote that the film was rubbish, but I wouldn't go by anything he says, as he hates horror films.

sth goes down badly: people do not like or do not approve of sth
Opp.: sth goes down well

His appointment to the post of general secretary went down badly with the unions.

His new book has gone down well with the critics.

to go for sb: to attack

The dog went for me as soon as I opened the gate.

to go off: (i) if an **alarm clock** goes off, it rings (ii) if **a bomb** goes off, it explodes (iii) if **meat** or dairy products (cream, milk, yoghurt, etc) go off, they go bad

I overslept because my alarm clock didn't go off.

At the beginning of the film, a bomb goes off outside the town hall.

This milk smells funny. Do you think it has gone off?

to go off sb/sth: to stop liking sb/sth that you used to like

I've gone off horror films. I can't stand them any more.

to go on about sth: to keep talking about sth in such a way that others get bored, impatient or irritated [Note: with same meaning but emphasising the fact that the speaker spoke for a long time: **to go on and on about**]

I wish he would stop going on about his new car.

She went on and on about her new job.

to go over sth: to carefully look at and check sth (particularly homework/plans/the facts/a story)

At the start of the class, our teacher always goes over our homework.

to go through with sth: to complete what you had planned; generally used in negatives (with **can't/couldn't**) and questions

When I saw all those people waiting for me to give a speech, I couldn't go through with it.

to go with sth: to match/co-ordinate with (for colours/patterns)

Does this tie go with this shirt?

Have

to have difficulty in doing sth: to find it difficult to do sth

I have (great) difficulty in remembering names.

He had no difficulty in persuading her to go.

to have had enough of sb/sth/doing sth: to be annoyed by sb/sth and not accept them/it any longer

I've had enough of the poor service in this supermarket. In future, I'll take my custom elsewhere.

to have misgivings about sth/doing sth: not to be sure if sth is good or right

The school had received some harsh criticism in the press, so we had misgivings about sending our children there.

to have no alternative but to do sth: the only choice sb will have is

If you are caught speeding again, we shall have no alternative but to take away your driving licence.

to have no hesitation in doing sth: (formal) not to need to stop and think about sth because you know that it is the right thing to do

She is determined and ambitious, so I have no hesitation in recommending her for this post.

sb has no intention of doing sth: there is no way that sb will do sth

I think they have no intention of paying me the money that they owe me.

to have no qualms about doing sth: not to have any moral doubts about doing sth

He knew she'd feel betrayed, but he had no qualms whatsoever about selling the story to the papers.

to have no recollection of sth/doing sth: (formal) not to remember sth/doing sth

He says he has no recollection of the incident.

to have (every/a perfect) right to do sth: to believe that what sb is doing is reasonable and fair
Opp.: to have no right to do sth

He had every right to complain. He paid a fortune for those chairs and they fell to pieces within a month.

"The assistants were rude and the manager refused to see me." "They had no right to treat you like that. You should complain."

to have the makings of sth: to have all the qualities necessary to become sth (these qualities still need to be developed, however)

He has the makings of an excellent golfer and I'm sure he'll soon be competing in major tournaments.

Practice

1. For each of the sentences, substitute the words in bold for an appropriate phrasal verb from the box below. Change the tense or form of the verb **go** when and where appropriate.

> go for – go through with it – go on about – go with – go off –
> go down – go about – go along with – go off – go by – go over

1. I don't know how we will **tackle the problem of** raising £4,000 by tomorrow. ....
2. I wish she would stop **continually talking about** how great her holiday was. ....
3. I've **stopped liking** rap music. It's become too aggressive and political. ....
4. My alarm clock **rings** at half past six every morning. ....
5. Let's carefully **re-examine and check** the plan again. ....
6. He says he is going to give up his job and sail single-handed round the world, but I doubt whether he has got the courage to **complete what he has planned**. ....
7. I don't think the best man's speech **was received** very well. Some of his jokes were in rather poor taste. ....
8. It's obviously a very good film – if the reviews are anything to **use in order to make a judgement**. ....
9. It **attacked** me. I don't know why. All I did was bend down and stroke it. ....
10. Yes it's a very nice shirt, but it is blue, and it doesn't **match** your trousers. ....
11. Like a fool, **I agreed to and participated in** his harebrained plan to join the Foreign Legion. ....

2. For questions 1 - 10, complete the second sentence so that it has a similar meaning to the first sentence, using 3 to 8 words. You must include the word given in bold, which cannot be changed in any way.

1. He says he doesn't remember a thing about the accident.
   recollection He says .... the accident.
2. Most English people find it very difficult to pronounce the Spanish 'r'.
   difficulty Most English people .... the Spanish 'r'.
3. "I'm sick and tired of your pathetic excuses," he said.
   enough He said .... their pathetic excuses.
4. As the only person not to receive a bonus, I think I'm perfectly entitled to feel upset.
   right As the only person not to receive a bonus, I think I .... upset.
5. Joe didn't think it was wrong of him to quit at such short notice.
   qualms Joe .... at such short notice.
6. I would certainly recommend David for the job.
   hesitation I .... David for the job.
7. If you do not settle your account within seven days, we will be obliged to begin legal proceedings.
   alternative If you do not settle your account within seven days, we .... you to court.
8. "There is no way that I will give in," Pat said.
   intention "I ....," Pat said.
9. She's only just started out, but, judging by her recent performance, she should become an excellent tennis player.
   makings She .... an excellent tennis player.
10. I'm not sure that it would be a good idea to trust him with all that money.
    misgivings I .... him with all that money.

112 Make (Combinations/Expressions)

Make (Combinations)

to make a booking: to reserve a seat in a theatre/a table at a restaurant/an airline ticket/a hotel room, etc

We do have a seat available for tonight's performance. Would you like to make a booking?

to make a comeback: to try and become popular/important again, having been out of the public eye for some time

He's too old to make a comeback. He can't sing any more.

to make a confession: to confess

I've got a confession to make. I'm not really a lawyer.

to make a discovery: to discover (often with regard to medicine/science)

It is one of the most important discoveries to be made this century.

to make a donation: to give money to a good cause/charity

Would you like to make a donation for the flood victims?

to make a fortune: to make a lot of money in business

He made a fortune selling second-hand cars.

to make a killing: to make a lot of money in a business transaction

If we sell it now, we'll make a killing.

to make a loss: to lose money

In its first year, our company made a loss of £40,000.

to make a mess: to cause untidiness

Look at the mess you've made. Clear it up right now.

to make amends: to compensate for having done sth bad to sb/for disappointing sb

I know I've let you down, but I promise I'll make amends.

to make an allegation: to allege (to claim that sth is true or to accuse sb of doing sth wrong, even though there is no proof to support your claim or accusation)

These are very serious allegations you are making.

to make an appointment: to arrange a time to see a doctor/bank manager, etc

Have you made an appointment with your dentist?

to make an arrest: to arrest sb

The police broke up the demonstration and made a number of arrests.

to make contact: to succeed in communicating with sb you would not normally communicate with

I've managed to make contact with a number of old university friends.

to make the team: to be good enough to be selected to play for a team

Even if he were to start training again, I doubt whether he would make the team.

Make (Expressions I)

It makes no odds: (i) it does not make any difference (ii) I don't mind

It makes no odds whether we run or hide. Either way they'll find us.

"Pizza or pasta?" "You choose. It makes no odds to me."

to make a beeline for: to go (often quickly) directly to sth or sb without paying attention to anything or anyone else that might be around

On entering the duty-free shop, she made a beeline for the perfume counter.

to make a big thing out of sth/to make a mountain out of a molehill: (informal) to exaggerate the importance of sth

Calm down. You're making a mountain out of a molehill.

to make (out) a (convincing/strong) case for sth: to provide (good) reasons for

Testing cosmetics on animals is, in my opinion, unacceptable and I have yet to hear anyone make out a convincing case for it.

to make a fool of oneself: to make oneself look stupid

I'm not going to do it. I'd only make a fool of myself.

to make a habit of: to repeatedly do sth undesirable

We ask you to hand in assignments on time. This is late. If you make a habit of doing this, you will be asked to leave.

to make a point of doing sth: to be very careful to do sth because you believe that what you are doing is important or necessary, or because you want other people to see that you are doing it

He made a (special) point of being sociable.

to make ends meet: to earn enough money to survive

On a salary like hers, it's not surprising that she finds it hard to make ends meet.

to make no bones about: to make no attempt to hide (often negative) feelings

He hates studying for school and he makes no bones about it.

to make sense: if sth makes sense you understand it

Why would she give up such a wonderful opportunity? It doesn't make sense.

to make one's way: to walk / travel (often slowly or with difficulty)

We couldn't see a thing in the dark. Slowly, carefully, we made our way down the stairs.

to make way for: (i) to move to one side so that sb/sth can pass (ii) to create a space for sth

A voice called out "Make way for the King!" and a golden carriage rolled into sight.

We'd have to knock down that wall to make way for a new desk.

228

Practice

1. *Decide which of the words below are used with the verb **to make**.*

1	an arrest	11	an appointment ......
2	contact	12	a mess ......
3	a blank	13	a discovery ......
4	a fortune	14	an allegation ......
5	a loss	15	blood ......
6	the line	16	level ......
7	a comeback	17	a conclusion ......
8	a booking	18	a killing ......
9	a confession	19	a donation ......
10	amends	20	the team ......

2. *Complete the following sentences with a word or phrase from the shaded box below.*

> a booking – our way – a fool – a point of – a big thing –
> way for – a habit – a beeline – case – no odds –
> no bones – sense – a mountain – ends

1 It doesn't make .... Why would he betray his own brother?
2 You won't be able to attend the seminar unless you've made ....
3 Knowing that she lacked confidence, he made .... singling out her painting for special praise.
4 On entering the shop, the children made .... for the sweet counter, scurrying directly towards it as if drawn by a huge, invisible magnet.
5 Earning less than the minimum wage and with four mouths to feed, Alison was finding it difficult to make .... meet.
6 We were too tired to talk. Neither of us spoke as we made .... back to the warmth of our cabin.
7 Jo makes .... about the fact that he doesn't like Bob. He openly criticises him and whenever he finds himself in his company, he ignores him.
8 Whilst I will never agree to privatisation of the railways, I have to admit that she made out a very convincing .... for it.
9 "I don't understand why you're making such .... out of my decision. Did I make .... of myself?" "No." "So why are you making .... out of a molehill?"
10 Sometimes I sleep in late on Sundays. It's nice but it does mean that Sunday has gone before I know it, so I try not to make .... of it.
11 Ours was one of the houses pulled down to make .... the new road.

12 It makes .... whether we win or lose today. We have already won the championship.

3. *The words in bold have been jumbled. Swap them around to make correct sentences.*

1 Speculators made a **mess** on the market while stock prices were rising. ....
2 As it's all for a good cause, I'll make a **comeback**. ....
3 **Amends** have been made, and I wish to deny them in the strongest possible terms. ....
4 The ageing film star was trying to make a **killing**. ....
5 Please clear up all this dreadful **donation** you've made. ....
6 How can I make **allegations** for the dreadful way I've treated you? ....
7 Jason makes a **point** of leaving the computer on whenever he leaves the room; it's very annoying. ....
8 His refusal to take the promotion just doesn't make **way**. ....
9 The receptionist made a **habit** of being pleasant on the telephone. ....

4. *Using the **make** collocations and the **make** expressions, answer the following questions in as many ways as you can.*

1 Why isn't he playing in this match?
....
....
2 Why was she fired and what is she doing now?
....
....
3 How's business?
....
....
4 You were robbed. What happened?
....
....
5 Why do you think she is a good teacher?
....
....

113 Make (Expressions VII/Phrasal Verbs)

Make (Expressions)

can't make it/sth: to be unable to go to a party/dinner/meeting, etc [Note: **Did you (finally) make it to?...**: Did you go to ... in the end? (implication that the person being addressed had previously thought that he/she might not have been able to go to the particular event)]

I'm sorry, John, but I can't make it to tomorrow's meeting.

to make a move: to leave; often prefaced with: **Let's/We ought to/ I'd better/It's time we ...**

It was late and he had an early start the next morning. "We ought to make a move," he said.

to make do with sth: to satisfy oneself with what one has as opposed to what one wants

The bed didn't arrive for three days. In the meantime, we had to make do with a mattress on the floor.

to make it 6 o'clock: one's watch/clock says it is 6 o'clock; more common in the question form: **What time do you make it?**: What time is it?

to make like sb: (American English) to behave as if one were sb (but in fact they aren't)

He makes like he's an expert on the subject.

to make yourself understood: to be able to say simple things in a foreign language

I know very little Portuguese, but I can make myself understood.

to make the best of sth: to do your best in a difficult situation

The settlers had to make the best of the few natural resources they had.

to make the most of sth: to get the maximum use or advantage of sth

I made the most of my time in Poland and learnt as much Polish as I possibly could.

to make (full) use of sth/sb: to use sth (fully)

Very few people make full use of the features this machine has to offer.

not to be able to make head or tail of sth: not to understand; normally used with reference to sth that has been written or said

He handed me a piece of paper. "See if you can understand it. I can't make head or tail of it," he said.

sb will make a good/an excellent...: sb has all the right qualities to be a good/excellent ... **Opp.:** sb will make a terrible/an awful/an appalling...

I'm so happy he's decided on a career in teaching. He'll make an excellent teacher.

sb's not going to make it: sb's not going to arrive somewhere in time for sth

He looked at his watch and then at the traffic ahead of him. "I'm not going to make it," he thought.

that makes a change: that's different from normal; used to express satisfaction or surprise that a good thing has happened

They're going to lower taxes. Well, that makes a change.

Make Phrasal Verbs

to be made up of: to be formed by or composed of

The selection committee is made up of former players, the team manager and members of the board of directors.

to make (a cheque/receipt) out to sb: to write sb's name on a cheque/receipt

Shall I make this cheque out to you or to Susan?

to make for somewhere: to go in the direction of

In the panic that ensued, hundreds of people were injured as they made for the exit.

to make sb/sth into sb/sth else: to transform sb/sth into sb/sth else

It was his strict upbringing that made him into the man he is today.

They've made that old cinema into a skating rink.

to make it up to sb: to do sth nice for sb having previously let them down

I know it's my fault that we haven't been on holiday, but I'll make it up to you, I promise.

to make off with sth: to steal sth and escape with it

The dog made off with the bone.

to make (sth) out: to be able to read or see; often used with: **can('t) / could(n't) wasn(n't) able to, etc**

Up ahead in the distance we could just make out the lights of our hotel.

to make up a set: to complete a set (things or people)

I'm looking for a sixth tea cup to make up a set.

to make up for doing sth: (i) to do sth nice for sb because you have previously behaved badly in some way (ii) to compensate, make a bad situation better

He made up for letting her down by taking her out to the most expensive restaurant in town.

We'll have to work extra hard to make up for lost time.

to make up sth (e.g. story): to invent sth, possibly in order to deceive, people

That can't be true. You've made it all up.

to make up your mind: to decide

Well, make up your mind; do you want to come, or not?

sth/sb isn't as bad/good/ beautiful, etc as everyone makes out: sth/sb isn't as bad/good/beautiful as everyone says

He's not as strict as everyone makes out.

230

Practice

1. Match a 'make phrase' sentence in Section A with a sentence in Section B. The sentence in Section B should be a logical extension of the 'make phrase' sentence. An example has been done for you.

Section A
0   He **makes like** the boss.   e
1   I **make it** twenty past.   ......
2   We **can't make it** tomorrow.   ......
3   Let's **make a move**.   ......
4   We should **make the most of it**.   ......
5   He **made full use of the** chance he was given.   ......
6   That **makes a change**.   ......
7   We're **not going to make it**.   ......
8   I couldn't **make myself understood**.   ......
9   He'll **make a** good manager.   ......
10 You'll have to **make the best of it**.   ......
11 I can't **make head or tail of** this.   ......
12 **Make up your mind** about the promotion.   ......
13 We are going to **make up** a bridge party.   ......

Section B
a   I don't speak a word of French.
b   We need one more player.
c   It's sixty miles away and it starts in half an hour.
d   He must have been half asleep when he wrote it.
e   He may think he is, but he isn't.
f   I've had enough of this party.
g   Sorry to cancel at such short notice but Sam's ill.
h   But I think my watch is fast.
i   It's not often the government admits they were wrong.
j   Things do not look good.
k   It's a beautiful day.
l   Now he's one of the best in his field.
m   He has all the right leadership skills.
n   Are you going to accept it or not?

2. Complete the following sentences with (an) appropriate preposition(s) from the box below.

> up of – with – out – off with –
> out – for – up for – out to – up – into

1   If his play is made .... a film, he'll become a millionaire overnight.
2   Thieves broke into her house last night and made .... £ 2,000 worth of jewellery.
3   The committee is made .... workers, union leaders and company directors.
4   It wasn't as bad as everyone made .... I thought it was rather good.
5   Could you make the cheque .... Links, Ltd., please.
6   "We haven't got any milk left. They've drunk it all." "I know, and the supermarket won't be open now. They'll just have to make do .... orange juice."
7   I made .... being rude to her by buying her a huge box of chocolates.
8   On arriving in Miami, we made .... South Beach, which we had been told was the nicest part of the city.
9   It was so foggy that I couldn't make .... the names on the street signs.
10 I know I said we would go out tonight, but I can't – something's come up at work. I'll make it .... to you, I promise.

3. Choose the correct item.

1   The exam wasn't as difficult as everybody made ....
    A off   B up   C out   D for

2   The athlete made .... the time lost through injury by training extra hard.
    A up for   B up to   C out to   D do with

3   'You don't expect me to read this without my glasses on! I can't make .... the small print'.
    A for   B into   C up   D out

4   Your appointment is in half an hour's time, so you'd better make .... now.
    A yourself understood   C a change
    B a move   D head or tail

5   What time do you make ....?
    A do   B it   C for   D out

6   They'll never make .... for the 8 o'clock train.
    A a good   B a move   C like   D it

7   That sounds incredible. They must have made it ....
    A in   B out   C up   D off

231

114 Put (Expressions/Phrasal Verbs)

Put (Expressions)

to put an end/a stop to sth: to stop an activity that is unpleasant, harmful or unacceptable

His decision/intervention/ruling put an end/stop to the rioting/quarrel/unpleasantness.

Someone should put an end to big game hunting.

to put effort into sth/doing sth: to work very hard to get sth done

He put a lot of/didn't put much effort into the dinner/preparing the dinner.

to put sb in the picture: to give sb information about a situation/some aspect of their job which they need, but do not have

None of the board members really knew what was going on, so a meeting was organised and the C.E.O. put them in the picture.

to put into words: to find the right words to express sth

How did I feel? It's difficult to put into words.

I can't put it down: (used in reference to books) to be unable to stop reading it

It was such a good book that I couldn't put it down.

to put on a play: to present a theatrical play for public performance

At the end of term the kids always put on a play.

to put paid to: to destroy

Bad weather put paid to their chances of winning the match.

Who put that idea into your head?: Who persuaded you that that was the truth?

You thought I hated you? Who put that idea into your head?

to put the blame on sb: to blame sb

They put the blame on the goalkeeper for the team's poor performance.

to put the finishing touches to sth: to complete the final details of sth (meal/essay/speech/cake, etc)

I just need to put the finishing touches to this project and it will be ready.

to put sth to the vote: to vote on whether or not to accept sth

The most democratic way of deciding whether this club wants to change its constitution is by putting it to the vote.

put together: combined

She's more intelligent than the two of you put together.

He ate more than the rest of the team put together.

to put two and two together: to make a simple connection between related facts and come to an obvious conclusion

How did I know that he leaked the information to the press? Well, I just put two and two together. He hates the minister and he has access to the information.

Put (Phrasal Verbs)

to put (sth) across: to successfully and effectively communicate your views or ideas to other people

He is not very good at putting his ideas across to other people, which is a shame, because some of his ideas are truly outstanding.

to put (money) by: to save money so that you can use it at a later date

Every month we put by £200 so that at the end of the year we'll have enough to visit our son in Australia.

to put (an animal) down: if a vet puts an animal down, he kills it painlessly because it is injured, sick or very old

The vet had to put the poor cat down as it was very sick.

to put (sth) down to: to say that sth is caused by

The doctors put his ill health down to the fact that he was overweight.

to put in for sth: to formally apply for sth (generally a pay rise, expenses, a job - particularly in the company for which you already work)

I hear you have put in for that job in the Accounts Department.

to put sb off: (i) to disturb sb while they are trying to do sth, to break sb's concentration (ii) to make sb feel that they do not want to do sth (iii) **to put sb off their food**: to make sb not want to eat

I've got to write these reports and I need to concentrate but all that noise from the radio is putting me off.

You should read this. It's called 'The Physics of Teleology'. Don't be put off by the title. It's not complicated and it's absolutely fascinating.

Watching the documentary on plastic surgery has put me right off my dinner.

to put sth on: (i) to switch on/plug in a device (ii) to begin to cook or heat sth

I went home and put the radio on.

I'll put the kettle on. Do you want a cup of tea?

to put sth out: (i) to extinguish (a fire) (ii) to take sth (the cat, the rubbish, etc) from the inside of your house and leave it outside your house, so as to give it exercise (the cat) or so that it can be collected (the rubbish) [Note: **to put sb out**: to cause sb inconvenience]

It took thirty firemen to put the fire out.

Have you put the rubbish out?

She looked at her brother. "I know I said we would only be staying with you for two nights," she said, "but would it put you out if we stayed for three?"

to put up with sb/sth: to tolerate sb/sth

Mary's boyfriend is so rude and aggressive. I don't know how she puts up with him.

We moved out of the city because I couldn't put up with the noise.

Practice

1. Complete the sentence beginnings in section A with a **put** ending from section B. Write the number of the **put** ending in the space next to the beginning it corresponds to. One has been done for you.

Section A

A John managed to lose all his money and his passport, and that ... **5**
B How you two have the nerve to criticise Jan's golf, I don't know. He's better than the two of you ....
C How did I know it was the butler who did it? Well, one minute the butler stands to inherit a substantial sum of money in his employer's will, and the next minute the employer is dead. I just ....
D Fox-hunting is a despicable sport, and it is time we ....
E It wasn't my fault, so don't ....
F I can't explain how I felt. It's difficult to ....
G There's only one way to decide who is going to take over from Tom. Let's ....
H A lot has happened since I've been away, so I'd appreciate it if you could ....
I The book was so good that I couldn't ....
J I'm looking for a new job?! Who on earth ....
K The drama club meets three times a month and at the end of each term we ....
L You're not trying hard enough, so ....
M I'll have the report ready by tonight. I've just got to ....

Section B

1 put a bit more effort into it.
2 put it down.
3 put into words.
4 put two and two together.
5 put paid to our holiday.
6 put together.
7 put an end to it.
8 put it to the vote.
9 put that idea into your head?
10 put the finishing touches to it.
11 put the blame on me.
12 put on a play.
13 put me in the picture.

2. Read the following passage and fill in the gaps with a suitable form of a **put** phrasal verb.

Michael, turn that programme off. I know it's the news but it's full of violence these days, enough to **1)** .... anyone .... their dinner. Change channels, then. Oh dear! Not much better, is it? Firemen **2)** .... a huge forest fire. Yes, Jane, the forests will still be there when we go on holiday. What's that? We haven't **3)** .... enough money for a holiday? There must be some mistake; I'm sure there was enough. Yes, I did **4)** .... a pay rise but no, I didn't get it. My boss just went on about how badly the firm was doing, how sales had plummeted and so on. He made me feel sorry for him, as if I should be giving him money. Yes, I know we can hardly make ends meet, but you know I'm no good at **5)** .... my arguments .... I **6)** .... it .... my lack of self-confidence. Well, you give me some suggestions for making economies. Perhaps we should have the cat **7)** .... That would save some money. No, I'm only joking. Listen, will you two stop squabbling! I don't see why I have to **8)** .... your noise on what is supposed to be my day off. Anyway, if we haven't got enough money for a holiday, then that's just too bad. What's all that racket now? The kettle's boiling - you **9)** .... it .... to make a cup of tea, you say? And the cat wants to go out? Well, don't just stand there **10)** .... the cat .... and bring me a cup of tea, then. Honestly, what a way to spend a Sunday!

3. Circle the correct item.

1 Did you put **down to / in for** that transfer to head office, then?
2 It would cost a lot to put **on / by** such a lavish musical.
3 The artist was busy putting **paid to / the finishing touches to** the painting.
4 You could tell that they had put **a lot of effort into / a stop to** making the party a success.
5 Put money **by / across** on my salary? And just how do you expect me to do that?
6 Put **up / out** the candles, the power has come back on.

115 Set (Combinations/Expressions/Phrasal Verbs)

Set (Combinations)

to set a date for sth: to decide the date on which sth (an exam, wedding or other important event, etc) will take place

We're getting married but haven't set a date yet.

to set a good/bad example: to behave in a way that shows other people how to behave

As a teacher, I always try to be punctual. That way, I set a good example to my students.

to set a precedent: to do sth or decide sth for the first time and thereby give support to, or establish rules for similar actions or decisions that follow; often used for a decision made by a court of law

If the court finds in his favour, this could set a precedent.

to set sb a target: to decide or tell sb that they have to achieve sth

If you don't set your employees targets, they lose motivation and your company doesn't perform as well as it should.

to set a trap for sb: to invent a plan to catch sb doing sth wrong

In scene one the villain sets a trap for the hero.

to set an exam: to give students an exam to do

They set us a strictly-timed multiple choice exam.

to set homework: to give students homework to do

He didn't set us any homework to do.

to set sail: to begin a journey by boat or ship

The sea was calm when we set sail for France.

to set sb/sth free: release sb who/ or sth which has been captive

Once they reached a clearing, they set the wild deer free.

to set the alarm (for): to adjust the alarm clock so that it rings (at a certain time)

Have you set the alarm?

to set the table: to arrange plates and cutlery on a table so that it is ready for a meal

Set the table. We're eating in 5 minutes.

to set up home somewhere: to start living somewhere in your own house

They set up home in Broadstairs.

to set up in business: to start doing business

We set up in business selling second-hand books last year.

to set your heart on sth: to really want sth that is often hard to do/ get

He set his heart on winning the gold.

Set (Expressions)

all set: ready to leave

Are we all set? Let's go then.

to be dead set against (doing) sth: To be totally opposed to sth

Her parents were dead set against her moving to Italy.

to be set in your ways: to be unable to change the way you do things because you have done them that way for a long time

I wouldn't like to share my flat with anyone after so many years of living on my own. I'm too set in my ways.

to be set to: to be ready to do sth/to have been arranged to happen

The meeting is set to start at 6 pm.

to be set up for life: to have so much money that you need never worry about money again

With the money from the inheritance, he was set up for life.

to set eyes on sb/sth: to see sb/sth (often for the first time)

The minute I set eyes on her, I knew I could trust her.

to set foot in/on: to enter

The minute I set foot in the café, I thought something strange was going on.

to set out with the intention of doing sth: to start doing sth with a particular objective in mind

I didn't set out with the intention of becoming a writer; I guess it just happened.

to set sb thinking: to cause sb to start thinking about sth

What you said about exploiting obvious business opportunities set me thinking. I've got an idea ...

to set your mind on sth: to be determined to do or achieve that thing

I know he can pass the exam if he sets his mind to it.

to set to work (+ing): to start doing sth in a determined way

Nobody knew where the witness was. He set to work finding her. He would leave no stone unturned.

Set (Phrasal Verbs)

to set aside: (i) for money: to save a certain amount of money (ii) for time: to reserve a certain amount of time for a particular purpose

Every month we would set aside £200 to have enough money to go to Paris.

Every day I set aside half an hour for my yoga exercises.

to set sb back: (informal) to cost sb

How much did that set you back?

to set sb down: to stop and let sb get off/out somewhere; also used for buses, taxis, etc

The bus will set you down outside my house.

"Do you want me to set you down here?" asked the taxi driver.

to set forth: (formal) to clearly explain an idea, policy, plan, etc

The President set forth his plan to privatise the railways in a speech at the party conference.

to set in: to start and seem likely to continue for sometime (for bad weather, doubt and panic)

234

I don't think we'll be playing football this afternoon. This rain has set in for the rest of the day.

to set off: to start a journey

We don't have to set off until midday.

to set (an alarm) off: to cause an alarm to ring

Every time a bird lands on his car it sets the alarm off.

to set out to do sth: to begin sth with the intention of achieving a particular goal

I don't want to be average. I set out to be the best pianist in the world, and I won't stop until I am.

to set up: to start a business

Links English Language Centre was set up in 1989.

to set sb up: to make sb look guilty of a crime they did not commit.

"I didn't do it! I've been set up!".

Practice

1. What can you set? Put a tick (✓) next to the things you can set and a (✗) next to the things you can't.

1	an animal free	8	a good example	14	someone a target .....
2	dumb	9	lucky	15	up home in .....
3	an exam	10	some homework	16	a trap .....
4	sail	11	a deal	17	up in business .....
5	the table	12	a precedent	18	a fire .....
6	a balance	13	a date	19	your mind on .....
7	your heart on				

2. Fill in the blanks with the missing set expressions listed below.

> set me thinking – set foot – set his mind on – set eyes – set up for life – set out with the intention of – set in his ways – dead set against it – all set

The minute I **1)** .... in his office I knew it was true. It was in the air. I hadn't seen Fester for months. He looked paler, older, wearier. "Where's May ?" I asked." She's gone," he murmured. May was thirty years his junior and from the moment he had **2)** .... on her he had fallen hopelessly in love. Ripples of concern had spread throughout the family but as a confirmed and solitary bachelor it never entered our heads that he'd go and marry her. He was too **3)** .... We were right. But he did make her his business partner in our family business. It was a scandal. The family were **4)** .... but there was nothing to be done. Old, lonely and enormously wealthy, Fester was easy prey. Inevitably, the minute May started work, she had **5)** .... relieving the old man of his considerable wealth. It was a year-long spending spree of epic proportions: cars, jewels, furs, even an apartment. By the time Fester had woken up to what was going on, she had nearly bankrupted us. So, there he sat. I tried to console him. He told me he was going to sell the company. I told him not to be ridiculous. He showed me the contract he had made with *Redston's*, our rivals. He was **6)** .... to sign it in half an hour. I stared at him in disbelief. He looked up and said " It's better this way. It's best for everyone." His words **7)** .... I was the sole benefactor of Fester's will, and the company was worth millions. I'd be **8)** .... If selling off two hundred years of family history would bring him some peace, who was I to interfere? Anyway, I knew Fester. Once he had **9)** .... something, there was no stopping him. There was nothing I could do. I shrugged my shoulders, turned round and walked out of his office.

3. Substitute the phrases in bold in the sentences with an appropriate **set** phrasal verb from the box below.

> set you back – set aside – has set forth – has set in – set off – set up – set up – set off – set out – set you down

1. I didn't do it. I was **the victim of a plan to make me look guilty**. ....
2. When I leave university I would like to **start** my own computer software business. ....
3. He didn't **mean to** break the world record. It just happened. ....
4. The government **has explained** its proposals for a new social security programme in a document called *Looking to the Future*. ....
5. The slightest fluctuation in temperature will **cause** the alarm **to ring**. ....
6. It looks as if the rain **is likely to continue** for the rest of the day. ....
7. That looks as though it must have cost a small fortune. How much did it **cost you**? ....
8. You can't go wrong. You don't have to worry about getting lost when you get to Oxford because the driver will **drop you off** right outside my college. ....
9. I always try to **reserve** at least an hour of every day for meditation. ....
10. If we want to get there by midday, we'll have to **start our journey** at four in the morning. ....

116 Take (Expressions/Phrasal Verbs)

Take Expressions

not to take kindly to: not to like sth and be annoyed by it

John takes great pride in his cooking and he won't take kindly to your making jokes about his soup tasting like washing up liquid.

to take advantage of sth: to use an opportunity or situation to get some kind of benefit from it [Note: **to take advantage of sb**: to exploit sb or a weakness in their character in order to get sth that you want]

I took advantage of my holiday in England to do lots of swimming.

He took advantage of her loneliness and trust to win her confidence.

to take an instant dislike to sb: to dislike sb the moment you meet them

My boss and I took an instant dislike to one another.

to take sth apart: to separate sth into pieces

The alarm clock was not working properly, so she took it apart to see what was wrong with it.

to take exception to: to be offended/made angry by

He took exception to the way his neighbours always parked their car outside his garage.

to take it for granted that: to believe or assume that sth is a fact because it is logical/natural

He took it for granted that we all understood French, and he started reading as a poem by Rimbaud. None of us understood a word.

to take sb for granted: not to treat sb with the respect they deserve and not thank them for their help; instead, you simply expect them always to be there when needed

She left him because she said he always took her for granted.

to take sth in your stride: to accept and deal with sth bad or unpleasant without worrying about it or getting upset

Most people would be devastated if they lost their jobs, but Geraldine seems to have taken it (all) in her stride.

sth takes its toll on your health: sth is having a bad effect on your health and making you ill

Too much work and too many sleepless nights had taken their toll on his health.

to take no notice of/not to take any notice of: not to pay attention

Perhaps he didn't see the sign or perhaps he took no notice of it.

to take pride in sth: to pay a lot of attention so as to do sth (e.g. your work, your cooking, etc) as well as you can and therefore to feel proud of what you have done

She was a woman who took a great deal of pride in her appearance.

to take priority over sth: to be considered to be more important than sth

Doing your homework takes priority over wanting to watch TV, Derek.

to take sb to court: to take legal action against sb

He was taken to court for not paying a parking fine.

to take your mind off sth: if you do sth to take your mind off another thing you do it so as to stop worrying or thinking about that other thing

The main reason I go hiking is to take my mind off all the problems I have at home.

Take (Phrasal Verbs)

to be taken aback: to be surprised

We were taken aback by the news.

The news took us aback.

to be taken in/to take sb in: to be deceived by

We were all taken in by his story.

He took us all in with his story.

to take sth in: to understand and remember

I didn't take any of it in.

Most people only take in 25% of what they read.

to take after sb: to resemble a member of your family, physically or in character

I take after my mother.

to take sth back: to withdraw what you have previously said

I saw him play yesterday and he was awful. I take back what I said about Tournquist being an excellent tennis player.

sth takes it out of you: sth makes you feel very tired

Teaching adolescents can certainly take it out of you.

to take it/sth out on sb: to make another person suffer (e.g. by being rude or aggressive) because sth or sb has annoyed you

So, you've had a bad day at work. There's no need to take it out on me. It's not my fault.

to take sb on: to give sb a job, to employ sb

We take on extra staff at Christmas.

to take up: to occupy/use (i) space (ii) time

It's a lovely sofa but it takes up half the living room.

It it's taking up too much of your free time, why not get someone else to do it?

to take sth up: to start a sport or hobby

I'm thinking of taking up tennis.

to take sb up on an offer: to accept sb's offer

I've offered him a three-year contract in Hong Kong but I don't know if he'll take me up on the offer.

Practice

1. *For questions 1 to 15, complete the second sentence so that it has a similar meaning to the first sentence, using 3 to 8 words. You must include the word given in bold, which cannot be changed in any way.*

1. We made the most of the sunny weather and had a picnic in the countryside.
   advantage We .... the sunny weather and had a picnic in the countryside.
2. She prides herself on her cooking.
   pride She .... her cooking.
3. He paid no attention to the 'No Parking' sign.
   notice He .... the 'No Parking' sign.
4. The needs of the poor should be given more importance than those of the middle classes.
   priority The needs of the poor .... those of the middle classes.
5. I made her very angry and upset when I said that her novel was amateurish and badly written.
   kindly She .... the way I described her novel.
6. If he had paid more attention to her, she wouldn't have left him.
   granted If he .... she wouldn't have left him.
7. He did some gardening to help him forget about his job interview the next day.
   mind He did some gardening to help .... his job interview the next day.
8. I dismantled the radio to see what was wrong with it.
   apart I .... to see what was wrong with it.
9. The long hours she works are beginning to ruin her health.
   toll The long hours she works are beginning to .... her health.
10. I am going to sue them if they print that article.
    court I am going to .... if they print that article.
11. She didn't like Bill the moment she set eyes on him.
    instant She .... Bill.
12. As she is a close friend, I naturally assumed that she would help me out.
    for As she is a close friend, I .... help me out.
13. Being dismissed didn't seem to bother him.
    dismissal He seemed .... stride.
14. I'm sure it was something you said that offended her.
    exception She must have .... said.
15. I admit that I was too critical of the film.
    back I .... about the film.

2. *For each of the sentences below, substitute the words in bold for an appropriate* **take** *phrasal verb. The phrasals you need to choose from appear in the box below.*

> taken in – take it out of me – take up – takes after –
> take on – taken aback – take up – take in –
> take it out on me – take them up on it

1. I know working a twelve-hour shift without a break is really going to **make me feel tired** – but I need the money. ....
2. The doctor told him to go on a diet and **start (playing)** squash. ....
3. How can I have been so stupid? I was completely **deceived** by him. ....
4. We couldn't cope with all the extra work we had, so we had to **employ** another secretary. ....
5. How you manage to **understand and remember** all that information, I just don't know. ....
6. I'd love to have that table, but our flat is too small and a big table like that would **occupy** too much space. ....
7. "Acme and sons" have offered me a job, and I've decided to **accept their offer**. ....
8. I know it's difficult for him at work but why does he always have to **make me suffer because someone or something has annoyed him**? ....
9. He's certainly not afraid to speak his mind. He **resembles** his father in that respect. ....
10. We were all somewhat **surprised** by the news that she intended to sue him. We thought they were friends. ....